619: THE HISTORY OF A FORGOTTEN SQUADRON

Second edition
published in 2005 by
WOODFIELD PUBLISHING
Bognor Regis, West Sussex, England
www.woodfieldpublishing.com

ISBN 1-903953-51-0

619

The History of a Forgotten Squadron

BRYAN CLARK

Woodfield

This book is dedicated to the memory of the crew of Lancaster aircraft EE109 PG-F and all the other young men of Bomber Command who died that we might live in a free country.

Also to a former WRAF officer, Dr Margaret Clark, for her support and tolerance and to our sons David, Matthew and Johnnie, the first two now the ages that Roy Trahair and Vinny Crookes were when they died in October 1943 and John the age that Mike Trahair was when his brother Roy went missing.

Without all of them this book would not have been written.

CONTENTS

Bryan Clark in 1977, at the time the wreck of EE109 PG-F was discovered.

Foreword

The Strategic Bombing Campaign of World War II was waged at a dreadful cost, both to this country and Germany, and few families were untouched by it. In Britain, our cities of London, Manchester, Liverpool, Bristol, Birmingham, Coventry, Glasgow and others had been bombed by the Luftwaffe in the early years of the War; but the cities of Germany suffered far more in the later years - from the summer of 1943 onwards - when the four-engined bombers of the RAF came into squadron service on a scale hitherto unknown and, together with the B17s of the USAAF, helped pound Germany into defeat in little more than two years. The air campaign paved the way for the successful Allied land offensive from 'D' Day onwards, but in the process a lot of ordinary people suffered. We remember this suffering in order to learn from it.

To meet the Strategic Bombing Campaign, new RAF squadrons were formed virtually overnight in the summer of 1943. One of them was No 619 Squadron, formed at RAF Woodhall Spa in Lincolnshire in April-June 1943. In twenty-three months of operations from June 1943 until April 1945 it lost 85 aircraft and almost 500 men as a main force squadron in No 5 Group of Bomber Command. My father was the first pilot captain killed on operations with the squadron.

Like many other squadrons raised to meet the strategic bombing campaign, No 619 Squadron was disbanded as soon as the War was over, and today it is largely forgotten. It does not even have a College of Arms approved squadron crest, and it is remembered only by the dwindling band of old men who in 1943/45 flew its Lancaster aircraft on what now seem to be almost primitive sorties over occupied Europe. Some 55,500 aircrew died in the 12,330 aircraft lost by Bomber Command during the War. If the injured and prisoners of war are included, the loss rate is close to 60% of all those who flew with

Bomber Command between 1939 and 1945, the highest loss rate of any branch of the British Armed Forces. These young men fought a war in the only way then possible, using technology that today seems antediluvian; but that is all there was then, and, remarkably, the democracies prevailed. It was, however, a much closer run thing than sometimes today we care to remember.

The author was a career officer in the post-War RAF, but he and I met after his RAF service when he was the Administrator of Trinity College, Bristol, an Anglican Theological College, training women and men for ordained and lay ministry in the Anglican Communion. He tells the story of the discovery of an aircraft of 619 Squadron in a river in Hannover in 1977, thirty-four years after it was lost when the crew were on their twenty-first operation. After leaving the RAF, the author continued his investigation to try to identify the crew and their families, and the result is this book. The crew had arrived on 619 Squadron on the day my father and his crew went missing.

In researching the story of this aircraft, the author has written a history of one of the forgotten squadrons of Bomber Command and has intertwined within it the human story of one Lancaster crew of seven men, their training, their operations, their families, and the difficulties their relatives faced in the very different world of October 1943 and the immediate post-war period.

The author concludes the story with his meeting in Hannover with the retired German Professor of Medicine, who as a fifteen years old boy was conscripted with his school class into the flak battery [3./521] defending that city and helped to shoot down this aircraft. In a similar operational life to 619 Squadron this one flak battery shot down twenty-five allied aircraft, including the one central to this story. They were defending the city from which our own Royal family came and with which we had strong links for 200 years until 1914. Three of the Professor's classmates did not survive the war.

Sixty years on we are sufficiently removed from the conflict to be able to remember the fallen on both sides of the conflict.

Bryan Clark's engaging and moving account of this squadron has given me previously unknown information about how my father (who was killed when I was eighteen months old) spent his last weeks on this earth. My thankfulness for these insights will be matched only by the gratitude of others who also have personal links with the squadron – and our relief that, through these meticulously researched pages, No 619 Squadron will no longer be forgotten.

The Rt Revd Nigel McCulloch MA
Bishop of Manchester
Bishopcourt, Manchester

Nigel McCulloch, now Bishop of Manchester, with his father, who was shot down in June 1943 [The Times]

Author's Preface

So much has been written about Bomber Command and the Second World War that I hesitate to add to the genre. I am moved to do so for a number of reasons. First, the story I have to tell is unusual. Not many people were involved during their RAF careers in the late 1970s in the recovery of the remains of an aircraft that went missing in 1943 or can speak from inside the RAF Police of the obstacles we encountered within the MOD in our attempts to identify the remains. Secondly, having read fairly extensively over the past couple of years in order to be able to put this one aircraft into context, I want to correct the impression I have read so often that the strategic bombing campaign achieved little or nothing and perhaps bordered on the criminal.

The campaign waged by Bomber Command, particularly from late 1942 onwards when the new generation of four-engined heavy bombers at last came into service, was fought for one very good reason and at a tremendous cost to the young men of Bomber Command and their families. By the nature of things these young men were amongst the brightest and best of their generation. War is awful and demeans us all, and I certainly do not wish to glorify it by anything I write. But sometimes – though not very often – war is justified, and the young men who died in the air war over Europe trying to defeat an evil regime knew that. As it was then, so now. We have had to relearn to our cost in recent years in the fight against terrorism, that democracy carries within it the seeds of its own destruction. It provides the freedom for those who are so minded to destroy it. Hitler knew this, and he used it to good effect. He did not seize power; he came to power through the ballot box. Evil prevails when good men do nothing. The strategic bombing campaign did much to shorten the war and to bring to an end an evil greater than war itself. It can also be argued that it prevented an even greater loss of life and freed the German people from tyranny. A most moving testimony to this was found in the visitors' book at the Commonwealth War Graves Commission cemetery in Berlin on a cold New Year's Day in 1993. Visiting what is an overwhelmingly Bomber Command Cemetery with my wife and young children, like all visitors we were overwhelmed by the row upon row of small neat white headstones, mainly in groups of seven, and by the ages on them of the young men buried there: Sergeants and Pilot Officers of 18 or 19; Warrant Officers and Squadron Leaders of 21, the latter veterans with gallantry awards and decorations. From the addresses accompanying the entries in the visitors' book, we were surprised to see how many of the visitors were German, often Berliners. In German, one Berliner had written simply and poignantly: 'I thank you for your sacrifice'.

I was also moved to begin my research by an article '*Let us remember the fatherless as well as the fallen*' written for the *Credo* slot in *The Times* on Remembrance Day 1996 by the Bishop of Wakefield, The Right Reverend Nigel McCulloch [now Bishop of Manchester]. I had known Nigel some years previously when as Suffragan Bishop of Taunton he was also the Chairman of the Finance Committee of the central body responsible for paying the fees of Ordinands training at the Church of England's theological colleges. At that time I was the Administrator of Trinity Theological College, Bristol, and so Nigel and I had met professionally on a number of occasions. In his *Credo* article Nigel wrote that he understood the situation of the fatherless, as his father had been killed on operations as a pilot with the RAF during the Second World War when he was a toddler. As a result, he had grown up in the post-war years without a father, and this had affected his outlook. He had not been able, for example, at theological college to share the excitement of others that the Aramaic word Abba, which is used by Jesus in the New Testament[1], means Daddy.

I wrote to Nigel thanking him for his wise article, and saying that he could not have known that I had served in the RAF, and I had certainly not known until then that his father had died in the RAF. We ex-

[1] St Luke's Gospel, Chapter 14, verse 36: '*Abba! Father! All things are possible for Thee; remove this cup from me; yet not what I will, but what Thou wilt*'.

changed letters. It was several years later when I was researching this book that I realised, almost inevitably, that his father had died with 'my' squadron, No 619. Indeed, his father had arrived on the Squadron in the first few weeks of it existence, and died on the day that Cyril Fuller and his crew arrived, and, as you will discover, without them this book would never have been written. Nigel's father and his crew were the first operational casualties of the 495 men the Squadron was eventually to lose in 23 months of operational life. As the story of Cyril Fuller and his crew lies at the heart of this book, it is a neat connection.

There is one more, personal, motive. It has irked me since 1977 that so little was done to tell the next of kin that EE109 had been found [or to be more precise re-found]. The stonewalling that seems to infect all Government departments effectively prevented a proper investigation from being carried out by the RAF Police special investigation branch, the military equivalent of the CID, in Germany in 1977. Similar obfuscation has affected my post-RAF research. It is an amazing fact that over fifty years after the end of the Second World war one can go to the Public Record Office and read documents about top secret wartime discussions of strategy, but you cannot get to the original records of the war-time dead or the immediate post-war investigations into Bomber Command's missing aircraft and their crews. I am not foolish enough to think this book will change any of that, certainly not in the short-term, but if enough people begin to ask questions, those records will have to be put into the public domain. And there is no reason why they should not be. The excuse that the files contain confidential information about the missing men does not stand up to even cursory examination. A few of the casualty files – very, very few – may contain information that is genuinely personal. But this information, and a lot more, can be obtained from the RAF Record Office anyway. I cannot even now get to the information that I provided for their files in 1977. It is simply administratively more convenient for the Ministry of Defence not to have to make the casualty files available. By now they ought to have been deposited in the Public Record Office at Kew.

Protecting the feelings of next of kin is also sometimes cited as a reason for keeping the files under lock and key. I can only reply that the next of kin I have spoken with are only too pleased to know at last something of what happened to their missing relatives. Many of them had spent years trying to find out. In any case, is it really for a Whitehall department to decide what the next of kin should be told? It is only because the 12,330 aircraft losses of Bomber Command occurred during the circumstances of total war that the files [one for each of the aircraft losses] are not openly available to next of kin and the public. That some of the information might upset relatives is not sufficient reason for withholding all of it. In any case, knowing well from my own RAF service the sort of records involved, the risk of there being much information of a really personal nature on the files is virtually nil. All that is on file is a précis of the service and medical histories of the men concerned, sufficient for the RAF to be able to identify them if identifiable bodies were ever found or the men turned up in post-war disguise, plus the details of post-war investigations to find out what had happened to aircraft and crews when this was not already known. It is this latter material that would most interest aviation historians for it includes the captured German documents on which most of it is based.

With the passage of time, no parents can still be alive. The youngest of the aircrew would themselves now be in their mid-to-late seventies, and so parents would have to be at least 100 to 120 years of age, or older. Not many brothers or sisters will still be alive either, unless much younger than the missing men. I do know personally two much younger siblings, who were aged only four when their older brothers went missing in 1943 and 1944, but they are the exceptions and even they are now in their 60s. The truth is that Whitehall has yet to be put under pressure to change the present arrangements. When it has been put under enough pressure, the casualty files will be released to the Public Record Office. For the moment it is easier to get information out of German records than from British. One can only think that the dead bomber crews would be turning in their graves.

Bryan Clark
Ashford Carbonel,
Ludlow, Shropshire

Acknowledgements

I have to thank so many people for their help with this book that it is inevitable I will overlook some. I could not in any case within the confines of publishing constraint hope to mention all of them. I hope those I have omitted will forgive me.

Particular mention must be made of the families of the crew of EE109 PG-F, especially Mike Trahair, the much-younger brother of rear gunner, Sergeant Roy Trahair, whose mother did not give up the search to find out what had happened to Roy until her death in the 1980s when she was over 90 years of age and whose archive of material was invaluable. I must also thank Mrs Reg Stevens, the widow of the East End policeman navigator Pilot Officer Reg Stevens; Simon Eaude, the nephew of the Air Bomber, Pilot Officer Leo Eaude; Mrs Frances Crookes and her daughter Ann, sister-in-law and niece of Sergeant Vinny Crookes, the nineteen years old mid-upper gunner; and Mr and Mrs Jim Adams, sister and brother-in-law of Sergeant Dick Sprackman, the wireless operator.

Of former 619 Squadron crew members, I must thank Group Captain Ronnie Churcher DSO MVO DFC, the founding flight commander of 'A' Flight under whose command the crew of EE109 operated and with whom Cyril Fuller flew his first operational flight to Krefeld on 21 June 1943 soon after joining the squadron; Wing Commander Robert Millward OBE DFC and Bar, the only surviving squadron commander; Flight Lieutenant John Howard DFC and Bar, the Air Gunnery Leader, still firing away at over 90 years of age; Flight Sergeant George Hexter DFM RCAF; Major Hubert 'Nick' Knilans DSO DFC USAAF; Robin Tate, Nick Knilans' bomb aimer on 619 Squadron and then 617 Squadron; Flight Lieutenant Stan Jones DFC DFM; Flight Lieutenant Bob Knights DSO DFC; WO Alec Bates; the late Steve Rew; Flight Sergeant George Allen, the ex-apprentice 'A' Flight fitter; and most of all Flight Lieutenant John Whiteley DFC, the 619 squadron association secretary, who has been an indefatigable guide and help and a most charming host. To all of these, I say a profound thank you for putting up with the naïve questions of a RAF policeman sixty years after the event.

Within my old police force, the Provost Branch of the RAF, I have to thank Air Commodore Richard McConnell, Squadron Leader Steve Atkins, Flight Lieutenant Tom Parkhouse and Herr Matthew Geuyen, my former interpreter at HQ P&SS Germany.

Amongst aviation historians, reporters and others I should like to thank the author Martin Middlebrook; Mike Hodgson of the Thorpe Camp Visitor Centre; author Alan Cooper; author Bill Chorley; Günter Leonhardt of the Luftfahrt-Museum Laatzen-Hannover e.V; Wolfgang Steinweg, Chefreporter of the *Hannoverische Allgemeine*; Colin Adamson and his editor Max Hastings of the *London Evening Standard*; David Collins of the Newark Air Museum at the former RAF Winthorpe; Beatrice Padley, retired librarian from Sheffield; Hallamshire Press of Sheffield, publishers of the work of George Cunningham, rear-gunner Vinny Crookes' boyhood friend; author Lionel Lacey-Johnson; French aviation enthusiast Alain Charpentier of the Loire; John Hey and Rex Roell, both Dutch aviation historians; Peter Rodway, Archivist of Alleyn's School; and Mr S.B. Taylor of the RAF Personnel Management Centre in Gloucester. All of these helped in various ways and gave me vital clues. Above all, however, I must thank Professor Dr Med Jürgen and Margot Probst for their extensive help and hospitality. In 1943 Professor Probst as a fifteen year old *Luftwaffenhelfer* was manning Flak Batterie 3./521 when it shot down EE109 over Hannover. During a visit by the author and his family to Hannover, he placed a red rose – a symbolic German gesture – on the grave of Roy Trahair, the rear gunner of EE109.[1]

[1] I would like to think that a lot of healing took place during the writing of this book on both sides of the wartime divide. It is one of the ironies of war that had EE109 crashed a hundred yards further on than it did it would have landed in the grounds of the Royal Palace, the Herrenhaus, in Hannover, from whence came our own Royal family. In 1943, the people of Hannover felt sure the RAF would not bomb their city because of our joint British/German heritage. They were wrong, of course, and the Herrenhaus was destroyed in the third of the four RAF raids of September/October 1943. Even more ironic is the fact that Professor Probst is descended from a long line of Lutheran ministers, one of

One official to whom I owe a considerable debt of gratitude, though he may not thank me for mentioning his name, is Mr Graham Day of the MOD's Air Historical Branch for his patient help and forebearance in facing the hostile questioning of a policeman who was intent on proving where Day's predecessors in office had gone wrong. Without his help, I could not have recovered as much information as I have [though I would have liked more]. I hope he might yet see the light and place his files in the National Archives.

Finally, I must thank my wife Margaret for tolerating my long absences in my study for hours on end writing this book. And I thank you the reader for bothering to read it.

Omissions, errors and howlers are, of course, entirely mine.

Bryan Clark
Ashford Carbonel
2004

whom administered the formal oath to the House of Hannover at the time of the Act of Settlement in 1707. That oath brought our two monarchies together in a personal union that continued until 1837 and would have continued beyond that had Queen Victoria been a man, probably until the Twentieth Century. One can only speculate, as one of the great 'what ifs' of history, whether Bismarck would have been able to coerce the German states into one nation in 1866/1871 had he faced a British king, and if not whether WWI could have happened, and if not that WWII could not have followed. On such slim strands of chance hang so much fate and history.

About the Author

An infant in Salford during the Luftwaffe Blitz of December 1940, the author joined the RAF as an apprentice at the age of sixteen in 1956 and served for 23 years. In 1977 he was the Squadron Leader in charge of the SIB of the RAF Police in Germany when the aircraft at the centre of this story was found in a river in Hannover by workmen building a new autobahn.

As an officer of the RAF Police, the author was responsible for security at a nuclear-armed 'V' Force base at the height of the Cold War, commanded a Counter Intelligence unit in the Gulf and was employed as a counter-terrorist specialist in Northern Ireland at Belfast Airport during 'the troubles' of the mid-1970s.

Now in semi-retirement, he is Clerk to the Governors of the Royal National College for the Blind, Secretary of the Corporation of an independent school, parent governor of his son's village school and a member of the Council of an Anglican Theological College. In the years since leaving the RAF, he has been the Administrator of Trinity College Bristol and the Bursar of Rossall School and Rossall Preparatory School in Lancashire.

He lives in the country near Ludlow with his wife, an academic historian and former WRAF officer, and their 'late extra' young son, where they breed Longhorn cattle, Manx Loughtan sheep and keep rare breed hens.

1. The Discovery

Every contact leaves a trace [Criminal investigators' dictum]

As he looked at the mangled heap of metal, abandoned perambulators, cast-off refrigerators and the other ugly debris of a modern urban society, dragged from the river by the German building contractors, Jim Condon could have been forgiven for thinking that this was indeed one of the more unusual cases to have come his way in his thirty years as an RAF Policeman. As the Flight Sergeant in charge of the Special Investigations section of the Provost & Security Services Detachment at RAF Gütersloh, a former WWII Luftwaffe base and now the northern-most Royal Air Force station in RAF Germany, he was usually called in to investigate the more serious kinds of crime: major theft, fraud, offences against people, the occasional drugs case and even more occasionally the more dramatic investigation, such as death in suspicious circumstances - the sort of thing that in the UK would be dealt with by the CID rather than the uniformed constabulary. He was, in effect, a CID officer serving in the RAF, working in plain clothes and dealing with the most serious of criminal activities involving British interests or British citizens, uniformed or civilian, in the northern bit of Germany. He handled only those cases that were too serious or complex for the normal RAF station policemen. More importantly, he was always called in whenever in his 'patch' of north Germany a sudden or suspicious death was reported or joint British and German police interests or jurisdiction were at issue. The workload was not enormous, for RAF officers and airman then, as now, were a decent, law-abiding lot, but every now and then, a big case would come his way. This was the nineteenth case to do so in the first three months of 1977. That it should have come to him was not in dispute: for all its unusualness, this was a killing, involving both British and German interests, and the victims had died thirty years previously during the Second World War.

Though his office at Gütersloh was next to those of the Station RAF Policemen, Condon answered, through his Provost Branch[1] officer, Flight Lieutenant Clive Watts-Morgan, a Welsh former Colonial Policeman, direct to his SIB Commanding Officer, a Squadron Leader of the Provost Branch, based two hundred miles away at the Headquarters of the Provost & Security Services for Germany, located at the main BAOR and RAF Headquarters complex at Rheindahlen, near Mönchen-Gladbach. This arrangement was intended to give investigators like Condon the independence from Station pressure and freedom of action to work on or off base, with people of all ranks, whether senior or junior to themselves, free from the sort of inhibitions that might influence or impede a Station policeman serving in a uniformed and hierarchical military service. Thus it was that earlier that day he had received a telephone call from Warrant Officer Mick Cattigan in the Special Investigations office at Rheindahlen instructing him to make immediate contact with Mr Hall, the British Services Liaison Officer, and Herr Verneke of the Public Order Department in Hannover to inspect the tangled remains dredged from the river, the Leine, near the centre of Hannover. Mixed in with the metal debris were human bones.

The Remains

In March 1977, German workmen, digging and dredging the Leine river at a point in the Calenberger Neustadt district of Hannover where the Weddigen Ufer runs alongside the riverbank and Emden Strasse is at right angles on the one side, and Morwegsgasse and Fischer Strasse

[1] RAF Police officers of commissioned rank are called Provost Officers and are members of the Provost Branch, having been gazetted in the London Gazette as *Assistants to the Provost Marshal*, which gives them the legal authority under the Air Force Act to carry out their duties as police officers without regard to the usual strict rank observance of a military service. Provost Officers are usually only personally engaged on the more serious cases or in those involving commissioned officers.

are on the other, began to drag to the surface more than just the accumulated debris to be found in any large urban waterway or canal. It should be said that the Leine is a canal on a scale unknown in Britain. It is a major waterway that bisects Hannover from north-west to south-east and it flows out from the north-west of the city through a series of waterways and canals across the plains of Niedersachsen for a hundred miles until it reaches the City of Bremen and joins the North Sea. Inland, from the North Sea to well beyond Hannover, the Leine and its tributaries form an important route for the passage of the large barges and their heavy cargoes on which German industry so depends. As a tidal river the Leine has a slow but significant current. The significance of all of this will become clear later.

The workmen were engaged in digging out the riverbed before constructing pile-driven concrete supports for an autobahn fly-over at the point opposite Emden Strasse. Here, the river is about 12 metres [39½ feet] wide and 4 metres [13 feet deep]. Beneath, in 1977, lay another two or three metres of accumulated silt and beneath that lay all the junk and detritus that in the years since WWII had found its way, intentionally and unintentionally, into the river and had sunk into the silt.

From this thick layer of silt, the workman began to dredge a pile of broken metal and other bits of flotsam and jetsam. It soon became clear, however, that there was something unusual about some of the debris. At first, the workmen were unsure what they had found, except that some of the chunks of metal were quite large and one piece was a length of the wing flap from a large aircraft. This piece provided the first real clue. Though covered with dirt and mud after thirty years in the silt, it was still recognisable as a piece of an aircraft of the type flown during the Second World War.

By the time Jim Condon arrived on the scene some hours had already passed since the workmen had first started recovering wreckage, and some small pieces of the wreckage had been taken away by them as souvenirs. Condon immediately began a search for identification marks or makers' plates on the larger pieces of wreckage, but none was found. What was found, amidst the sludge-covered debris, was a gold coloured cigarette case with the initials 'MK' on it [which, we later concluded, probably had nothing to do with the aircraft], some fragments of bone and twelve rounds of belt-fed ammunition stamped with the date 1942. The ammunition was badly swollen and encrusted with rust and mud, and the German Explosives Ordnance [Bomb Disposal] technicians, who had been called to the scene, decided it was in too dangerous a state to be retained as evidence. They destroyed it on site. The bone fragments were labelled and added to the collection of thirty or so bones already recovered

Condon then had a quiet word with the foreman, and he in turn spoke with his workmen. This resulted in a number of souvenirs being returned, one of which was the maker's plate from a Mark 28 Merlin engine. This proved at last that the aircraft had belonged to the RAF and that it was probably a Mark III Lancaster bomber.

Condon arranged for the area of the river search to be widened, fearing by now that bombs might lie in the silt. The German bomb disposal team swept the river electronically for 500 metres either side of the spot where the engine had been found. The result was a relief, if disappointing in terms of police evidence. The EOD team concluded that there was nothing of significance within the kilometre stretch of the river searched, and certainly nothing with the mass of a bomb. A 24-hour uniformed RAF Police guard was then mounted over the wreckage.

Of the thirty bones, some at least seemed to be human in origin, the most obvious being a number of long-bones [leg/arm]. All the bones were tagged by Condon and his team as police evidence and taken to the Hannover Public Order Department for examination by a pathologist. He duly pronounced them to be parts of at least two human skeletons. The nature of the enquiry was now confirmed. It was a police investigation to try to identify human remains. No skulls or other evidence that would help identification had been recovered, and so Condon's SIB boss at Rheindahlen sent a signal [a sort of telegram or e-mail] to the department of the Ministry of Defence in London that held war-time aircraft records asking for help in identifying the aircraft.

Meanwhile, house to house enquiries were being carried out by Condon and his team in the immediate area of the river with the help of German interpreters, because, even while first surveying the debris on the river bank, Condon had been approached by a dear old lady, who had come out of a nearby house and told him that she could tell him 'all about that aircraft'. It had crashed during the War on the night of 18th October 1943, in the process taking the roof off her house. Consequently, she remembered the date well. After hitting her roof, the aircraft had ended up straddling the river with its nose embedded in the mud on the opposite bank and the front part lying on top of a barge that had been moored there. The tail was facing Emden Strasse, and the crash had effectively blocked the river. She recalled seeing 'some' bodies of the crew on the riverbank the following morning, and she remembered that they had looked very young. Even then, at the height of the war, and faced with the remains of men who only hours previously had been dropping bombs on her city and her people, she told us she 'had felt so sad for their mothers, because she knew how they were going to feel'. She had noticed that one of the uniforms had sergeant's stripes on the arm. The bodies had been taken away and, she thought, some of the wreckage had been removed later by the German authorities, but the part of the aircraft we had found had been pushed into the river as the quickest way of reopening it again to barge traffic.

The old lady still lived in the house, at the junction of Emden Strasse and the Weddigen Ufer, facing the river. At this point Emden Strasse runs at right angles away from the river and Weddigen Ufer runs alongside the river bank on the southern side. The housing on this side of the river was of pre-war stock, and so would have been there at the time the Lancaster came down in 1943. On the other side of the river there was an open area with some modern post-war housing.

The possibility of dredging the river in the hope of finding further human remains was discussed with the British Liaison Officer for the Hannover area and officials of the Hannover Public Order Department and also with civil engineers at the site [who were excavating prior to sinking concrete supports for an autobahn fly-over]. All were of the view that, given the nature of the river and the riverbed and the absence of any other large pieces of wreckage during the search by the bomb disposal people, and the manpower that would be involved in searching perhaps miles of river, with a fast current that could have carried wreckage and remains a long way from the crash-site, widening the search was not a practical proposition. The investigators knew, of course, that a Lancaster aircraft usually flew with a crew of seven, but at this stage they had no way of knowing whether all the crew had been in the aircraft when it had crashed or if any had survived. As information was obtained at the site, it was passed on through the SIB Headquarters at Rheindahlen to the civilian official in charge of the records of missing aircraft and personnel in the OAR [Operational Aircraft Records] department of the Ministry of Defence.

Within 24 hours, the local Hannover newspaper, the *Hannoversche Allgemeine Zeitung*, carried its first article about the aircraft having been found, beneath a photograph of a length of wing flap about 2 feet wide and perhaps twenty feet long in front of a pile of dredged debris, with the by-line *Hervor kamen die Trümmer eines Bombers*: 'Hence came the rubble of a bomber'. The article read:

> *'Memories of the bombing of the Second World War were awakened following the discovery yesterday morning at the channelling works along Morwegsgasse in the shadow of the Bremer Damm the wreckage of a war-plane. Probably the remains of an Allied bomber, it would have been shot down in an air raid and crashed into the Leine. The workmen on the site met an obstacle to their [hydraulic] ram and had to use an excavator. To date they have a ten-metre piece of wing, landing gear and other unidentified pieces. The Site Clerk of Works, Herbert Weigt, contacted the City Water Department to warn a bomb disposal team. There is no immediate danger. Despite this, a temporary halt has been called to the work. On Monday, the Military authorities and Fire Services will renew efforts with special equipment to find other parts of the wreckage. The sludge will be washed off the remains, to expose any munitions, and the nationality of the aircraft can probably then be announced. There is no trace of the crew of the machine.'*

The next article in the newspaper came five days later, under the heading *Neue Funde im Wrack des abgestürzten Flugzeugs*: 'New find in the wreck of the destroyed aircraft'.

The article read:

'The Lower Saxony Bomb disposal team yesterday made further finds at the raising of the WWII warplane. The wreckage was found, as already announced, at works on the Morwegsgasse. Testing of the bottom of the Leine showed wreckage strewn along a 20 metre stretch of the river bed. After cleaning off the mud, parts of an ammunition belt with machine gun bullets was exposed. The team also found a thigh bone and a further skeletal part mixed up in the mud and sludge. Whether it is a human bone will be clarified in the next few days. The clearance operation will continue today.'

Forty-eight hours later, a further article appeared, together with three photographs taken by a free-lance photographer, Andreas Conrad. The first photograph showed Bombenräumer [Bomb Disposal Man] Gerhard Laudsems holding upright a blade [as tall as him] of a propeller from the aircraft, with a pile of debris behind him, another showed the site of the excavation with the Bremer Damm in the background and the excavating crane to the fore, and the third showed in close detail a section of bomb release clips from the bomb bay mechanism. The photographs accompanied an article '*Der Bomber stürzte fast senkrecht herunter*' [the Bomber fell almost straight down]. The article also claimed to contain an eyewitness report, and the pathologist's opinion that the bones were parts of the skeletons of at least two crew members. The article read:

A week after its discovery, the aircraft wreck in the Leine can be identified as an Allied machine. Identifiable construction marks, especially the English writing on the hydraulic and oil filters, leave no doubt. From the two bomb carriers found in the sludge it can definitely be said to be a bomber or fighter-bomber. On the second day of the work bones were found. A pathologist of the North City Hospital has meanwhile confirmed that they are the remains of two men.

The office in charge of the operation will undertake to make contacts with American officials. Possibly through old aircraft plans the identity of the plane and its crew can be established.

In the meantime several readers have contacted this paper with memories of the crash of an allied warplane and the location of the crash-site. A complete picture cannot be reconstructed, and the information on time, aircraft type and other identity is contradictory.

Bernd-Jürgen Könnecker, who lives on Weddigen Ufer, remembers the account given by his father, who has since died. By this account the wreck is of a two-seater Canadian fighter, which crashed in October 1944. The machine came down directly over the roof of their house and crashed on the Weddigen Ufer. Both crew were killed on impact.

Carla Röhde, who lives in a neighbouring house, gives information on the date of the crash. By her description the aircraft would have been shot down in a nocturnal raid in 1943. When she came back home in the morning from a bomb shelter in the Altstadt, the river bank was strewn with wreckage. A dead crewman was lying in the street. Frau Röhde states that the wreckage was later thrown in the river.

Dr Med Jürgen Probst gives a further clue. The former Flakhelfer remembers that a four-engined British Lancaster bomber was shot down at 2018 on 18 Oct 43 over Calenberger Neustadt. Dr Probst writes: 'According to official records, the main part of the wreck fell on Weddigen Ufer. The machine was hit by Flak Batterie 3./521, which covered that part of the City. The bomber exploded at once and fell almost vertically down.'

The size of the oil-cooler and propeller blade found by the recovery team, lead to the conclusion that the wreck was more likely a heavy bomber than a fighter. The aircraft type will be confirmed by an expert.

The next article appeared on 21 March 1977, and it read:

'Bombermotor geborgen' [Bomber engine safe] beneath a photograph by Andreas Conrad of the remains of an in-line engine block.

'An engine block was found at the weekend at the excavation site of the aircraft wreck. The motor has a provable maker's mark on it. As reported, the machine was probably shot down during a raid on Calenberger Neustadt in October 1943. British experts will today seek to identify the aircraft. From information from the military police at the NATO base at Gütersloh, it will probably he possible to identify the aircraft engine from its serial number. A further piece of information is the discovery of a propeller with three blades.

The final article appeared in the newspaper the following day:

After aircraft experts of the RAF identified the wreckage on the Leine riverbank as the remains of a four-engined Lancaster bomber, we can report that the recovery operation has been closed. All bomb release clips were open, and so there is no risk of unexploded bombs being in the river sludge. The RAF will see to the removal of the wreck. The remains of the crew will be buried. British officials will concern themselves with their identity and squadron. The tunnelling works in Morwegsgasse, which have been interrupted for two weeks to permit the recovery of the wreck, will recommence.'

Jim Condon's house-to-house enquiries along the Weddigen Ufer produced little more than the accounts that had appeared in the *Hannoversche Allgemeine Zeitung* but some important facts were established. First, Dr Med Jürgen Probst had a copy of a record of all aircraft shot down by his flak battery during the period 1943/1944 and it included a Lancaster shot down at 2018 on 18th October 1943 that had fallen on the Weddigen Ufer. This was the only aircraft to fall on the Weddigen Ufer during the war. Second, Dr Med Klaus Riehm who lived in nearby Emden Strasse and had done as a boy in 1943, by reference to his late father's diary, could also date the crash to the 18th October. His house had been hit by incendiary bombs that same night!

All the witnesses were also agreed that the wreckage had been strewn along the length of Emden Strasse, that 'some' bodies of 'enemy flyers' were found in Emden Strasse and that the remains of the aircraft had come to rest in the Leine. Dr Riehm remembered seeing 'at least one' body. Frau Röhde thought there had been at least two. There was some suggestion that one had been found in a garden in Emden Strasse. To take the enquiry on further, we now needed details from the casualty file[2] at MOD. How many men were missing, what height were they, was there anything on their records that might help the police enquiry?

The human bones were escorted from Gütersloh as police evidence by F/Sgt Allen, Mick Cattigan's deputy at HQ P & SS, and after being held as police evidence for a while by the Squadron Leader SIB, they were conveyed by a police investigator [to ensure continuity of evidence] to the RAF pathologist at the RAF Hospital Wegberg, a few miles from Rheindahlen. This would have happened in any event, but it was actually done at the specific request of OAR, Ministry of Defence. The pathologist at the RAF Hospital was a flight lieutenant specialist of the RAF medical branch and the RAF Police in Germany regularly worked with him, knew him well and there was nothing unusual in involving him in a police enquiry. But events were now to take a far from normal turn.

To act on the request of OAR had been a mistake. So far, this had been a properly constituted police investigation by the RAF's official police investigative body in Germany. The Command Provost Marshal was also the Coroner's Officer for RAF Germany, and so it was perfectly proper that the police should be called in to investigate a case of 'sudden death' even if it had occurred the best part of 34 years previously. At the end of the police enquiry, the Coroner's Officer would have to assist the senior officer at Headquarters RAF Germany, who acted as Coroner, to decide what conclusion to reach about the human remains, thought to be RAF, now in police custody.

It was at about this time that it began to be clear that the flow of information between the RAF Police in Germany and the MOD's OAR(RAF) Branch was in one direction only. The civilian official at OAR refused to release any information about the aircraft that had been lost on 18th October, 1943 or to provide any information that might identify the crew. Indeed, he appeared to believe that it was 'his' investi-

[2] A casualty file is held at MOD for every aircraft lost during WWII, regardless of the number of actual 'casualties'.

gation and that the RAF Police would do his bidding. After a couple of signals to him from the Squadron Leader SIB, putting the contrary view, it became clear that the police investigation was being impeded; indeed, that it couldn't be taken any further. The flight lieutenant pathologist had concluded, like the German pathologist before him, that the bones were the remains of at least two men, and that using standard calculations for establishing height from long bones, he could say that they were within the height range of all six missing crew members of the aircraft that had been shot down on 18th October 1943! This information, we discovered, had been supplied to him direct by the MOD, and the RAF Police were only officially informed about this by OAR in early 1978 when they were told that instructions had been issued by OAR to the RAF Hospital Wegberg for the bones to be buried as 'unknown airmen'. The RAF pathologist found himself in an impossible position between the MOD on the one hand and the RAF Police on the other. It is fairly certain he had been told not to release any information to the RAF Police, but to a huge extent he relied on us to be able to produce the background information he needed for his report. Officially he was not supposed to tell us what he knew. There could now be no doubt that the OAR and the RAF Police had completely different views as to whose enquiry this was. The police investigation was suspended, in the vain hope that the OAR would realise that the best hope of bringing the enquiry to a satisfactory conclusion lay in cooperation. It was not to be.

Eventually we received a copy of the medical report, probably unofficially [but as the relevant Police files in Germany are now thought to have been destroyed following the ending of the Cold War, the closure of Gütersloh and the rundown of the RAF presence in Germany] the author cannot be sure. The RAF Police investigation never reopened. The evidence needed to close it had been taken out of police hands.

The pathologist was provided with a resume by the Squadron Leader SIB, RAF Germany of the circumstances in which the human remains had been found, and this was attached as an Annex to the medical report sent by the pathologist to OAR. [This is probably how the RAF Police came to have a copy of his report – the pathologist could hardly not give us a copy of a report based on our own police enquiry.] Today even the Annex [on file at the Air Historical Branch of MOD] cannot be viewed. From memory, however, the medical report concluded that all, or most, of the missing men were within the height range calculated by the pathologist from the bones. If one had been very small or very tall, he might have been identified or eliminated. Today, of course, with the advent of DNA testing a totally different approach would be taken, and, whether MOD liked it or not, the RAF Police would insist on an approach being made to relatives to obtain DNA samples, with whoever had the information needed for this to be done being subpoenaed if necessary to release it so that next of kin could be traced. It is not likely, therefore, that the bones would be released from RAF Police custody. With the benefit of hindsight, things would be different today.

In February 1978, after repeated requests from the RAF Police UK Headquarters at Rudloe Manor [who kept a watching brief on overseas cases] for the case of the war-time Lancaster to be concluded, a memo was sent to the Group Captain in charge of police policy at MOD, asking him to take up with the Head of OAR the matter of their behaviour in impeding a police enquiry. The memo was written in the strongest terms in the hope that the Head of OAR would be told, first, that it was not in his gift to dispose of police evidence, and, second, that he had impeded an official investigation. Whether the message was ever delivered, the author does not, and would not expect to know, but he can say that he wrote the memo and was the Squadron Leader in charge of the SIB in Germany.

According to the Commonwealth War Graves Commission's registers, the bones recovered from the Leine in March 1977 were buried as 'unknown airmen' on 4th April 1978 at Hannover Limmer [CWGC] Cemetery in graves 5 and 6, Row A, Plot 10, not far from the resting place of the only member of the crew of EE109 with a known grave, Sgt Roy Trahair, the rear gunner, who is buried in Grave 7, Row C, Plot 3. The Hannover Limmer Cemetery is about four kilometres from the place where EE109 came to rest on the night of 18th October 1943.

2. No 619 Squadron and RAF Woodhall Spa

What is needed is a humanity strong in will and firm in the determination to preserve itself. Freedom must discover its virility.
[Thomas Mann. *The Coming Victory*]

The RAF's No.619 Squadron was never famous. It is unknown to the airmen and women of the present-day RAF, and many of their predecessors – those, say, who served in the RAF in the fifty years after 1950, would not have heard of it either. But for a brief period during the Second World War, it was a typical main force operational squadron of Bomber Command, flying Lancaster aircraft in No.5 Group of Bomber Command, one of the 21 new squadrons brought into being virtually overnight to meet the needs of the strategic bombing campaign and then unceremoniously disbanded just as quickly when the war was over. In between, its crews lived and died in the almost surreal world inhabited by Second World War bomber crews, where in the morning you could be enjoying the peaceful rural idylls of Lincolnshire yet that night be hundreds of miles away dropping bombs on Berlin or some other distant German city, knowing that any moment could be your last as a night-fighter closed in for the kill or one of the barrage of flak shells filling the sky around you exploded close enough to take you, your six fellows, your 12,000lb bomb-load and your 102 feet of fuel-filled wings into a fiery oblivion.

A former Luftwaffe night-fighter pilot, who was shot down by his own flak over Hannover on 18th October 1943, but was able to bale out successfully, has told the author that '*the fighting technique* [of the night-fighter pilot] *was to try to hit the fuel tanks* [in the wings] *and set them alight ... this they did for their own protection, or they might* [otherwise] *be blown up by the bombs on board* [the night-fighter pilots often getting to within a hundred feet or so of the bomber in the blind spot beneath it] ... *damaging the bomber in the area of the tanks and engines also left open the possibility that the crew might be able to parachute out of the burning, but still flying, machine*'.[1] Like many of the German *Wilde Sau* [Wild Boar] night-fighter pilots, this man had previously flown bombers, and so he had seen the effect from both sides of the fence and knew only too well what he was talking about.

A retired German professor of medicine, who as a fifteen year-old *Luftwaffenhelfer*, was a member of flak batterie 3./521 based on the Sports Platz near the Masch-see in the centre of Hannover, told the author '*I have observed this* [the explosion that erupted if the bomb-load was hit] *myself ... if a bomber took a hit on its bomb bay, the explosion would destroy the machine and cause the death of the crew*'.[2] This same man said that they were told in the flak teams that a flak shell exploding within 12 metres [40 ft] of an aircraft would bring that aircraft down; that they did not have to achieve a direct hit with their radar-guided Sprenchender Kanonier [anti-aircraft gun] & FunkMessGerät Fabrikat Telefunken *Würzburg* [radar]. During the twelve months from 26th July 1943 to 18th June 1944, Flak Batterie 3./521 shot down 25 aircraft, including Cyril Fuller's Lancaster aircraft EE109 PG-F of 619 Squadron, the rediscovery of the remains of which in 1977, almost 34 years after it was lost, inspired this book.

Specifically, during the four Bomber Command raids on Hannover in late September and early/mid October 1943, Flak Batterie 3./521 shot down twelve of the RAF's attacking force of heavy bombers: five Lancasters, four Halifaxes and three Stirlings. Of these four raids, only the third - that of 8th October - caused significant damage, when a Bomber Command force of 504 aircraft [282 Lancasters, 188 Halifaxes,

[1] Letter to author, via Prof Dr Med Jürgen Probst, in June 2001.

[2] Ibid.

26 Wellingtons[3] and 8 Mosquitoes] attacked the city on a clear night and the Pathfinders were finally able to mark the centre of the city accurately. This resulted in a most concentrated attack, with a creep-back of only 2 miles, all within the built-up area. This was probably Hannover's worst attack of the war. Local reports describe extensive damage in the centre of the city and in many other parts except the west.[4] The electrical supply and telephone network failed at the beginning of the raid and many water mains were quickly broken. A large area of fire quickly developed in the centre and south-central districts. Acting on instructions from the Party Headquarters and local air-raid posts, the population was shepherded to collecting places in open areas between the fires. This action, it is believed saved many lives, but 1,200 people were killed and 3,345 were injured, 449 seriously so. A further 6,000-8,000 people received treatment for eye injuries caused by the smoke and heat. Of the physical damage, 3,932 buildings were completely destroyed and more than 30,000 others damaged in varying degree. RAF reconnaissance photographs show that the important Continental rubber factory and the Hanomag machine works were badly hit.[5]

Particularly relevant to our story, the hutted barracks of the flak batterie received a direct hit and was largely destroyed [see photograph]. Looking back on photographs taken at the time, Jurgen Pröbst commented:

> *'On this attack my Flak batterie was hit and the greater part of the barracks around it were lost. The bomb crater, in which soldiers*

---

[3] This was the last occasion on which the twin-engined Vickers-Armstrong Wellington bomber, the work-horse of the early years of the campaign, with its unusual Barnes Wallis fabric-covered 'geodetic' design, was used in a raid by Bomber Command, the 26 aircraft involved being provided by No 300 [Polish] and No 432 [Canadian] Squadrons.

[4] An article in the Hannoversche Allgemeine Zeitung of 5/6 Oktober 1968 includes an aerial photograph taken during the raid by an Australian bomber pilot, showing bombs falling on the city. On a clear night, the positions of Flak Batterie3./521 and the crash site of 619 Squadron's EE109 can also be seen.

[5] Middlebrook and Everitt, The Bomber Command War Diaries [Midland Publishing Ltd, 1996] p 437/438.

sought shelter, shows what power the high explosive bombs had. For a short time the batterie was u/s as the electrical connections between the command radar and the guns were destroyed. One sees that the opponents on both sides had given themselves nothing, even if we lost no personnel in this attack. One of the pictures shows our radar machine, which carries the silhouettes of shot-down bombers on its parabola. The one marked with the 'x' is the crew we are researching.[6]

Unfortunately for the crew of EE109, the guns of flak batterie 3./521 were not permanently damaged on the 8th October. Ironically, this the most successful raid from the RAF's point of view, was the only one of the four in which Cyril Fuller and his crew did not participate, as they were that week taking a few days, well-earned break at their homes with their families, having completed two-thirds – twenty - of their tour requirement of thirty operations following their part in the attack on Hagen on 1 October.

On the other three nights, because of thick cloud over the city [10/10 at 10,000 ft plus], the RAF's bombs fell mainly in fields and woods to the north and north west of the city.

But back to the story of 619 Squadron.

A sister squadron of the more famous dam-busting squadron, No 617, both in terms of the proximity of its squadron serial number[7] and the bases, aircraft and aircrew it used, No 619 Squadron came into being on 18th April, 1943 'on a mainly cloudy day, with good visibility

---

[6] Letter to the author in December 2000.

[7] RAF Squadron serial numbers had reached as far as No 695 by the end of the War. No 618, the missing serial between No 617 and No 619 did exist as a squadron but never went into action. It was formed on 1 Apr 43, with Mosquitoes, with the intention it would use a variant of Wallis's bouncing bomb [used by 617 in the attack on the Ruhr dams in May 43] to attack German warships. This plan never came to fruition, and, though 618 was deployed to the Far East in Oct 44 for use against Japanese warships, the absence by this time of suitable naval targets led to the squadron being disbanded on 29 Jun 45 without having ever dropped a bomb in action.

but a fresh westerly wind building up by mid-day'[8]. The Squadron's first commanding officer, Wing Commander I J McGhie, was posted in from 57 Squadron at RAF Scampton and found himself the commander of a newly-numbered unit at RAF Woodhall Spa with no aircraft and only his adjutant, Fg Off GM Burdett, and three crews of seven men each, captained by F/L CSR Bell DFC, F/O SE Harrison DFM and Sgt W McCleod, all operationally experienced crews left behind by 619's predecessors at Woodhall, No 97 Squadron, to form the nucleus of the new squadron. The rest of 97 Sqn had been posted out to Bourn to become one of the elite squadrons of the Pathfinder force being put together – in the teeth of much opposition[9] - by Air Vice-Marshal Donald Bennett within 8 Group, Bomber Command. The following day an experienced engineering officer, F/L M C Mitcham was posted in from No 1485 B & G Flight to take up duties as squadron engineering officer, and notification was received that P/O WW Fuller, then completing a course at the School of Aircraft Engineering, RAF Henlow, near Hitchin in Bedfordshire, would shortly be posted in as the Electrical Officer.

The following day, a steady stream of ground crew personnel, administrative and disciplinary staff started to arrive: senior NCOs, junior NCOs, aircraftmen and WAAFs. By the end of that day 619 had 62 people on its strength.

On the 22nd April, Flying Officer [acting Flight Lieutenant] RC 'Ronnie' Churcher DFC, an experienced pilot who had flown Manchesters [on 106 Squadron at Coningsby] at the same time as many of the pilots that were later to become well known in Bomber circles[10], was

---

[8] The Squadron diarist, perhaps for want of much else to say, carefully recorded the weather conditions day by day.

[9] Air Vice-Marshal D C T Bennett, *Pathfinder*, [Crécy Publishing Ltd, 1998], first published 1958.

[10] P/O J Aytoun [later S/L on 619], P/O S Cockbain [later S/L QFI at 1661 HCU Winthorpe], Sgt S E J Jones [later F/Lt DFC DFM on 619], S/L P C Ward-Hunt, P/O AJF Rayment [later F/L on 619], P/O H B Martin [later Air Marshal Sir Harold KCB, DSO and bar, DFC and 2 bars, AFC – obituary The Times, 4 Nov 1988], Sgt E Dampier-Crossley [later F/L DFC on 619], P/O L T Manser [later posthumous VC],

posted in from 1660 CU with the acting rank of Squadron Leader to take over 'A' Flight. At the age of twenty-one, he was a flying officer, holding two acting ranks above his substantive rank. F/Off PSF Walmsley and crew were next to be posted in, from 1654 Conversion Unit RAF Wigsley, and notification was also received that day of the imminent posting in of two other experienced pilots, F/Lt E Dampier-Crossley DFC RAAF, a New Zealander serving in the Royal Australian Air Force and his crew from 1660 CU, and Acting F/Lt CO Harrison and his crew from 50 Squadron, RAF Syerston, just off the old Fosse Way between Nottingham and Lincoln.

On the 23rd April, further notifications were received of the imminent postings in from No 1660 Conversion Unit RAF Swinderby of another four pilots and crews: Sgt DJ Coomber, Sgt D V Jordan, Sgt K McCulloch and Sgt T Metcalfe. The squadron diarist noted rather hopefully that '*although these crews have completed only one or two operations, they will be given the benefit of the Commanding Officer's many years of flying experience and the support of their "gen"* [sic] *crew colleagues*'. Less than two months later, and after only a handful of operations by the Squadron, Sgt [by then Pilot Officer] McCulloch and his crew, and Sgt Jordan and his crew, were all dead, as also was the experienced New Zealander Dampier-Crossley and his crew. By the end of August, Sgt Metcalfe [by then a F/Sgt and towards the end of the War given a posthumous DFM] and five members of his crew were also dead [one survived to be taken pow], and five members of Sgt Coomber's crew were dead. Coomber, by then a Pilot Officer with a DFM, and the seventh member of his crew were prisoners of war. Twenty-eight men, trained at considerable expense over a year and more, had joined the new squadron in April, and after two months of operations twenty-five were dead.

The 24th April, a day of '*thin variable cloud and very good visibility*', saw the arrival of the 100th member of the squadron to be posted in, and by the end of that day the total strength stood at 107. Easter Monday that year fell on the 26th April, and the squadron was given

---

F/O Gunter [later S/L on 619], F/O H E Maudslay [killed as S/L DFC during the dams raid].

the afternoon off as a general holiday. That day another pilot was posted in from 57 Squadron: New Zealander F/O J D Henderson RNZAF. The following day, F/O J A Howard was posted in from 1485 B & G Flight as the squadron gunnery officer. Today, at the age of 90, John Howard still has vivid memories of his time on the squadron:

> *'As gunnery leader I had no crew and such trips as I did were usually when a rear gunner was unfit for some reason or another, or on odd occasions when a new crew arrived minus a rear gunner. It took from Apr 43 to Mar 44 to do 13 operational trips [with Jock Abercromby, Ronnie Churcher, Gerry Scorer and others]. Jock Abercromby's last trip with 619 was to Berlin when we had with us as passenger/observer Edward Morrow, who was War Correspondent for Columbia Broadcasting. Two other broadcasters went that night with other squadrons and failed to return. Abercromby was then posted to 83 Pathfinder Sqn but went missing on his second trip. Wing Co. Jeudwine replaced Abercromby in December 43 but lost his rear gunner on a trip to Berlin some time in February. I filled in as rear gunner on 1 Mar 44 and as his RG remained in hospital with severe frostbite, it was arranged that I would continue as a crew member. I had become rather tired of being the squadron odd job man. However, in May 44 we were posted as a crew to 54 Base on Master Bomber duties and did our last trip as such on 5th June 1944 for D Day.*[11]

In explaining that he had no memory of Fuller and his crew, even though he flew with them as an observer on a fighter affiliation exercise in EE109 on 27 Jun 43, Howard says '*unhappily one became very hardened to the news on return to base of those who had gone missing even when someone in the missing crew was by way of a pal.*'[12]

By the 28th, the diarist was recording that stationery and publications were now arriving from APFS and that with the help unstintingly given by the parent station, RAF Coningsby, the squadron was quickly

[11] Letter to author August, 2000.

[12] Ibid.

becoming organised. So much so, that a detachment of 619 squadron personnel was being trained in marching to take part in the forthcoming 'Wings for Victory Week' parade, of which the diarist believed '*with the short period of instruction daily* [they] *will, we are sure, reflect credit on the squadron*'.[13] In 1943 the RAF was new enough to believe still that an air force, like the Army from whence it came, marched to victory. The other important event of the day was the weather: *little or no cloud, misty at first variable, cloud, good visibility in the afternoon, showers in the evening.*[14]

The next day, the 29th April, must have been the most momentous so far in the Squadron's eleven days of existence. Two aircraft arrived, a Lancaster Mk I and a Lancaster Mk III from 617 Squadron. The diarist recorded '*we are now leaving the embryo stage*'.[15] Steve Rew, a member of the ground crew of 619 Squadron throughout the whole of its operational life, was less kind about these events.

> *'Between April 18th and the 30th, 250 men and women arrived including ... 7 complete aircrews [making ten in all] the Engineering Officer, 'A' flight commander, and the Bombing, Navigation, Signals and Gunnery leaders. 'A' and 'B' Flights were formed with a Flt Sgt in charge of each, and some ground equipment such as engine trestles and trolley accumulators (batteries for engine starting etc., mounted on wheels, together with a charging set) had been acquired. More important on the 29th two aircraft arrived. They were a Mk I and a Mk III [Lancaster] and came from 617 Squadron where they had been used as training aircraft, but they were obviously a long way from having been new when 617 Squadron got them. 617 Squadron letters [AJ] were painted out and one aircraft was issued to each flight.*

Later he records the dreadful technical condition of these two aircraft, as one of the many laments of the young erks [airmen] posted to

[13] 619 Sqn ORB entry for 28 Apr 43.

[14] Ibid.

[15] Ibid.

the new squadron: *'A' Flight's had the [magneto] leads crossed to disguise the most appalling mag. drops.* [16]

At the end of this first month of 619's existence, the diarist was able to write: 'the last day of the month showed us with two aircraft, ten complete crews, 31 WAAFs and 202 other ranks. With five DFC and four DFM holders, the squadron has a nucleus around which it is hoped to form an efficient fighting unit.'[17] As usual, the state of the weather was also recorded: '3/4 cloudy, occasional rain and drizzle mist, further rain and drizzle in the afternoon closing about 1730 hours; visibility very variable all day from 1500 yards to 6 miles.[18]

The Signals Leader, F/L Gilmour, had arrived at the Squadron the previous day, and so the new squadron began the month with all the Headquarters officer posts filled except the flight commander of 'B' Flight, the Medical Officer and the Electrical Officer. Group HQ telephoned on 1 May to ask whether the eight ground crews it had instructed eight squadrons in the Group to send at the rate of one each had all arrived? They had not! So far, 619 had received one sergeant fitter and one sergeant rigger. The sergeant fitter was George Allen, a young ex-Halton apprentice [569012], who for almost the entire operational life of the squadron was to look after three aircraft in 'A' Flight, including for the first six months the one usually flown by the 'A' Flight Commander, Ronnie Churcher. This aircraft, ED977 PG-A, the first of two 619 Sqn aircraft to be named *Nulli Secundus* [Second to None], was the Squadron's veteran with 46 operations flown by the time it was lost on 5/6 Jan 44 in an operation against Stettin.

George Allen had joined the RAF as a 'Trenchard Brat' at Halton in the 33rd Entry, finishing his training at Christmas 1938. After the outbreak of war, like many other ex-apprentices, he volunteered for aircrew training and was sent to Canada to be trained as a pilot. His flying instructor in Canada, on the Harvard training aircraft, was

[16] Chris Rew, privately published booklet, circulated within the 619 Sqn Association in the 1970s.

[17] Ibid.

[18] Ibid.

another ex-Halton apprentice from the 30th Entry. Unlike the author's experience as an ex-apprentice in the post-war RAF, where being an ex-apprentice sometimes seemed like the RAF equivalent of a Masonic handshake, George found that his near contemporary '*had it in for me*'. As a result, George was 'chopped' from pilot training and recommended for flight engineer training instead, an obvious aircrew route for a qualified fitter. Instead, however, he was posted to 619 Squadron, and when he plucked up the courage to ask his boss, the Engineering Officer, about his flight engineer training was told '*forget it*'; the Engineering Officer was not going to give up a skilled fitter. And so George Allen completed his war as a Lancaster engine fitter, and as a consequence survived to tell the tale. The chances are that as a Flight Engineer he would not have done. In a photograph taken for PR purposes in 1943 with other ground crew in front of Nulli Secundus, George is able to identify Cpl Jock Mitchell, AC 'Taff' Evans, AC 'Ginger' Thomas and probably F/S Mullins, 'an old-sweat Chiefy', [who extraordinarily was awarded a Military Medal, after being mentioned in despatches three times].[19]

But back to early May, 1943. Chris Rew described Woodhall Spa as:

> *'a typical war-time dispersed bomber airfield with three runways, a perimeter track, some 40-odd concrete dispersal points, and two corrugated iron hangars on opposite sides of the airfield. Near one of the two hangars was a collection of brick-built huts collectively known as the Technical Site or 'Tech Site'. One hut was occupied by the Station Commander, Group Captain H L Patch [post-war Air Chief Marshal] and his Station Headquarters staff, while the others were offices, stores and workshops for the various technical sections – Electrical, Armament, Instrument, Radio etc. Within a radius of perhaps half a mile from the tech site were the Sergeants' Mess and the communal or 'Com Site' for the airman, and at perhaps quarter miles radius from these focal points were a number of 'Domestic Sites' comprising groups of huts in which the troops lived. The difference in accommodation for officers, NCOs and airmen lay primarily in the*

[19] Letters to author in October 2000.

> *number of men per hut, for although the Officers' Mess was a commandeered hotel in Woodhall Spa* [author: today the Petwood Hotel, with its famous memorial bar to 617 Sqn, who succeeded 619 in this rather splendid building] *only the more senior officers were able to sleep there, the others using one of the hut sites. The airfield had been completed late in 1941, and No 97 Squadron had been in occupation with Lancasters since the summer of 1942.*[20]

Woodhall Spa lay almost on the perimeter of the larger and much better known RAF Coningsby. Today, the former RAF Woodhall Spa is typical of so many other derelict East Anglian airfields, except that one small part of it is still used by the RAF for testing the engines of the Tornado jet aircraft now based at Coningsby. And so a road sign in red still records the name of this once active operational station. Apart from the Tornado test section, what remains of the rest of the old airfield is used by a commercial quarrying company. As a result, instead of the hum and activity of a RAF station at war, the only noise to be heard is that of the wind whistling across the flat plains of Lincolnshire and the drone of lorries grinding past with their heavy loads. The landscape is dominated not by an air traffic control tower but by the derrick-like, distant towers of the quarry. It is still possible to stand, however, on a remaining section of runway from which, some sixty years ago, first 97 Squadron, then 619 Squadron and finally 617 Squadron flew some of the most dramatic and significant air operations of the Second World War. But just as few of today's officers and airmen have heard of 619 Squadron, few of them have heard of RAF Woodhall Spa. It has long ceased to be an important place-name in RAF circles.[21] Some airmen may, if WWII buffs, have visited the village of Woodhall Spa and seen the dam-like memorial to 617 Squadron, but they will probably not have realised that the remains of the airfield are still evident only a mile away. At the former domestic site at Thorpe, a local group has started to

---

[20] Rew, op cit.

[21] The airfield was closed in 1945. Part was later used by 92 MU for the storage of bombs, and for a few years in the late 1950s/early 1960s the airfield gained a brief new lease of life as a location for Bloodhound surface-to-air missiles.

preserve the few buildings still intact, as the Thorpe Camp Visitor Centre. Much had already gone, however, the post-war use of the airfield not having had history or preservation in mind.

The Centre is on a part of what was formerly No 1 Communal Site, built in 1940 with a planned life of ten years. That site originally had on it the Officers' and Sergeants' accommodation and Messes, the Airmen's Dining Hall and the NAAFI, the ration store and other stores and the latrine and ablutions blocks. Today, only the Airmen's Dining Hall, the NAAFI and the ration store still stand, for at the end of the war the RAF vacated the site, and it became a target for squatters until it was taken over by Horncastle District Council, which converted the buildings into temporary council housing. By the early 1960s the buildings were no longer fit for this use, and by 1987 the site was totally derelict. The Woodland Trust acquired part of the site, and the Thorpe Camp Preservation Group was allowed by the Trust to restore the salvageable buildings. [22]

In many ways Woodhall Spa was like so many of the huge number airfields commissioned during WWII, a monument to the amazing development that saw the number of RAF airfields increase in total so dramatically. Between 1939 and 1945 some 444[23] airfields were constructed in UK at the cost of about £200M.[24] By 1942 a peak labour force of 60,000 men was employed in the UK solely on the task of airfield construction for the RAF and USAAF. Ernest Bevin[25] decreed that some 28,000 men due to be called up for the forces were to be left

---

[22] I am grateful to Mike Hodgson, of the Preservation Group, for this information from his Centre brochure.

[23] David J Smith, *Britain's Military Airfields 1939-45* [Patrick Stephens Ltd 1989], p54. Smith has also produced a list of airfield projects that were NOT completed – about 90 – and the list is thought to be incomplete!

[24] Prof Robin Higham in his book, *Bases of Air Strategy, the building of Airfields for the RAF 1914-1945*, [Airlife Publishing Ltd, 1998] records that during 1939-1945 the number of airfields used by the RAF and USAAF increased from 52 to 740 in the UK alone. Overseas, the Royal Engineers and later the RAF Construction Branch built about 1,000 more.

[25] Ernest Bevin [1881-1951], Minister of Labour in the war-time coalition government and a member of the post-war Labour Cabinet.

in the building industry until October that year. He stated also that the country's entire building manpower was to be devoted to the project and that all public and municipal work would have to be postponed. There was friction with Churchill over this as the Prime Minister was most concerned about the effect on civilian morale of facing a further winter living in bomb-damaged houses that received only temporary repairs. Bevin prevailed, however, and repair work was suspended until 1943. At one time a third of Britain's total construction labour force was engaged in the work of airfield construction. Much Irish labour was attracted to this country and rewards were high, giving rise to criticism that the men who built the aerodromes earned more than the pilots who flew from them [the pilots sometimes taking off for Berlin while the work was still progressing]. Time wasting and slackness also attracted criticism, and in the case of the Irish it was said that their efficiency depended on the influence of the local priest. Apart from the vast labour force engaged in this enormous construction project, a Class 'A' airfield was also likely to consume some 20 miles of drain, six miles of water main, four miles of sewer, ten miles of roadway and four and a half million bricks.[26]

All of this, of course, was of no concern to the men and women of the fledgling 619 Squadron in May 1943. Their airfield and domestic sites already existed, even if not standing comparison with the nearby pre-war permanent stations, such as Waddington, Scampton, Coningsby and Hemswell. And so on the 2nd May 1943, a third aircraft arrived, and the first pilot to fly with 619 Squadron, Sgt D.V. Jordan and his crew, took off that day from Woodhall on a training flight. Jordan and his crew were to die barely six weeks later during a raid on Krefeld. But the squadron now had three aircraft, twenty officers, 80 senior NCOs [57 of them aircrew], 298 other ranks, 30 WAAFs, and the weather was '*good with fine visibility until 1800 hours, when cloudy and clearing at midnight*'!

The following day, 3rd May a second training flight took place, and on the 4th two aircraft and crews [S/L Churcher and Sgt Metcalfe] took

---

[26] Smith, ibid, Chapter 4.

part in a Bomber Command 'Bullseye' Exercise.[27] On 6 May the second flight commander, S/L GR [Gerry] Scorer arrived from RAF Fiskerton, but the next day the squadron was grounded. All three aircraft were u/s [unserviceable]. The next day saw the arrival of two experienced crews, F/O SEJ Jones DFM and his crew, and F/L Dampier-Crossley DFC, whose imminent arrival had been signalled on 22nd April. A new squadron needed some captains with credibility if those coming straight out of training [and that was the majority] were to be encouraged and were to pick up anything from that experience before it was too late.

The Squadron reached a significant turning point on 9th May. '*The CO decided there were enough personnel now to hold a parade*'. Unfortunately, it rained, and so the parade was held in a hangar, where '*immediately after the CO had spoken to the troops*', the two padres, S/L Hitchens and S/L Jones held a short drumhead service. Thirteen WAAFs, twenty-two officers and 270 airmen took part. The next three days were spent desperately trying to find things to keep over three hundred idle hands occupied, but by the 12th May the situation could no longer be disguised and the diarist recorded 'everyone disgruntled....time is passing, only four aircraft, and shortage of ground staffs'.

The following day must have sent Squadron spirits soaring: seven new Lancaster Mk III aircraft arrived bright and shiny from the manufacturers. These were part of the consignment of aircraft in the EE106 to EE117 series of aircraft registration numbers about which we shall be hearing more shortly.

From then on the process of getting the new Squadron operational began to move at a rapid pace. An Army officer, Major Mullock, gave a lecture on flak, F/L CSR Bell DFC carried out 'a height check with full load' and on the 14 May the new Squadron was allotted the code letters PG. These were now painted on the aircraft, each aircraft being allocated in addition a third identifying letter. From now on the aircraft will be referred to in this way, for example, EE109 PG-F.

---

[27] A bombing training exercise, against a British city at night, designed to see whether the crews really could achieve a bullseye. Few could [not because they were not proficient but because they did not have the equipment to permit them to do so].

The next couple of days were occupied with various flying training exercises – Command Bullseyes, cross country navigational trips, and then on 17th May a party was held in the Officers' Mess at Woodhall attended by W/C Guy Gibson and the surviving crews from No 617 Squadron, who in the early hours of that morning had returned from the attack on the Ruhr dams. The following day the Squadron was delighted when Sgt DL May, the air bomber [bomb aimer] in F/S W McLeod's experienced crew, scored a direct hit on the practice bombing range from 20,000 feet, using the ABS bombsight. Sadly Sgt May was killed only a month later on 21/22 June when their aircraft [EE116 PG-Q] was hit by flak during an attack on *Freidrichshaven*. Twenty-four hours later, on returning to Woodhall from *Blida* in North Africa, to which they had flown after the raid with the other four 619 Squadron aircraft, so as to be able to attack *Spezia* on the return leg, F/S McLeod and the rest of the crew completed their operational tour. Another 48 hours and Sgt May would have completed his tour of duty as well.

The 22nd May saw the beginning of the air-testing of all the aircraft, and the same day a formation of aircraft from the Squadron led by the Squadron CO, W/C John McGhie, flew over Boston as part of the 'Wings for Victory Week' campaign. Since the beginning of May, the Squadron crews had flown almost 115 hours of training. One month on since John McGhie had found himself the Commanding Officer of nothing, he had a Squadron, which, if not yet operational, was rapidly becoming so.

The 23rd May saw the arrival of three more captains and crews [Sgt FW Shirley, Sgt WJ Douglas and Sgt RT Hughes]. Sgt Shirley and all his crew [except the flight engineer Sgt Simes] plus Sgt Douglas, who was flying as second pilot, and two members of the ground crew, F/Sgt AP Price and Sgt PJ Cooper, were to be killed while flying an aircraft [EE113 PG-K] on an air test on 9th June forty-eight hours before the Squadron flew its first operational sortie. F/Sgt Price was an ex-Halton apprentice instrument fitter. It is thought their aircraft crashed into the North Sea, but this was never confirmed for certain, though in the absence of any other evidence, it seems that his must have happened. Sgt Hughes alone, by this time commissioned, and his crew completed most of their first tour of operations with No 619 before being posted to another new Squadron, No 630, on 15th November, 1943.

On 27th May the Squadron carried out its first 'fighter affiliation exercise', in which Bomber crews practised being stalked and attacked by fighter pilots, who at least would not actually shoot them down. On this day also the Squadron sent away the two aircraft it had received for training purposes from No 617 Squadron, the ground crews only too pleased no long to be responsible for trying to keep them serviceable.[28]

By the 31st May, the Squadron could put ten aircraft in the air simultaneously for training, had seventeen crews and nineteen aircraft, had flown 191 hours and 31 minutes in training and had a strength of forty officers, 120 Senior NCOs, 335 other ranks and 39 WAAFs. The only serious deficiency remained a shortage of sergeant fitters, which the diarist noted were 'the key men of the flight ground staff', of which only a quarter of the Squadron's established strength had arrived. Thus, by the end of the first full month in existence, the Squadron was rapidly approaching operational status, and within a fortnight would be flying its first mission with hostile intent.

On 1st June two more crews arrived, captained by F/O WED Bell and Sgt CA Goddard. Sgt Goddard and his crew were killed on 6th September during an operation against *Mannheim*. F/O Bell survived to retire as a Wing Commander with a DFC. He died in 1966. The following day, 2nd June, the Air Officer Commanding No 5 Group, Air Vice-Marshal the Hon Sir Ralph Cochrane, made the first of a number of visits he was to make to the Squadron over the next two years, to welcome them into the Group.

On 6th June another crew arrived, captained by Sgt OA O'Leary. They were to die on the attack on the Experimental Rocket Establishment at *Peenemünde* on 17/18th August, when the Squadron lost three aircraft including its Commanding Officer, John McGhie. But for the moment, the Squadron had a strength that was rapidly approaching its establishment. On 8th June, P/O DM Joss and his crew arrived. Tragi-

[28] These aircraft, W4921 and W4929, were sent by No 619 Sqn to No 1654 Conversion Unit, where novice crews had to try to fly them instead.

cally, they were to be lost on 2nd October while returning from the *Hagen* raid, crashing in the Bristol Channel off Llantwit Major, along the coast from Cardiff. All were killed. The reason for this happening could not be established, but obviously they were massively off course.

In chronological order, however, the Squadron suffered its first casualties on 9th June, when PG-K was lost on an air test, as already mentioned. Two days later, on 11th June, the Squadron participated in its first operation, sending twelve aircraft to *Dusseldorf*. Only ten of the aircraft are known to have bombed. On this the night of its operational debut, the squadron lost its first aircraft on operations: ED978 PG-B captained by Flight Lieutenant CO Taylor, the Deputy Flight Commander of 'A' Flight was lost. They had been shot down by a night-fighter over Belgium and crash-landed near Tongeren in the Limberg province. Taylor evaded capture, with the help of the Belgian *Maquis,* but his crew did not and spent the next two years as prisoners of war. Taylor returned to flying duties as an instructor, his experience of the *Maquis* and the escape routes being too much of a liability for further operational flying.

Another aircraft, PG-L captained by F/S Metcalfe was forced to jettison its bombs into the North Sea and return back to base early when the instrument gyros ceased to function.

In addition to being the day of the Squadron's debut into the world of Bomber Command operations, June 11th was a fine summer's day, and Chris Rew, a member of the 619 Squadron ground crew for most of the Squadron's existence, wrote an account of that day for the Squadron Association some twenty years or so ago, describing how the ground crew sweated in the hot sun as they loaded up the aircraft for the first time with real bombs, a 4,000 lb 'cookie' and a dozen or more small bomb containers of 150 x 4 lb incendiary bombs into each aircraft. Chris died some years ago, and I hope his family will not mind if I quote from what he wrote, as it describes so graphically what that first step into operations was like on this typical main force bomber squadron:

> *The bomb winches were very low geared, and the inside of the aircraft was uncomfortably like an oven. Now and again, throughout*

the day there would be the sound of a Merlin [engine] running up to check that some snag was cleared, and over the whole camp was an atmosphere of expectancy and tension. Ops were on, and everyone was secretly hoping that their work wasn't going to let the side down.

In the late afternoon the crews were briefed by the CO and the Met Officer, and the Navigation, Bombing, Gunnery, Signals and Engineer leaders briefed their own specialist groups. The crews had their tea and wandered down to the crew room to collect their equipment and put on their flying clothing. For many of them this was a new experience, the climax of months of training, but for a few, the more senior crews, it was by no means new. They had already completed one 'tour' of about 30 operations, and had just had a few months so-called 'rest' as instructors on training units, passing on to the newcomers their hard-won experience. All of them, however, had one thing in common, even if they would not admit it – butterflies in the tummy; not exactly fear, but a kind of nervous excitement. Corny jokes were cracked, and the occasional temper got frayed, just as in every crew-room in Bomber Command whenever ops were on. They gathered up their equipment and went outside and stood or sat in groups outside the crew-room waiting for the buses to take them out to their aircraft. Eighty-four men, some in their early twenties, but a few doddering old grandfathers in their early thirties, and quite a number who were not yet legally responsible for their actions.[29] *At last the crew buses, looking like over-grown shooting brakes,*[30] *started to arrive and the crews scrambled onto them.*

Out on the dispersals where the aircraft stood, big and black against the setting sun, which glinted on the polished perspex, there was also an atmosphere of tension. Everything was ready, the pitot head covers, static vent plugs and wheel covers were being removed, and the trolley accumulators were in position behind the aircrafts' starboard wheels, with their leads plugged in. There were two ground crew men on duty on each aircraft, who regarded the kite as their

[29] At that time the legal age of responsibility was 21 years of age.

[30] Shooting brakes were vehicles used by shooting parties and can best be described as large estate cars or small buses.

own, merely allowing the aircrew to fly it. They were Engine or Airframe mechanics and regarded themselves as the kin-pins of the squadron, referring to the other trades – Armament, Electrical, Instruments, Radio and Radar – collectively as 'gash' trades. Everyone had been working hard all day, doing inspections, checking and re-checking services and systems. The aircraft had flown on test and then been re-fuelled and bombed up. Now in the cool of the evening, everything was ready, and their labours were about to bear fruit. The undercarriages of the aircraft were shorter than usual under the weight of fuel and bombs, and the big bomb doors were open, revealing the dark green cylindrical shape of the 'cookie' and the shiny rectangular cans of incendiaries. The stage was set, and ready for the entrance of the night's principal actors.

They arrived in the crew-buses driven by WAAFs and piled out with their flying kit, parachutes and bags, dumped their kit and stood around smoking and chatting among themselves and to the ground crew. At last, the skipper said 'Well chaps, we'd better be moving'. And they began to climb into the aircraft, the ground crew helping with their loads. The ground crew took the latter away and the door was shut. The aircrew settled down in their positions and started checking the intercom and other equipment. At last the Flight Engineer slid back his window, leant out, and shouted 'OK to start up: switch on ground.' One of the ground crew replied 'OK Starboard Outer straight across'. He then climbed onto the trolley accumulator and up into the starboard undercarriage, while his mate seated himself on the towing arm of the trolley accumulator with his thumb hovering over the button. He watched while the man in the undercarriage unscrewed the priming pump, turned the outboard cock on and primed the pump. When this was done, he pressed the button and shouted 'Contact Starboard Outer'. The Flight Engineer replied 'Contact Starboard Outer' and pressed the starter and booster coil buttons. As the engine turned the ground crew man operated the priming pump until the engine fired. Then the engineer flicked on the idle cut-off switch and the engine settled down to a discontented grumble. When it was running, the men on the trolley acc. ran across, ducked under the bomb doors and swung himself up into the port undercarriage to prime the port engines, while the man in the starboard undercarriage screwed down the pump and turned the cock off before jumping down and pressing the button on the trolley acc. When all four engines were running, the ground crew unplugged the trolley acc. and dragged it clear of the aircraft and watched the big bomb doors slowly close. Then came the long wait while the engines warmed up. After what seemed like several hours, they saw the engineer duck down to look at the temperature gauges and come up with his hand on his microphone switch. Each engine in turn was then run up, its note rising to a roar, dropping and rising again as the CSU control was checked, and then gradually increasing [sic] to a crescendo as take-off power was reached. Then it started to diminish, steadied, and the sensitive ear could detect the difference as each magneto was checked, and finally died away to a discontented grumble again. After all four had been run up, one of the ground crew ran through the blustering gale of the slipstream to the door, clutching the foolscap booklet that was the Form 700 to his chest, opened the door, scrambled in head first, went forward to the cockpit, opened the 700 at the appropriate pages and handed it to the skipper for signature. When it had been signed, he uncrossed his fingers and went back down the fuselage to the door, jumped out, shut the door and ran clear of the slipstream. He put the 700 in the homemade tent beside the dispersal, and stood by the wing tip of the aircraft, watching the pilot and waiting. At last the pilot looked at his watch and waved 'chocks away'. The two ground crew men ran in behind the big propellers and pulled on the ropes attached to the chocks in front of the wheels. One was stuck, so the man had to sit down and thump it with both fees. At last it came clear and he dragged it out to the wing tip, giving the pilot a thumbs up sign at the same time. There was a hiss of compressed air as the brakes were released, a light increase in the engine noise, and she started to roll out of the dispersal, leaving behind her a giant's breath of a slip-stream, strongly flavoured with the clean acrid smell of 100 octane. She swung round onto the taxi track and nosed her way up to the perimeter track where she had to halt to let another aircraft come past. Then she turned onto the perimeter track and taxied towards the downwind end of the runway in use, where she joined the queue of aircraft waiting to take off.

At the head of the queue was PG-B, with Wing Commander McGhie in the pilot's seat. A green Aldis lamp flashed from the control caravan and he swung her round on to the runway, taxied up it for a few yards to straighten out the tail wheel, and applied the brakes again. A quick burst of throttle on each engine to clear the plugs, and again he was waiting. He must have felt reasonably satisfied at that moment. The hard work of the last two months was about to show results. Not only had the Squadron produced the twelve aircraft required of it, but the little crowd of watchers standing by the caravan was of encouraging proportions, and this was quite a useful indicator of morale. He clipped on his oxygen mask, tightened his straps, and ran a knowledgeable eye over the instrument panel. The pre-take off checks had been completed, the gyro was set and un-caged and all was ready. At last the green Aldis lamp shone again: he pulled the control column back and switched on his microphone: 'Zero Boost'. The Engineer repeated 'Zero Boost' and started to move the throttles forward, until the boost gauge needles were vertical and the aircraft was beginning to shudder, torn between the thrust of the engines and the restraint of the brakes. Wing Commander McGhie released the parking catch on the brake lever, but held the brakes on with his left hand. His right hand grasped the throttles, his left hand released the brake lever and he pushed the throttles forward to full power, his wrist twisted so that the port outer engine reached full power first. He could feel the Engineer's hand against his, backing him up in case one of the levers should slip from his grasp. The aircraft started to move and he kicked on starboard rudder and gave a momentary gentle squeeze on the brake lever to stop her swinging to port. The Engineer started reading out the airspeed indicator readings: 'Fifty....Sixty'... he eased the control column forward to bring the tail up – 'Seventy......Eighty......Ninety.....One Hundred......One Ten'...the end of the runway was getting very close...'One Twenty'....he eased the control column back and suddenly the bumping and rocking ceased. 'Airborne......One Thirty'. Then, as he spoke 'Undercarriage up...Flaps up...Climbing power'. He listened with satisfaction as the

Engineer replied 'Undercarriage up and locked... flaps up... climbing power, sir'.

At five hundred feet he started a gentle turn to starboard and flew back on a reciprocal heading. He saw another aircraft airborne, one just lining up on the runway and the other nine moving up in the queue, and he would not have been human is he had not felt a momentary pride of achievement in watching <u>his</u> squadron getting airborne. Then he recalled himself, asked his navigator for the first course and swung the aircraft gently round on that heading.

[Chris Rew, ground crew, No 619 Sqn 1943/45]

On 12th June twelve aircraft were sent to Bochum, and all returned safely, though not without incident. The pilot of one aircraft, Sgt DJ Coomber in ED981 PG-V, lost consciousness because, unknown to him, his oxygen supply had failed. It was only when the navigator realised the aircraft was going round and round in gentle circles that the crew found that the pilot was no longer conscious. The Flight Engineer soon revived Sgt Coomber, using the emergency oxygen bottle, but by this time they were 150 miles off course and would have been at least an hour late over the target. The crew were concerned about this, but Coomber's response was 'so what?', a typically light-headed reaction to anoxia. His crew prevailed upon him to jettison their bomb load and to return to base, where on arrival he called up Air Traffic for permission to land and, receiving it, proceeded to do so. He called again when he was clear of the runway and was rather surprised to receive a second permission to land. He pointed out that he had already landed and received an urgent: 'V Victor pancake'. As he taxied round he gradually realised that he was not at Woodhall Spa but Bardney, ten miles away. One can imagine that he had his leg pulled mercilessly in the bar about this incident, but the medics were most interested to have on their hands a survivor of oxygen starvation, a condition about which not much was known at that time. [Coomber and his crew were finally brought down in the same aircraft on 23/24th August, crashing on the Baltic coast near Keil, while taking part in the first of the winter of 1943/1944 *Battle of Berlin* raids. He and his Flight Engineer, Sergeant GA Stamper, were taken POW, but the rest of the crew were killed.]

On 14th June the AOC again visited Woodhall and listened in to the crew briefing and debriefing before and after the operation to *Oberhausen*, when No 619 sent six aircraft. One aircraft did not return: ED980 captained by P/O K McCulloch had been shot down over Holland and all seven members of the crew killed, becoming the Squadron's first operational fatalities. A photograph of P/O McCulloch, holding his baby son in his arms, accompanied an article his son wrote for the *Credo* slot in *The Times* for Remembrance Day 1996 under the title '*Remember the fatherless as well as the fallen*'. The baby, Nigel McCulloch, is now the Bishop of Manchester and living only a few miles from where the Lancaster was built in that city.

On the day that Pilot Officer McCulloch and his crew were lost another new crew arrived on the Squadron, direct from their training at No 1661 Conversion unit, RAF Winthorpe, near Newark, having spent the previous two weeks with the No 5 Group Finishing School at RAF Fiskerton. To them quite directly this book owes its origin. Had the author not been in charge of the police investigation that followed the discovery of their aircraft in the River Leine in Hannover in March 1977, his post-RAF research into them, their families and their Squadron this would not have happened. That new crew consisted of Sergeant Cyril Fuller [pilot], Sgt George Wilson [flight engineer], Sgt Reg Stevens [navigator], Sgt Leo Eaude [air bomber], Sgt Dick Sprackman [wireless operator], Sgt Vincent Crookes [mid-upper gunner] and Sgt Roy Trahair [rear gunner]. We will return to them again in the Chapter 3.

In this way a new Squadron was born. A year or so later No 619 Squadron was itself to spawn another new Squadron, No 227, in much the same way. By the end of June, after less than three weeks of operations No 619 Squadron had taken part already in ten Bomber Command operations, flown 80 sorties and lost three aircraft and crews [plus another flak-damaged aircraft written-off after crash-landing at Woodhall on returning from Gelsenkirchen]. In just over two months since John McGhie had surveyed his non-existent command, the Squadron had become fully operational and already becoming a distinct entity with its own squadron loyalty and sense of pride. Since the middle of April when the Squadron had consisted of only John McGhie and his three veteran crews from No 97 Squadron – and no aircraft - a total of thirty-three crews had been posted in and the Squadron had taken delivery of some twenty or so Lancaster aircraft to call its very own.

As we shall soon be meeting some of those aircraft and the crews that flew them, this is probably a good time to make a point about the different Marks of Lancaster aircraft. Most RAF squadrons, No 619 included, flew only two types, the Mark I and the Mark III and most squadrons had both. This is not as odd as it may seem, for the two were essentially the same, the only major difference being the engines. The introduction of the four-engined heavy bombers had made a huge impact on the production demands placed on the manufacturers of the engines they used, especially the Merlin engines installed in both the Lancaster and the Handley Page Halifax. What is more, this engine was also used in many other aircraft, including the Spitfire and Hurricane fighters. By 1943, the 18,000 engines per year that the Rolls-Royce plants at Derby, Crewe, Glasgow and Ford's at Old Trafford could manufacture were quite simply not sufficient to keep pace with demand, and so Ford had suggested that their Packard plant in America be allowed to produce the engine under licence. This met with British immediate approval because Churchill wanted to see the eggs spread over as many baskets as possible to reduce the risk of production being interrupted by German bombing.

Packards were given the 20,000 Rolls Royce master drawings, which had already been deposited in America at the USAAF's Wright Field base, in 1940, as a precaution after the fall of France, and an enormous portion of Ford's car producing capacity was set aside for the production of the Merlin engine. Though at first the American engineers were said to have found some difficulty in working to Rolls Royce tolerances, the first American-built engines were rolling off the production lines within a year. The new American-built engines were designated Merlin Mk 28s to distinguish them from the British-built Merlin Mk 22s. This was important, for though there were no external differences when the engines were installed in the aircraft and cowled, there were important internal differences. The American version used different carburettors – an American Bendix rather the British S.U. – and an American magneto. As the engines of aircraft in service were automatically changed after a certain number of flying hours had been completed, it was quite possible for what was originally a Mark I Lancaster to become a Mark III, and vice-versa, by a simple switch of engine type, depending on the availability of replacement engines, and there were even reported cases of aircraft flying with one set of engines inboard and a different set outboard. Later production models of the Lancaster used several other variants of the British-built engines, No 619's PB203, PB210 and PB245 being fitted with Mark 38 Merlins, and RA527, RA588 and RA590 with Mark 24s. SW254 PG-S [the penultimate aircraft lost by 619] was also fitted with Mark 24s.

Other variants of both the aircraft and the engines did exist, but not usually in 5 Group and not in large numbers. For example, No 635 Squadron [No 8 Group] was the only Squadron to operate with the much more powerful [1,635 hp compared with the 1,420 of the Mk 28] Mark 85/87 variant engines in the Mark VI version of the aircraft. Canadian squadrons in No 6 Group flew the Mark II Lancaster with radial Bristol Hercules engines and Canadian-built Mk Xs with Mk 38 and later Mk 224 engines fitted. One Lancaster, a Mark VI flown variously by No 7, No 106 and No 635 Squadrons, had Merlin engines of the types 38, 85, 68, 102,150, 620, 621, 630 and 631 installed in succession![31]

Meanwhile, however, the 619 Squadron ground crew were most impressed by the superb toolset supplied with the American Mk 28 engines, which is understandable as the author knows of one war-time fitter at RAF Waddington, a motor mechanic and garage owner in civvie street before the war, who was so exasperated by the shortage of tools on his squadron that he went home to Wales to bring tools back from his garage to supplement the official British issue.

This is probably also a good time to say something about the ground crews who serviced Bomber Command's aircraft in all weathers, often

[31] Robertson '*Lancaster – The Story of a Famous Bomber*' [Harleyford 1964].

in the open. Their's was not an easy life, and the working conditions could at best be unpleasant. Like the aircrew, their lives revolved around the rhythm of bomber operations, with long periods of boredom punctuated by brief snatches of near pandemonium. Aircraft 'snags' had to be fixed as quickly as possible, because one could never know how long it would be before the aircraft would be required for another operation. When the time for operations came, the usual procedure was for two ground crew to attend each aircraft, and for one of those two to be on duty eight, nine or ten hours later when the aircraft returned from ops. This imposed long hours of duty, sometimes almost round the clock. In theory every Lancaster had a ground crew of four engine fitters and two riggers, but squadrons were rarely up to strength, and the usual size of a ground crew on 619 Squadron was two fitters and a rigger. After the aircraft had departed on night operations, the ground crew would go down to the cookhouse for a late supper, after which they would return to the flight office where a few decrepit beds and biscuits provided for the long wait until the aircraft returned.

There they sat, talked, snoozed, played cards, smoked [the dangers to health were not then known] and generally passed the time until 'their' aircraft returned. In a very real sense, it was indeed 'their' aircraft. Different crews might, and did, fly it, but they always serviced it, and sometimes they were fonder of the aircraft than the aircrews that flew it. Would 'their' aircraft come back? Would the aircrew look after it properly? Until long after the departure, and possibly not until her return, the ground crew would not know the target. They might be able to make a shrewd guess, based on the amount of fuel taken aboard or the bomb load, but this could only be guesswork and was often wildly wrong. As the sound of an aircraft's returning engines was heard, the ground crew office would fall silent while the assembled men waited for the telephone call telling them which aircraft it was and instructing the representative of that ground crew to get out to his dispersal pan to see his aircraft back in. As the aircraft were usually returning in darkness, this meant signalling the taxi-ing aircraft with a hand-held torch so that the pilot could be guided in the dark back to the dispersal from which he and his crew had set off eight hours or more earlier, by a man on foot running backwards as fast as he could to avoid being run over by the monster rapidly heading towards him with four propellers spinning madly, and waiting to devour him if he got it wrong. Chris Rew wrote that the returning aircrew were invariably asked three questions by the ground crew: 1. have a good trip? 2. any snags? 3. where was it? Snags would then be listed, signed by the pilot and the aircraft formally handed back, via the Form 700, to the ground crew, after which control locks, wheel covers, pitot-head cover, etc, would be fitted.

For the ground crew man concerned, this was one of the most satisfying experiences of the job. 'His' aircraft was back, and for a while he could sit in her, happily listening to the metallic sounds of the engines and the systems as they cooled. Again, to quote Chris Rew, it did not require a man with much imagination to whisper 'Good old girl, well done'. The feelings of the man, or men, left in the flight office were, of course, quite different. Would their aircraft be returning? Had she been shot down? If air traffic had no news of their aircraft, they could only hope and wait. Perhaps the aircraft had been diverted? Perhaps it had crash-landed at Woodbridge or one of the other emergency airfields, after getting back despite being badly damaged? Then there was always the awful thought, at that early hour of the morning, had they, the ground crew, been in any way to blame? More often than not, the empty space on their dispersal would not be filled again by that aircraft. It would not return, and the young men the ground crew had seen off a few hours previously were more likely to be dead than to be prisoners of war. The boy the WAAF had danced with only a few days ago would not be coming back. Within twenty-four hours his mother would be receiving an OHMS telegram regretting that he was missing on operations, followed by a letter from the Squadron Commander expressing his own sadness at the loss. Considering the size of the task involved, and the many other commitments that faced them, the Squadron Commanders made an amazingly good job of the sad task of writing to the mothers [or occasionally the wives]. No doubt, this was because they knew only too well that the next letter to be written might well be to their own next of kin, as happened in the case of three of No 619 Squadron's six war-time commanding officers.

For the moment, however, we will leave the operations being flown by the new Squadron, as a full list of these is contained in Chapter 4, together with details of the more interesting operations, as seen from the wider strategic or tactical perspective. I have done this because I wanted to provide a full, definitive list but without the narrative becoming too bogged down by pages and pages of detail. Also at the end of Chapter 4 are a number of tables, showing the Commanding Officers of 619 Squadron, the operations flown in simple chronological order, a list of the decorations awarded by name and aircrew category [though this list will be incomplete, as awards were often announced long after the recipient left the Squadron, in some cases posthumously at the end of the War, and the author has personally found three that were not previously known to the Squadron Association], a list in order of arrival of all aircraft captains known to have flown with the Squadron, with date of arrival and departure, an alphabetical list of all those killed in action, a list of aircraft losses arranged by call-sign, and finally, by way of a typical example, details of the operations flown by Sgt/F Sgt/Pilot Officer Gordon Taylor during his tour of operations with the Squadron from mid-1943 through to the Spring of 1944. He was a contemporary of the many early members of the Squadron killed in action, but he survived to fly post-war as an airline pilot with Aer Lingus.

A squadron is shaped to a very large extent by the character and personality of its commanding officer. A post-war No 8 Group medical report stated emphatically that 'The morale of a squadron was almost always in direct proportion to the quality of leadership shown by the squadron commanders, and the fluctuations in this respect were most remarkable'.[32] Guy Gibson was one type of successful RAF commander at squadron level. Not terribly cerebral, in many ways a typical product of the English public school system, the perpetual school prefect. Cheshire was another type: quieter, thoughtful, self-effacing and introverted. Willie Tait, the other big 617 Sqn 'name' was from yet another mould. Almost embarrassingly shy, lacking in natural charisma,

---

[32] Hastings, op cit, p.216.

he led by operational example.[33] These were all, of course, very young men. By 1943 the older pre-war officers were either dead or in senior command appointments. Promotion was rapid as a consequence. Some were squadron leaders at 21; others group captains in their mid-twenties. By and large, the RAF officer corps was less class-bound than that of the Army or even the Navy. It drew its officers – and NCOs – mainly from the grammar schools rather than the public schools, and the differences between those who were commissioned and those who were not were not as wide – socially, educationally or culturally – as they were in the other armed forces. In today's jargon, they would be called the upwardly mobile, but in the more class-ridden days of the time, some concern had been expressed at a high level amongst some of the senior officers of the pre-war RAF that the RAF appeared not to be capturing more of the middle and upper classes.

No 619 Squadron was fairly typical. In 1943 most of its aircraft captains – the pilots – arrived from training as sergeants. True, they were soon commissioned, usually backdated to the time they had completed operational training. But by late 1944, captains and other commissioned members of the crews were arriving as flying officers. It has often been said that Harris arranged for this to happen so that men who were in constant danger of being shot down would at least, if they survived as prisoners of war, have a better rate of pay accruing for their return home than they would as NCOs. It also foreshadowed the post-war decision by the RAF to commission all aircrew, and the decision pretty well effective by the end of the war that pilots of multi-engined aircraft should be commissioned officers. Many progressed through officer ranks fairly quickly. Within 619 Squadron, it was not unusual for a pilot to arrive as a flying officer and to leave as a squadron leader flight commander, and all this during the course of a tour of only six months or so on operations [Table 5 of Chapter 4 shows a number of examples of this happening]. Often, of course, it was quite literally a case of dead

---

[33] Tait served on in the post-war RAF, retiring in the 1970s as an Air Commodore. I remember a RAF colleague of mine, a war-time pilot, pointing Tait out to me one day when we were standing on a tube station platform while serving at MOD in the early 1970s. To a young RAF officer he looked surprisingly ordinary!

men's shoes. Even the squadron commanders, and certainly the flight commanders, were expected to fly fairly regularly – perhaps half as often as other crews - on operations, and flak and night-fighter cannon were totally unaware of the rank or experience of the crew of the aircraft they were attacking.

By the nature of things most of the aircrew losses were amongst the younger men. For a start, there were far more of them, but some older men were lost on operations, volunteers from other safer RAF occupations who had answered the call for flight engineers, or air gunners, or even navigators. At least two air commodores were lost on operations [Air Cdre AM Wray DSO, MC, DFC and bar, AFC, aged 48; and Air Commodore R Ivelaw-Chapman, as a pow]. One of the oldest squadron commanders lost was W/C VJ Wheeler, DFC and bar, MC and bar and Order of St Stanislaus (Russia), who died at the age of 46 while commanding No 207 Sqn in March 1944. The famous bomb expert, S/L 'Talking Bomb' Richardson, made his first operational flight since 1918 on 28 Aug 42 when he flew on an operational mission, twenty-four years later. At least three station commanders and one G/Capt flying as a Squadron Commander were also lost on operations, including RAF Coningsby's G/Capt AC Evans-Evans [see Chapter 4, Dortmund-Ems Kanal, 24th February, 1945]. He was 43 years of age. He had taken with him that night all of No 97 Squadron's specialist leaders, and one of those to die with him was S/L WG Wishart, DSO, DFC and bar, the squadron navigation officer, who was 22 years of age and had flown 84 missions.

No 619's commanding officers were younger men. The first, W/C IJ McGhie, was killed on the Peenemünde raid of 17/18 August 1943 within four months of founding the squadron and after only two months of operations. He was a married man from Aberdeen and lived with his family in the village of Woodhall Spa. By one of those awful coincidences, on the very night he died his family would have been affected by a Luftwaffe raid on the village of Woodhall Spa, and the No 617 Squadron memorial is built on the site of a hotel damaged in that raid and later demolished.

John McGhie was succeeded by W/C 'Jock' Abercromby, who stayed with the Squadron until 4th December 1943 and then died during a Berlin operation on 1/2 January 1944 soon after leaving to join No 83 Pathfinder Squadron. He was 33 years of age and his parents lived in Brechin, Angus. Abercromby has excited much controversy in recent years because of his belief that a bomber pilot should fly a straight and level course so as to provide his gunners with the best opportunity of spotting and shooting down an approaching enemy fighter. This was not a view shared by most bomber pilots, including his immediate predecessor as CO of 83 Squadron, G/Capt John Searby, the master bomber on the Peenemünde raid.[34] At least one experienced junior officer dared to disagree with Abercromby about his 'stable platform' view, and he survived and Abercromby did not, though it would be extremely unfair to attribute these matters to anything more than chance.

Abercromby was succeeded by W/C John Jeudwine DSO OBE, a pre-War regular officer and an ex-Cranwell cadet. It may be coincidence, but more awards and decorations were made during Jeudwine's stint as CO than any other. There could be a logical explanation, of course, in that most of the remaining crews by Jeudwine's time were experienced and so deserving of awards, but it is noticeable that the only ground crews to be given awards with 619 during its twenty-three months of operational existence seem to have been during Jeudwine's spell as CO. Jeudwine was a rather aloof, reserved bachelor and his life revolved around the RAF and flying. But he gained the respect and trust of his Squadron, both aircrew and ground crew:

> *"... a rather dour man, obstinate, bold and hard ... but he was a better man than Cheshire or Gibson."*
>
> [F/L RG 'Reg' Hutton, Engineer Leader]

---

[34] Searby [Edited Middlebrook], '*The memoirs of G/Capt John Searby DSO DFC*' [William Kimber 1988] p165-6 and 193. See also Walter Thompson DFC, *Lancaster to Berlin* [Goodhall 1985] p191-193 and Middlebrook, *The Berlin Raids* [Penguin 1990] p204/205.

"... a typical Regular RAF officer, tall, thin, sunburnt, wrinkled and older than average for a bomber skipper...rather aloof, perhaps shy, pre occupied and perhaps even a little sad ... I think he must have had a mental barrier against women, while he was always very polite he had a sort of coldness towards them ... there was one red haired WAAF driver who drove the crew bus ... immediately she heard that the Wing Commander had landed she would take the bus straight across the airfield, disregarding the perimeter track and regardless of other passengers..."

[W/O Alec Bates, who flew as Jeudwine's wireless op]

"Jeudwine was certainly a fine airman and good leader ... he did not expect anyone to do what he could not do himself... in ranks we were poles apart but he always joined in on a crew party and encouraged the ground crew to come along... as a result our aircraft was always spotless and kept in good order."

[a member of Jeudwine's ground crew]

"G/Capt Jeudwine often mixed with the air crews, and I spoke to him on several occasions, but I cannot claim to have known him well... he was a popular station commander [at RAF Strubby, later in the War] very experienced but never domineering over junior officers, whom he always encouraged and supported... I once returned from a raid on the Ruhr and he was in the control tower... my landing was not the best I ever made in a Lancaster and over a drink in the Mess he pulled my leg about the ropey landing... in a fit of bravado I challenged him to a landing competition to judged by the squadron commander... I have to admit he won and it cost me a round of drinks. [F/L John Whiteley DFC].[35]

It is typical of John Jeudwine's professional approach to leadership that just before he relinquished command of 619 Squadron, when a fitter appeared before him on a charge of having failed to spot flak damage to a radiator hose in John's own aircraft, damaged during an attack on Bourg Leopold, and this had resulted in John having to return early

[35] *Global Warrior, the Story of G/Capt John Jeudwine DSO OBE DFC,* op cit.

from the next raid [when he was master bomber], John dismissed the case as senior subordinate commander, with the words: 'He would have needed X-ray eyes to have found it'.

Jeudwine left the Squadron with a DFC on 22 May 1944, when he was posted to No 83 PFF Squadron at RAF Coningsby for Master Bomber duties, taking most of his 619 Sqn crew with him. After a hectic tour as a Master Bomber he was posted, first, as Base Operations Officer at Coningsby and, then, as a G/Capt to RAF Dunholme Lodge as Station Commander. His Base Operations duties were taken over by Wg Cdr Guy Gibson, who soon afterwards was killed while returning from a 'last' operation as master bomber, this time on an operation against Mönchen-Gladbach in September, 1944. John had served as a master bomber at the same time as Willie Tait and W/C Simpson of 97 Squadron, and he had taken over from W/C John Woodruffe, one of the greatest of them all. After a brief spell as Station Commander at Dunholme Lodge, he moved to Strubby as Station Commander, where once more he was with 'his' squadron, No 619, and we will hear more about that in a moment. Then finally, when Strubby was on the point of closing down at the end of the war [No 619 Squadron had moved to RAF Skellingthorpe in June 1945] John was posted on 10th September as Station Commander of RAF Little Staughton, a Pathfinder station in No 8 Group, located in Bedfordshire, about five miles from St Neots. Here, just after mid-day on 19th October 1945 he took off at 1255 hours on an air test in a single seater Typhoon Mk 1B fighter. Six minutes later at 1301 he crashed close to the north side of the airfield and was killed. He was 32 years and 3 months old, and was on his third command as a Group Captain. There cannot surely be any doubt that but for his untimely death, John Jeudwine's name would have been well known to my generation of young officers in the 1960s, probably as a senior air officer. He was a remarkable man, and the story of his life, and escape from Java in March/April 1942, is well worth reading.[36]

---

[36] *Global Warrior*, by Alain Charpentier, Lionel Lacey-Johnson and Geoffrey Jeudwine [published 1999 by Lacey-Johnson].

But let me leave the last word to Sgt George Allen, the ex-Halton apprentice who serviced Jeudwine's aircraft, Nulli Secundus:

> *As the War progressed we moved to Strubby ... I saw G/Capt Jeudwine again... Alec Henshaw, the Castle Bromwich Spitfire test pilot used to land in the afternoon, leave his new Spitfire by the Control Tower and get on a bike and cycle home to Mablethorpe [about 4 miles away]... returning in the morning... the last Christmas of the war I remember G/Capt Jeudwine serving the SNCOs their dinner as ops had been cancelled... one day in 1945 the tannoy came on to say that the Allies were in Berlin... after the War was over I was selected to fly to Gatow [Berlin] with G/Capt Jeudwine... I had never seen anything like it...I was given the job of riding in the back of a trooper, telling visiting Lancaster crews the various places we were passing and visiting – for which I was briefed... the last time I remember seeing G/Capt Jeudwine he was looking up to the Dome of Hitler's Chancellery through which a bomb had dropped smack in the middle'.*
>
> [Sgt George Allen, 619 Sqn ground crew 1943/45].

Jeudwine was succeeded as CO of No 619 Squadron by W/C JR 'Dick' Maling DFC, after a brief interregnum during which S/L Bill Whamond[37] held the fort. Maling arrived on 23rd May and was the CO for only two months before being lost during a raid on Stuttgart on 25/26th July. He and three other members of his crew survived as POWs but three were killed. He in turn was succeeded by W/C AR 'Robert' Milward, who remained CO until completing his third tour of ops in February 1945. Today he is the only former CO still in touch with the Squadron Association [and possibly the only one still alive] and he usually chairs the annual re-union dinners of the Association. Robert Milward had previously commanded No 30 Squadron in Greece

[37] At that time Bill Whamond was one of the two flight commanders on No 619 Squadron, and like a number of other more experienced No 619 captains had flown previously on No 106 Sqn under Guy Gibson. After the war, he was a Doctor. He died a couple of years ago.

and Crete, before taking it on to Egypt where it re-equipped with Hurricanes. In a letter to the author, Robert Milward said:

Strangely, I had known Dick when he was a test pilot at Drigh Road in Karachi pre-war. I was then in 39 Squadron at Risalpur and we used to carry out operational exercises on the air firing and bombing ranges at Karachi. [Later]... I was completing my Lancaster course at Syerston and rang Dick to arrange to have lunch with him. In the event he went missing that evening and instead of lunch I took over his squadron! When I last heard of him he was running a vineyard in New Zealand.

You will be aware that I had been involved in operations before taking over 619 Squadron... when the war broke out I was a flight commander in 39 Squadron, and we were operating against the Italians from Aden, and then moved up to the Western Desert. I was promoted to S/L and given command of 30 Squadron in Greece. After a fairly 'hot' war we were finally driven out of Greece via Crete and back to Egypt where after re-equipping with Hurricanes I was posted to command 67 Squadron, just being formed in the Far East with Brewster Buffaloes, a poor exchange for the Hurricane! After a brief but extremely active war against the Japs I found myself back in India preparing to take a new fighter wing in Imphal. Instead, I got a severe attack of dysentery and came home after seven years in the East. A long stay in Halton Hospital[38] got me back onto flying, and having flown fighters or light bombers all my flying life, I put great pressure on Air Ministry to be posted to 2 Group. It was not to be and Harris' net was cast far and wide; so somewhat unwillingly I found myself in Bomber Command, preparing for a third tour, and a new role, in Lancasters.

It could have been worse. The Lancaster was a fine aircraft, although a trifle big by any standard! Harris' iron grip on Bomber Command strategy had temporally been weakened by preparations for the invasion and by the German V1 bombing. Instead of the long and devastating role of nightly strategic bombing of cities, many of our

[38] The RAF Hospital at RAF Halton, near Wendover, Buckinghamshire.

sorties were daylight raids on V1 rocket sites or marshalling yards etc, returning from time to time to long-range night attacks on cities such as Munich or Bremen. There was no doubt which was the more popular with the aircrew!

The selection of crews for operations was always a tricky problem. I had to ensure that the crew lists were prepared before the target was known. The only exception to this rule was that I would ensure if possible that new crews had experience up to the task involved.

As far as administration was concerned, I had enormous help from 'Adj Clarke', as he was universally known, who was loved and respected by all.

Of the three squadrons I commanded, 619 was the most exacting. Coming into Bomber Command it was obvious that the stresses and strains of a long term of strategic bombing operations had taken its toll. Morale had been pushed to its limit, and crews coming close to completion of their tours suffered in particular. I have often been asked whether I found the close attention paid to squadron affairs by G/C Jeudwine in any way difficult to handle. I have to answer 'yes', but not to the extent that I could not handle it. I could understand how he felt but could never quite get on his wavelength. He seemed to have little interest in anything other than operations, and seemed to me to have a close to impenetrable mind. Oddly, though we had both been involved in the Far East war, we never discussed it.

After initial over-zealous attempts at running the squadron for me when at Dunholme Lodge, I moved the squadron to Strubby and Jeudwine did not take over the station for some weeks. We had no further troubles over command.

Throughout the whole of my time with 619 Squadron I was well supported by my flight commanders and could not have wished for a better backing than I got from all members of the Squadron. Those who continue to attend our re-unions carry the spirit of those days forward to the present and have every reason to be proud of their past.

W/C Milward relinquished command on 21st February 1945, as the bombing war was nearing an end, and his successor W/C SG Birch saw the squadron through until the end of the war. He in turn relinquished command on 14th June 1945 to a Rhodesian W/C SE Flett, who took the Squadron to Skellingthorpe, south west of Lincoln at the end of June, and was in command when it disbanded virtually overnight on 18th July 1945, the instructions to do so being received barely 24 hours previously! W/C Birch died in 1979 after retiring from the RAF as a G/Capt MVO OBE. W/C Flett moved on to No 44 Squadron, the Rhodesian bomber squadron, when No 619 disbanded.

No 619 Squadron had flown its first operation to Düsseldorf on 11th June, 1943. It flew its last operational sorties, to Berchtesgaden and 'Gardening', on 25th April 1945. On both occasions it lost an aircraft and its crew. The Berchtesgaden raid was the last major Bomber Command operation of the war. The Master Bomber controlling the raid was W/C Maurice Smith, formerly a flight commander on No 619 Squadron. The squadron had flown on some of the major raids of the war: Berlin [all 19 raids of the winter of 1943/44], Hamburg, Hannover, München, Köln, Stuttgart, Essen, Nürnberg, Peenemünde, Dresden, Milan, Mannheim, Leipzig, Düsseldorf, Mönchen-Gladbach, in support of the Allied Expeditionary Force and finally Berchtesgaden. In doing so it had lost 85 aircraft and almost 500 men. It also supplied several of the handful of specialist master bombers *[eg, W/C John Jeudwine and W/C Maurice Smith]*.

In this short time it had operated from four airfields: RAF Woodhall Spa [to Jan 44], RAF Coningsby [to Apr 44], RAF Dunholme Lodge [to Sep 44] and RAF Strubby [to the end of the War], all in Lincolnshire. During the brief spell at Dunholm Lodge it had carried out just over 1,000 sorties in 72 operations at a cost of 34 aircraft lost. Any crew joining the squadron at that time had only a one in three chance of surviving their tour. It was at this time that the Squadron came to know Colonel Craycroft-Amcott's family of Hackthorne Hall, just to the north of the airfield, who allowed members of the Squadron to make use of the grounds of the Hall and to swim in the ornamental lake. Though the Squadron never got round to having an officially [College of Arms] approved crest – one of only a few RAF squadrons not to have done so - the unofficial squadron crest displays a heron with a battle axe and bears a close resemblance to the Craycroft-Amcott family crest of a stork with a battle axe, the stork having being changed to a heron in the Squadron's crest at Colonel Craycroft-Amcott's suggestion, there having been herons using the lake in the grounds of Hackthorne Hall at the time 619 Squadron enjoyed the Craycroft-Amcott's hospitality.

During twenty-three months of operations, the Squadron's air gunners had claimed eight enemy aircraft and a flying bomb destroyed, one aircraft probably destroyed and three aircraft damaged.

3. Lancaster EE109 crew history & final flight

Lancaster aircraft serial number EE109 was one of a batch of 247 Mark IIIs delivered to the RAF between March 1943 and June 1943 by A.V. Roe of Chadderton, Manchester. The order for this and another 619 Lancaster aircraft had been placed by the Air Ministry in 1941, and the manufacturer had begun to fulfil the contract from November 1942 onwards. As far as No 619 Squadron was concerned, EE109 was simply one of a batch of new aircraft in the ED/EE series delivered new by the manufacturer on 23rd May 1943 just as the Squadron was starting to form up from scratch, at Woodhall Spa.

In the same series of aircraft, No 619 Squadron also received ED977, ED978, ED979, ED980, ED981, ED982, ED983, EE106, [EE109], EE110, EE111, EE112, EE113, EE114, EE115, EE116, EE117 and EE118. Later it was to receive EE147, EE149, EE150 and EE170 second hand from No 617 Squadron, EE134 second hand from 49 Squadron, EE168 second hand from No 97 Squadron and, new, EE198. All twenty-five of these aircraft were to be lost on operations with No 619 Squadron, except EE118, which was transferred immediately after arrival to No 156 Squadron, with whom it was struck off charge in October 1943 after having been damaged in a crash the previous month. Indeed, so rapidly were Bomber Command's aircraft being lost at this stage of the War that only two of the original twenty-five aircraft survived more than six months, and of these one [ED977] only just got beyond that landmark, as it was lost on operations on 5/6 January 1944, by that time a veteran with 440 hours on the clock and 46 operations to its credit. The other [EE116] survived against the odds for ten months until 11/12 April 1944 when it failed to return from Aachen with 560 hours on the clock. Though ED977 is always spoken of as the Squadron's longest serving veteran aircraft, with only 440 hours on the clock when it was lost on 5/6 January, its claim has to give way to EE116 with 120 hours more flying time and three months more operational service to its credit. So far as is known no other 619 Squadron aircraft exceeded the operational service of these two.

Like the other aircraft in this series, EE109 was fitted with four Mark 28 American-built Merlin engines [see Chapter 2 for an explanation of engine types]. Thirty-three years after being shot down by flak over Hannover, it was to be one of EE109's Mark 28 engines that would lead to the identification of the wreckage.

Following its arrival with No 619 Squadron, EE109 was given the code letters PG-F, the first two being the Squadron code letters and the third the aircraft's individual callsign. It was one of four aircraft coded PG-F to be lost in twenty-three months of operations [the last, LM756, being the very last aircraft lost by the Squadron on 25 April 1945 on the raid against Hitler's Eagle's Nest at *Berchtesgaden* in the Bavarian alps].

In its five months of service with No 619 Squadron, EE109 PG-F flew on twenty-eight operations, fourteen of them with Cyril Fuller and his crew. When it came to grief over Hannover city centre at 2018 hours on the night of 18 October 1943, after being struck by flak fired by Flak Batterie 3./521, it had flown 282 hours [plus 2 hours 28 minutes that would not have been recorded on the Form 700].

There can no doubt that EE109 was considered by Cyril Fuller and his crew to be 'their' aircraft. Apart from flying fourteen of their twenty-one operations in it, the surviving flying log books show that they also flew many of their training flights in it, the first on 16 June 1943, only two days after arriving on the Squadron from No 1661 Conversion Unit. It seems likely that it was Fuller and his crew that gave the aircraft its nickname '*Meathound*', and that is certainly the belief of two of the families. The nickname can be seen on the nose of the aircraft in a number of surviving photographs. The only non-standard equipment fitted was *Monica*, a device intended to give the crew early warning that an aircraft was on their tail.

The crew that regarded *Meathound* as their aircraft was captained by Cyril Fuller. Born in Peckham, London, on 20 October 1912, he was quite a bit older than the average first tour pilot when he was posted onto operations with No 619 Squadron on 14 June 1943. At the age of 30 years and eight months, he was nine years older than his flight commander, S/L Ronnie Churcher, and only a few years younger than his squadron commander, John McGhie until 17/18 August and then Jock Abercromby, and he was only two days short of his 31st birthday when he died on 18 October 1943. Unmarried, his next of kin were his parents, Charles and Mary Fuller of 135 Thornsbeech Road, Catford, London SE6, and he had one sibling, his sister Nellie, who is believed to have been much the same sort of age as him. His parents died in Catford in the 1950s and Nellie in Eastbourne in the mid 1990s in her mid-eighties. There are, thus, now no surviving near relatives.

His father was a Tram Inspector, and the family would today be considered upwardly mobile or middle class, but no doubt in the culture of the times they would have regarded themselves as more or less working class. Cyril was obviously quite bright, because at the age of 12 he secured a London County Council scholarship from Lyndhurst Grove School, Camberwell, to Alleyn's, an old-established public school in Dulwich. The scholarship took effect from 1 August 1924 and was an 'Article 20' award. The boy entered Alleyn's on 17 September 1924 and remained there until leaving from the Lower Sixth on 21 December 1929, having matriculated in the summer of 1928. He left to take up accountancy, and his last employment before the War was with McCory & Sons in Fenchurch Street. When he left Alleyn's, his family was living at 12 Crofton Road, SE5.

At Alleyn's, Cyril was a house prefect, a Lance Corporal in the OTC [Officer Training Corps] and was awarded his School football colours in 1929. His last three term reports written by masters WR Morgan and CE Hack in 1929 remarked 'very fair progress – unobtrusive', 'a good boy, always cheerful' and 'a good worker with a fair brain, of which he makes good use'. The Alleyn Magazine for his final year records, regarding his membership of the football team, 'C. Fuller shaped well at outside left, but he scarcely ever put in a shot, a remarkable lapse in a player who can shoot so well'. His sporting prowess was not restricted to football. On the cricket field that summer he represented his house, Tulley's, in the inter-house cup final, scoring 30 in the first innings and 10 in the second, and taking two catches when his house was in the field, one in each innings. Tulley's won the cup comfortably, scoring 269 in the first innings and 214 in the second, compared with Brading's 296 and 86.

Six months after the outbreak of the Second World War, on the Leap Year day of 1940, 29 February, Cyril Fuller became a full-time Territorial Reservist as a Gunner in the Royal Artillery. On 18 October he was promoted Lance Corporal, but on 7 June 1941 he transferred to the Royal Air Force with the service number 657008 to train as a pilot.

As an AC2 he completed the formalities of 'signing on' at 9 Recruit Wing before being posted to an aircrew basic training unit, No 54 Group, at Torquay. This training completed, he was promoted Leading Aircraftman and posted on 18 September to Southern Rhodesia for flying training. The initial training course was undertaken at Bulawayo and was followed by Elementary Flying Training at No 28 EFT School, Wolverhampton. After this, Fuller received his elementary pilot's wings [known as budgie wings in the RAF], was promoted sergeant and on 28 March 1942 was sent to No 23 Service Flying Training School, Heaney [S. Rhodesia]. This course lasted six months, at the end of which he was posted to No 33 Flying Instructors' School, Belvedere [S.Rhodesia]. Flying training now completed, he returned to the UK and was posted to No 29 Operational Training Unit at RAF North Luffenham on 20 October 1942. It was here that he was to meet the other members of his crew.

Leo Eaude, born in 1918, was five years younger than Cyril, the fourth of the six children of George Henry Eaude [1867-1948] and his wife Agnes [neé Wilson 1886-1967]. At the time of the Millennium in 2000, Leo's two eldest sisters were still alive, but one has since died. The first four Eaude children, including Leo, were born at 639 Lord Street, Southport and the last two in nearby Birkdale. The Eaudes are an old

Lancashire Catholic family. Their father was a coal merchant, and they were quite well off until the depression in the 1930s hit business. Leo's next nearest older brother, Philip also served in the RAF, retiring as a Wing Commander. Sadly, he died without knowing that his brother's aircraft had been found in 1977. Before joining the RAF, Leo, like Philip, worked in the Treasurer's Office in Southport. By 1943 his parents were living at 7 Dover Road, Birkdale but after Mr Eaude's death in 1948 Agnes returned to Nottingham. In the postwar years, when the families were still trying to find out what had happened to their sons, it was from Birkdale and then Nottingham that Mrs Eaude corresponded with the other mothers.

Like his pilot, Leo was a bachelor, and photographs suggest a rather serious, shy-looking young man, old for his years, and one would guess the obvious companion for the older pilot. Leo's father was 50 when Leo was born and 76 when he went missing, something that has always seemed to the author to be particularly poignant [as an older father of sons]. Also like Cyril Fuller, Leo underwent initial flying training *as a pilot* abroad. His logbook shows that he completed his initial training in Canada, having joined the RAF in July 1940 at the Blackpool reception centre, not far from his home town of Southport, and been allocated the service number 1354355.

Between February and April 1942, he received tuition as a pilot on Tiger Moth aircraft at No 31 Elementary Flying Training School, De Winton, Alberta, in Canada, completing a total of over 71 hours flying. He flew his first solo flight on 6 March and by the time he moved on to No 32 Service Flying Training School, Moose Jaw, for advanced flying training on Harvard II and Oxford aircraft, he had flown 35 hours 20 minutes as a pilot. He was withdrawn from pilot training on 20 June having by then flown 140 hours, including over 66 as first pilot. From August to November 1942 he underwent air gunner, navigation and air bomber training on Fairey Battle and Avro Anson aircraft at No 31 Bombing and Gunner School, RAF Picton, Ontario and No 33 Air Navigation School, RAF Mount Hope, Ontario, before qualifying as an Air Bomber on 6 November.

In training he had dropped 92 bombs and fired off 1,200 rounds of ammunition. He was then posted to RAF North Luffenham in Rutland, just off the A1, near Oakham, where he joined up with Cyril Fuller. It is easy to see why these two men, both older than average and both having trained abroad, would have been drawn together when crews were being formed by self-selection at North Luffenham.

The navigator, Reginald 'Reg' Stevens, was a London policeman, whose beat was his native East End, where he worked through the Blitz dealing with the disruption and mayhem caused by the Luftwaffe bombing. He was the youngest of three brothers, born on 6 November, 1913, and he was the nearest in age to Cyril of the crew of EE109. He was also the only married member, with a young wife aged 23 at the time he went missing. They had no children, and his wife is still alive now in her 80s. She did not remarry. While Reg was away in the RAF, his wife worked in a munitions factory, starting each day at 7.30 am and working through until 6.30 pm in the evening, her family moving out to Essex after their home in the East End was destroyed in the Blitz.

Reg's parents and brothers died some years ago, and after his death his widow and parents did not keep in touch. There could be many reasons for this, of course, but it is clear that bereaved mothers often felt they had been treated less fairly than the [usually young] widows, who were awarded a gratuity, whereas any payment being made by an unmarried airman from pay to his mother was stopped thirteen weeks after he was posted missing. It has to be remembered that this was a time when it was normal for young men to make deductions from pay to their mothers to supplement the family budget, and so the loss of a son caused not only emotional turmoil but often a loss of income as well. Reg never spoke to his young wife about his operations with 619 Squadron '*he just wanted to forget about it while he was on leave*'. When he returned to the Squadron from leave a week or so before the final fatal flight, his widow said '*it was the only time he did not want to go back*'. His name is inscribed on a memorial at Scotland Yard to Metropolitan Police officers lost during WWII. '*He went through a lot in the East End and was then killed in the RAF!*' Like two other members of his crew, and so many other young men from the United Kingdom and the

Dominions, Reg was a volunteer in a very real sense. As a policeman he did not have to join the Armed Forces at all, let alone volunteer for aircrew duties. He did so because of what he had seen in the Blitz of London.

These three older-than-usual young airmen, 30, 25 and 29 years of age respectively, were drawn together in the self-selection process for forming crews that the RAF had adopted at OTUs such as North Luffenham. They would have trained together through the last two months of 1942 until in the January of 1943 they were joined by the other members needed to complete the crew, a Wireless Operator, two Air Gunners and a flight engineer.

The wireless operator was Richard Stephen Sprackman, a farmer's son from Bridgeyate, Warmley, on the south western edge of Bristol. Though in a protected occupation as a farm worker on his father's farm, Dick Sprackman had found a way around the restriction by moving a few miles to work on an uncle's farm where his occupation was not protected, and so like Reg Stevens he was a real volunteer. Unlike the other three, he was much more the sort of age of a typical bomber crewmember and was only 20 when he died in October, 1943. With a shock of wavy fair hair, he was a good-looking boy, and in other circumstances would have been busy courting rather than facing the discomfort and danger of life as a bomber crewman. He had one sister within a year or so of him in age, and she and her husband live today in Weston-Super-Mare, half an hour's travelling time from the farm where she and Dick grew up. Dick's is one of three EE109 flying logbooks known to have survived. He joined up at a recruit centre in Oxford.

The mid-upper air gunner was even younger than Dick Sprackman. Vincent 'Vinny' Crookes was a bricklayer's apprentice from Sheffield, born on 23 March 1924 in the heart of the old city of Sheffield. At the time of his death he was 19 and seven months and had been serving in the RAF from August 1942, when he had joined at the age of 18½. He had one older brother, George, two years older than Vinny, who until his death in 1996 spent years trying to find out what had happened to his brother's aircraft. Today, Vinny's nearest relatives are his brother's widow, Frances, and her daughter, Ann, the neice Vinny never knew. In a normal world, Ann could have expected to have known an uncle in what was and is a very close family and probably to have had cousins to have played with as she grew up. When Vinny was about 11 or 12 years of age, his parents moved out to a new estate of modern houses being built on the western rural edge of Sheffield, and his father, the foreman of a Timber Merchants in Sheffield and involved in the building of the estate, had his choice of house. Thus it was that Vinny spent his teenage years in Norton Park Crescent, Sheffield 8, in a house with such modern plumbing and sanitary arrangements as were to amaze his friends from the inner city when they visited.

His mother was a quiet, shy, house-proud lady, and Vinny and George were her especial joy. She never recovered from Vinny's loss, and her only consolation was that her older boy George who spent the War in the equally dangerous job of torpedo boat crewman in the Royal Navy did survive. She had already lost her eldest son, Kenneth, of bronchial pneumonia at about the time Vinny was born. The Crookeses are a through-and-through Sheffield family, taking their name from a nearby village of that name, and like the other families of the crew of EE109 were very much the type of family that was emerging as the new middle class from the depression of the between-the-wars years.

Vinny joined up at the huge recruit depot at RAF Padgate in Lancashire on 27 Aug 42 'for the duration of the present emergency'. On completing basic training he was promoted Leading Aircraftman and started air gunner training on 5 December. Two months later on 6 February 1943 he qualified as an air gunner and was promoted Sergeant. He was still eighteen years of age.

Ten days later on 16 February 1943, he was posted to No 29 OTU, RAF North Luffenham, 1943 where he joined the crew of Cyril Fuller, Leo Eaude and Reg Stevens.

Growing up in Sheffield his particular childhood friends were George Cunningham and Norman Blackwell, and their childhood antics were later to form the basis of two books, with beautiful Lowry-esque paintings that George Cunningham was to publish in the late

1980s/early 1990s.[1] George describes Vinny thus: *Vinny had straight, very fine fair hair, which fell over this forehead. One of his front teeth was rather prominent and he had the habit of sucking in air past it when he got excited.* The books describe in hilarious details the antics of schoolboys, unsophisticated adventures in a different, less affluent and less commercial age, with an evocative account of George's visit by tram to the Crookeses in their new home, and the amazement of seeing for the first time in his life a modern bathroom with hot water coming from a tap. There is a poignant painting of George waving farewell to Vinny before departing back to the inner city, and the final chapter of the second book, *More George!*, is more or less a tribute to Vinny, with a photograph of him as a sergeant air gunner, and the remarks passing between George and Norman, as a plane drones overhead on VE night "*I wish owd Vinny could have made it,* murmured Norman, echoing my own thoughts…at the age of twenty I had come out of [the War] as a half-trained die-sinker, a fire fighter who had never doused a conflagration and a part-time soldier who hadn't fired a shot…[and Vinny was dead]". Vinny's name is inscribed on a Scout memorial in Sheffield. Like Reg Stevens, the only occasion Vinny was reluctant to return to operations was after the period of leave in early October 1943 immediately before the fatal flight.

The other gunner to join the burgeoning crew at North Luffenham was Roy Trahair. A Cornishman from St Austell, Roy was eighteen months older than Vinny Cookes, born on 9 October 1922. His parents, Richard Treeve Trahair and Emily Linna Trahair, had been born in the late Victorian period at the end of the Nineteenth Century, and he was the third of three brothers and a sister. Then came a late extra, Mike, who had just started school when Roy went missing in October 1943, having nine days previously spent his twenty-first birthday at home on leave. Much of the content of the letters Roy wrote home from Woodhall to his parents is concerned with enquiries about the progress of his young brother, Mike. Mike's only memory of Roy is of

[1] The books *By George!* and *More George!* are published by the Hallamshire Press of Sheffield and are joyous, evocative, descriptive works of art. From them one can feel and smell the Sheffield in which Vinny Crookes grew up in the 1930s.

being with him during that leave, when Roy, a keen photographer, took a photograph of Mike in his new outfit for starting school. Today, Mike is an accountant in his early 60s.

Like Vinny, one of Roy's brothers saw active service with the Royal Navy, and his father had served in the Army during the Great War. Roy was designed to be a rear gunner. Only 5'3½" tall, he could squeeze into the cramped turret at the back of the Lancaster more easily than most men. Roy joined the RAF at Weston-Super-Mare on 7 October 1941, two days before his 19th birthday. He had attended an aircrew selection board the previous day and been recommended for wireless operator/air gunner training. He then spent two months on the Reserve until being called up and sent to 3 Recruit Centre, RAF Padgate, on 19 December. Ten days later he was posted to No 10 Recruit Centre, and after basic training, was posted to the Recruit Despatch Unit, Blackpool on 2 March 1942 for W/Op training. Three weeks later he ceased W/Op training and was posted to RAF Peterhead to await an Air Gunner's course. On 6 July 1942 he was posted to the Aircrew Reception Centre, Regents' Park, London, for reassessment, following which he went to No 14 Initial Training Wing, Bridgnorth for six weeks and was then posted to No 4 Air Gunnery School, Morpeth, on 30th August. Six days later he fractured his wrist and was sent on sick leave for 21 days. This resulted in him being re-coursed from No 10 Air Gunners' Course to No 15, which he successfully completed at the end of November 1942, being reclassified as a Sergeant Air Gunner on 8th December 1942. He was then sent on leave with the intimation of an overseas posting. A week later he was posted instead to 29 OTU, RAF North Luffenham, where he was to join Cyril Fuller's crew.

The remaining member of the crew was George Arthur Wilson, the Flight Engineer. He hailed from Battersea, London, and his parents were William and Clara Edith Wilson of Stanley Grove, Queenstown Road, SW8. He was 21 when he died in October 1943, and his service number indicates that he joined the RAF at Cardington. His is the only family the author has not been able to trace. A crew photograph taken in the summer of 1943 in front of EE109 shows him with dark wavy hair and suggests that, along with the former policeman Reg Stevens, he was taller than other members of the crew. It is not clear at what point he joined the others in training as an operational crew.

The majority of the crew first flew together as a crew in Wellington Mk III EJ905 on 28 January 1943 at 29 OTU, RAF North Luffenham. Air Gunner Roy Trahair recorded the event in his diary with the cryptic note '01.10'. [The flight had been of one hour and ten minutes' endurance.] Thereafter, though occasionally flying with other pilots, the crew members flew together more often than not. By the end of March, Roy Trahair had flown 28 of his 45 training flights in Wellingtons at 29 OTU with Cyril Fuller as pilot and had added 34 hours 20 minutes day flying and 22 hours 55 minutes night flying to his totals of 85.35 and 27.05 respectively.

During April they flew a further eleven training flights, all except one with Cyril Fuller as pilot, but on 10 April they also flew their first mission with hostile intent in Wellington Mk III BK545 on a nickelling [leaflet dropping] raid to Lyons, a flight time of 6 hours 20 minutes, landing on return at Ford. Roy Trahair kept a copy of the leaflet dropped. F/L ES Kennedy, the officer commanding No 'C' Flight signed off their logbooks for April.

In May, Roy Trahair spent two weeks with the No 5 Group Training Unit at RAF Fulbeck on No 7 Course where he completed 8 hours and 30 minutes of Ciné Gun fighter affiliation practice, before returning to No 1661 Conversion Unit, RAF Winthorpe, near Newark, for heavy bomber conversion training with the remainder of the crew. They started on the twin-engined Manchester, which by now had been relegated to a training role, and flew four exercises in Manchesters L7430, L7401 and L7302 before on 22 May making their first flight in a Lancaster [ED434]. They had now flown *for the first time* a four-engined heavy bomber and the type of aircraft in which, in only three weeks time, they were to begin their operational careers. After a further fifteen flights in various Lancaster aircraft [W4253, W4258, W4249, W4947, W4217 and ED323] and a total of 23.25 flying hours by day and 10.45 by night they were adjudged ready for an operational unit. Wg Cdr FG Woodward, the Chief Instructor No 1661 CU signed off their logbooks.

On 14 June 1943 they arrived at RAF Woodhall Spa for a tour of thirty operations with No 619 Squadron, which was then – operationally speaking – three days old. On the evening of their arrival, the Squadron despatched six aircraft on a bombing raid to Oberhausen, and one did not return [ED980, captain P/O K McCulloch – seven crew killed]. This was their introduction to an operational squadron. It had been the squadron's third operation and already they had lost two aircraft [and one in training]. It was P/O McCulloch and his crew's second operation, his first three days previously having been in the rank of sergeant pilot.

Between 16 June and their first operation [to Mulheim on 22/23 June in ED977], Cyril Fuller and his crew flew six training flights in EE109 PG-F, the aircraft that they were to come to regard as their own. By the time they flew on their first operation they had gained a further 4 hours 40 minutes experience by day and completed two *Bullseye* exercises by night [7 hours 55 minutes in total].[2]

I will not attempt here to produce a list of the operations in which Cyril Fuller and his crew took part, as a full list with comments is attached at Table 1 of this Chapter, but in addition to the four operations completed by the end of the month – including bringing back a flak-damaged aircraft from the third and crash-landing at base – they also flew four training exercises, three by night including one night firing by the gunners and one fighter affiliation exercise by day. Three of the exercises were in EE109 and one in EE149, the former 617 Squadron aircraft.

July saw them depart on five operations and undertake a further ten training exercises, all of the operations and all except one of the training excises in EE109. This added 36 hours and 15 minutes to their flying totals. The logbooks were signed by S/L Ronnie Churcher, the flight commander of 'A' Flight and the Squadron CO, W/C IJ McGhie.

In August they flew a further five ops and six training exercises, three of the ops in EE109, one in ED977 PG-A *Nulli Secundus* [to Nürn-

[2] A Bullseye was a mock attack on a British city when searchlights would be switched on to give the crews some idea of what the real thing might be like.

berg] and one in EE114 PG-B [to Berlin – the opening raid of the series of 19 operations against that city during the course of the Winter of 1943 and Spring of 1944]. In the course of doing this they added a further 43 hours 55 minutes flying time to their logbooks. This month their logbooks were signed off by F/L SEJ Jones, deputy flight commander of 'A' Flight and by Cyril Fuller, as a commissioned pilot. He, Leo Eaude and Reg Stevens had been commissioned as pilot officers, first appearing as such in the Squadron Operational Record Book for the operation to Berlin on 23 August 1943 but officially promoted with effect from 23 May 1943, when they had completed the first stage of their Heavy Conversion training.

In September they flew a further six operations and ten training exercises. Four of the operations were flown in EE109 and two in ED977 PG-A. Six of the training exercises were also flown in EE109. This month they added a further 55 hours exactly to their logbooks, again for obvious reasons, mostly flown at night. Ronnie Churcher and Fuller signed the crew members' log books.

October was a brief month. After the operation of 5 hours 45 minutes to Hagen on 1st October, the crew went home on leave for a week. They had completed twenty ops and had only one third of their tour remaining. On the way back to the Squadron a week later, most of them met up in London and travelled back together on the train. Leo Eaude treated them all to dinner. During the day of 18 October they flew an hour's refresher training before setting off at 1750 from Woodhall Spa to Hannover on their last flight. The logbooks were then signed off by Ronnie Churcher, showing 1 hour flown by day and 5 hours and 45 minutes by night. After that comes the all too familiar rubber stamp impressions: DEATH PRESUMED and CENTRAL DEPOSITORY, ROYAL AIR FORCE – AUG 1946.

Table 3.1. The Operational Record of P/O Cyril Fuller DFC and his Crew – June to October 1943

Op	*Date*	*Target*	*Aircraft*	*Comments*
	14 June			*Posted to No 619 Squadron, Woodhall Spa, from No. 1661 Conversion Unit [Lancasters], Winthorpe, Nottinghamshire. All seven crew were sergeants.*
1.	21 June	Krefeld	ED977 PG-A[1]	*Sgt Fuller flew as second pilot with S/Ldr Churcher his Flt Cdr ['A' Flt].*
2.	22 June	Mulheim	ED977 PG-A[2]	*First op together as crew.*
3.	24 June	Wuppertal	EE106 PG-C[3]	*This aircraft FTR from Antheor Viaduct on 16/17 Sep 43.*
4.	25 June	Gelsenkirchen	EE149 PG-U[4]	*Ex-617 Sqn aircraft. Badly damaged by flak; crash-landed on return to base.*

---

[1] The 619 Sqn ORB records the aircraft as being ED957 but this is an error, as this serial number was never issued [to any aircraft in the RAF] and S/Ldr Churcher's logbook shows that he was flying his usual aircraft, ED977 PG-A *Nulli Secundus*, that night. ED977 went on to fly more operations [46] than any other aircraft on the squadron until it failed to return on 5/6 January 1944 during the raid on Stettin [crashed in the target area: F/Off AG Day and crew all killed – buried Poznan Old Garrison Cemetery].

[2] Again the ORB incorrectly shows the aircraft to be ED957. Roy Trahair's logbook shows that this first operation as an operational crew was flown in ED977.

[3] EE106 failed to return from the operation against the Antheor Viaduct on 16/17 Sep 43, a joint 619/617 Sqn operation, led by 619's CO W/Cdr W Abercromby, and designed to put 617 'back in the saddle' after the disastrous raid on the Dortmund-Ems Canal two nights previously, when 617 had lost five out of eight aircraft and crews, including the remnant of Guy Gibson's dam-busting crew. S/Ldr Churcher took over control of the raid from W/Cdr Abercromby when the latter's R/T went u/s after the first two aircraft had bombed. The crew of EE106 survived after ditching off Opporto, being rescued by Portuguese fishermen. The Pilot, F/Lt SEJ Jones DFC DFM survived the war and then flew with BOAC for 35 years. His navigator, F/Off AD Holding joined 617 Sqn and died in a flying accident on 20/21 January 1944.

Table 3.1 The Operational Record of P/O Cyril Fuller

5.	28 June	Cologne	EE109 PG-F	*First of 13 ops in this 'their' aircraft.*
6.	3 July	Cologne	EE109 PG-F	
7.	24 July	Hamburg	EE109 PG-F	
8.	25 July	Essen	EE109 PG-F	
9.	27 July	Hamburg	EE109 PG-F	
10.	29 July	Hamburg	EE109 PG-F	
11.	2 August	Hamburg	EE109 PG-F	
12.	7 August	Milan	EE109 PG-F	
13.	10 August	Nürnberg	ED977 PG-A	*S/L Ronnie Churcher's aircraft, Nulli Secundus.*
14.	15 August	Milan	EE109 PG-F	
15.	23 August	Berlin	EE114 PG-B[5]	

[4] EE149 was an ex-617 Sqn aircraft. It was badly damaged by flak during this raid on Gelsenkirchen but was brought back by Cyril Fuller and his crew and crash-landed at base, surely an irony when Fuller and his crew were to succumb to flak eighteen ops later. EE149 was written-off as beyond economic repair.

[5] EE114 PG-B failed to return from a raid on Leipzig on 20/21 Oct 43, having returned early with engine trouble from the operation against Hannover two nights previously when Fuller and his crew were lost. [The ORB incorrectly records the aircraft serial number as EE144, but that was a 617 Sqn aircraft lost on the Dortmund-Ems Canal raid on 16 Sep 43: EE144 AJ-S, S/Ldr GW Holden DSO, DFC and the remnant of Guy Gibson's dam-busting crew from May 1943. Holden had only recently taken over from Gibson.]

16.	3 September	Berlin	ED977 PG-A	*Fuller, Eaude and Stevens now P/Off.*[6]
17.	6 September	Munich	ED977 PG-A	*Fuller's fifth trip in Nulli Secundus.*
18.	22 September	Hannover[7]	EE109 PG-F	*F/Off JK Cox*[8] *flew as second pilot.*
19.	23 September	Mannheim	EE109 PG-F	*Bombed at 2153 from 20,000 feet.*
20.	27 September	Hannover	EE109 PG-F	*P/Off B Arden*[9] *flew as second pilot.*
21.	1 October	Hagen[10]	EE114 PG-B[11]	*Fuller and crew went on leave for a week after this op.*
22.	18 October	Hannover	EE109 PG-F	*Shot down by flak over target at 2018*

---

[6] Sgt LB Geller and P/Off R Perkins flew as navigator and air bomber respectively in place of P/Off Reg Stevens and P/Off Leo Eaude during the operation to Berlin on 3rd September 1943. F/Off P Ingleby flew in place of Stevens on the trip to Munich on 6th September 1943. [Stevens and Eaude ill?]

[7] The raid on Hannover on 22 September was the first of a series of four in less than a month. The last of the four on 18 October was the least successful of the series with thick cloud covering the target and most of the bombs falling in open country north and north west of the city. Ten days previously on 8 October weather conditions had been much better, and on a clear night Hannover suffered its most damaging raid of the War. Cyril Fuller and his crew were on leave at the time of this raid, Roy Trahair celebrating his 21st birthday with his parents, brothers and sisters at home in St Austell, Cornwall.

[8] F/Off JK Cox and three of his crew were killed on 2/3 January 1944 while en route to Berlin in LM423 PG-H [shot down by a nightfighter near Kleve]. Three of the crew survived as POWs.

[9] P/Off Arden survived the war to retire as W/Cdr B Arden DFC.

[10] On this operation Sgt Whitehead flew as second air bomber.

[11] See note 5. Roy Trahair's logbook, written up after his death, records the aircraft as EE109. Whether this is right or whether the ORB is right we will probably never know.

Sgt LB Geller was a member of P/Off 'Nick' Knilans' crew and flew with him to Hannover on 27th September 1943. F/Off Phil Ingleby and P/Off R Perkins appear later as members of F/Off Arden's [new] crew. Bob Knights has written that he knew Phil Ingleby well on both 619 and 617 Squadrons. 'He was one of the 'characters' on 619 and flew with Bob once as navigator on a trip to Berlin on 16th December 1943. 'He came to 617 in about April 1944 but unfortunately was killed when flying with a Canadian pilot called Duffy in a Mosquito. They lost a wing and crashed into the Wash.'

P/Off James Horne had flown as second pilot with F/Sgt GG Taylor to Frankfurt on 4th October 1943, having arrived on the Squadron from 1654 CU on 5th September. He was on his second operation as second pilot when lost with Fuller and his crew on 18th October. He was married, and his wife was living in South Brixham, Devon at the time of his death. His religion was recorded as Church of Scotland, and so there may have been a Scottish connection.

Table 3.2 The Operational Flights of EE109 [PG-F]

	Date	*Target*	*Pilot/Captain*
1.	21 June 43	Krefeld	F/Off WED Bell[1]
2.	28 June 43	Cologne	Sgt C Fuller
3.	3 July 43	Cologne	Sgt C Fuller
4.	8 July 43	Cologne	Sgt HL Vickerstaffe[2]
5.	12 July 43	Turin	P/Off T O'Shaughnessy[3]
6.	24 July 43	Hamburg	Sgt C Fuller
7.	25 July 43	Essen	Sgt C Fuller
8.	27 July 43	Hamburg	Sgt C Fuller
9.	29 July 43	Hamburg	Sgt C Fuller
10.	2 Aug 43	Hamburg	Sgt C Fuller
11.	7 Aug 43	Milan	Sgt C Fuller
12.	9 Aug 43	Mannheim	P/Off HL Vickerstaffe
13.	10 Aug 43	Nürnberg	Sgt C Fuller
14.	14 Aug 43	Milan	F/Lt F Pullen[4]
15.	15 Aug 43	Milan	Sgt C Fuller
16.	17 Aug 43	Peenemünde	F/Lt F Pullen
17.	27 Aug 43	Nürnberg	P/Off HL Vickerstaffe
18.	30 Aug 43	Mönchen Gladbach	P/Off J Heffernan RCAF[5]

---

[1] F/Lt Bell survived his tour of operations with 619 Sqn, despite having had to abandon one aircraft, EE111 PG-S, over the Humber estuary on 26/27 Nov 43 when returning from Berlin. He completed his tour and finished the War as W/Cdr WED Bell DFC. He died in 1966.

[2] Sgt Vickerstaffe was commissioned, survived his tour of operations and was awarded a DFC.

[3] P/Off O'Shaughnessy completed his tour and went on to 617 Sqn. As F/Lt TV O'Shaughnessy he was killed in a flying accident on 20 Jan 44 when ED918 AJ-F crashed off the beach at Snettisham, Norfolk. He is buried in Great Crosby Roman Catholic Cemetery and his navigator, F/Off AD Holding, another former 619 Sqn member, who survived the ditching of EE106 PG-E off Opporto by F/Lt SEJ Jones on 16/17 Sep 43 during the raid on the Antheor Viaduct, was also killed. He is buried in Birmingham (Brandwood End) Cemetery. ED918 AJ-F was one of the special aircraft adapted to take Barnes Wallis's bouncing bomb and had been flown by F/Sgt Ken Brown of 617 Sqn during the Dams raid in May 1943.

[4] F/Lt Pullen was posted mid-tour to No 50 Sqn.

[5] P/Off JAF Heffernan RCAF was killed with all his crew in JB123 PG-D during a raid on Berlin on 2/3 Jan 44.

TABLE 3.2 THE OPERATIONAL FLIGHTS OF EE109

19.	31 Aug 43	Berlin	F/Off NB Morrison RCAF[6]
20.	2 Sep 43	Gardening	P/Off J Heffernan RCAF
21.	3 Sep 43	Berlin	W/Cdr W Abercromby[7]
22.	22 Sep 43	Hannover	P/Off C Fuller
23.	23 Sep 43	Mannheim	P/Off C Fuller
24.	27 Sep 43	Hannover	P/Off C Fuller
25.	29 Sep 43	Bochum	P/Off C Firth[8]
26.	7 Oct 43[9]	Stuttgart	F/Off NB Morrison RCAF
27.	8 Oct 43	Hannover	F/Off NB Morrison RCAF
28	18 Oct 43	Hannover	P/Off C Fuller *Shot down by flak*

[6] F/Off NB Morrison RCAF survived his tour with 619 Sqn and was awarded a DFC.

[7] W/Cdr W Abercromby DFC and Bar was posted to 83 [Pathfinder] Sqn, Wyton, on 4 Dec 43 and was succeeded as CO of 619 Sqn by Wg Cdr JR Jeudwine OBE DFC. Abercromby was killed during a raid on Berlin on 1/2 Jan 44 when his aircraft exploded while outbound and crashed near Vechta. The navigator Sgt LH Lewis was thrown clear and was the only survivor. Abercromby and the other seven members of his crew are buried in the Sage War Cemetery.

[8] P/Off C Firth and his crew, with an average age of 22, failed to return from the raid on Leipzig on 20/21 Oct 43 while flying EE114 PG-B, the aircraft they were also flying two nights previously when they had been obliged to return early from the raid on Hannover because of engine trouble.

[9] Roy Trahair's flying logbook, written up for October 1943 by someone else after he failed to return from Hannover on 18 October, records that EE109 was used by Cyril Fuller and his crew on their penultimate operation, the raid on Hagen on 1 October 1943. The Squadron ORB records that they used EE114 PG-B. If EE109 was used that night, the total of operations flown in the aircraft before it was lost is 29 not 28, but we will probably never know for sure, as the person writing up Roy's logbook posthumously may have wrongly jumped to the conclusion that as Fuller and his crew usually flew EE109 if it was available, they must have been flying it on the Hagen operation. No one else flew EE109 to Hagen, and no one else is recorded as flying EE114. [I mention this only because there are several examples in the ORB of the same aircraft serial number being shown against two crews for the same operation].

Table 3.3 Aircraft Despatched by 619 Squadron to Hannover on 18 October 1943

Aircraft	*Pilot*	*Take off time*	*Bombing time*	*Debrief report*	*Landing time*	*Flight time from take off to bombing*
ED977 PG-A	W/Cdr W. Abercromby	1702	2028	Bombed at 20,500 feet. Cloud 10/10 at 10,000 feet.	2243	3 hrs 26 minutes
JB123 PG-D	F/Sgt GG Taylor	1715	2018	Bombed at 20,500 feet. Cloud 10/10 at 15,000 feet.	2231	3 hrs 03 minutes.
DV326 PG-P	F/O RD Rayment	1716	2021	Bombed at 20,300 ft. Cloud 8-10/10 at 14/15,000 feet.[1]	2242	3 hrs 05 minutes.
DV328 PG-L	F/O B Arden	1717	2019	Bombed at 20,400 feet. Cloud 10/10 at 15,000.	2237	3 hrs 02 minutes.
EE111 PG-S	F/Lt WED Bell	1719	2021	Bombed at 20,200 feet. Cloud 10/10. [2]	2247	3 hrs 02 minutes.
EE134 PG-Y	F/O RE Knights	1721	Aborted	Oxygen leak in front of rear gunner.	2044	3 hrs 01 minute.
EE116 PG-Q	F/O M Hamilton	1722	2023	Bombed at 19,500 feet. Cloud 8-9/10 at 8-10,000 feet.	2229	2 hrs 55 minutes.
JA867 PG-X	F/O MA MacDonald	1723	2018	Bombed at 20,300 feet. Cloud 9/10.Hit by flak.	2257	2 hrs 50 minutes.

[1] Reported seeing an explosion lasting 20 seconds at 2018 from 20,500 feet.

[2] Reported seeing a large red explosion at 2015 from 21,000 at 52.35N/09.30E.

TABLE 3.3 AIRCRAFT DESPATCHED BY 619 SQUADRON TO HANNOVER ON 18 OCT 1943

EE114 PG-B	P/O C Firth	1725	Aborted	Returned to base early. Engines running hot.	2006	2 hrs 54 minutes
EE168 PG-R	F/Lt AH Tomlin	1726	2020	Bombed at 21,300 ft. Cloud 8-9/10 at 14/15,000 feet.[3]	2238	2 hrs 50 minutes
JA847 PG-C	F/O EK Williams	1737	2027	Bombed at 20,000 feet. Cloud 9/10 at 12,000 feet.	2255	2 hrs 28 minutes.
EE109 PG-F	P/O C Fuller	1750	2018	Shot down by flak near centre of the target. Bombs had been released.		

Of the eleven crews and the eleven aircraft that survived this raid, Wing Commander Abercromby DFC and Bar was killed on 1/2 Jan 44 during a raid on Berlin soon after leaving 619 for 83 [Pathfinder] Squadron, RAF Wyton. P/Off Firth and his crew, with an average age of 22, were lost in EE114 PG-B on their next operation [on 20/21 Oct 43 to Leipzig].

F/Off Rayment [by now Flt/Lt] and crew were lost, believed crashed in the sea in DV381 PG-B, on 26/27 Nov 43 during a raid on Berlin, one of four 619 Squadron aircraft lost that night, three of them crashing or being abandoned in England when returning to base. Of this three, EE111 PG-S with Flt/Lt Bell and crew on board was abandoned over the Humber estuary and EE168 PG-R with Flt/Lt Tomlin and crew aboard crashed near Hutton Cranswick airfield, Yorkshire. Both crews survived their ordeals and went on to complete their full tour of operations with 619.

JA847 PG-C was lost on 2/3 Dec 43 during a raid on Berlin [F/Off JF Bowyer RCAF and crew, three killed, four POW], one of two 619 Squadron aircraft lost that night. JA867 PG-X was lost on 16/17 Dec 43 during another raid on Berlin [P/Off GB

[3] Reported seeing a large blue explosion at 2015 from 20,500 feet.

Loney and crew all killed]. JB123 PG-D was lost on 2/3 Jan 44 during another raid on Berlin [P/Off JAF Heffernan RCAF and crew all killed].

ED977 PG-A, the Squadron's longest serving aircraft having flown 46 missions, was lost on 5/6 Jan 44 during a raid on Stettin [F/Off AG Day and crew all killed]. F/Off EK Williams RCAF and crew were lost on 24/25 Feb 44 [in LM419 PG-N] during the raid on Schweinfurt [the flight engineer Sgt JR Trail, the navigator F/Off AG Knight, the bomb aimer F/Off CH Clarke and the wireless operator Sgt PS Smith surviving as POWs; F/Off Williams and both his air gunners, F/Sgt Glazebrook RAAF and Sgt W Walch are buried in Dürnbach War Cemetery].

DV328 PG-L was lost over Berlin on 24/25 Mar 44 [P/Off P Thompson RNZAF and crew all killed and buried in the War Cemetery in Berlin], having completed eleven Berlin operations. EE116 PG-Q was abandoned, on fire, from 16,000 feet on 11/12 Apr 44 during a raid on Aachen [Flt/Lt H J Moore, the pilot, and F/Sgt T A Jones, the wireless operator, survived as POWs, the rest of the crew died and are buried in Bergen op Zoom War Cemetery].

Thus, of the twelve aircraft that took off for Hannover on 18 Oct 43 only two – DV326 PG-P and EE134 PG-Y - survived operations with 619 Squadron and they possibly only because they were transferred to No 5 Lancaster Finishing School at RAF Syerston before they could be lost. DV326 had completed ten Berlin operations, DV328 eleven, JB123 ten and the doyen of them all, *Nulli Secundus* ED977 PG-A, eight to Berlin. DV326 survived the handling of the trainee pilots of the Finishing School and the War and was finally struck off charge on 15 Jan 47. EE134 was struck off charge on 31 Mar 45.

Perhaps more surprisingly, of the twelve crews that took off for Hannover that night, seven survived their tours with 619 Squadron: F/Sgt Taylor (later Flt/Lt DFC), F/Off B Arden (later Wg Cdr DFC), Fg Off ML Hamilton (later Sqn Ldr DFC), Flt/Lt WED Bell (later Wg Cdr DFC), Fg Off RE Knights (later Flt Lt DSO DFC), Fg Off MA MacDonald and Flt/Lt AH Tomlin (later Sqn Ldr DFC and Bar). Four crews [those captained by Abercromby, Firth, Rayment and Williams] were lost within four months. Fifty-seven years on, of the twelve pilots, only Bob Knights, who went on to have a distinguished second tour with 617 Squadron, is still alive.

Table 3.4 Aircraft Lost During the Raid on Hannover 18/19 October 1943

[All-Lancaster raid, 360 aircraft taking part: 18 missing/crashed = 5%]

Squadron	*Base*	*Aircraft*	*Take off*	*Time hit/down*	*Cause*
7	Oakington	JA917 MG-P	1748	2100	Not known
7	Oakington	JB347 MG-V	1749	2035	Not known
9	Bardney	ED499 WS-X	1743	2030	Not known
44	Dunhome Lodge	R5901 KM-X	1746	2036	Not known
97	Bourn	JB220 OF-O	1738	Not known	Not known
100	Grimsby	DV159 HW-J	1749	Not known	Not known
101	Ludford Magna	DV230 SR-T	1715	Not known	Not known
101	Ludford Magna	DV266 SR-U	1721	Not known	Fighter
103	Elsham Wolds	JB147 PM-C	1720	2030	Not known
103	Elsham Wolds	JB279 PM-E	1730	2010	Not known
103	Elsham Wolds	JB349 PM-G	1733	2045	Not known
115	Little Snoring	DS683 KG-R	1815	2235 At base	Fighter
115	Little Snoring	DS769 KG-H	1805	Not known	Not known
207	Spilsby	W4276 EM-L	1721	Not known	Not known
207	Spilsby	LM326 EM-Z	1716	2030	Not known
426 (Crew 408)	Linton-on-Ouse	DS717 OW-?	1741	2154 Ditched. Crew picked up	Out of Fuel
460	Binbrook	ED985 AR-C2	1716	2005	Not known
467	Bottesford	W4240 PG-A	1708	2030	Not known
619	Woodhall Spa	EE109 PG-F	1750	2021	Flak

In the 17 aircraft that went missing [that is, excluding DS717, whose crew ditched off the Suffolk coast and were all picked up safely when they drifted ashore two hours later, and DS683, whose crew got back to base on two engines with one dead and two injured aboard] were a total of 124 men. Thirteen of the 17 aircraft had seven men aboard, 3 had eight and 1 nine. Of these124 men, twenty-two became POWs, and the rest [102] were killed. Fifty-seven are buried in the Hannover Limmer War Cemetery, eight in the Reichswald Forest Cemetery, ten in Becklingen War Cemetery and twenty-seven, including seven of the crew of the 619 Squadron aircraft, EE109, have no known grave. Of the squadrons involved, 100, 101, 103 and 460 Squadrons were in 1 Group; 115 Squadron was in 3 Group; 9, 44, 207, 467 and 619 Squadrons were in 5 Group; 408/426was in 6 (RCAF) Group; 7 and 97 Squadrons were in No 8 (Pathfinder) Group.

4. The Operational Record

Aircraft losses of No 619 Squadron in 23 months of operations incorporating a list by crews[1] of those members of the Squadron who gave their lives in the cause of freedom

The Eternal god is thy refuge, and underneath are the Everlasting Arms.[2] [Deuteronomy Ch 33, v 27]

[1] I have followed the convention of only identifying the Service to which aircrew belonged if they were serving in the Dominion or Allied air forces, for example in the RAAF, RCAF, RNZAF, SAAF, or [rarely] the USAAF. Other aircrew, so far as is known, were serving in the RAF or RAFVR, though some of these would have been citizens of Commonwealth and other countries.

[2] This verse from Deuteronomy was the theme of a Chaplain's Prayer used during WWI by the Royal Flying Corps and then by the Royal Air Force in the years up to WWII.

June 1943 – May 1945

9 JUN 43 EE113 PG-K LANCASTER MK III

Lost without trace on air test over the North Sea. F/S Price, an instrument fitter and ex-Halton apprentice, and another ground tradesman had accompanied the aircrew on the air test. These were the first casualties suffered by the Squadron since it started forming in April.

Casualties:	Sgt F W Shirley	Pilot	+
	Sgt W J Douglas	Second Pilot	+
	Sgt W A Robinson	Navigator	+
	Sgt J J Wemyss	Air Bomber	+
	Sgt P Fox	W/Op	+
	Sgt D M Gray	Air Gunner	+
	Sgt J H Bambridge RCAF	Air Gunner	+
	Sgt P J Cook	Ground tradesman	+
	F/Sgt A P Price	Instrument fitter	+

11/12 JUN ED978 PG-B LANCASTER MK III

Took off at 22.37 from Woodhall for *Düsseldorf.* Shot down by night-fighter, crashing at Tongeren [Limberg], Belgium. This was the night of the Squadron's operational debut, with twelve aircraft taking part. The pilot evaded capture and got back to UK on 3 Sep 43 after being assisted by the Belgium *Maquis.* The rest of the crew were taken POW. Taylor returned to flying as an instructor.[3] He was the first deputy flight commander of 'A' Flt.

Crew	F/Lt C O Taylor	Pilot	Evd
	Sgt W C Anderson RCAF	Flight Engineer?	Pow
	F/O S E Harris	Navigator	Pow
	Sgt R Evans	Air Bomber	Pow
	Sgt D E Inggs	W/Op	Pow
	Sgt J H Henderson	Air Gunner	Pow
	Sgt R E Chisholm RCAF	Air Gunner	Pow

[3] Had he returned to operations and been shot down again the knowledge F/L Taylor had gained of the *Maquis* and their escape routes could have put them and others at risk.

14/15 JUN **ED980 PG- LANCASTER MK III**

Took off from Woodhall at 2315 for *Oberhausen*. Shot down by night-fighter [Hptm Hans-Dieter Frank of I./NJG1] and crashed at 0056 at Schijndel [Noord Brabant] 7 km W of Veghel, Holland. Six of the crew rest in Eindhoven [Woensel] General Cemetery, but Sgt Van Camp, a Canadian citizen serving in the RCAF, lies in Groesbeek Canadian War Cemetery. The pilot's young son, Nigel McCulloch, a toddler in 1943, is now the Bishop of Manchester. Before knowing about his father's service with 619 Squadron, the author had met and knew Nigel in the 1980s when the former was Administrator of Trinity Theological College in Bristol and Nigel was Chairman of the Church of England's central body responsible for paying the fees of ordinands training at the Church's colleges.

Casualties:	P/O K McCulloch	Pilot	+
	Sgt R E Tofts	Flight Engineer	+
	F/O H Forshaw	Navigator	+
	Sgt N C Richards	Air Bomber	+
	Sgt L Timms	W/Op	+
	Sgt P J Ruane	Air Gunner	+
	Sgt R H Van Camp RCAF	Air Gunner	+

These were the Squadron's first operational fatal casualties.

20/21 JUN **EE116 PG-Q LANCASTER MK III**

One of five aircraft involved in a raid on *Freidrichshaven*. All five bombed successfully and then flew on to Blida, N Africa. Sgt D L May, the bomb aimer in F/S McLeod's crew was hit by flak and killed. A month earlier on 18 May, Sgt May had scored a direct hit from 20,000 ft during a training exercise, using the ABS bomb sight. On their return from North Africa, all five aircraft successfully completed an attack on *Spezia* and then flew back and landed safely at Woodhall. With these two ops F/S McCleod and his crew completed their tour of operations. EE116 was lost on 11/12 Apr 44 when it failed to return from Aachen. It will be remembered that F/S McLeod and his crew were one of the three crews left behind at Woodhall by 97 Sqn to form the nucleus of the new 619 Sqn.

21/22 JUN **EE198 PG-H LANCASTER MK III**

Took off from Woodhall at 2323 for a raid on *Krefeld*. Crashed in the Astense Peel near Opheusden [Noord Brabant], 10 km SSE of Helmond, Holland. All were taken for burial in the military cemetery at Venlo. After the War their remains were re-buried in the Jonkerbos War Cemetery. Their average age was 23.

Casualties:	Sgt D V Jordan	Pilot	+
	Sgt W A Davies	Flight Engineer	+
	F/O W M Girdwood	Navigator	+
	Sgt E Stanley	Air Bomber	+
	Sgt B Howe	W/Op	+
	Sgt F Burton	Air Gunner	+
	Sgt W J Parkes	Air Gunner	+

25/26 JUN **EE149 PG-U LANCASTER MK III**

Took off Woodhall 2245 for a raid on *Gelsenkirchen*. A/c badly damaged by flak but successfully crash-landed on return. After technical inspection the aircraft was struck-off charge as beyond economical repair. No injuries reported [but this crew eventually succumbed to flak over *Hannover on 18 Oct 43* – and hence this book about them and their Squadron]. All survived.

Crew	Sgt C Fuller	Pilot
	Sgt G A Wilson	Flight Engineer
	Sgt R Stephens	Navigator
	Sgt L Eaude	Air Bomber
	Sgt R S Sprackman	W/Op
	Sgt V Crookes	Air Gunner
	Sgt R Trahair	Air Gunner

28/29 JUN **ED979 PG-** **LANCASTER MK III**

Took off from Woodhall at 2258 for a raid on *Köln*. Shot down by night-fighter [Maj Günter Raduach, I./NJG1], crashing near Aalst [Noord Brabant] 5 km S of Eindhoven, where all were buried in Woensel General Cemetery. Sgt Walker RCAF was reburied after the War in the Canadian War Cemetery at Groesbeek.

Casualties:	Sgt T P Murphy	Pilot	+
	Sgt J Adsetts	Flight Engineer	+
	P/O E Harper	Navigator	+
	P/O A Mackay	Air Bomber	+
	Sgt N E Rivers	W/Op	+
	Sgt J H W Walker RCAF	Air Gunner	+
	Sgt R A Grace	Air Gunner	+

10/11 Aug **EE112 PG-T** **Lancaster Mk III**

Took off from Woodhall at 2146 for *Nürnberg*. All rest in Durnbach War Cemetery. F/L Dampier-Crossley RAAF came from Rotherham, Canterbury, New Zealand, and his flight engineer came from Drumcondra, Dublin, in the Irish Republic. This was an experienced crew, and one of the first to be posted in to the Squadron to form the nucleus of the new Squadron.

Casualties:	F/L E Dampier-Crossley DFC RAAF	Pilot	+
	P/O G B P Patterson	Flight Engineer	+
	F/O J MacA McLean DFC RAAF	Navigator	+
	F/O A H Blazer	Air Bomber	+
	F/S F Dawson	W/Op	+
	F/O P C Moxham	Air Gunner	+
	Sgt J Wardle	Air Gunner	+

12/13 AUG **JA844 PG-J LANCASTER MK III**

Took off from Woodhall at 2141 for *Milan*. Bombed successfully from 21,000 ft at 0132. On returning to England, after crossing the Sussex coast at Selsey Hill, JA844 was about one mile inland when it was struck by another aircraft [Lancaster ED361 of No 207 Squadron], which passed below and in front of JA844 from the port side, the port rudder of ED361 striking the port wing tip of JA844, causing that wing's trailing edge to curl up about 3 or 4 feet. This put the aircraft into a steep dive to port, causing the starboard outer and port outer engines both to catch fire. The pilot managed to level the aircraft at about 1,000 ft, extinguish the fires, feather the engines, and make for the nearest airfield [thought to be Shoreham]. The crew called 'Darky' [meaning an aircraft was in trouble and needed to land immediately at any available airfield] but this failed to elicit a response and a distress flare was fired. Because another aircraft was observed half-way down the runway, P/O Arden attempted to make a circuit. Realising that this was not going to succeed, he took the aircraft out to sea and was flying parallel with the shore when the port wing suddenly dropped and the aircraft was levelled only just before it hit the water. This had happened so suddenly that the crew had not had time to take the correct ditching action. They came down about 500 yards from the shore, just off Littlehampton and were in the water for about 45 minutes before being picked up by an Air Sea Rescue launch from 29 ASR Unit, Littlehampton. By this time Sgt Jones, the navigator had drifted away from the dinghy in the darkness and was not seen again. The mid-upper gunner, Sgt Les Maddaford, died in Littlehamton Hospital from injuries and shock. The events of that night are recorded in detail in the Squadron ORB and also in a letter sent by Sgt A V Howarth, the W/Op, to the father of Les Maddaford on 31 Aug 43.[4]

Crew:	P/O B Arden	Pilot	
	Sgt A W Shepherd	Flight Engineer	
	Sgt D V Jones	Navigator	+
	P/O R Perkins	Air Bomber	
	Sgt A V Howarth	W/Op	
	Sgt L T C Maddaford	Air Gunner	+
	Sgt A Finch	Air Gunner	

[4] I am grateful to Mr John Maddaford, brother of Sgt Maddaford, for making this letter available to me.

P/O Arden flew again, starting back as second pilot with P/O Cyril Fuller soon after this incident, and he went on to complete his tour, retiring from the RAF as a wing commander with a DFC. Attempts to trace him at his last known address in Witney, Oxfordshire in 1977 have failed, and it seems likely he is now dead. P/O Perkins and Sgts Howarth and Finch also went on to complete their tours. The 207 Sqn aircraft was abandoned, crashing at Plaidstowe: one crew member [F/S K E Goodsell] was killed.

17/18 AUG — ED982 PG-D LANCASTER MK III

Took off from Woodhall at 2144 for the raid on the *Peenemünde* rocket site, coordinated by master-bomber G/Capt John Searby, another ex-Halton apprentice. Crashed in the Baltic, the 26th of 45 aircraft to be downed that night. F/O Warren's body was washed ashore and taken to Greifswald for burial on 11 Sep. His grave is now in the Berlin 1939-45 War Cemetery. The bodies of the other crew members were never found, and they are commemorated on the Runnymede Memorial.

Crew on 10th op.	P/O A J Pearce	Pilot	+
	Sgt W H Humphrey	Flight Engineer	+
	F/O J M Warren	Navigator	+
	F/O L G Davis DFM	Air Bomber	+
	Sgt T B Barrie	W/Op	+
	Sgt R D Deugard	Air Gunner	+
	Sgt C B Francis	Air Gunner	+

17/18 AUG **EE117 PG-L LANCASTER MK III**

Took off from Woodhall at 2151 for *Peenemünde*, flown by the founding CO. Shot down by night-fighter [Lt Hans Meissner of II./NJG3, flying a ME110 from Schlewig/Jagel with Untoffz Josef Krinner, radar operator, one of their three successes that night in the space of only nine minutes[5]]. All eight members of the crew are buried in Aabenraa Cemetery, Denmark. Crew on seventh operation, some on second tour. Probably the 38th of 41 a/c shot down that night. F/S Horsham had joined the RAF as an apprentice.

Casualties:	W/C I J McGhie DFC[6]	Pilot	+
	F/S P J Horsham	Flight Engineer	+
	F/O E G Prest RCAF	Navigator	+
	P/O P M Goldsmith RAAF	Air Bomber	+
	WO F A Thompson RCAF	W/Op	+
	Sgt W A Mitchell	Air Gunner	+
	Sgt A C R Chapman	Air Gunner	+
	F/S V G Stabell RAAF	Second Pilot	+

[5] Martin Middlebrook, *The Peenemünde Raid* [Penguin Books 1988, p 183/184].

[6] W/C IJ McGhie was married and with his family lived in Woodhall Spa village while he commanded 619 Squadron. On the night of the attack on Peenemünde [17/18 Auguust 1943] the Luftwaffe bombed Woodhall Spa village, and John McGhie's family must have been affected by this attack. The Royal Hotel and Winter Gardens in Woodhall village was destroyed. A large memorial to 617 Sqn, with more than a passing resemblance to the Möhne Dam, has been built on site of the hotel, now an area open to the public, and which was given by the hotel owners to Woodhall Urban District Council after the War. There is a smaller memorial to 619 Squadron within the compound at the part of the former airfield still used by the RAF. The 617 Sqn memorial bears the names of the 206 members of the Squadron who died during the War. The 619 Squadron memorial does not list names, but 619 Squadron lost 495 members after coming into existence a month later than 617.

17/18 AUG **EE147 PG-P LANCASTER MK III**

Took off from Woodhall at 2155 for *Peenemünde*. Crashed near Anklam-Lassan, Germany. All now lie in Poland in the Poznam Old Garrison Cemetery. Crew on their 9th operation. Probably the 29th aircraft down that night.

Casualties:	P/O O A O'Leary RCAF	Pilot	+
	Sgt T Underdown	Flight Engineer	+
	F/S R Crossley	Navigator	+
	Sgt J T Hubbard	Air Bomber	+
	Sgt J H Shaw	W/Op	+
	Sgt D G Cox	Air Gunner	+
	F/S L F English RNZAF	Air Gunner	+

23/24 AUG **ED981 PG-V LANCASTER MK III**

Took off for *Berlin* from Woodhall at 2007. Crashed 300 metres off the beach at Surendorf, 19 km NNW of Keil, where the five that died are buried in the War Cemetery. F/S Castle's service number indicates that he had joined the RAF, post-Oct 1925, as a civilian, probably as a fitter or mechanic, possibly an armourer, an obvious source of recruitment for air gunners. Sgt Stamper had joined the RAF as an apprentice. Sgt Gardner was ex-Army.

Casualties:	P/O D Coomber DFM	Pilot	pow
	Sgt G A Stamper	Flight Engineer	pow
	Sgt W H Cade	Navigator	+
	Sgt H R Snell	Air Bomber	+
	Sgt K R Wallace	W/Op	+
	F/S A Castle	Air Gunner	+
	Sgt L Gardner	Air Gunner	+

31 AUG/1SEP **EE115 PG-G LANCASTER MK III**

Took off for *Berlin* from Woodhall at 1954. Outbound, crashed near Höxter, where on 4 Sep the six that died were laid to rest. After the War, they were reburied in Hannover Limmer War Cemetery. F/S Metcalfe's DFM was not gazetted until 10 Apr 45.

Casualties:	F/S F G Metcalfe DFM	Pilot	+
	Sgt W G Mycock	Flight Engineer	+
	F/S R W Gollogly	Navigator	+
	Sgt H E Kilburn	Air Bomber	+
	Sgt F C Dryden	W/Op	+
	Sgt H D Watkins	Air Gunner	pow
	Sgt R L Measor	Air Gunner	+

31 AUG/1 SEP **JA848 PG-R LANCASTER MK III**

Took off for *Berlin* from Woodhall at 2000. Shot down by a night-fighter and crashed near Jüterbog, where the six that died were buried. After the War they were reburied in the Berlin 1939-45 War Cemetery.

Casualties:	F/S G W Bower RCAF	Pilot	+
	Sgt F Hudson	Flight Engineer	+
	F/S E P Jones	Navigator	pow
	Sgt R H Crooks	Air Bomber	+
	Sgt W McGill	W/Op	+
	Sgt P A Musso RCAF	Air Gunner	+
	Sgt R Jones	Air Gunner	+

5/6 SEP **JB133 PG-L LANCASTER MK III**

Took off at 1938 from Woodhall for *Mannheim*. While flying straight and level about 80 km from the target suddenly burst into flames. The order to abandon was given but before anyone could comply the aircraft disintegrated, crashing near Waldfishbach- Burgalben, about 9 km NNE of Pirmasens. The six crew members that died are in the Rheinberg War Cemetery. The only survivor, Sgt Gostling, was thrown out of the aircraft as it broke up and landed safely to be taken pow.

Casualties:	F/S C A Goddard	Pilot	+
	Sgt K A Metcalfe	Flight Engineer	+
	Sgt F E Gostling	Navigator	pow
	Sgt R V Forsdick	Air Bomber	+
	Sgt F Sumner	W/Op	+
	Sgt W Kershaw	Air Gunner	+
	Sgt E E Nicholls	Air Gunner	+

16/17 SEP **EE106 PG-E LANCASTER MK II**

Took off from Coningsby at 2006 for the *Antheor Viaduct* as part of a joint 617/619 force under W/C Jock Abercrombie, the new CO of 619 [on an operation intended to put 617 'back in the saddle' again after the disastrous raid on the Dortmund-Ems Kanal, near Ladbergen, the previous night when 617 had lost five crews, including the remnant of Guy Gibson's crew and F/L L G Knight DSO MID RAAF and his crew, which was the one that had made the final breach in the Möhne Dam four months previously]. Thought to have been hit by Flak over the target, the aircraft was ditched off Opporto and the crew rescued by Portuguese fishermen. The pilot and rear gunner had earned their DFMs while serving with 106 Squadron [Gibson's squadron before he took over 617]. After a brief spell of internment the crew was returned home and completed its tour of ops. F/O Holden later joined 617 Sqn and lost his life in a flying accident on 20/21 Jan 44. Stan Jones was born in Broad St, Ludlow, where the author now lives and after the war flew as a pilot with BOAC for 35 years. He told me he had been recruited to 619 by Ronnie Churcher who knew him from 106 Sqn days.[7]

Crew:	F/L S E J Jones DFM	Pilot	int
	Sgt A E Brookes	Flight Engineer	int
	F/O A D Holding	Navigator	int
	Sgt G E Deschaine	Air Bomber	int
	F/S R G Faux	W/Op	int
	Sgt C S Cook	Air Gunner	int
	P/O A W E Cartwright DFM	Air Gunner	int

[7] Telephone conversation with the author 29 Oct 2000.

29/30 SEP **ED983 PG-W LANCASTER MK III**

Took off from Woodhall at 1821 for *Bochum*. On return in low cloud struck high ground at 0005 at Cadwell Hill, five miles west of Mablethorpe. Of those that died, Sgt Cooper and F/O McKay RCAF were buried in Cambridge City Cemetery, while the others were taken to their home towns for burial [Sgt Billingham was cremated at Wandsworth].

Casualties:	P/O E Mearis	Pilot	+
	Sgt P Bowditch	Flight Engineer	inj
	Sgt R L Cooper	Navigator	+
	F/O A C McKay RCAF	Air Bomber	+
	Sgt R Armstrong	W/Op	inj
	Sgt J A G Billingham	Air Gunner	+
	Sgt R T E Davies	Air Gunner	+

1/2 OCT **EE110 PG-U LANCASTER MK III**

Took off from Woodhall at 1825 for *Hagen*. Crashed on return in Bristol Channel off Llantwit Major, some 12 miles SW of Cardiff. Six bodies were recovered at Barry but that of F/O Joss was found on the opposite side of the Channel at Portishead. All were taken to their home towns for burial or cremation.

Casualties:	F/O D M Joss	Pilot	+
	Sgt T Monoghan	Flight Engineer	+
	P/O C F Bale	Navigator	+
	F/O F V Anderson	Air Bomber	+
	Sgt P Engel	W/Op	+
	Sgt J Lowe	Air Gunner	+
	F/S K G Mortlock	Air Gunner	+

3/4 OCT **JB131 PG-T LANCASTER MK III**

Took off from Woodhall at 1844 for *Kassel.* Engaged by enemy night-fighter twice and rear gunner, Sgt G H Jackson killed. The pilot, Sgt H C Knilans RCAF [later Lt USAAF], an American who went on to win an immediate DSO with 619 and a DFC with 617 Sqn has written movingly about this incident in his war diaries [see p. XXX], as he personally cut his gunner's body from the damaged turret on landing back at Woodhall at 0039.

Casualty: Sgt G H Jackson Air Gunner +

8/9 OCT **ED839 PG-C LANCASTER MK III**

When taking off from Woodhall at 2258 for *Hannover*, swung and slid to a stop with its undercarriage wrecked. A fire broke out and The aircraft was totally destroyed. None of the crew was injured. The captain was F/O J G Thompson RCAF. Because of the state of the Woodhall runway, the other seven 619 aircraft had to land elsewhere on their return, six at Coningsby and one at East Kirby.

18/19 OCT **EE109 PG-F LANCASTER MK III**

Took off at 1750 from Woodhall for *Hannover*. Hit by flak over the target and crashed near centre of Hannover. Two bodies were recovered in 1943 but today only one, Sgt Roy Trahair, has a known grave [Hannover Limmer War Cemetery].Two unidentified bodies were buried as unknown airmen at Limmer Cemetery in early 1978 [Plot 10, Row A, graves 5 & 6] after the remains of this aircraft were discovered in the Leine river in Mar 1977 during the construction of an autobahn fly-over. Next of kin were not informed. P/O Horne had just joined the squadron and was on his second op as second pilot [the first with F/S GG Taylor a few days previously]. He left a young widow, as also did Reg Stephens, the navigator, a former London policeman who had survived the Blitz on his native East End when on duty in 1940/1. His widow, 23 at the time, never remarried and is still alive in her 80s. The others were all unmarried. The youngest was Vincent Crookes, the mid- upper gunner from Sheffield, who was 19 year of age.

Casualties:	P/O C Fuller DFC	Pilot	+
	Sgt G A Wilson	Flight Engineer	+
	P/O R Stephens	Navigator	+
	P/O L Eaude	Air Bomber	+
	Sgt R S Sprackman	W/Op	+
	Sgt V Crookes	Air Gunner	+
	Sgt R Trahair	Air Gunner	+
	P/O J Horne	Second Pilot	+

20/21 OCT EE114 PG-B LANCASTER MK III

Took off at 1718 from Woodhall for *Leipzig*. Nothing further was heard from this aircraft at take-off. Crashed at Langwedel and all buried at Hannover Limmer Cemetery. The same crew and aircraft had to return early from the Hannover raid the previous night with engine problems. Sgt Weighell was an ex-apprentice. The average age was 22. P/O Christopher Firth [22] was the son of Stephen and Elizabeth Firth & husband of Audrey Firth of Dunston, Gateshead.

Casualties:	P/O C Firth	Pilot	+
	Sgt G M Weighell	Flight Engineer	+
	F/S C N D Wright RCAF	Navigator	+
	Sgt D Demaine	Air Bomber	+
	Sgt G W Dilnutt	W/Op	+
	Sgt M Jones	Air Gunner	+
	Sgt A G Osborne	Air Gunner	+

26/27 NOV DV336 PG-U LANCASTER MK I

Took off at 1719 from Woodhall for *Berlin*. Crashed 0200 on return coming down just to the south of Elvington airfield, Yorks. Sgt Pearse, P/O Salt and Sgt Knights RAAF all rest in Harrogate [Stonefall] Cemetery. Three others are buried in other United Kingdom cemeteries. Sgt Wilcher has no known grave and is commemorated on panel 169 of the Runnymede Memorial.

Casualties:	P/O K J Mears	Pilot	+
	Sgt L Pearse	Flight Engineer	+
	Sgt D W Blundell	Navigator	+
	P/O GG Salt	Air Bomber	+
	Sgt A R Wilcher	W/Op	+
	Sgt W W N Knights RAAF	Air Gunner	+
	Sgt H V Birch	Air Gunner	+

26/27 NOV **DV381 PG-B** **LANCASTER MK I**

Took off at 1722 from Woodhall for *Berlin*. Nothing further heard. Believed to have crashed in sea. Five are commemorated on the Runnymede Memorial. F/L Rayment and Sgt Lynch rest in Becklingen War Cemetery. F/S Cook had survived the ditching of EE106 off the coast of Portugal on 16/17 Sep 43 and may be the air gunner, 'Jock' Cook, identified on the back of a photograph taken by Roy Trahair before he went missing on 18 Oct 43.

Casualties:	F/L R D Rayment	Pilot	+
	Sgt M J Lynch	Flight Engineer	+
	F/O J Kellett	Navigator	+
	Sgt W Archibald	Air Bomber	+
	F/S J T Richards	W/Op	+
	F/S C S Cook	Air Gunner	+
	F/S J A Fowler	Air Gunner	+

26/27 NOV **EE111 PG-S** **LANCASTER MK III**

Took off at 1714 from Woodhall for *Berlin*. Abandoned over the Humber Estuary at 0232 while returning to base, crashing onto Fourholme Sands. No injuries reported.

Crew:	F/L W E D Bell	Pilot
	Sgt M V Pink	Flight Engineer
	F/S J A Featherstone	Navigator
	F/S J A Walsh	Air Bomber
	Sgt J Webster	W/Op
	F/O T K Graves	Air Gunner
	F/O J Kemp	Air Gunner

26/27 NOV EE168 PG-R LANCASTER MK III

Took off at 1728 from Woodhall for *Berlin*. Crashed on return at 0235 one mile east of Hutton Cranswick airfield, Yorkshire, where attempting to crash-land. No injuries reported.

Crew:	F/L A H Tomlin DFC	Pilot
	F/S E G Cass	Flight Engineer
	P/O T A Peatfield	Navigator
	F/S J Simkin	Air Bomber
	Sgt H W Thompson	W/Op
	Sgt W Dunham	Air Gunner
	F/S P D Mitchell	Air Gunner

The night of 26/27 November was the squadron's worst night for losses in its first six months of operations, losing this night four out of its sixteen aircraft taking part in this raid on *Berlin*. It was redeemed slightly by the knowledge that the crew of the aircraft piloted by P/O Hubert 'Nick' Knilans, the American flying with the RAF via the RCAF, claimed a Ju 88 shot down and a Me 110 damaged. These two a/c had attacked Knilans' Lancaster ED859 PG-V while it was on the outward trip, damaging the port inner engine, which had had to be feathered, but they went on to bomb the target and get back safely, landing at Spilsby. It was following this incident that Knilans was recommended on 29 November by 619's CO, W/C Jock Abercromby for an immediate award of a DSO, which was subsequently confirmed and announced to the Squadron on 8 December.[8] F/S Learmonth, the mid-upper gunner, was awarded an immediate DFM. Meanwhile, W/C Abercromby had been posted as a G/Capt to command No 83 [PFF] Squadron and was killed in early January during another attack on Berlin.

[8] For a full list of decorations awarded members of the squadron, see Table 4 of this chapter.

2/3 DEC **EE170 PG-N LANCASTER MK III**

Took off at 1641 from Woodhall for *Berlin*. Hit by flak north of Magdeburg and burst into flames. As the crew prepared to bale out, the aircraft exploded. Sgt Cross regained consciousness at 5,000 ft and landed safely, but with several broken ribs. The rest were killed and are buried in the Berlin 1939-45 Cemetery.

Casualties:	P/O J F Ward	Pilot	+
	Sgt G W Cross	Flight Engineer	pow
	P/O E T Hargreaves	Navigator	+
	Sgt J H Duncan	Air Bomber	+
	Sgt J W Scott	W/Op	+
	Sgt R Smithers	Air Gunner	+
	Sgt G W Arlett	Air Gunner	+

2/3 DEC **JA847 PG-C LANCASTER MK III**

Took off at 1643 from Woodhall for *Berlin*. Crashed into the Tegel, a heavily wooded area near Berlin where F/O Bowyer is buried. The two air gunners were never found and are commemorated on the Runnymede memorial.

Casualties:	F/O J F Bowyer RCAF	Pilot	+
	Sgt E C Parrot	Flight Engineer	pow
	F/S T G Conway	Navigator	pow
	F/O G F F Staker	Air Bomber	pow
	Sgt E B Thornhill	W/Op	pow
	P/O R W McManaman		
	MID RCAF	Air Gunner	+
	Sgt A C Leitch	Air Gunner	+

This night the Squadron lost two of its ten aircraft taking part in this attack on *Berlin*. Weather conditions were good over the target with some low cloud, and the returning crews thought the raid had been successful with fires seen burning some 150 miles away on the return flight. The surviving eight aircraft all landed at Coningsby on return. One crew reported seeing a large explosion at 2020.

16/17 DEC **JA867 PG-X LANCASTER MK III**

Took off at 1630 from Woodhall for *Berlin*. Crashed at Eberswald Finow, where the crew were buried. Since 1945 their remains have been transferred to Berlin 1939-45 cemetery.

Casualties:	P/O G B Loney RCAF	Pilot	+
	F/S J Gray	Flight Engineer	+
	F/O H A De Vries	Navigator	+
	F/O M Gennis	Air Bomber	+
	Sgt L Banks	W/Op	+
	Sgt D Corbitt	Air Gunner	+
	Sgt R F Dearden	Air Gunner	+

16/17 DEC **EE150 PG-F LANCASTER MK III**

Took off at 1635 from Woodhall for *Berlin*. Outbound badly shot up by nightfighter, but with great skill and determination the crew completed their mission. On return to Woodhall at 0140 crashed near the airfield's outer beacon. F/L Tomlin received an immediate first bar to his DFC and F/S Brookes an immediate DFM. F/L Tomlin and four members of his crew had also crashed landed on return from Berlin on 27 November in EE168. Once again no injuries were reported.

Crew:	F/L A H Tomlin DFC	Pilot
	F/S A E Brookes	Flight Engineer
	P/O T A Peatfield	Navigator
	F/S A Aveline	Second Navigator
	F/S J S Simkin	Air Bomber
	Sgt R W Thompson	W/Op
	Sgt W Dunham	Air Gunner
	Sgt E S Evans	Air Gunner

During this evening's raid on *Berlin* the squadron lost two out of fifteen aircraft. Because of thick cloud over the target [10/10ths] the crews were not able to see or photograph the results of the attacks, but reported that the bombing was concentrated on the marker flares and that if they had been accurately laid then the bombing would also have been accurate. Crews reported seeing the glow of the fires in *Berlin* from 50-70 miles away on the return leg. A raid on *Frankfurt* took place on 20/21 December when fifteen aircraft of 619 were detailed. Two failed to take off, and one returned early after a fire broke out after take off and the crew had to jettison their bomb-load. Nonetheless, the remaining 13 aircraft reached the target and dropped 560 tons of bombs, though once again weather conditions were not good [9/10ths at best] and the bomb drop could not be plotted accurately. The glow of fires on the clouds indicated that once again much of a German city was alight. On 29/20 December fifteen aircraft were again detailed for *Berlin*, but one scrubbed, and only fourteen went to the target. All got back safely. Again, the weather was bad with 10/10ths cloud and plotting the bomb drop was impossible, and once again the glow of fires indicated that *Berlin* was again suffering. This was the last operation of 1943 for No 619 Squadron, an operation ordered for the night of New Year's Eve being cancelled because of bad weather. The new CO, W/C John Jeudwine, a pre-War Cranwell cadet, had taken part in four raids in his first month in charge, including two against Berlin and his first, on the first day with the squadron, to *Leipzig* as second pilot with S/L R Aytoun in DV326 PG-P on 3 December. His predecessor, W/C Jock Abercromby flew his last operation with No 619 Sqn on 2 December to *Berlin* in JB123 PG-D. A month later to the day he was killed en route once more to Berlin, but this time as a pathfinder with No 83 Sqn.[9]

[9] W/C W Abercromby was the son of David Grewar Abercromby and Euphemia Abercromby of Brechin, Angus, and he was 33 years of age when he died. He is buried in Sage War Cemetery, Plot 8.F.12.

1944

The New year began as it had finished with another raid on *Berlin* on the night of ½ January. This time fourteen aircraft of No 619 Squadron took off, but one [LM420 PG-R] returned early with three engines out of use, having jettisoned its bombs over the North Sea at position 53.24N 01.30E thirty- five minutes after take-off. Once again weather conditions were bad over the target with 10/10ths cloud at 20,000 ft, and the general opinion of the crews was that the raid was not successful in terms of target concentration or accuracy. The next night, 2/3 January, another raid on *Berlin* was ordered, and 619 Sqn provided ten aircraft. One [PG-O} returned early with engine problems, having jettisoned its bombs over the North Sea position 52.22N 02.39E fifty-seven minutes after take-off. Once again there was 10/10ths cloud over the target. The missing aircraft were:

2/3 JAN **JB123 PG-D LANCASTER MK III**

Took off at 2326 from Woodhall for *Berlin*. Crashed at Wense, 4km NNW of Wendeburg. Most of the crew were taken for burial at Fallingbostel on 6 Jan. Since 1945, six have been reburied in the Hamburg War Cemetery. W/O Evans, who gained his DFM with No 106 Sqn in Mar 43, rests in Celle War Cemetery. The pilot was an American citizen from Los Angeles, serving in the RCAF.

Casualties:	P/O J A F Heffernan RCAF	Pilot	+
	Sgt K W Cheshire	Flight Engineer	+
	F/O L C Keeling	Navigator	+
	F/O A B Bearcroft	Air Bomber	+
	F/O W J C Lord	W/Op	+
	F/S K M MacDonald	Air Gunner	+
	W/O E S I Evans DFM	Air Gunner	+

2/3 JAN **LM423 PG-H LANCASTER MK III**

Took off at 2343 from Woodhall for *Berlin*. Attacked by a night- from the port quarter and abandoned at 21,000 ft near Kleve. The dead are now buried in the Reichswald Forest War Cemetery. It is not known whether the two Braids were related.

Casualties:	F/O J K Cox	Pilot	+
	Sgt G K Hawkins	Flight Engineer	pow
	F/O G M Braid	Navigator	pow
	F/O R W Braid	Air Bomber	pow
	Sgt C G Payne	W/Op	+
	Sgt D Burden	Air Gunner	+
	Sgt J Cooksey	Air Gunner	+

5/6 JAN **ED977 PG-A LANCASTER MK III**

Took off at 0018 from Woodhall for *Stettin*. Crashed in the target area, where the funeral of Sgt Stuart was reported on 12 Jan. With the other six members of the crew, he now lies in the Poznan Old Garrison Cemetery. This was the No 619's longest serving aircraft with 46 ops completed and was often flown by S/L Churcher, the Flt Cdr of 'A' Flt. Ironically this was also the last 619 Sqn aircraft lost from Woodhall Spa.

Casualties:	F/O A G Day	Pilot	+
	Sgt W D Holliday	Flight Engineer	+
	Sgt T Bell	Navigator	+
	F/L A E Wesson AFM	Air Bomber	+
	Sgt R W Carpenter	W/Op	+
	Sgt E E Watson	Air Gunner	+
	Sgt M Stuart RAAF	Air Gunner	+

15/16 FEB **DV330 PG-O LANCASTER MK III**

Took off from the Squadron's new base, Coningsby, at 1637 for *Berlin*. Crashed in the Baltic. The bodies of Sgt Carpenter and F/O Parry RCAF were washed ashore in Germany and both now lie in Berlin 1939-45 War Cemetery. Three others were recovered from Danish waters and are interred in Svino Cemetery. The bodies of Sgt Cole and F/S Little were not recovered and they are commemorated on the Runnymede memorial.

Casualties:	F/O R M Rumble RCAF	Pilot	+
	Sgt J V P Cole	Flight Engineer	+
	F/S R H Little	Navigator	+
	F/O W H C Pateman	Air Bomber	+
	Sgt G H Carpenter	W/Op	+
	F/O R C Parry RCAF	Air Gunner	+
	F/O P J Coleman	Air Gunner	+

This was the first aircraft lost by No 619 Sqn from RAF Coningsby, to which station the squadron had moved on 9th January. Three days later 619 had been joined at Coningsby by 61 Sqn from Skellingthorpe, whilst No 617 Sqn moved from Coningsby into the accommodation at Woodhall vacated by 619. Meanwhile 619 had sent without loss eleven aircraft to *Brunswick* on 14/15 January, thirteen aircraft to *Berlin* on 20/21 January [ME568 PG-F returned early with two engines on fire], seven to *Magdeburg* and two on a diversionary raid to *Berlin* on 21/22 January, fourteen to Berlin on 27/28 January [ED859 PG-V returned early with its Gyro, ASI and altimeter unserviceable], fourteen to *Berlin* on 28/29 January, eleven to *Berlin* on 30/31 January and twenty to *Berlin* on 15/16 February when F/O Rumble and crew were lost. The twenty aircraft put up on 15/16 February was the single biggest total the Squadron had ever put into the air for a single operation and was a prodigious achievement. In fact, it was better even than twenty, for one 619 Sqn pilot also flew that night to *Berlin* from East Kirkby in a 630 Sqn aircraft, returning with a seriously injured rear gunner.

Once again on the three *Berlin raids* in late January and the one in mid-February the weather over the target had closed in with 10/10ths cloud. Bomb plotting and raid photography was not possible, but the fires in Berlin could be seen from 100 miles away, and the target was described on 28/29th January as being 'one mass of flames'. On 6th January two of 619's more experienced crews, those of Nick Knilans [by now a Lt

USAAF but having opted to remain in Bomber Command] and Bob Knights were posted out to join No 617 Sqn. On 20th January another former 619 Sqn pilot, F/L T V O'Shaughnessy and three crew, including another ex-619 man, F/O A D Holding, were killed when their 617 Sqn Lancaster ED918 AJ-F crashed on the beach at Snettisham, Norfolk, 35 minutes after take off from Woodhall. ED918 had taken part in the raid on the *Sorpe Dam* on 16/17 May 43 with F/S Ken Brown at the controls. It will be remembered that F/O Holding was the navigator of EE106 PG-E when it ditched off Opporto on 16/17 Sep 1943 during the raid on the *Antheor Viaduct*.

On 19/20 February and 20/21 February, No 619 sent nineteen aircraft to *Leipzig* [one borrowed from 61 Sqn] and fifteen to Stuttgart. All bombed and returned safely. Over *Leipzig* [a raid which ranks with the Nürnberg raid of 30/31 March 1944 in the annals of Bomber Command disasters] cloud was 10/10ths and over Stuttgart up to 7/10ths.

24/25 FEB **LM419 PG-N LANCASTER MK III**

Took off at 2008 from Coningsby for *Schweinfurt*. Shot down by night-fighter, whose fire is believed to have caused the port wing to break off. The three members of the crew that died are buried in Dürnbach War Cemetery.

Casualties:	F/O E K Williams RCAF	Pilot	+
	Sgt J R Trail	Flight Engineer	pow
	F/O A G Knight	Navigator	pow
	F/O C H Clarke	Air Bomber	pow
	Sgt C B Smith	W/Op	pow
	F/S J G L Glazebrook RAAF	Air Gunner	+
	Sgt W Walch	Air Gunner	+

The Squadron sent nineteen aircraft on this raid and all bombed and returned home safely except LM419. The following night the Squadron sent thirteen aircraft to *Augsburg*. Twelve got to the target, bombed and returned safely but ED497 PG-Z returned early with unserviceable supercharger and hydraulics. For once weather conditions were good with clear sky over the target, and PFF marking was reported to be good.

17 MAR **ED597 PG- LANCASTER MK III**

During a *training flight* from Coningsby both ASIs failed and the pilot [F/S N W Donnelly RNZAF] tried to abort take-off, but the aircraft ran off the end of the runway and the undercarriage collapsed. The aircraft was struck-off on 29 March. No injuries were reported.

24/25 MAR **DV328 PG-L LANCASTER MK III**

Took off at 1853 from Coningsby for *Berlin*. Crashed south of Teltow, 16 km SW of the centre of Berlin. All seven crew are buried in the Berlin War Cemetery.

Casualties:	P/O P Thompson RNZAF	Pilot	+
	Sgt B F Gratwicke	Flight Engineer	+
	Sgt J B Campbell	Navigator	+
	F/O J V Leyland	Air Bomber	+
	Sgt J D Pedley	W/Op	+
	Sgt L Minshull	Air Gunner	+
	F/S J Hay RAAF	Air Gunner	+

30/31 MAR **DV328 PG-L LANCASTER MK I**

Took off at 2213 from Coningsby for *Nürnberg*. On return they crashed-landed at Woodbridge airfield, Suffolk having had two Engines knocked out by flak. None of crew was injured but the the aircraft was consumed by fire. Sadly, this crew died within months: Sgt Woodcock during the raid on *Salbris* on 8 May; and the rest of the crew, plus Woodcock's replacement F/S Broll, on 24 July during the *Kiel* operation.

Crew:	Sgt J Parker	Pilot
	Sgt N M Rice	Flight Engineer
	F/S G A Grigg	Navigator
	F/S A D Aumell RCAF	Air Bomber
	Sgt W A Sharp	W/Op
	Sgt A Dickson	Air Gunner
	Sgt J H Woodcock	Air Gunner

Also during the month, ten Squadron aircraft had been to *Chateauroux* on a clear night with a full moon on 10/11 March as part of a 54 Base effort involving thirty aircraft. Nine of the aircraft were awarded an aiming point hit [and the tenth was not only because of camera failure], having met no fighter of flak resistance and having bombed from between 7,500 and 10,000 ft. It was believed the target had been destroyed. The AOC 54 Base, A/Cdre Sharpe, flew that night as second pilot with W/C Jeudwine.

On 15/16 March 619 sent sixteen aircraft to *Stuttgart*, the third raid on that city in as many weeks, and though the weather was good on the flight to the target there was up to 7/10ths cloud over the city. The 619 crews thought that the PFF markers seemed to be scattered, and they suspected that the fires they could see were probably decoys in woods. The rear gunner of P/O K Roberts' crew, F/S G C King RAAF, in LM378 PG-J fought off and claimed as destroyed a Ju88 that began firing short bursts of cannon at them from only 50/75 yards distance as they left the target area. One cannon shell blew off the port fin and port rudder, but the aircraft got safely back to base. Roberts was awarded an immediate DFC and King an immediate DFM.

On 18/19 March the squadron sent fifteen aircraft to *Frankfurt*. With only light cloud over the target, the ground markers were seen clearly from 20,000 ft, and the bombing was believed to have been concentrated. W4127 PG-D made an early return because of engine trouble, having jettisoned in the North Sea, off Orfordness, from 10,500 ft all its bomb-load except 600 x 4 lb and 16 x 30 lb bombs.

On the 22/23 March eighteen 619 aircraft went to *Frankfurt* again as part of a very large force, and all bombed the target successfully. Conditions were favourable at take off and along the route. Cloud over the target was 5/10ths and the flak was ineffective, though several aircraft were coned by searchlights. All returned safely.

On 24/25 March the squadron once again got eighteen aircraft off, this time for *Berlin*. Though conditions had been just good enough for take-off, they deteriorated rapidly and strong winds were met en route, blowing many crews off course and into heavily defended areas. There was no cloud, however, and numerous combats took place with night-fighters, and search lights were a nuisance. One fire over the target was estimated to be six miles in length. The winds made for a high crossing speed over the target and bombing was difficult and consequently not that accurate. P/O Thompson RNZAF in DV328 PG-L failed to return [see above] and one aircraft ED866 PG-E returned early with engine trouble, having jettisoned its bomb load over the North sea from 11,000 ft. P/O Thompson and his crew were on their second trip, their first op having been to Frankfurt two days previously.

On 25/26 W/C H Y Humphreys and his crew, attached to No 619 Squadron for operational experience, flew on an operational trip to *Aulnoye* in ED859 PG-V. W/C Humphreys was attached to the squadron prior to taking up appointment as Commanding Officer of No 57 Sqn.

On 26/27 thirteen aircraft were sent to *Essen*, continuing the Battle of the Ruhr. Although the Met department had forecast that it would be clear over the target there was 10/10ths cloud, and it was difficult to judge the effectiveness of the raid.

On 30/31 the squadron prepared seventeen aircraft for *Nürnberg* but one did not take off because the W/Op was ill. Of the sixteen remaining, ED866 PG-E returned early because of intercom failure, having jettisoned all except 1,200 x 4 lb incendiaries over the North Sea. The other fifteen reached the target and bombed on a clear night with 8/10ths cloud over the target and much fighter and flak activity. On returning Sgt Parker in LM418 PG-S crash-landed at Woodbridge – see the report above.

11/12 APR **LL784 PG-W LANCASTER MK I**

Took off at 2043 from Coningsby for *Aachen*. This aircraft exploded over Holland, two survivors parachuting to safety as POWs. The others are buried at Eindhoven [Woensel]. The pilot was a graduate of Edinburgh University and a boxing half blue. He had been posted in to 619 Sqn from 617 Sqn as a F/O on 21 Oct 43 W/O Munro had completed a previous tour with 61 Sqn, his DFM being gazetted on 11 Jun 43.

Casualties:	S/L JWED McGilvray DFC	Pilot	+
	Sgt I R F Haberfield	Flight Engineer	+
	F/O E A Drake	Navigator	pow
	F/O A K Baker	Air Bomber	pow
	P/O J L Pritchard	W/Op	+
	Sgt R Hillier	Air Gunner	+
	W/O A A Munro DFM	Air Gunner	+

11/12 APR **EE116 PG-Q LANCASTER MK III**

Took off at 2040 from Coningsby for *Aachen*. Abandoned, on fire from 16,000 ft over Holland in the vicinity of Tilburg, the aircraft crashing at Waarde [Zeeland]. The dead are buried at Bergen op Zoom War Cemetery, Sgt Lang in the Canadian section.

Casualties:	F/L H J Moore	Pilot	pow
	Sgt R G Giddings	Flight Engineer	+
	F/O P M Wood	Navigator	+
	F/O P R Butler	Air Bomber	+
	F/S T A Jones	W/Op	pow
	Sgt H G Lang	Air Gunner	+
	Sgt H F Shearsby	Air Gunner	+

This was the last operation from Coningsby, for two days later 619 Squadron received orders to move to Dunholme Lodge, a satellite of Scampton, and the third base in eleven months of operational life.

20/21 APR **W4127 PG-D** **LANCASTER MK I**

Took off at 2207 from Dunholme Lodge to bomb the railway yards at *la Chapelle*. The aircraft came down near Poix-de-la-Somme, where six members of the crew were buried within hours, a certain irony given the pilot's surname.

Casualties:	P/O P H French	Pilot	+
	Sgt J Atkinson	Flight Engineer	+
	F/O E T Tinker RCAF	Navigator	+
	F/O J S Thomson RNZAF	Air Bomber	+
	Sgt R Thompson	W/Op	+
	Sgt R H Hortie RCAF	Air Gunner	evd
	Sgt J W Randall	Air Gunner	+

P/O French arrived as a Sgt with his crew on 1st April from No 5 Lancaster Finishing School and flew his first operation as a second pilot with S/L Bill Whammond on 10th April in LL783 PG-C to *Tours* [when the CO of 619 Sqn, W/C John Jeudwine, had acted as Master of Ceremonies, ie, Master Bomber]. On 18/19 April he and his crew – as shown above but with Sgt P A Sigurdur RCAF as rear gunner - flew to *Juvisy* on their first op in ND728 PG-N. French was, therefore, on his third op, five of his crew on their second op and Hortie on his first op with that crew when they perished.

23/24 APR **ME747 PG-Q** **LANCASTER MK I**

Took off from Dunholme Lodge and crashed in the sea two miles during *night cross-country exercise*, killing all seven crew. Only two bodies were recovered. Sgt Veal was buried at Emery Down, Lyndhurst and Sgt Emsley in Camberwell. The Sqn ORB says 'believed to have been shot down by enemy intruder'.

Casualties:	Sgt J Broomfield	Pilot	+
	Sgt F E W Veal	Flight Engineer	+
	Sgt D W A Kersey	Navigator	+
	Sgt K W P Hunt	Air Bomber	+
	Sgt G T Wilks RAAF	W/Op	+
	Sgt E G Emsley	Air Gunner	+
	Sgt F L Tucker	Air Gunner	+

This crew would appear to have been shot down before they had completed even one operation, as there is otherwise no trace of them in the ORB. The ORB records the W/Op to have been Sgt Martin.

24/25 APR **ME723 PG-X** **LANCASTER MK I**

Took off at 2055 from Dunholme Lodge for München. Hit by flak and crashed at 0144 some 3 km S of the Speichersee at Aschheim, where all were buried, but their bodies we transferred to Dürnbach War Cemetery in 1948. W/O Schofield had won an immediate DFM for his gallantry during a raid on *Stuttgart* in March, when his air bomber on that occasion, F/S G E Hexter RCAF, though wounded, had refused to leave his post and also received a DFM. George Hexter is still alive and a member of the 619 Squadron Association. The author is grateful to him for recent help.

Casualties:	W/O D Schofield DFM	Pilot	+
	F/S A Baker	Flight Engineer	+
	F/S R Withinshaw	Navigator	+
	F/S E Brunt	Air Bomber	+
	Sgt D W Golding	W/Op	+
	Sgt J A Durkin	Air Gunner	+
	P/O E N Powell	Air Gunner	+

26/27 APR **LL904 PG-S** **LANCASTER MK I**

Took off from Dunhome Lodge at 2127 for *Schweinfurt.* Those seven who died are buried in Dürnbach War Cemetery.

Casualties:	F/S E Whinfield	Pilot	+
	Sgt H Goldberg	Flight Engineer	+
	WO2 J C Horne RCAF	Navigator	+
	F/S G J Langridge RCAF	Air Bomber	+
	Sgt D W Chick	W/Op	+
	F/S R A Wickham	Air Gunner	+
	Sgt J E Watson	Air Gunner	+
	F/S F S Young RNZAF	Second pilot	pow

This crew had been posted in from No 1661 CU on 8 Jan 44 and were on their 18th operation [F/S Whinfield's 19th, as he had flown his first op as second pilot on 21 Jan with P/O GG Taylor in LM378 PG-J to *Magdeburg*]. The crew had flown to *Berlin* on their first two ops on 27/28 Jan and 28/29 Jan in ME569 PG-X. In all they had flown to *Berlin* and *Stuttgart* on three separate occasions, to *Frankfurt* twice and also to *Ausburg, Essen, Nürnberg, Tours, Aachen, Juvisy, La Chappelle, Brunswick* and *München*, twelve of their ops in DV326 PG-P.

They were on their second trip to *Schweinfurt* when they died, and this was their first operation in LL904. The mid-upper gunner, F/S Wickham, had previously flown as rear gunner in the crew of F/L WED Bell. The New Zealand second pilot, F/S Young had been posted in with his crew four days previously on 22nd April from No 51 Base and this was his first trip with the squadron, his death leaving his crew without a pilot. F/S Whinfield shared a room with Sgt George Allen, the ex-apprentice fitter, who remembers the RAF Police arriving in the early hours of the morning to remove Whinfield's belongings after he failed to return from this operation.[10] Sadly, this was an experience all too well known to ground crew senior NCOs.

26/27 APR — LL919 PG-W — LANCASTER MK I

Took off at 2132 from Dunholme Lodge for *Schweinfurt.* Crashed at Landeville in the Province of Haute-Marne and on the northern edge of the Forêt du Pavilion, 13 kms SE of Joinville, France. The six who died are buried in Landeville Churchyard.

Casualties:	F/L G G C Gunzi	Pilot	+
	F/S E G Cass	Flight Engineer	+
	F/O N Vlassie RCAF	Navigator	+
	F/S J W Mills	Air Bomber	pow
	Sgt A Pickstone	W/Op	+
	F/S LL Fiendell RCAF	Air Gunner	+
	Sgt K Frank	Air Gunner	+

This crew, with Gunzi then a Sergeant, had been posted on to the Squadron on 30 Dec 43 from No 1668 CU and had completed at least 15 operations. Gunzi flew his first op on 14/15 Jan 44 as second pilot with the American pilot, Lt Nick Knilans in ED859 PG-V to *Brunswick*, and the crew flew their first op together on 28/29 January to *Berlin* [Gunzi by now a P/O]. Eight of their operations were flown in the aircraft in which Gunzi had first flown with Nick Knilans, ED559 PG-V. On two ops at least, the flight engineer, navigator and bomb aimer were not the regular members of his crew.

[10] Conversations with and letters to the author Aug/Oct 2000.

During April the Squadron had participated in ten operations: On the 5/6th of the month fifteen aircraft were prepared for a raid on *Toulouse*. ND728 PG-N did not take off because of wireless and generator problems and LL784 PG-W returned early because the R1155 radio was not working. The weather was clear over the target and little opposition was met, but on returning to England most of the aircraft had to land away from base because of bad weather.

On 10/11th April eighteen aircraft were sent to the railway marshalling yards at *Tours* on an operation led by the 619 Squadron CO, W/C John Jeudwine, who was the Master of Ceremonies [later known as Master Bomber]. ND728 PG-N returned early, this time with engine trouble when the starboard inner engine failed. The target was bombed from 5,000-7,000 ft, and the raid was judged to have been a success, the diarist recording that 'the yards appeared to have been well plastered'. The following night sixteen aircraft went to the marshalling yards at *Aachen*. This time they bombed from maximum height, but once again there was little opposition. On this occasion, however, two aircraft failed to return, both with experienced pilots and crews: S/L McGilvray and F/L Moore.

For the next week, the squadron was busy moving base from Coningsby to Dunholme Lodge, but on 18/19th April fourteen aircraft went to the marshalling yards at *Juvisy*. This time they dropped their bombs from 8,000-10,000 ft, and once again there was little opposition. The raid was again adjudged to have been a success with a good concentration of bombing on the target. On 20/21st April fifteen aircraft were prepared for an attack on the marshalling yards at *La Chapelle*, but LM378 PG-J did not take off because of pressure failure. The aircraft again bombed from 8,000-10,000 ft, and again the bombing was reported to be very concentrated, but this time they met a little more opposition than previously, presumably the enemy having twigged that a concerted campaign was being waged against the French marshalling yards. One 619 Squadron aircraft, W4127 PG-D failed to return.

On 22/23rd sixteen aircraft took off for *Brunswick* and all successfully bombed the target in what was believed to have been another concentrated raid, although haze over the target prevented photography. Post-

War analysis shows that the raid was not a success. The initial marking by 617 Sqn was accurate, but a thin layer of cloud hampered visibility, and there were also problems with communications between the bomber controllers. JB134 PG-G [Sgt Wadsworth] was attacked by a Ju88, but fire was returned and the rear gunner [Sgt F H Joy] claimed the enemy fighter as destroyed. It had been a near miss, however, with the elevators of JB134 damaged by cannon shells, the fuselage pock-marked with splinters and holes in the top of the rear turret. Nonetheless, this aircraft and all the others made it safely back to base. Sadly, Wadsworth, Joy and the rest of this crew were to die within days anyway. There is a very moving illuminated tribute to this crew on the board commemorating No 619 Squadron at the Lincolnshire Aviation Heritage Centre at East Kirkby.

On 24/25th fifteen aircraft were sent on the long trek to *München* [P/O Gunzi and his crew in LL919 PG-W, the aircraft in which they were to die 48 hours later during the raid on *Schweinfurt* were airborne, for example, for 10 hours and 16 minutes]. All bombed successfully in another concentrated attack and again opposition was said to be light. One aircraft [ME723 PG-X] failed to return. Target photography was prevented by fire tracks, and one pilot reported seeing decoy red spot and green flares being set off about 3 miles NNW of the town. Others reported being able to observe the red glow of the fires on the return journey from 100 to 150 miles away.

Two days later on 26/27th April, thirteen aircraft – two of the original fifteen having been scrubbed – were sent to *Schweinfurt.* Two aircraft were lost, it is thought because inaccurate wind forecasts probably sent them off track and into heavily defended areas. Strong head winds also delayed the PFF Lancasters and the low level marking provided for the first time by Mosquitoes of 627 Squadron was also inaccurate. As a consequence the raid was a failure. After debriefing P/O Olsen and his crew were informed that they had completed their tour of operations and would be posted off operational duties. They had arrived on the Squadron, with Olsen then a Sergeant, seven months previously on 27 Sep 43 from 1660 CU.

On 28/29 April ten aircraft were detailed for a raid on an aircraft factory in *Oslo*. Nine bombed successfully from 5,000-8,000 ft with practically no opposition, but DV326 PG-P returned early because the intercomm failed, jettisoning 10 x 1,000 lb MC bombs over the North Sea and bringing one 1,000 pounder and a five hundred pounder back with it when it landed after almost four hours in the air. During April 1944 the Squadron had dropped 659 tons of bombs.

3/4 MAY **JB134 PG-G LANCASTER MK III**

Took off at 2147 from Dunholme Lodge for *Mailly-le-Camp*. En route to the target crashed at Courboin, 10 km SE of Château-Thierry. All are buried in Courboin Communal Cemetery. The three DFMs and the DFC were awarded posthumously.

Casualties:	P/O D A Wadsworth DFC	Pilot	+
	Sgt J R Burgess	Flight Engineer	+
	F/S A C Shenton	Navigator	+
	F/S J Bengston	Air Bomber	+
	Sgt H G Brady DFM	W/Op	+
	Sgt J H Maltby DFM	Air Gunner	+
	Sgt F H Joy DFM	Air Gunner	+
	Sgt A Naylor	2nd Air Bomber	+

It will be remembered that this was the same crew and aircraft that fought off a Ju88 night-fighter and shot it down ten days previously during the raid on *Brunswick*. They had been posted into 619 some time before 14/15 Jan 44 when they made their first trip as a crew to Brunswick in the aircraft in which they eventually perished, JB134 PG-G. In between they had completed at least 21 operations, fifteen in JB134, and were on their 22nd when shot down. P/O Wadsworth flew the first of his four operations in that rank on 26/27 Apr to *München*. His other ops were completed as a Sergeant.

7/8 MAY **ND730 PG-O LANCASTER MK III**

Took off at 2152 from Dunholme Lodge for *Salbris* to bomb an ammunition dump. Crashed at Champigny-en-Beauce in Loir et Cher, 14 km NNW of Blois. All eight are buried in Orleans New Cemetery. As far as can be established Fred Fuller [born Finchley], whose wife Marjorie lived in Muswell Hill and father in East End Road, London N2, was not related to Cyril Fuller [born. Peckham], who was killed in Oct 43 with 619 Sqn over Hannover, and whose parents lived in Catford.

Casualties:	S/L F E Fuller	Pilot	+
	Sgt R C Reid	Flight Engineer	+
	F/O C K Plunkett	Navigator	+
	F/O N A Loranger RCAF	Air Bomber	+
	F/S J Hill	W/Op	+
	Sgt J Booth	Air Gunner	+
	Sgt J H Woodcock	Air Gunner	+
	F/S A G Holke RCAF	Second Navigator	+

This crew had been posted in from No 1661 CU on 8 Jan 1944, Fred Fuller as a F/L. F/L Fuller flew his first operation with 619 as a second pilot in EE116 PG-Q to *Berlin* on 27 Jan 44 with F/O M L Hamilton as captain [who was posted out to 617 Sqn a fortnight later on 15 Feb 44]. Fuller's bomb aimer, P/O Loranger RCAF, flew that same night to *Berlin* as second bomb aimer in EE134 PG-Y with F/O JG Thompson. Fuller and his crew flew together on their first operation the following night, also to *Berlin*, and had completed at least 17 operations [Fuller and Loranger 18] when they came down on the night of 7/8th May on the *Salbris* raid. Fuller flew his last four operations [from 22/23 April] as a Squadron Leader. He and Loranger had flown on five of the 1943/44 winter Battle of Berlin raids and the rest of the crew on four of them.

9/10 MAY **LM446 PG-H** **LANCASTER MK I**

Took off at 2210 from Dunholme Lodge to attack the Gnome and Rhône works at *Gennevilliers*. Came down at Aubergenville in Seine-et-Oise, 12 km ESE of Mantes-la-Jolie. The seven who died are buried in Aubergenville Communal Cemetery.

Casualties	P/O J M Aitken RNZAF	Pilot	+
	Sgt F A Towse	Flight Engineer	+
	F/S S Levy	Navigator	+
	Sgt R E Hickling	Air Bomber	+
	Sgt J R Presland	W/Op	+
	Sgt F F Dring	Air Gunner	+
	W/O L Rhodes	Air Gunner	pow
	F/S K Goodwin	Second Pilot	+

This crew had been posted in from No 5 Lancaster Finishing School on 8 March 1944, the pilot and rear gunner as flight sergeants. Ten days later Aitken, by then a P/O, flew as second pilot in LM446 PG-L to *Frankfurt* with P/O R W Olsen as captain and Sgt Hickling flew on the same raid as second air bomber with P/O F G Secker as captain in LL783 PG-C. Aitken and his crew flew together on their first operation together four days later, also to *Frankfurt*, and by the time they came down on the *Gennevilliers* raid they had flown at least 13 ops [Aitken and Hickling 14].

21/22 MAY **NN695 PG-X** **LANCASTER MK I**

Took off at 2258 from Dunholme Lodge for *Duisburg*. On the home run they were caught by an intruder night fighter over East Anglia and crashed near East Wretham airfield, Norfolk. Those who died are buried in various cemeteries in UK, the Canadian P/O Bandur RCAF in the Brookwood Military Cemetery. The rear gunner, F/O Baker was aged 38 and well above the usual age for Bomber Command aircrew in 1944. He is buried in Cambridge City Cemetery. The ORB records that Sgt Leeson was the only survivor, and it is thought he parachuted to safety.

Casualties:	F/O R H Redshaw	Pilot	+
	Sgt L J Richardson	Flight Engineer	+
	P/O S B Bandur RCAF	Navigator	+
	Sgt K Leeson	Air Bomber	
	Sgt K W Harmer	W/Op	+
	Sgt R A McKay	Air Gunner	+
	F/O F J Baker	Air Gunner	+

This crew joined the squadron on 28 April from No 51 Base. On 3 May Sgt Leeson flew as a second air bomber with F/L K Roberts RAAF in LM378 PG-J on the raid against *Mailly-le-Camp*, while F/S Bandur RCAF flew as second navigator with S/L F E Fuller in ND730 PG-O. F/O Redshaw and his crew flew their first operation together on the night of 7 May dropping mines in the sea off the Friesian Islands [Nectarine I] while the squadron sent thirteen other aircraft to Salbris. From then until they were lost a fortnight later they had completed a further three operations and were on their 4th/5th when shot down by the intruder.

During May No 619 Squadron had taken part in ten operations, eight of which were part of the transportation offensive, that is the softening up process of the German supply routes in readiness for the Normandy Landings in early June. In the process the Squadron had lost four aircraft, a relatively light proportion, though three of the crews had a lot of experience.

On 1st May a new crew [captain P/O GA Baker] flew on a cross-country exercise by day. P/O GG Runnalls and F/O RH Redshaw were detailed to fly a similar excise by night. Three weeks later Redshaw and his crew were dead. Baker and four members of his crew died on the Wesseling raid on 22 June. Runnalls, however, went on to complete his tour and to be awarded a DFC [not recorded in the Squadron ORB but the citation discovered in the PRO by the author].[11] That same evening twelve aircraft were despatched to *Toulouse,* led by W/C John Jeudwine in LL778 PG-A [the second *Nulli Secundus,* replacing the original, ED977, lost on 5/6 January]. The twelve captains included the flight commanders, Squadron Leader FE Fuller and Squadron Leader WN Whamond. All twelve aircraft bombed the target and got home safely to base arriving back between 0500 and 0600 the following morning. That day a new crew was posted in [P/O MHA Davis, captain].

On the night of 3/4th May twelve aircraft took part in the raid against the German military camp at *Mailly-le-Camp,* an operation involving 346 Lancasters and 14 Mosquitoes. W/C Leonard Cheshire was the 'Marker Leader' but after accurate marking the raid did not go according to plan, and as a result 44 Lancasters [11.6%] were lost, including 619's JB134 PG-G captained by P/O DA Wadsworth DFC with his experienced and much decorated crew. After marking, Cheshire had ordered the main force to come in and bomb but the main force controller, W/C LC Deane, could not transmit the order to the waiting Lancasters because his VHF radio set was being drowned by an American Forces broadcast.[12] German night-fighters arrived while the Lancasters were circling the target and took a high price of the bombers.

On 7/8th May thirteen aircraft were sent to *Salbris* and one, the new crew captained by F/O Redshaw was sent on a 'gardening' trip dropping mines in area Nectarine I [the Friesian Islands]. All bombed but S/L FE Fuller and crew were lost, together with a second navigator who

---

[11] AIR 2/8750 p451, the citation signed by the Station Commander G/Capt J R Jeudwine and the Base Commander [R B Casey?] on 15 Apr 45.

[12] For a full account of the disastrous raid on Mailly-le-Camp read Chapter 15 of Lionel Lacey-Johnson's book *Point Blank and Beyond* [Airlife 1991]. Lt Col Lacey-Johnson, a retired Army Intelligence Corps officer and photographic interpreter, was inspired to write the book because his brother Nigel died in the raid as the navigator of a Lancaster aircraft of No 101 Squadron from RAF station Ludford Magna.

had joined them to gain experience from the newly arrived crew of F/S AJ Buckley.

On 9/10th May twelve aircraft were sent to *Gennevilliers*. Eleven bombed successfully, one having to return early with engine and rear turret problems [the new crew captained by P/O Baker]. This time P/O JM Aitken RNZAF and his crew did not return.

On 11/12th May fifteen aircraft were despatched to *Bourg-Leopold*, led by W/C Jeudwine in PG-A. All aircraft reached the target area, except PG-A, W/C Jeudwine having to return early because of engine trouble. Of the remaining fourteen, only six bombed, the remainder being instructed not to bomb but to take their bombs back to base. This was to be Jeudwine's last operation as CO of No 619 Squadron for on the 13th May he received the immediate award of a DFC and on the 15th May relinquished command of the Squadron on being posted to 54 Base, Coningsby for master bomber duties. His crew was posted to No 83 Squadron to join him. The squadron diarist recorded: '*the members of the squadron regret the departure of their commanding officer but are happy to learn that he and his crew will be controlling future operations*'.

On 16th May S/L WH Whamond assumed temporary command of the Squadron.

On 19/20th May sixteen aircraft were sent to *Amiens*. All reached the target but only three bombed, the rest being instructed not to bomb but to take their bombs home. Once again against a target in France every precaution was being taken to avoid civilian casualties, and in the event that haze or cloud obscured the target it was deemed better not to bomb. That night returning crews reported up to 10/10ths cloud over the target.

On the 20/21st fifteen aircraft were detailed for a raid on *Duisburg*. In the event one failed to take off [LM420 PG-R, captain F/S Morcom] and two others [LL904 PG-S, captain F/S Wingate and LL808 PG-D, captain P/O Davis] returned early with a failed starboard inner engine and an unserviceable wireless transmitter respectively. On this operation F/O Redshaw and his crew were lost.

On 22/23rd May fifteen aircraft were prepared for an attack on *Brunswick.* One [LL969 PG-G, captain P/O Dougherty] failed to take off and another [LM536 PG-Q, captain P/O Runnalls] returned early after the pilot had a fit of dizziness. The returning crews reported that if the PFF marking was accurate, then it should have been a successful raid.[13]

On 27/28th May fourteen aircraft were sent to *Cherbourg.* Amongst the captains were S/L Whamond and a new flight commander, S/L LB Gunter. All the aircraft took off and reached the target and once again returning crews reported that if the PFF marking was accurate it should have been a good raid.[14]

On the last day of the month and overnight into June, twelve aircraft were sent to *Maisy,* led by the new Commanding Officer, W/C JR Maling in PG-A *Nullie Secundus.* All aircraft took off and arrived at the target but conditions were such that they were ordered not to bomb but to return to base.[15] On returning, they all had to be diverted to other stations and satellites as bad weather had clamped out Dunholme Lodge.

During May a total of *fifteen* new crews had arrived on the Squadron, including the new Commanding Officer [W/C JR Maling, from 51 Base with effect from 23rd May] and a replacement Flight Commander [F/L acting S/L LB Gunter]. This compared with seven new crews in April. The outgoing CO, John Jeudwine, had been awarded an immediate DFC, as also had the gunnery leader [F/L JA Howard], the dead pilot [P/O DA Wadsworth] and his wireless operator [Sgt HG

---

[13] Middlebrook and Everitt report in *The Bomber Command War Diaries* [first published Viking 1985] that the raid was a failure. The target had been covered by cloud, and Brunswick City records show that few bombs fell in the town, there were no casualties and most of the bombs fell in the surrounding countryside. A photo reconnaissance aircraft flying over the target an hour after the attack found it completely free of cloud.

[14] This time, *The Bomber Command War Diaries,* ibid, record that the 272 aircraft involved in the operation [208 Lancasters, 49 Halifaxes and 15 mosquitoes] carried out raids on five coastal-battery positions and that all the targets were bombed satisfactorily. Only one Lancaster and one Mosquito were lost.

[15] Ibid, p518, '68 Lancasters of 5 Group raiding a coastal gun battery found it covered by cloud and only six aircraft bombed'.

Brady - immediate DFM] and the flight commander [F/L acting S/L WN Whamond]. There were also two non-immediate DFCs for F/L A Sandison and F/O ACE Lance. The Squadron had dropped 525 tons of bombs in May during 652.02 hours of operational flying [659 and 834.43 respectively in April]. After twelve months of operational service, 619 was most definitely an effective fighting unit, as had been the hope of its diarist in the days the Squadron had been forming from nothing at Woodhall Spa a year previously.

6/7 JUNE LL783 PG-C LANCASTER MK I

Took off at 0055 from Dunholme Lodge to bomb communications - railway and road centres – in the area behind the *Normandy battlefield.* Came down between Baupte and Carentan not far from the main railway line from Cherbourg to Carentan. Jack Forrest, the Flight Engineer, and Reg De Veill survived the crash but the others were killed. According to the CWGC records, only F/S Tucker has a known grave, but according to a French researcher four members of the crew are buried near the crash site and only the pilot, F/L Roberts RAAF, has no grave, his body having been consumed in the fire that destroyed the aircraft after it hit the ground with Roberts still at the controls. The others had baled out but were too low to survive and their bodies were found by French partisans in nearby fields with the parachutes still attached and were buried locally. The French researcher holds the local *Maquis* records, and so he is likely to be right.

Casualties:	P/O K Roberts DFC RAAF	Pilot	+
	Sgt J F J Forrest	Flight Engineer	pow
	W/O J E Lott	Navigator	+
	F/S W H De Veill	Air Bomber	pow
	F/S J H Tucker	W/Op	+
	F/S L E Williams	Air Gunner	+
	F/O G H Wyand	Air Gunner	+

In 1995 the French authorities arranged for a memorial to be unveiled at the site of the 1944 crash in the presence of the family of F/L Kimberley Roberts RAAF, the pilot from Bunbury, Australia and the two surviving crew members. The local Bunbury newspaper also carried the story of recent investigations at the crash site, together with the interesting information that F/L Roberts always flew with a WWI German Iron Cross around his neck as a lucky talisman. He had been given the Cross before he departed for England by a friend's father, a pilot in the Royal Flying Corps during WWI, who had been given it by a German pilot as a memento after an aerial duel over Belgium on 8 June 1917. After shooting the RFC pilot down, the German pilot had landed, shaken hands with him and given him the Iron Cross he was wearing on his uniform as a memento. The German pilot was Hermann Goering![16]

21/22 JUNE LL808 PG-D LANCASTER MK I

Took off at 2329 from Dunholme Lodge for *Wesseling.* Those who died are buried in Rheinberg War Cemetery. This crew had arrived on the Squadron precisely two months previously.

Casualties:	P/O P Johnson	Pilot	+
	Sgt M E Mansbridge	Flight Engineer	pow
	F/S G H Trantor	Navigator	pow
	F/S J Vaughton	Air Bomber	+
	Sgt R Brown	W/Op	+
	Sgt G I Martin	Air Gunner	pow
	Sgt T H Tuckwell	Air Gunner	pow
	F/O P A Pearson RAAF	2nd Air Bomber	pow

[16] I am grateful to Alain Charpentier, a French WWII aviation enthusiast, for this and other information about the memorial and the investigations he undertook at the site of the crash.

21/22 JUNE LL977 PG-H LANCASTER MK I

Took off at 2307 from Dunholme Lodge for *Wesseling*. Outbound, hit by flak at 17,000 ft near Aachen. In the explosion that followed F/L Saunders was thrown out of his cockpit. The remainder died and are buried in the Rheinberg War Cemetery.

Casualties:	F/L D C Saunders	Pilot	pow
	Sgt C W Goodwin	Flight Engineer	+
	F/S J E Whittome[17]	Navigator	+
	Sgt C W Flewelling RCAF	Air Bomber	+
	W/O C W Goodwin	W/Op	+
	Sgt A J Handford	Air Gunner	+
	Sgt J P Halpin	Air Gunner	+
	Sgt J O Johnston	2nd Air Bomber	+

21/22 JUN ME846 PG-C LANCASTER MK III

Took off at 2301 from Dunholme Lodge for *Wesseling*. The aircraft is believed to have come down near Deurne. The two air gunners are buried in Schoonselhof Cemetery, Antwerp, but P/O Davis has no known grave. He was 20 and the gunners 19.

Casualties:	P/O M A H Davis	Pilot	+
	Sgt W D Belshaw	Flight Engineer	pow
	F/S L E J Taylor	Navigator	pow
	F/S P E Knox RAAF	Air Bomber	pow
	Sgt T A Newberry	W/Op	pow
	Sgt G H Moggridge	Air Gunner	+
	F/S J E R Bowering RCAF	Air Gunner	+

[17] Unusually the pilot survived when the rest of the crew died, the freak outcome of an explosion. In 1977/78 the author as the S/L in charge of the Special Investigation Branch in Germany and his F/L deputy scattered the ashes of the widow of a F/S Navigator on her husband's grave in the Rheinberg War Cemetery. It had been her dying wish that this be done, and her son a Sergeant in the Lancashire Constabulary was able to send us her ashes as a police exhibit. We were probably in breach of all sorts of British rules and European directives, but we felt it was the least we could do.

21/22 JUN **ED859 PG-V[18] LANCASTER MK III**

Took off at 2312 from Dunholme Lodge for *Wesseling*. Shot down by a night-fighter and crashed at Hetzerath, 3 km SW of Erkelenz. All were buried locally at Hetzerath but since the War have been reinterred in the Reichswald Forest War Cemetery.

Casualties:	F/S J A Buckley	Pilot	+
	Sgt J R Wallis	Flight Engineer	+
	F/O L J McKinnon	Navigator	+
	Sgt M L Morrison RCAF	Air Bomber	+
	Sgt A J Walker	W/Op	+
	Sgt K F Rice	Air Gunner	+
	Sgt A L Jamieson	Air Gunner	+

21/22 JUN **ND986 PG-S LANCASTER MK III**

Took off at 2324 from Dunholme Lodge for *Wesseling*. Hit by flak and fell into the Rhine between a road bridge and a rail bridge at Duisburg. The bodies of all the crew were recovered and buried at Düsseldorf in the Nordfriedhof. After the war they were moved to the Reichswald Forest War Cemetery. Note that this crew had within it men from three Dominion air forces and well as the RAF.

Casualties:	P/O K E Crawford RAAF	Pilot	+
	Sgt W A Loose	Flight Engineer	+
	F/S G N Rackley	Navigator	+
	F/O K A Galloway RNZAF	Air Bomber	+
	Sgt A R Ward	W/Op	+
	Sgt T E G Howe RCAF	Air Gunner	+
	Sgt J Cutting	Air Gunner	+

[18] ED859 was one of the Squadron's oldest aircraft. It had belonged previously to No 156 Squadron, and was on its 71st operation with 630 hours flown when it went missing.

21/22 JUN **NE151 PG-W LANCASTER MK III**

Took off at 2310 from Dunholme Lodge for *Wesseling*. The five who died are buried in Rheinberg War Cemetery.

Casualties:	P/O G A Baker	Pilot	+
	Sgt A C Dalman	Flight Engineer	+
	WO2 S Malick RCAF	Navigator	pow
	Sgt E N Kullberg RCAF	Air Bomber	+
	Sgt L Sargent	W/Op	pow
	Sgt E D Kidd	Air Gunner	+
	Sgt H J Cossey	Air Gunner	+

During June 1944, the squadron had taken part in most of the operations designed to support the Normandy Landings, one experienced crew being lost on D Day itself when the Squadron was tasked with destroying road and rail centres so as to prevent the German Army from attacking the beachhead. Suddenly the target names have a decidedly French ring: *Wimereaux, La Pernelle, Caen, Pontaubault, Etampes, Caen, Ornay-sur-Odon, Beauvoir, Pommereval and Marquise*, but the Squadron also took part in the disastrous raid on *Wesseling* when the German night-fighters got amongst the bomber stream and extracted a high price in aircraft and crews. It was the blackest night of the War for No 619 Squadron [though Revigny a month later came close to matching it with five aircraft lost]. The *Wesseling* raid alone cost the Squadron six aircraft and 44 aircrew [32 killed and 12 POWs]. That represented 37.5% of the aircraft and crews despatched. It was also a disaster for Bomber Command, which that night lost 39 aircraft, all Lancasters. With a year's operations under its belt, and already on its third Commanding Officer, No 619 Squadron was indisputably in the thick of it, as the list of awards and decorations announced this month proves, if that were needed: fifteen DFCs and 2 DFMs. Perhaps, even more telling are the ten mention in dispatches, seven of them going to ground crew: F/S TA Gould [Engine Fitter IIE], F/S FJ Mullins [Airframe Fitter IIA], Cpl WF Copson [Engine Fitter IIE], LAC RW Houghton [Airframe Mechanic], LAC J Lynch [Airframe Mechanic], LAC JJD Stephens [Engine Mechanic] and LAC AC Turner [Engine

Mechanic]. The two Flight Sergeants had, inevitably, trained as Trenchard brats - Halton apprentices – the very backbone of the RAF. These ground crew worked in all weathers around the clock, usually outside and often in the atrocious weather conditions of Lincolnshire. On other squadrons they did not always receive the recognition they deserved. It says a lot for the leadership of John Jeudwine that he saw their worth and took the trouble to pay tribute in this way. Aircrew and ground crew alike today always speak of him in the most glowing terms. That his social skills were geared to the world of pre-War bachelor Mess life does not matter. He inspired his officers and his men, and there is little doubt that had he survived [he was killed in a flying accident weeks after the end of the War] he would have risen to the highest ranks in the RAF, and his would have been a name known to my post-War generation of officers. He was as single-minded in his pursuit of the air war as Harris and Trenchard, and he was a product of the latter's academy at Cranwell. This was Trenchard's legacy to the RAF, then only 25 years old. Cadets like Jeudwine, and apprentices like Gould and Mullins were the mainstay of a system of training and group loyalty that modern management gurus can only dream about. Into this system slotted the temporary 'exigencies only' wartime airmen.

By June 1944 some of the electronic aids that were eventually to tip the balance in favour of the allied air forces had started to come into service. On 3rd June, for example, No 619 Squadron received instruction in the theory and manipulation of the H2S radar bombing set and also practised using the Monica Mk V tail protection system, which was intended to give warning of the presence of other aircraft. The latter was of limited value in a bomber stream of several hundred!

During June 1944 the Squadron had dropped 702 tons of bombs and flown 707.32 hours of operations.

7/8 JULY **ME745 PG-L** **LANCASTER MK I**

Took off at 2220 from Dunhome Lodge to attack the flying boat base at *St Leu D'Esserant*. Crashed at about 0145 near Precy-sur- Oise. The pilot and four of the crew evaded capture, but the two air gunners were killed. Both lie in Boran-sur-Oise Communal Cemetery. F/S B McDonagh came from Co Sligo in Eire.

Casualties:	F/L C C Johnston	Pilot	evd
	Sgt W A Clark	Flight Engineer	evd
	F/L T J Lakes	Navigator	evd
	F/O M A Cockman	Air Bomber	evd
	F/O D W Cotter RAAF	W/Op	evd
	Sgt J I S Patterson RCAF	Air Gunner	+
	F/S B McDonagh GM	Air Gunner	+

18/19 JULY **LL969 PG-G** **LANCASTER MK I**

Took off at 2256 from Dunholme Lodge to destroy a railway bridge at *Revigny*. Shot down by a night-fighter while approaching the AP. Crashed at St Utin [Marne]. Only the rear gunner survived. The others are buried in St Utin Churchyard.

Casualties:	F/O S B Morcom	Pilot	+
	Sgt J E Mackintosh[19]	Flight Engineer	+
	F/S S Whitehurst	Navigator	+
	F/S W H G Lebatt	Air Bomber	+
	F/S W J Thomas	W/Op	+
	Sgt A Myres	Air Gunner	+
	F/S C E Ratchford RCAF	Air Gunner	evd

[19] Sgt Mackintosh was 19 years of age and was the son of Col EEB Mackintosh DSO and Mrs MC Mackintosh [nee Talbot-Ponsonby] of St John's Wood, London.

18/19 JULY **JB186 PG-O LANCASTER MK III**

Took off at 2250 from Dunholme Lodge for *Revigny*. Outbound, was intercepted by a night-fighter and came down at Auger-St-Vincent. Only the bomb aimer survived. The others are buried in Augur-St-Vincent Communal Cemetery. Sgt Lewis evaded capture, getting back on 10 September.

Casualties:	F/O A H J Begernie	Pilot	+
	Sgt F C Bright	Flight Engineer	+
	Sgt W S A Birks	Navigator	+
	Sgt B G Lewis RCAF	Air Bomber	evd
	Sgt A Marper	W/Op	+
	Sgt J Geddes RCAF	Air Gunner	+
	Sgt W F Hinett	Air Gunner	+

18/19 JULY **LM378 PG-J LANCASTER MK III**

Took off at 2302 from Dunholme Lodge for *Revigny*. Outbound, was intercepted by a night-fighter and crashed at 0115 at Montreuil aux-Lions, 16 km WSW of Château Thiery. Only the Flt Eng survived. The others are buried in the British Cemetery Montrueil aux-Lions, along with soldiers killed in the Great War.

Casualties:	F/O F F Molinas DFC RAAF	Pilot	+
	Sgt J A Nealey	Flight Engineer	evd
	F/S A W Habergham	Navigator	+
	F/S L Morgan	Air bomber	+
	Sgt A E Curtis	W/Op	+
	Sgt R B Cox	Air Gunner	+
	Sgt M Loosli	Air Gunner	+

18/19 JULY **LM640 PG-L LANCASTER MK III**

Took off at 2303 from Dunholme Lodge for *Revigny*. Outbound, intercepted by night-fighter and crashed at Villiers-St-Genest, Oise. All seven crew were killed but only four have a known grave – in the local French community churchyard.

Casualties:	F/O H J Wilson RCAF	Pilot	+
	Sgt T Mullen	Flight Engineer	+
	F/O A G Britten RCAF	Navigator	+
	F/O E L Morrison RCAF	Air Bomber	+
	F/O R Logan	W/Op	+
	F/S J F Mara RCAF	Air Gunner	+
	Sgt G A Garbutt RCAF[20]	Air Gunner	+

18/19 JULY **PB245 PG-Z LANCASTER MK III**

Took off at 2258 from Dunholme Lodge for *Revigny*. Shot down probably by night-fighter and crashed at Ussy-sur-Marne. All seven members of the crew were killed.

Casualties:	F/O N W Donnelley RNZAF	Pilot	+
	Sgt S W Ling	Flight Engineer	+
	WO2 J K Johnson RCAF	Navigator	+
	F/O D I Grant RNZAF	Air Bomber	+
	Sgt R T W Harwood	W/Op	+
	W/O J F R Tate	Air Gunner	+
	Sgt T F Frogley DFM	Air Gunner	+

[20] Unusually for a RAF Squadron this crew had five members from the RCAF.

23/24 JULY **PB208 PG-S LANCASTER MK III**

Took off from Dunholme Lodge at 2300 for *Keil*, the first major raid on a German city for two months [629 aircraft, 519 Lancs]. Came down in the sea, probably in the area of Nissum Fjord as WO2 Aumell RCAF is buried in Denmark at Sondre Nissum. The others have no known grave.

Casualties:	F/O J Parker	Pilot	+
	Sgt N M Rice	Flight Engineer	+
	P/O G A Grigg	Navigator	+
	WO2 A D Aumell	Air Bomber	+
	Sgt W A Sharp	W/Op	+
	F/S J Broll	Air Gunner	+
	Sgt A Dickson	Air Gunner	+

This was the crew, with the pilot then a sergeant, that had crash-landed at Woodbridge on 31 March on their return from Nürnberg. The rear gunner on that occasion, Sgt J H Woodcock, died on 8 May during the Salbris operation, his place having been taken by F/S Broll. They were close to completing their tour of operations, having arrived on the Squadron on 13 February.

24/25 JULY **LM643 PG-E LANCASTER MK III**

Took off at 2227 from Dunholme Lodge for *Donges* to bomb an oil depot. Came down at Montoir-de-Bretagne [Loire-Atlantique]. Five are buried at Escoublac-la-Baule Communal Cemetery, while F/S Murphy RCAF is buried at Montour-de-Bretagne and Sgt Ward in Pornic War Cemetery.

Casualties:	F/O R W Orbell	Pilot	+
	Sgt J R Ward	Flight Engineer	+
	F/O J J Kommes RCAF	Navigator	+
	F/S D M Murphy RCAF	Air Bomber	+
	Sgt G H Lucas	W/Op	+
	Sgt J R Scott	Air Gunner	+
	Sgt S Sinclair	Air Gunner	+

25/26 JULY **ND935 PG-K LANCASTER MK III**

Took off at 2106 from Dunholme Lodge for *Stuttgart*. Crashed at about 0230. The three who died are buried at Choloy War Cemetery in France.

Casualties:	W/C J R Maling	Pilot	pow
	Sgt J D White	Flight Engineer	pow
	F/O B Murray	Navigator	pow
	F/O G S MacRae RCAF	Air Bomber	pow
	Sgt H Parrott	W/Op	+
	F/S J R Kellum RCAF	Air Gunner	+
	Sgt J Harper	Air Gunner	+

This casualty meant that the Squadron had lost its commanding officer, W/C J R Maling, the fourth CO in thirteen months of operations.

26/27 JULY **LM484 PG-H LANCASTER MK III**

Took off at 2126 from Dunholme Lodge for *Givors* to bomb rail communications. Believed to have crashed near St-Loup [Rhône]. All lie in Pornic War Cemetery. Sgt Graham was aged 36 and well above average age for wartime aircrew at this stage of the War. He was the son of Harry and June Graham of Bradford and husband of Catherine Graham of Bradford, Yorkshire. This crew had arrived on the Squadron seven days previously.

Casualties:	F/O R G Turvey RAAF	Pilot	+
	Sgt E Graham	Flight Engineer	+
	F/S T F Galbraith RCAF	Navigator	+
	Sgt J H Gilliver	Air Bomber	+
	F/S R Rothwell RAAF	W/Op	+
	Sgt J G Pearce RCAF	Air Gunner	+
	Sgt R J Thair	Air Gunner	+

26/27 JULY **PB346 PG-J LANCASTER MK III**

Took off at 2119 from Dunholme Lodge for *Givors*, as above, the aircraft having been borrowed by No 44 Sqn [F/O D N McKechnie and his crew]. Crashed on fire near la Boissiere-sur-Evre. All the crew members were killed. F/O McKechnie came from Southern Rhodesia, No 44 [Rhodesia] Sqn RAF being proud of its badge and connections.[21]

28/29 JULY **LM536 PG-Q LANCASTER MK III**

Took off at 2158 from Dunholme Lodge for *Stuttgart* the third raid on that city in four days. The thirteen aircraft of 619 Sqn were part of a force of almost 500 aircraft, 494 Lancasters and 2 Mosquitoes, from Nos 1, 3, 5 and 8 Groups. It was a bright moonlit night and the night-fighters got amongst the bomber stream, shooting down 39 Lancasters. For the fighter crews it was like a duck-shoot. In all 40 Lancasters were lost that night at the cost of over 250 men of Bomber Command. W/O Patterson and his crew had joined the Squadron on 11 March and were very near the end of their tour. They crashed at 0230 near Gräfenhausen, 9 km from Pforzheim. All were buried at Gräfenhausen initially but their bodies now lie in the Dürnbach War Cemetery.

Casualties:	W/O J Patterson	Pilot	+
	Sgt L E Lilley	Flight Engineer	+
	F/S S D G Rice	Navigator	+
	F/S F H Hall	Air Bomber	+
	Sgt R Rodger	W/Op	+
	Sgt E H Hunter	Air Gunner	+
	F/S D R Butler	Air Gunner	+

If the night of the *Wesseling* raid on 21/22 June had been the blackest night for 619 Squadron in its first year of operations, July 1944 must count as its blackest month. It had lost twelve aircraft and eleven crews in fourteen operations, including its Commanding Officer and some very experienced crews nearing the end of their tours of operations. Ten

[21] After the declaration of UDI by the Ian Smith Government in Southern Rhodesia in 1965, No 44 [Rhodesia] Sqn RAF, then flying Vulcan bombers from RAF Waddington, was told quietly to drop its Rhodesian emblem, but this instruction was largely ignored by the aircrew, who were proud of the connection.

of the raids were against *targets in France*, in support of the Allied troops now moving forward across that country, and three were against the German city of *Stuttgart*. The other was against *Kiel*. The targets in France were road or rail centres, German communication centres and oil depots, and flying bomb sites. Between 4 July and 30 July, the Squadron had visited *Creil, St Leu D'Esserant, Culmont Chalindrey, Villeneuve, Caen, Revigny, Courtrai, Donges, Givors* and *Cahagnes*. It had cost the squadron 77 airmen, of whom 65 were dead. During the month the Squadron had dropped 921 tons of bombs and flown 1,163.55 hours of operations.

3/4 AUG **ME568 PG-F** **LANCASTER MK I**

Took off at 1145 from Dunholme Lodge for *Trossy* to attack a flying bomb storage site. All seven crew were killed. Six rest in Marrisel French National Cemetery and Sgt Forrest at Villeneuve-St-Georges. F/S Lyford's brother was also killed in the RAF.

Casualties:	W/O R Bennett	Pilot	+
	Sgt E C T Davies	Flight Engineer	+
	F/S F P Lyford	Navigator	+
	F/S A Griffiths	Air Bomber	+
	F/S W Cobb	W/Op	+
	Sgt R A Forrest	Air Gunner	+
	Sgt M Cody	Air Gunner	+

This crew had arrived on the Squadron on 3 May and were well into their tour of operations.

5 AUG **LM420 PG-R LANCASTER MK III**

Took off at 1108 from Dunholme Lodge for *St Leu D'Esserant* to bomb a flying bomb storage site. The target was identified [F/L WF Jordan] visually but on the run up at 15,000 the aircraft took a direct hit from heavy flak beneath the nose cone. The air bomber, F/S JC Speckman, was badly injured and the Flt/Eng, Sgt FW Belt, went forward and pressed the release button, bombing at 1335. F/S Speckman died of his injuries after the aircraft had landed at Dunholme at 1440, the first aircraft back by an hour. They had obviously rushed Speckman back for treatment, but to no avail.

Casualty: F/S J C Speckman Air Bomber +

9/10 AUG **ME866 PG-W LANCASTER MK I**

Took off from Dunholme Lodge at 2052 for *Chatellerault* to bomb oil storage dumps in the Forêt de Chatellerault. Possibly collided with a 50 Sqn aircraft over Thure, a village 7 km from the target. Six died but the Navigator, P/O HJ Cleland survived and evaded capture.

Casualties:	F/O L A Hall	Pilot	+
	Sgt A W Taylor	Flight Engineer	+
	P/O H J Cleland	Navigator	evd
	F/S R Smellie	Air Bomber	+
	F/S A W Pope	W/Op	+
	Sgt E L Colley	Air Gunner	+
	Sgt E F Christy RCAF	Air Gunner	+

12/13 AUG **ME855 PG-X** **LANCASTER MK I**

Took off at 2036 from Dunholme Lodge for *Brunswick*. Was caught by a night-fighter whose fire smashed the rear turret and mortally wounded the rear gunner, F/S Willis. The other six were taken POW. Willis is buried in Sage War Cemetery. F/O Guest had previously completed a tour with No 144 Sqn, his DFM being promulgated on 26 May 1942. S/L Gunter, as a F/L, had been a flying instructor at No 1661 CU, RAF Winthorpe, near Newark, at the time Cyril Fuller and his crew went through Winthorpe on heavy conversion training, having previously completed a tour of ops on Manchesters [as also had Ronnie Churcher (also later 619), Dampier-Crossley (619), AJF Rayment, Henry Maudslay (617), Micky Martin (617), Steve Cockbain (1661 CU), PC Ward-Hunt (Gibson's flight commander on 106) and Leslie Manser (VC)]. There was thus a bit of the 'old firm' about the higher echelons of Bomber squadrons by 1944.

Casualties:	S/L L B Gunter[22]	Pilot	pow
	P/O E Poulter	Flight Engineer	pow
	F/L E Parsons	Navigator	pow
F/L G F Ruddock	Air Bomber	pow	
	F/O C F Guest DFM	W/Op	pow
F/S G T Short	Air Gunner	pow	
	F/S R A Willis MID	Air Gunner	+

[22] As a F/L, LB Gunter had been at No 1661 CU, RAF Winthorpe, near Newark, Nottinghamshire as an instructor in 1943 at the time Cyril Fuller and his crew went through on heavy conversion training, though on another flight from them. He was, however, the instructor at that time of the late S/L JF Grime DFC, who went through training at the same time as Fuller and his crew, completed a tour on Lancasters with No 207 Sqn at RAF Langar and then went on to be a flying instructor [and acting CFI] at Winthorpe. John Grime was known personally to the author, in a capacity unconnected with the RAF, and the author went to his funeral in June 1997. Winthorpe airfield still exists and is used today by light aircraft and gliders. Part of the site is now the Nottinghamshire Air Museum and is well worth a visit.

29/30 AUG **LM656 PG-M LANCASTER MK III**

Took off at 2036 from Dunholme Lodge for *Königsberg* to bomb this important German supply port. For the 5 Group aircraft, like those from 619 Squadron, this meant a 950 mile route to the target. This aircraft was lost without trace and the missing crew have no known graves. They are commemorated on the Runnymede Memorial. Most probably they came down in the sea.

Casualties:	F/O F E Eley	Pilot	+
	Sgt H C Keatley	Flight Engineer	+
	F/O T de Vries RCAF	Navigator	+
	F/O D F Gay	Air Bomber	+
	Sgt J C Coverley	W/Op	+
	F/S W F Fraser RCAF	Air Gunner	+
	F/O G D Danielson RCAF	Air Gunner	+

The statistics for August give a fairly clear idea of the way the war is going: twenty operations were flown, no doubt partly the result of the better weather to be expected at this time of year, but also a reflection of the control of the air that the Allies were winning over French air space. As in the previous two months, the Bomber Command was able to fly operations by day, taking advantage of the Allied fighter day cover that could be provided for relatively short haul attacks on targets in the occupied Low Countries and France, as well as by night [taking advantage of the greater targeting accuracy now made possible by electronic and technological advances and a manufacturing and training base that at last was producing aircraft and crews faster than attrition from flak and night-fighter losses]. Losses are also down – only four, compared with twelve the previous month – and this despite the steadily increasing tonnage of bombs dropped [921 tons] and the operational hours flown [1,163.55]. During the month, the Squadron had visited *La Breteque/Siracourt, Bois de Cassan* [twice], *Trossy St Maximin, St Leu D'Esserant, Secqueville, Chatellerault, Bordeaux, Givors, Brunswick, Gardening* [twice], *Brest, Deelen, Stettin, L'Isle Adam, Darmstadt, Königsberg* [twice] and *Auchy Le Hesdin.* Most of the effort had been in support of the Allied land forces and even the long trips to German cities were made in the main to cut off the flow of materiel from important supply ports. More and more of the aircraft of the main force squadrons were now fitted with the sort of radar aids previously only available to the Pathfinder squadrons, and reports can now be seen in the records of aircraft having turned back to base on 'boomerangs', that is early returns, with faults they could not have had a year previously, for example H2S sets not working properly.

11/12 SEP — LM191 PG-O — LANCASTER MK I

Took off at 2048 from Dunholme Lodge for *Darmstadt*. Crashed at 0015 near Hausen vor der Höhe [Bad Schwalbach]. All were killed and are buried in Dürnbach War Cemetery. This crew had joined the Squadron on 13 July and were well into their tour.

Casualties:	F/O C B Dockrey RCAF	Pilot	+
	Sgt A Archer	Flight Engineer	+
	F/O E J A McNair RCAF	Navigator	+
	F/O J R Potts RCAF	Air Bomber	+
	Sgt E D Bone	W/Op	+
	Sgt H J Depotex	Air Gunner	+
	F/S E K Carlson RCAF	Air Gunner	+

11/12 SEP — LM209 PG-H — LANCASTER MK I

Took off at 2045 from Dunholme Lodge for *Darmstadt*. Crashed at 0030 into a wood about 1 km to the south of Darmstadt airfield. The wreckage lay undiscovered until May 1947 when examination of a large crater in the wood led to the recovery of the bodies of the crew. They are now buried at Dürnbach War Cemetery. This crew had arrived on the Squadron in mid June [the pilot as a F/L] and were well into their tour.

Casualties:	S/L R A Squibbs	Pilot	+
	Sgt A Furnival	Flight Engineer	+
	F/S J Singer	Navigator	+
	F/O J F Parry	Air Bomber	+
	Sgt J Davison	W/Op	+
	Sgt D Greenley	Air Gunner	+
	WO1 LG Evans RCAF	Air Gunner	+

A previous attack on Darmstadt in August had failed, and so this attack was launched by 5 Group, using 226 Lancasters and 14 Mosquitoes. This time 5 Group's own marking techniques were so accurate that a huge fire was started in the centre of the city and in the suburbs to the south and east. Property damage was almost total and the deaths of 8,433 people were reported to the police, including almost 500 foreign workers and 368 prisoners of war. The post-War US Strategic Bombing Survey[23] estimated that there might have been another 5,000 unreported deaths and that 49,200 people were made homeless. Post-War Darmstadt city guides have quoted figures of 12,300 dead and 70,000 homeless. This raid, with its high casualties and massive destruction of property was cited at the time and has often been since, as an example of 'terror warfare' at its worst. Having visited modern-day Darmstadt, I know the raid is still the source of much sensitivity. Darmstadt was a major rail centre, but as *Middlebrook and Everitt*[24] have suggested it is perhaps likely that it was chosen because it was a medium-sized city at a time when Bomber Command was running out of bigger targets.

19/20 SEP **PB405 PG-S LANCASTER MK III**

Took off at 1904 from Dunholme Lodge for *Mönchen-Gladbach*. All killed and are buried in Venray War Cemetery. F/S Stobbs had just arrived on the Squadron and was flying as second bomb aimer. F/L Leonard and his crew had arrived on the Squadron in mid June and were well into their tour of ops.

Casualties:	F/O L W Leonard	Pilot	+
	Sgt D J Carter	Flight Engineer	+
	F/S J M Davies	Navigator	+
	F/S J W C Mabbutt	Air Bomber	+
	W/O J Webster	W/Op	+
	Sgt W Johnson	Air Gunner	+
	Sgt J R Sutherland	Air Gunner	+
	F/S J K Stobbs	2nd air bomber	+

[23] Effects of City Raids, p. 9a.

[24] Martin Middlebrook and Chris Everitt *The Bomber Command War Diaries* [first published by Viking 1985].

26/27 SEP **ED602 PG-X LANCASTER MK III**

Took off at 0025 from Dunholme Lodge for *Karlsruhe*. Lost without trace. All are commemorated at Runnymede.

Casualties:	F/O R W Pettigrew RCAF	Pilot	+
	Sgt A Moir	Flight Engineer	+
	F/O J W Thompson RCAF	Navigator	+
	F/S A M B McDonald	Air Bomber	+
	Sgt H E Smith	W/Op	+
	Sgt G P Adams RCAF	Air Gunner	+
	Sgt P C Lowe	Air Gunner	+
	F/O T E Kerslake	Second pilot	+

This crew had joined the Squadron three months previously on 1 July and were well into their tour of operations by this stage. F/O Kerslake had been posted in with his crew from No 51 Base three days previously. This was his first operational flight, and his crew members were now left pilot-less before they had even started their tour. This was the last 619 Squadron aircraft to be lost from Dunholme Lodge, for on the 27th September an advance party, under the command of F/L MV Rees, had begun the move of the Squadron from Dunholme Lodge to RAF Strubby, about four miles from the Lincolnshire coast near Mablethorpe, and the following day the main party moved there under the command of F/L MG Clarke. The 29th September was spent getting aircraft ready and stores unpacked, but by the 30th the Squadron was practising high level bombing and fighter affiliation exercises from its new base. It was to remain at Strubby for remainder of the War, moving to Skellingthorpe in June 1945 for disbandment.

In the month of September the Squadron had flown 187 sorties to twelve targets, including attacks on two airfields, three harbour defences, various flying bomb storage sites and seven cities, dropping 813 tons of bombs in the course of flying 1,030.20 hours operationally. Four aircraft were lost, all with experienced crews, three to flak and the fourth to a cause unknown. The courage of its aircrew had seen the award of twelve medals for gallantry: five DFCs and 7 DFMs. The Squadron had visited *Brest, Deelen, Mönchen-Gladbach, Le Havre, Darmstadt, Stuttgart, Boulogne, Bremerhaven, Mönchen-Gladbach/Rheydt* [a second time], *Münster/Handorf, Karlsruhe and Kaiserslautern.* Thirteen new pilots and crews had arrived during the course of the month, including the Canadian pilots and brothers [AE and GM McMorran] who were both to lose their lives in the last few weeks of the War. The raids on Mönchen-Gladbach and Darmstadt devastated those cities and caused huge loss of life and destruction of buildings. By now a more reasonable man might have been suing for peace, but Hitler was determined – as one can today imagine some modern day dictators also being determined – to defend his dictatorship to the last of his citizens, and sadly the destruction was to continue for another six months. By now it was clear that the Allies had near control of much of the air space over France and the Low Countries and the air power to strike almost at will and with devastating force. The German bombing of British cities in the early years of the War had caused much damage for its day, and it is debatable whether Britain could have taken much more without the British war effort and morale beginning to suffer. The difference between then and now was, of course, that the British Government could not have continued the War if it had forfeited the support of the people. The Allied bombing of Germany at this stage of the War was far more efficient and effective than the German bombing had been, and Hitler was beginning to reap Harris's whirlwind. But he was not susceptible to public opinion.

The Master Bomber on the second raid on Mönchen-Gladbach was W/C Guy Gibson VC DSO DFC. He and his experienced Navigator S/L JB Warwick DFC were killed on the return leg when their De Havilland Mosquito, borrowed from No 627 Squadron, RAF Coningsby, crashed in Holland. The cause of the crash has never been established. It may have been a consequence of flak damage, as Gibson was over the target for a long time and was one of the last to leave it, or there may have been engine failure. Aviation Historian Alan Cooper, who has written a biography of Gibson, believes it could have been the result of a simple failure to switch cocks from one fuel tank to another, something even an experienced Mosquito crew found difficult and something a pilot and navigator not familiar with the aircraft type could easily overlook [and Gibson and Warwick were not experienced on the type]. By now virtually all the aircraft on main force squadrons, such as No 619 Squadron, carried H2S, Gee, Monica Mk V and other radio and radar aids, and with the accurate targeting techniques now being used by 5 Group's own marking force, such precise targets as flying bomb stores, airfields and harbours were being wiped out. Bomber Command had come full circle. Ironically, it was in this role of supporting the ground forces that the RAF had at last really come into its own. But it had been a long haul, and it was not over yet.

4 OCT 44 **LM681 PG-W LANCASTER MK III**

Took off at 1725 from Strubby on a *minelaying* trip. Hit by cannon or rocket fire and a fire started slightly forward of the mid-upper turret. The hydraulics, intercom and emergency air supplies were knocked out, ammunition exploded and the bomb doors holed. The the aircraft was crash-landed at 2340 at Carnaby without flaps or wheels. The mid-upper and rear gunners had fought the fire and the former, Sgt F Webster, been badly burned. He was rushed to hospital at Raunceby, and a replacement gunner joined the crew, but by 4 November Sgt Webster [by now a F/S] had rejoined the crew as mid-upper gunner, with his replacement and the original mid-upper rotating as rear gunner.

Captain:	F/O DH Strachan RNZAF	Pilot
Sgt F Webster	Air Gunner	inj

23 OCT **ME787 PG-J** **LANCASTER MK I**

Took off at 1512 from Strubby for a raid on the *Flushing* Gun emplacements. Hit by flak twice while in the target area and a fire started in the bomb bay, resulting in the bombs having to be jettisoned and the crew ordered to bale out. Four did so over the target and two more over England, where they were hospitalised because of their burns. The pilot crash-landed at Woodbridge. It is assumed that Pearson, Bates, Fryer and Bell survived, as there is no trace of them in CWGC records or in POW listings. S/L Purnell returned to operations with a new crew, except for Lock and Young, on 16 Jan 45. He and Lock completed their tour of operations and were awarded DFCs.

Casualties:	S/L RG Purnell	Pilot	
	F/O KR Pearson	Flight Engineer	n/k
	F/O RT Bates	Navigator	n/k
	F/O DB Fryer	Air Bomber	n/k
	F/S WI Bell	Rear gunner	n/k
	F/O SCW Lock	W/Op	inj
	F/O FRA Young	M/Upper gunner	inj

During the month of October the Squadron had participated in 143 sorties to 11 targets and had lost no aircraft, the first month free of losses in its entire existence. This 100% record was marred, however, by the loss of four of the crew of ME787 PG-J on 23 October during the course of a raid on the *gun emplacements at Flushing*, as detailed above. They had to bale out over the target area after their aircraft was hit twice by flak, causing a fire in the bomb bay. Two other members of the crew baled out over England badly burned, and the pilot, S/L RG Purnell, crash-landed at Woodbridge. The Squadron took part in many of the support operations that were beginning to make victory at last look inevitable. The crews had been – in increasingly large numbers as the attrition rates of aircraft and crews diminished – to *Wilhelmshaven, Bremen, Veere/Flushing, Brunswick, Westkapelle, Nürnburg, Flushing, Bergen, Westkapelle* and twice Gardening. In the course of these operations 560 tons of bombs had been dropped and 707.05 hours flown operationally. Already, the weight of bombs dropped and the hours flown were reducing, but what was being done was being done to far greater effect than had been the case a year previously.

During October Squadron personnel [and former personnel] received eight awards, four DFCs and four DFMs, including an immediate DFC to F/O DH Strachan RNZAF and an immediate DFM to his mid-upper gunner, Sgt F Webster, for their gallantry in dealing with the fire and then bringing back LM681 PG-W from a Gardening trip after it had been damaged by cannon shell or rocket. Ten new crews were posted in and four left on completion of their tours. At last crews were beginning to survive their tours of operations in reasonable numbers. The pilots of all the new crews posted in for first tours were now all in the rank of flying officer, if commissioned, as also were many other commissioned members of crews, the AOC-in-C having won the battle with the Air Ministry to have his heavy bomber aircraft captains and commissioned aircrew promoted to that rank on reaching operational squadrons. This had the effect, of course, of increasing their pay slightly [which is believed by former aircrew to have been the real purpose of Harris' move]. On the other hand, it increased the rank differential [and pay] between the commissioned and the non-commissioned elements of the crews. If one gunner were commissioned and the other not, one would fly and be paid as a flying officer, the other as a sergeant. Harris' persistence had solved one problem by creating another. It is noticeable that RCAF officers and NCOs were promoted earlier than RAF counterparts.

This month a new Bomber squadron was formed, and it is worth commenting on how this was done. No 227 Squadron was formed on 7th October by 'A' Flight operating as a third flight of No 9 Squadron at RAF Bardney and 'B' Flight as the third flight of No 619 Squadron at RAF Strubby. This continued until 19th October when 'B' Flight ceased to operate at Strubby and moved to No 227's new base at RAF Balderton on 21st October. As a consequence W/C HR Black, the new CO of 227 Squadron, and his crew, flew with 619 Squadron on the operations to Wilhelmshaven and Bremen on the 5th and 6th October. In this way were new squadrons formed, and as a result Bomber Command was now a huge organisation with 110 operational squadrons on some 73 stations.

1 NOV **PB540 PG-Z LANCASTER MK III**

Took off at 1407 from Strubby for a daylight raid against the oil installation at Meerbeck, *Homberg*. Hit by heavy flak, the port tail plane and aileron controls were severed. It was crash-landed at Woodbridge, where it burst into flames on landing. The captain and the other three front cabin crew were killed and the other three injured, the rear gunner, Sgt Ralston, seriously.[25]

Casualties:	F/L LE Tanner	Pilot	+
	Sgt RJ Ward	Flight Engineer	+
	Sgt MG Gibson	Navigator	+
	Sgt AP Goddard	Air Bomber	+
	Sgt JR Fletcher	W/Op	inj
	Sgt JF Barton	Air Gunner	inj
	Sgt R Ralston	Air Gunner	ser. inj

6/7 NOV **LM742 PG-S LANCASTER MK III**

Took off at 1629 from Strubby for the *Mittelland Kanal* at Gravenhorst. The three crew members killed now rest in the Reichswald Forest Cemetery.

Casualties:	F/O EW Hookings	Pilot	pow
	Sgt HJH Tait	Flight Engineer	pow
	F/L L Croney	Navigator	pow
	Sgt RG Walters	Air Bomber	pow
	F/S RB Templeton RAAF	W/Op	+
	Sgt AC Norris	Air Gunner	+
	Sgt EF Wood	Air Gunner	+

[25] The Squadron's 18 aircraft were part of a force of 228 aircraft from 5 Group that attacked the oil installation at Homberg. Because of 10/10ths cloud over the target, the raid was not successful and had to be repeated the following night using *G-H* and a also week later. The crews experienced intense flak over the target, and all except two of the Squadron's aircraft were hit, though only one seriously. This aircraft, PB540 PG-Z, with F/L LE Tanner and crew on board, was hit by heavy flak, and the port tail plane and aileron controls were severed. It was crash-landed at Woodbridge on return, where it burst into flames on landing and the captain and three other members of the crew were killed

6/7 NOV **NN723 PG-J LANCASTER MK III**

Took off at 1631 from Strubby for the *Mittelland Kanal* at Gravenhorst. Crashed into the North Sea. Six of the crew were never found, but Sgt Hogg's remains were found after the War on *Ameland* and identified after an Interpol investigation.

Casualties:	F/S JLB Webster	Pilot	+
	Sgt B H Brodie	Flight Engineer	+
	Sgt JA Harrison	Navigator	+
	F/S CK Morton	Air Bomber	+
	Sgt L Kennedy	W/Op	+
	Sgt ES Bicknell	Air Gunner	+
	Sgt RJ Hogg	Air Gunner	+

6/7 NOV **PB205 PG-B LANCASTER MK III**

Took off at 1635 from Strubby for the *Mittelland Kanal* at Gravenhorst. On returning was one of two aircraft to land at *Hethal*, near Norwich. This aircraft crash-landed, but the crew [F/O JA Lavigner RCAF] but none of the crew were injured.

The sixteen 619 Squadron aircraft taking part in this attack were part of a force of 242 aircraft from 5 Group [235 Lancasters and 7 Mosquitoes] that attempted to cut the *Mittelland Kanal* at its junction with the *Dortmund-Ems Kanal*. The marking force had difficulty finding the target, but the crew of one low-flying Mosquito of 627 Squadron were so successful that their marker fell into the water of the canal and was extinguished. Only 31 aircraft, none of them 619's, bombed before the Master Bomber called off the attack. All 619's captains then jettisoned some of their bomb loads to reduce landing weight before returning to base, but two aircraft landed at *Hethal*, near Norwich, one of them with the consequences mentioned above. Thus, it was recorded that the squadron had lost three aircraft and two crews without dropping a bomb. This is strictly true, but PB205 was repaired and was back in operation with the Squadron within weeks[26], before being passed on to No 1661 CU at Winthorpe, then to 20 MU and finally being struck off RAF charge in May 1947. NN723 had flown only 16 hours when it was lost, and LM742 not many more at 60. On 8 Nov Lt MH Meter SAAF flew over to *Hethal* to pick up the crew of PB205.

11 NOV **PB356 PG-G LANCASTER MK III**

Took off 1635 from Strubby for *Harburg* where the aiming point was an oil refinery. No details are available as to what happened to this aircraft but only three bodies were found [Sgts Sanders, Nixon and Patterson], and they are buried in Hamburg Cemetery.

Casualties:	F/O PC Clapham	Pilot	+
	Sgt JGD Sanders	Flight Engineer	+
	F/S LW Bennett	Navigator	+
	F/O NEH McConnell RCAF	Air Bomber	+
	Sgt JC Richardson	W/Op	+
	Sgt G Nixon	Air gunner	+
	Sgt R Patterson	Air Gunner	+
	F/L KW Whitefield	Second pilot	+

F/O Clapham and his crew had arrived on the Squadron on 12 August, and so were well into their tour. F/L Whitefield, the second pilot, had arrived on the Squadron with his new crew from No 51 Base four days previously, and this was his first operational flight with the Squadron. Once again a new crew was left pilot-less before it had even started its tour of operations.

During November 1944 the Squadron had participated in ten operations, all except one all-5 Group all- Lancaster affairs led by low-flying, target-marking Mosquitoes specialists, and, weather permitting, the raids were becoming increasingly more effective and devastating. In the process, 619 Sqn had lost four aircraft [five if PB205 is allowed], four crews and one new captain on his first operation as second pilot. Ten replacement crews had been posted in, of which one lost its pilot

[26] F/O KR Hickmott RCAF was flying this aircraft to Gydnia on 18/19 December when he and F/O DH Strachan RNZAF in PB842 PG-Y attacked the cruiser *Lutzen*.

immediately, as already mentioned, and two were to be lost within four weeks of their arrival, showing that although the severe attrition rates of Summer of 1943 through to the Summer 1944 were no longer the norm, flying bombing operations against targets with flak protection was still an extraordinarily dangerous business. Several times, all or the majority of the aircraft despatched came back with flak damage. The bomb tonnage dropped during the month continued to fall as did the operational hours flown [to 571 tons and 862.09 respectively]. Of particular interest to the author, the last few days of the previous month and throughout this month had also seen the operational dêbut of the present Association Secretary, John Whiteley, to whom he is particularly indebted for help and guidance over the past eighteen months.

The operations flown during the month – Homberg, Düsseldorf, Dortmund-Ems Kanal, Gravenhorst, Harburg, Düren, Gravenhorst, Trondjheim, Gardening and München – paint a telling picture of the way the War was proceeding. The Homberg and Harburg attacks were directed against oil installations [and in the end it was lack of fuel that grounded the Luftwaffe and kept the fighters out of the air]; the Dortmund-Ems and Gravenhorst [Mittelland-Ems] attacks were aimed against the German canal supply system; the Düren raid was in support of the American First and Ninth Armies as they faced the German Army across the Rhine near Aachen [and involved the use of 1,188 heavy bombers of Bomber Command and 1,239 heavy bombers of the USAAF, which dropped in excess of 9,400 tons of bombs]; and the Trondjheim raid was against the U-boat pens. Only the operations to Düsseldorf and München were of the type that Cyril Fuller and his contemporaries would have recognised from eighteen months previously, and even they were different, qualitatively and in the marking technique used. By November 1944, 5 Group had developed into a formidably accurate and weighty bombing force, whose strength was increasing week by week exponentially as the German ability to repulse the attacks weakened exponentially. The outcome of the War was now becoming obvious to all except the German dictator and his closest acolytes, and much suffering could have been avoided by his recognition of this fact.

4/5 DEC **LM751 PG-O LANCASTER MK III**

Took off at 1642 from Strubby for *Heilbronn*. The two gunners survived as POWs. The rest of the crew died and are buried in Dürnbach War Cemetery.

Casualties:	F/O RH Schaeffer RCAF	Pilot	+
	Sgt LG Weir	Flight Engineer	+
	F/O PP Awad RCAF	Navigator	+
	F/O FL Meredith RCAF	Air Bomber	+
	Sgt JL Swanson	W/Op	+
	Sgt JR Keilty RCAF	Air Gunner	pow
	Sgt JE Nisholaiff	Air Gunner	pow

4/5 DEC **ND932 PG-U LANCASTER MK III**

Took off at 1642 from Strubby for *Heilbronn*. Six of the crew were killed and they lie in Dürnbach War Cemetery. P/O Shantz RCAF had married in Lincoln.

Casualties:	F/O SV Chambers RCAF	Pilot	+
	Sgt A Pascoe	Flight Engineer	+
	Sgt JC Reed	Navigator	+
	P/O IW Shantz RCAF	Air Bomber	+
	F/S JD Galliard	W/Op	+
	F/S R Prunkle RCAF	Air Gunner	+
	F/S GH Goudy RCAF	Air Gunner	pow

This was the only attack of the war on this unimportant town, whose only claim to being of strategic [or tactical] significance was that it stood on the main north/south railway line. Once again it was an entirely 5 Group effort, using 282 Lancasters, and 10 Mosquitoes as markers. It was a devastatingly efficient operation. In a matter of minutes, 1,254 tons of bombs were dropped on the town. The post-War British Bombing Survey Unit estimates that the attack had wiped out 82% of the built-up area of the town. It is believed that about 7,000 people died. No 619 Sqn lost two of its 16 aircraft, both with Canadian captains [F/O Schaeffer and F/O Chambers], and 5 Group lost 12 Lancasters in all. F/O Schaeffer and his crew had arrived on the Squadron only three weeks previously, but F/O Chambers and his crew had been with the Squadron since 24th July [Chambers arriving as a W/O] and were nearing the end of their tour; thus is war capricious. F/O Awad was an American citizen serving in the RCAF.

During the month of December, the Squadron had participated in eleven major operations and 'vegetables'[27] were laid on three other occasions.

After *Heilbronn*, there was an attack by another entirely 5 Group force [of 255 Lancasters and 10 Mosquitoes] on the railway yards and town centre at *Giessen* on the 6th December. Damage to the town and the railway yards was severe. No 619's PB699 PG-Z [F/O ET Pennells RCAF] received damage from machine guns and flak, but returned to base safely.

On the 8th, 10th and 11th of the month, the Squadron contributed 42 sorties towards the operations against the *Urft Dam* at *Heimbach*, near the ground forces *battle area in the region of Aachen*. Once again these operations were undertaken entirely by 5 Group, using the Group's own specialist markers. On the first occasion the raid was *G-H* –led, and the crews had to bomb through 9/10 cloud. Bombs were seen to land on the spillway and the dam walls, but the walls were not breached. On this first raid against the Dam, seven of 619's aircraft were instructed not to bomb and had to jettison some of their load on the way home to reduce landing weight. Driving sleet at Strubby caused all except four of the aircraft to divert, mostly to Boscombe Down but one to Tarrant Rushden. On next operation against the Dam, on the 10th, two 619 Squadron aircraft collided while taxying and the remaining thirteen were recalled after only half an hour in the air. On the 11th, for the third time of asking, 5 Group returned to the *Urft Dam*. This time many direct hits were scored, but once again it seems that the Dam was not breached.

On 17th December, fourteen aircraft [17 took off, but there were three early returns] participated in another entirely 5 Group attack, this time on the railway yards and the old city centre of *München*. The returning crews reported that extensive damage had been caused. Out of 280 Lancasters and 8 Mosquitoes, only 4 Lancasters were lost, none

[27] Anti-shipping mines, so called because they resembled turnips.

from 619. The Squadron Commanding Officer, W/C RA Milward, who wrote the ORB this month [it was usually done by the adjutant], noted: '*this effort of early returns was the worst record the squadron has suffered for some time*'. [Two aircraft had returned with engine problems and one with navigational difficulties.]

The Squadron was able to put four aircraft up at very short notice on Boxing Day to make an attack against German positions in the *Ardennes battle area*. On 28th December, five aircraft were sent to attack shipping at *Horten* and on 30th December eighteen to bomb the German supply bottleneck at *Houffalize*. In the event, this turned out to be the last operation of the last full year of the War. An operation detailed for 31st December was cancelled at short notice. There was, however, one last fling: a lone Gardening trip on New Year's Eve by F/O WJ Franks and his crew in ND957 PG-M, who returned with one hour and six minutes to spare in which to celebrate the Old Year.

Only one new crew had been posted in during the month. Once again the tonnage of bombs dropped had decreased [from 571 to 439 tons] but the operational flying hours were up [from 862.09 in November to 955.48 in December]. W/C JN Tomes, who had been flying with the Squadron since 24th November, was posted out on 13th December as the new Commanding Officer of No 57 Squadron, in succession to W/C H Y Humphreys, who had also completed his operational attachment with No 619 Squadron.

1945

4/5 JAN 45 **ND728 PG-N LANCASTER MK III**

Took off at 0122 from Strubby for *Royan*, a town near the mouth of the Gironde and close to the port of Bordeaux, where a German Garrison was refusing to surrender to 12,000 Free French fighters appointed by Gen de Gaulle. Many French civilians were killed. An American officer was blamed for having passed an incorrect message to SHAEF that the town was clear of all but collaborators. Sgt Bartholomew is buried in Soulac-sur-mer Communal Cemetery. The other members of the crew have no known grave.

Casualties:	F/O D Gray RAAF	Pilot	+
	Sgt A Johnson	Flight Engineer	+
	F/S EA Morley	Navigator	+
	F/S H Insley	Air Bomber	+
	W/O LJ Symonds	W/Op	+
	Sgt R Brown	Air Gunner	+
	Sgt WB Bartholomew	Air Gunner	died of inj.

7/8 JAN 45 **ND957 PG-M LANCASTER MK III**

Took off at 1654 from Strubby for *München.* Crashed on return leg near St-Pierre, probably because of weather conditions. All were killed and now rest in Villeneuve-St-George Old Cemetery. This crew had joined the Squadron on 20 Nov 44.

Casualties:	F/O CK Flockhart RAAF	Pilot	+
	Sgt PS Graves	Flight Engineer	+
	Sgt RW Price	Navigator	+
	F/S RW Keightley	Air Bomber	+
	F/S EA Smith RAAF	W/Op	+
	Sgt TL Letchford	Air Gunner	+
	F/S AF Murdoch	Air Gunner	+

13/14 JAN **PB842 PG-Y LANCASTER MK III**

Took off at 1652 from Strubby to attack the oil plant at *Pölitz*. Bombed successfully but while clearing the target area came under attack from a Me 410, which in turn was claimed destroyed by return fire from the rear gunner, F/S FW Roots. With its No 1 port fuel tank ruptured the aircraft was flown to Sweden and landed at Rinkaby. In due course, repairs were carried out and the crew with a Swedish officer accompanying them ferried it to Linköping, where it was stored until broken up for scrap in 1946. Most of the crew left Stockholm for home by Dakota on 10 Mar.

Crew:	F/O BP Curran RAAF	Pilot	int
	Sgt DH Drew	Flight Engineer	int
	F/S RI Wilson	Navigator	int
	F/S MPB Quigley	Air Bomber	int
	Sgt J Haigh	W/Op	int
	F/S FAM Blakeley	Air Gunner	int
	F/S FW Roots	Air Gunner	int

Up to 16th January 1945, the Squadron had participated in eight operations in the first month of the New Year and lost three aircraft in the process, but repeated snow squalls, frost and fog, either at the base or over potential targets, prevented further activity, despite heroic efforts at snow clearance, which kept the runways open almost as fast as they were being put out of action again by fresh falls of snow. It was a winter to be remembered. Despite this, the Squadron dropped a total of 420 tons of bombs in 878.34 hours of operational flying [compared with 439 tons and 955.48 hours in December].

All except one of the eight ops were of a tactical nature or in support of ground troops. On New Year's Day nineteen aircraft had returned again to the *Mittelland Kanal*, and once more the canal banks were left pockmarked by bomb craters and the walls breached in some places. On returning, the weather was such that all but one aircraft had to be diverted to *Tain* in the North of Scotland.

On the 4th January the squadron sent seventeen aircraft to *Royan*, to attack a German Garrison, on an operation that led to the deaths of many French civilians [through no fault of Bomber Command but stemming from poor intelligence sent to SHAEF by an American officer with a tactical air force unit]. It was one of the almost inevitable cock-ups of war, but it was a sad mistake all the same, especially as the attack was delivered with the considerable precision for which Bomber Command, and 5 Group in particular, was now becoming known. In the process, the Squadron lost an aircraft and its crew [ND728 PG-N], F/O D Gray RAAF and crew, one of only four Lancasters lost that night.

The next day [5th] at short notice, having been stood down after operations the night before, the Squadron sent ten aircraft to *Houffalize* again, once more in direct support of ground troops, this time to attack a concentration of enemy transport and men that had been reported by the Army. The target was again bombed with great accuracy. With deteriorating weather conditions on their return, all but one of the Squadron's aircraft were diverted – this time to *Topcliffe*, near Thirsk in Yorkshire.

On the following day [6th], the Squadron sent two aircraft to drop mines in *Gydnia harbour*.

Twenty-four hours later on 7th January, the Squadron contributed sixteen aircraft in an attack on *München*, which again devastated the city centre and was held to have caused severe damage. It was to prove to be the last major attack on that city of the war. Sadly, the Squadron lost another aircraft, this time ND957 PG-N with F/O Flockhart RAAF and crew. All were killed. They had crashed in France, it is thought as a consequence of the bad weather encountered that night. News of their deaths was reported to the Squadron the following day.

On the 13/14th January, 619 Squadron sent fifteen aircraft as part of an entirely 5 Group on the long journey to *Pölitz* to attack a synthetic-oil plant with a considerable degree of success. Though planned as a blind-bombing attack, weather over the target was found to be better than anticipated, and the Mosquito low-level markers were able to mark the plant decisively. This was one of an increasing number of attacks on distant oil plants in Eastern Germany, and it was lack of fuel that eventually defeated the Luftwaffe. One aircraft returned early and another [PB842 PG-Y, F/O BP Curran RAAF], having bombed, was caught in the target area by a Me 410. Though the rear gunner, F/S FW

Roots, fired back and claimed the Me 410 as destroyed, F/O Curran was obliged to land in neutral Sweden with a ruptured fuel tank. The aircraft was repaired but scrapped in 1946. The crew were interned, but returned to UK in a Dakota in March. A colour photograph of PB842 PG-Y taking off from Strubby in 'late 1944' was published some years ago by Keith Woodcock.

On 14 January the Squadron sent fourteen aircraft as part of a joint 1 and 5 Groups force to attack another oil installation, this time at *Merseburg,* which reconnaissance said had left the oil plant 'in a shambles'. This was another spectacular success for Bomber Command, so much so that it was specifically mentioned after the War by *Albert Speer*, the German Minister of Armaments, as having been a particularly severe set-back the German war effort. German tanks and aircraft were now running out of fuel, which made them as useless as if they had been destroyed. On returning the aircraft were once again diverted, this time to *RAF Middleton-St-George*, today Teeside Airport.

On 16/17 January, the Squadron despatched 17 aircraft to attack the synthetic-oil plant at *Brux* in Czechoslovakia, the fourth such attack on far distant oil targets in recent days. *Speer* also mentioned this attack as having had a considerable impact on their oil production.

During the month F/O DH Strachan DFC RNZAF and F/O R Bateman and their crews completed their tours of thirty operations and were stood down.

2/3 FEB 45 **PB210 PG-V LANCASTER MK III**

Took off at 2007 from Strubby for *Karlsruhe*, one of 20 aircraft despatched by 619 Sqn as part of an all-5Group force of 250 Lancasters and 11 Mosquitoes. Because of thick cloud, the raid was a complete failure, but it cost the Group 12 aircraft, including this one. It was the last major RAF raid of the War on this city. Only a few bombs fell on the city.

Casualties:	F/L EJF Smith	Pilot	pow
	Sgt H Bowden	Flight Engineer	+
	F/S EA Rex	Navigator	+
	P/O DC McNie RCAF	Air Bomber	+
	F/O EJ Mortis	W/Op	+
	F/S P Turner	Air Gunner	+
	Sgt JRA Ramsey	Air Gunner	+

This crew had joined the Squadron on 29 July 44, and were nearing the end of their tour of operations.

8/9 FEB 45 **ME314 PG-W LANCASTER MK III**

Took off at 1709 from Strubby as part of the first wave, 5 Group- marked attack on the synthetic-oil plant at Pölitz. Missing without trace, but the ORB records that they met "appreciable fighter opposition", and another 619 aircraft returned badly shot up and with a dead rear gunner and a seriously injured W/Op. It is likely, therefore, that this aircraft was shot down over the sea.

Casualties:	F/O HT Hesketh RAAF	Pilot	+
	Sgt T H Fullwood	Flight Engineer	+
	F/O RA Hudson	Navigator	+
	F/S JFE Moyle RCAF	Air Bomber	+
	Sgt AC St Leger	W/Op	+
	F/S JL MacDonald RCAF	Air Gunner	+
	F/S LE Marsh RCAF	Air Gunner	pow

This crew had arrived on the Squadron two months previously on 8 Dec 44 and were getting towards the middle of their tour. Only F/S Moyle's body was recovered, and he is buried in the CWGC 1939-1945 Cemetery in Berlin. F/S LE Marsh was the only survivor.

8/9 FEB 45 **PA180 PG-G LANCASTER MK III**

Took off at 1736 from Strubby, one of four aircraft tasked with laying mines in the area of Pölitz while eleven more attacked the oil installation. As they approached the mine-laying area they were attacked by a fighter and sustained heavy damage. The rear gunner was killed, the w/op seriously injured and the M/U gunner injured. The pilot brought the aircraft back safely to base, landing at 0105.

Casualties:	F/O R Dickinson	Pilot	
	Sgt GH Broughton	Flight Engineer	
	Sgt TT Turnbull	Navigator	
	F/S WL Reeves	Air Bomber	
	F/S A Horne	W/Op	s/inj
	Sgt JB Cracknell	Air Gunner	inj
	Sgt V Pascoe	Air Gunner	+

The aircraft was repaired and went on to fly with 9 Sqn from July 1945 when 619 disbanded. It was scrapped in May 1947. Sgt Cracknell was back on ops by 19th February, but several different W/Ops joined the crew for that and the next few trips [F/S EF Belcher, F/L W Clegg, F/S WL Reeves] plus replacement rear gunners for the dead Sgt Pascoe [F/S W Fifield, Sgt TA Best, and F/S J Wilkes].

During February 1945 the Squadron had contributed 153 sorties to twelve operations, mainly once again attacks against tactical targets chosen to starve the enemy of materiel and troops. A total of 529 tons of bombs were dropped in 1,096.20 operational flying hours [compared with 420 tons and 878.43 hours in January]. In the process 619 had lost two aircraft and a number had been damaged, one [PA255 PG-V], captain S/L Osborne, crash-landing at *Carnaby*, after being engaged by three nightfighters and the rear gunner shooting down two of them during one of two attacks this month on the *Mittelland Kanal*. In the mêlée a bomb had broken loose in the bomb bay and prevented the wheels from being locked down, Osborne landing at *Carnaby* with the wheels up. [The aircraft was repaired and went on to fly with No 9 Sqn and then with No 617 Sqn before being struck off charge in August 1947.]

Other targets this month were: *Siegen, Karlsruhe*, the *Dortmund-Ems Kanal* [twice], a *synthetic-oil plant at Pölitz, Dresden*, a synthetic-oil plan near *Leipzig* [twice], and *Gardening* [twice].

On the First of the month the Squadron sent twenty aircraft to *Siegen*. This was an attack on an important rail centre not far behind the ground troops frontline. Unfortunately, most of the attack was misdirected, either because of strong winds or decoy fires, and most of the bombs fell in the surrounding countryside, killing 128 people.

The next day, the Squadron sent 20 aircraft to *Karlsruhe*. Once again this was an entirely 5 Group affair, involving 250 Lancasters and 11 Mosquitoes. Cloud over the target caused the raid to be a complete failure. This was a lucky escape for *Karlsruhe* as it was the last major RAF attack of the war on the city. It cost the RAF, however, twelve Lancasters, four from one squadron alone [No 189 Squadron], and one from No 619 Sqn [PB210 PG-V], F/L EJF Smith and crew. Smith survived as a POW, but the other six members of his crew were killed. They are buried at Dürnbach War Cemetery.

On the 7th, the Squadron sent eleven aircraft to the *Dortmund-Ems Kanal.* This night, 177 Lancasters and 11 Mosquitoes of 5 Group again attacked the canal, 619's eleven all taking off at around 1600 hours, in the late afternoon. Although the crews thought it had been a successful attack, later photographs showed that the canal banks had not been damaged, most of the bombs falling in nearby fields. Three other crews went out on a mine-laying operation. All returned safely.

The following night the Squadron despatched 14 aircraft to *Pölitz*. This was a large scale attack by Bomber Command, using 475 Lancasters and 7 Mosquitoes, in two waves; the first wave was marked using the 5 Group method of low level marking; the second using the Pathfinders of 8 Group. In good weather both waves were extremely successful, and much damage was caused to the synthetic-oil plant. Speer mentioned this raid in his post-war interrogation. Twelve Lancasters were lost, one of them 619's ME314 PG-W [F/O HT Hesketh RAAF and crew]. Six members of the crew were killed, only the rear gunner surviving as a POW, and only one of the dead has a known grave. Three of 619's crews laid mines in the area of *Pölitz*. PA180 PG-

G [F/O R Dickinson] was attacked by a fighter while in the process of laying a mine, and abandoned the mission with a dead rear gunner, a seriously wounded W/Op and an injured M/Upper Gunner. Despite the aircraft sustaining heavy damage, the pilot got it safely back to base.

On the 13th February the squadron sent thirteen aircraft as part of the first wave of the infamous attack on the Medieval market town of *Dresden*. Their thirteen aircraft were airborne in 9½ minutes. The crew debriefings record that the target was lightly defended and no fighters were encountered. This first wave was an entirely 5 Group affair, using low level marking. During this wave, 244 Lancasters dropped 800 tons of bombs, but because of cloud the attack was only moderately successful. A second wave three hours later in clear weather, using 8 Group Pathfinders, to mark, and 529 Lancasters, to drop 1,800 tons of bombs, was fearfully accurate. Then the following day 311 heavy bombers of the USAAF dropped another 711 tons of bombs on Dresden. Dresden was destroyed and at least 35,000 people, and probably more, died in the conflagration that followed. More than any other operation of the War, this is the one that has caused so much controversy, though the part the USAAF played is usually forgotten, and blame is often laid entirely on Harris's shoulders. This is not fair. The reasons for choosing *Dresden* that night are complex and many. Aside from Harris's determination to prove that area bombing could achieve all that he and others claimed of it, it is disingenuous to blame him alone. He was carrying out a strategy handed down to him, albeit with enthusiasm. Bomber Command lost 6 Lancasters that night, and three others crashed, two in France and one in England. After the war, it suited the occupying *Soviet Union* and its puppet regime, the *DDR,* to retain a blackened *Dresden* as a ruin for anti-Western propaganda purposes. When the author visited Dresden in 1991 and 1992, like so many other places in the East, including the Soviet sector of Berlin, it was only just beginning to emerge from ruins. On the first occasion the German tour guide was delighted to see the city emerging from its 45 years of blackened hibernation. On the second, the guide, an unreconstructed communist, regretted the passing of a way of life that had served her quite well [when speaking in English, she presented a different front]. The famous church is now being rebuilt, and Britain has made some symbolic contribution towards the reconstruction. The Devil doesn't always get the last laugh.

The following day the crews were still resting from the previous night's operation when they were summoned by tannoy for an operation against another synthetic-oil plant, this time *Rositz*, south of *Leipzig*. They took off around 1645, with F/O Hickmott taking a new pilot, W/O Potter, as second dickie. All attacked the target and returned safely, but F/O Dunsmore and crew in PA198 PG-J were later than the rest because they had been attacked by fighters and had to return on three engines. Also, F/L JW May in NG483 PG-N landed at *RAF Manston*, Kent, with both inboard engines out of action and both tyres burst following an attack by a nightfighter. Once again, this was an entirely 5 Group affair, using 224 Lancasters and 8 Mosquitoes. Damage was caused to the southern end of the oil plant. Four Lancasters were lost, none from 619 Sqn.

The operations, many to long distance targets, had been conducted at a fast pace until half way through the month, so much so that by the middle of the month [the 15th February] the Squadron actually reached the point where it no longer had any fully serviceable aircraft available. There was then a race on to repair the many minor defects and to replace the power plants in three aircraft. In the event it did not matter, because on the 16th February there were no operations, and instead the crews cleaned their aircraft in the morning and attended a lecture on German signals intelligence by the Station Signals Officer in the afternoon. The next day there were still no operations and so a film showing of 'The Airborne Lifeboat' was arranged, but the projector broke down after the first reel! For the third day in succession there were no operations on the 18th, and local flying was arranged to keep the crews in flying practice. Various aircraft were collected from repair at *East Kirkby* and *Woodbridge*.

The operations to *Leipzig* and the *Mittelland Kanal* took place on the 19th, 21st and 22nd February. On the 25th February a conference took place at 55 Base Headquarters to discuss plans for forming up for daylight attacks in the future. G/C John Jeudwine, W/C RA Milward and W/C SG Birch attended [the latter having just taken over 619 Squadron from W/C Milward], as also did the two Canadian brothers, both now Flight Lieutenants, AE and GM McMorran.

On the 19th, eighteen 619 Sqn aircraft took part in another entirely 5 Group attack, this time consisting of 254 Lancasters and 6 Mosquitoes, against *Böhlen* near *Leipzig*. They took off late in the evening at around 2150. The raid failed because only the faintest glow of a TI could be seen, probably because the Controller [Master Bomber], Wing Commander EA Benjamin DFC and bar, was brought down by flak over the target. Post-raid reconnaissance showed that damage was superficial and bombing very scattered. W/C Benjamin is buried in the CWGC 1939-1945 Cemetery in Berlin. Unusually, his aircraft - a Mosquito - was the only one missing that night. No Lancasters were lost.

On the 20th, once again 5 Group returned to the *Mittelland Kanal* at *Gravenhorst* with a force this time of 154 Lancasters and 11 Mosquitoes. The raid was abandoned because of cloud and all 619's aircraft returned safely with their bomb loads. No aircraft were lost.

The following night, 5 Group went back again to *Gravenhorst*, but this time the take-off was earlier, all 619 Squadron's aircraft being airborne in a ten minute interval soon after 1700 hours, and on this occasion the aircraft were able to bomb the target in bright moonlight. F/O LW O'Brien RAAF in ME472 PG-R returned with the port wing damaged, and examination suggested that he had actually been struck by the German fighter aircraft that had attacked him. S/L PS Osborne, the newly-promoted Flight Commander of 'B' Flight, in PA255 PG-V crash-landed at *Carnaby* because of damage caused by a loose bomb which prevented him getting the undercarriage down. W/C SG Birch arrived after an operational attachment with 50 Squadron at *Skellingthorpe*. He took over the Squadron the next day, 22nd February, when W/C RA Milward completed his second tour of operations.

On the 24th February 5 Group went back to the *Dortmund-Ems Kanal*, this time with 165 Lancasters and 12 Mosquitoes. Tellingly, by this stage of the War, No 11 Group [Fighter Command] was able to supply a fighter escort. No 619 Sqn contributed 12 of the Lancasters.

All got back safely, but because cloud had covered the target they restricted themselves to dropping only one x 1,000 lb bomb each and bringing the rest back to base. Nine Lancasters were lost and four crashed in *France* and *Holland.* One of those crashing in *Holland* was an 83 Sqn Lancaster captained by the Station Commander of RAF Coningsby, G/Capt AC Evans-Evans DFC, a legendary figure with a huge personality and equally huge frame. His aircraft had been shot down by a night-fighter, and he and the other seven members of the crew are buried at Eindhoven. He was 43 years of age, and his navigator, S/L WG Wishart DSO, DFC and Bar, was 22. In addition to these two decorated officers, the crew contained F/L WC Fitch, with a DFC and a GM, and F/O DAJW Ball, with a DFM. Being shot down was largely a matter of luck, and crew experience often made little or no difference.

The month also saw the award of more decorations to 619 Squadron: three DFCs and a DFM.

7/8 MAR　　NG286 PG-Y　LANCASTER MK III

Took off at 1816 from Strubby for the oil refinery at *Harburg*. The Canadian captain was one of two brothers who had joined the Sqn together in Sep 44. The brother was also killed in April 1945. Four members of the crew survived as POWs. The three dead crew members have no known grave.

Casualties:	F/L GMS McMorran RCAF	Pilot	+
	Sgt K Phillips	Flight Engineer	pow
	F/O HE Hanson RCAF	Navigator	pow
	F/O T Turner RCAF	Air Bomber	pow
	F/S VW Lambert	W/Op	+
	Sgt SJJ Maton	Air Gunner	+
	F/S E Dellow	Air Gunner	Pow

7/8 MAR **PB699/G PG-Z** **LANCASTER MK I**

Took off at 1822 from Strubby for *Harburg*, as above. No details are known, but the crew all lie in Hamburg Cemetery [Ohlsdorf].

Casualties:	F/O CP Sparkes RNZAF	Pilot	+
	F/S DR Lloyd	Flight Engineer	+
	F/O RN Fergusson RNZAF	Navigator	+
	F/O CL Eyles	Air Bomber	+
	F/S PN Black RNZAF	W/Op	+
	F/O PB Eynon	Air Gunner	+
	Sgt J Bryce	Air Gunner	+

It will be recalled that F/O Sparkes and his crew had returned early from the *Sassnitz* operation on 6th March in this same aircraft with the starboard outer engine feathered, and F/L EJF Smith had returned early in it on 13th January with the rear turret u/s.

11 MAR **LM207 PG-E** **LANCASTER MK I**

Took off at 1211 from Strubby for *Essen* as part of a 1,000 bomber raid – the largest so far in the War with 1,079 aircraft taking part including 750 Lancasters! While on the outward leg, got into difficulty and tried to land at Evere [Brussels] airfield in Belgium. Wrecked when overshot the runway, fortunately without injuries to the crew.

Crew:	F/O EH Hooker	Pilot
	Sgt GPT Pullen	Flight Engineer
	F/S RK Appleton	Navigator
	WO2 MS Reside RCAF	Air Bomber
	Sgt J Schofield	W/Op
	F/S FV Verney RCAF	Air Gunner
	Sgt WHP Barnett	Air Gunner

F/O Hooker and crew were flown back to Strubby from Down Ampney on 13 March and were back on operations again to Würzburg three days later [16/17 March]. How different from 1943.

16/17 MAR **NG503 PG-W** **LANCASTER MK I**

Took off at 1757 from Strubby for *Würzburg* on third operational trip. All are buried in Dürnbach War Cemetery. This crew had joined the squadron seven days previously. The aircraft had been been issued to the Squadron new on 13 Feb 45 and was the last of a batch of 400 built by the Armstrong Whitworth factory, Baginton between Jul 44 and Feb 45. All 400 had Merlin 24 engines.

Casualties:	F/O TE Farrow RCAF	Pilot	+
	F/S EK Ireland	Flight Engineer	+
	F/O L Tilley RCAF	Navigator	+
	F/L CW McBride RCAF	Air Bomber	+
	Sgt J Macpherson	W/Op	+
	F/O JD Johnston RCAF	Air Gunner	+
	F/S H Mino RCAF	Air Gunner	+

20/21 MAR **PD425 PG-T** **LANCASTER MK I**

Took off at 2347 from Strubby as part of an entirely 5 Group force to attack the synthetic-oil installation at Böhlen, near Leipzig, an attack that devastated the plant and finally put it out of production. S/L Palmer, a Rhodesian, was gaining operational experience on attachment to 619 Squadron, prior to posting to No 44 Sqn. He and four members of his crew, most starting a second tour, were killed. Two were taken pow. The Flight Engineer, F/O Ricketts, had been awarded his DFM during a tour with 625 Sqn. The navigator, F/L Raw was 35, well above the usual age for operational aircrew by this stage of the War. The five dead are buried at Hannover War Cemetery.

Casualties:	S/L CM Palmer	Pilot	+
	F/O FJ Ricketts DFM	Flight Engineer	+
	F/L LC Raw	Navigator	+
	F/O DI Thomas	Air Bomber	pow
	F/L WF Graham	W/Op	+
	Sgt GRJ Miles	Air Gunner	pow
	Sgt PC Wiseman	Air Gunner	+

During March 1945, No 619 Squadron had participated in twelve operations, ten of a tactical nature and in direct support of the ground forces. In the process it had flown 178 sorties in 1,159.24 hours of operational flying, dropped 720 tons of bombs and lost five aircraft [but only four crews].

It is clear that by now the Allies had domination of the air, though on the longer trips to such distant targets as the oil refinery at *Böhlen*, near Leipzig, there remained a significant danger to the bomber crews, and losses still occurred. If anyone thought that the Luftwaffe was now a spent force, they were soon disabused of this idea when on the night of 3rd/4th March the Luftwaffe launched Operation *Unternehmen Gisela*. Close on 200 night-fighter intruders were sent that night by the Luftwaffe across the North Sea to lie in wait for returning bomber aircraft and to shoot them down when they attempted to land at home airfields. At least nineteen and possibly more bombers were brought down in this way, but at a high cost to the Luftwaffe, which lost twenty-five night fighters [not, it has to be said, so much as to RAF or allied guns as to the natural consequences, and technical and other hazards, of operating at night deep into hostile enemy territory, something RAF Bomber Command had also learned to its cost in 1943/44]. By contrast, when during the 1,000 bomber raid on *Essen* on 11th March F/O Hooker and his crew had got into difficulties and been obliged to land near *Brussels*, though the aircraft was written off, they were back at Strubby and on operations again within three days, something that would have been unthinkable even a year previously. It is also clear that the RAF supply chain for aircraft, aircrew, armaments and fuel was now functioning in a way the Luftwaffe could only dream about. During March 619 Squadron had lost four crews but had gained ten [plus two on attachment for operational experience before being posted to other squadrons]. The Luftwaffe had started with a considerable advantage, but through poor leadership and bad management it had forfeited its head start and was now rapidly losing the battle. Clearly, it was now only a matter of time, and the end was in sight.

The first attack of the month was against that old favourite, the *Dortmund-Ems Kanal*, on 3rd March. This was another all-5 Group attack, involving 212 Lancasters and 7 Mosquitoes, this time against the *Ladbergen aqueduct* of the Dortmund-Ems Kanal. The aqueduct was breached in two places and put out of use. No 619 Squadron contributed 15 aircraft, including two detailed for a Gardening operation at the southern end of the Oslo Fjord. Seven Lancasters were lost, but all of 619's got back safely, although PB590 PG-O [F/O GM Proctor RNZAF] had an engine knocked out of its mounting by flak and RA527 PG-M [F/O R Dickinson] lost the use of an engine when its radiator was hit by flak over the target. W/C Birch's gunners in aircraft PD441 PG-B, Sgt JD Longworth and Sgt EM Martin, claimed a flying bomb shot down near the target area. It was probably aimed at the port of Antwerp. On return to base, enemy intruders were active, and although all the aircraft got down safely, the airfield was badly shot-up.

The 5th March night saw another attack on the synthetic-oil plant at *Böhlen*, near Leipzig, and once again it was an entirely 5 Group operation, with 248 Lancasters and 10 Mosquitoes taking part. The target was covered by cloud, and the crews had difficulty seeing the wanganuis ordered by the Master Bomber. One of 619 Squadron's captains brought his bombs back because he had been unable to see the target, but some damage was done to the plant. Four Lancasters were lost, but all of 619's eighteen got back safely. The aircraft had had to climb to 15,000 ft on the way to the target to get above ice-producing cloud, and four aircraft sustained damage to the Perspex from ice flying off the propellers. Two aircraft had trouble with flak.

On 6th March, No 5 Group attacked the port, harbour installations and shipping at *Sassnitz* on the island of *Rügen* with a force of 191 Lancasters and 7 Mosquitoes. Considerable damage was caused to the northern end of the town and three ships were sunk. No aircraft were lost. No 619 Sqn contributed 13 aircraft [it should have been 14, but F/L GMS McMorran RCAF in NG286 PG-Y was unable to take off because the rear turret was completely unserviceable and the aircraft also had a substantial oil leak]. F/O CP Sparkes RNZAF in PB699/G PG-Z was obliged to return early with the starboard outer engine feathered. The attack was only partially successful because of late arrivals, caused by a change in wind strength, and cloud obscuring the TIs. One 619 Squadron captain brought his bomb load back. Three of 619's aircraft successfully laid mines in the area of the target. With the completion of this operation, two captains completed their tour of ops [F/O K Hickmott RCAF and F/O GM Proctor RNZAF].

The next night, 7th March, No 5 Group once again returned in force to the oil installation at *Harburg*, this time with 234 Lancaster aircraft and 7 Mosquitoes. It was an accurate attack, but 12 Lancasters were lost, including two from No 619 Squadron and four from No 189 Squadron, which had lost a similar number on the *Karlsruhe* operation on 2 February, only a month previously. F/O ET Pennell's crew in NG503 PG-W claimed an Me410 shot down. The missing 619 aircraft were NG286 PG-Y [F/L GMS McMorran RCAF] and PB699/G PG-Z [F/O CP Sparkes RNZAF]. Four of McMorran's crew survived as POWs but all of Sparkes' crew were killed.

On 11 March, Bomber Command returned to strategic bombing with a 1,000 bomber daylight raid on the city of *Essen*. No 619 Sqn contributed 15 aircraft, all taking off at around noon. There was little opposition and despite 10/10ths cloud over the target 4,661 tons of bombs were dropped onto *Essen* accurately by *Oboe*-directed sky markers. The Sqn ORB records that it was thought to have been a successful raid, and that the controller [Master Bomber] had directed the bombers onto red and blue puffs of smoke over the target. It was also the largest number of aircraft sent on a raid so far – 1,079, including 750 Lancasters! This was the last raid of the War on *Essen*, which was now in ruins, despite earlier raids having often produced disappointing and costly results. *Essen's* pre-War population of 648,000 had fallen to 310,000 by the end of the War, almost half having left for quieter parts. No 619 Sqn's missing aircraft was LM207 PG-E [F/O Hooper], which was wrecked in Belgium on the outward leg while attempting to land at *Evere* airfield and overshot the runway, fortunately without loss of life. The ORB records the aircraft as having landed at 1510 whereas the rest of the aircraft landed at around 1700. Presumably 1510 was the time down in Belgium. The ORB also states that: '*the attack was of great tactical value to our Western Front Armies in blocking communications behind the German front*'. The same evening, three crews planted 'vegetables' in *Oslo Fjord.* All returned safely.

The following day, 12th March, Bomber Command returned to *Dortmund.* This was another raid of great tactical significance. This time, 1,108 aircraft took part in a daylight raid and only two were lost. Another record tonnage of bombs was dropped – 4,851 tons – and again the result was devastating. A post-War survey reported '*The final raid...stopped production so effectively that it would have been many months before any substantial recovery could have occurred*' [Webster and Frankland, *The Strategic Air Offensive against Germany 1939-45* HMSO 1961 Vol III p.264]. The sixteen aircraft of 619 Sqn all got back safely but PD441 PG-B [F/O FW Seazell, on his first operation as captain] had its starboard outer petrol tank removed by a bomb dropped by a Halifax flying overhead near the target.

Two nights later, on 14th March, No 5 Group returned to tactical operations with a night attack on a synthetic-oil refinery at *Lützkendorf*, near Leipzig, involving 244 Lancasters and 11 Mosquitoes. Photo reconnaissance later suggested that moderate damage had occurred. Eighteen Lancasters were lost [7.4%], proving that even at this late stage of the War bombing distant targets was still a risky business. The early return was PA180 PG-G [F/O WD Cowling RCAF], from which the front escape hatch had blown off. Because of deteriorating weather the other aircraft were directed on return to land at *RAF Upwood.*

On 16th March, No 5 Group visited the city of *Würzburg* with another entirely 5 Group operation, involving 225 Lancasters and 11 Mosquitoes. No 619 Sqn contributed 15 aircraft to what turned out to be another devastating attack, the briefing and take-off in late afternoon being watched by officers from the RAF Staff College. 1,127 tons of bombs were dropped in only 17 minutes and a post-War survey suggested that 89% of this old cathedral city had been destroyed. Six Lancasters were lost, including 619's NG503 PG-W [F/O TE Farrow RCAF on his third operational trip] and two of 619's aircraft came back on only three engines [F/O GG Runnalls in LM657 PG-Q; and F/L JW May in NN751 PG-H]. The early return, in LM649 PG-P with the port outer engine unserviceable, was S/L CM Palmer, a Rhodesian attached to the Sqn for operational experience.

On the 20th March, the Squadron sent fifteen aircraft, all taking off just before midnight, as part of another entirely 5 Group affair, comprising of 224 Lancasters and 11 Mosquitoes. The target was once again the synthetic-oil installation at *Böhlen*, near Leipzig. This accurate attack finally put the plant out of action, and it was still out of action when captured by American troops several weeks later. Nine Lancasters were lost including 619's PD425 PG-T [S/L CM Palmer, the Rhodesian on attachment to 619 for operational experience]. Palmer came from Marandellas in Southern Rhodesia. He and four members of his crew were killed, the other two being taken POW. His Flight Engineer, F/O FJ Ricketts DFM had been decorated on a previous tour with 625 Sqn, and his navigator, F/L LC Raw, at the age of 35 was above the usual age for operational aircrew by this stage of the War. Another new pilot got back safely, however. LM657 PG-Q, piloted by F/S DR Irvine RCAF on his first trip as captain, was holed by a fighter attack but got back safely to base, landing 1¼ hours after the others. F/S Irvine was in the RCAF and his crew contained three other Canadians and three RAF. F/O NA Gampe RAAF in PB590 PG-O returned early with the starboard inner engine feathered.

The following night, 21st March, the squadron sent twelve aircraft as part of the force of 151 Lancasters and 5 Mosquitoes used in another entirely 5 Group attack, this time against enemy oil supplies, the target being the *Deutsche Erdölwerke refinery* near *Hamburg*. The attack was again devastatingly accurate with twenty petrol storage tanks destroyed, so much so that they were still out of action at the War's end. Some of the bombs fell, however, on the *Wilhelmsburg* district of *Hamburg* and thirty-one German civilians were killed, together with about a hundred foreign workers whose camp was hit. F/O AR Whittaker in NN751 PG-H lost an engine as he crossed the Danish coast on the outward leg but continued the attack on three engines and got back safely, an hour after the others.

On the evening of 23rd March, No 619 Sqn despatched 14 aircraft as part of an attack by Nos 5 and 8 [PFF] Groups with 195 Lancasters and 23 Mosquitoes against the town of *Wesel*, in direct tactical support of the 21st Army Group. The Sqn ORB records that the attack was carried out in bright moonlight and was entirely successful as the Army was seen to be crossing the river and to take the town against only feeble opposition. The *Stadt Wesel* claims to have been the most bombed town of its size in the entire war. It is said that 97% of the buildings were destroyed and that a population of 35,000 in 1939 had fallen to 1,900 by 1945. No aircraft were lost this night.

This turned out to be the last operation of the month for 619 Squadron. On 25 March, the Station Commander, G/Capt John Jeudwine, who as a wing commander had commanded No 619 Squadron from December 1943 to May 1944, gave aircrew a talk about operations in the Far East up until the fall of Java. One wonders whether he told them the interesting story of his leadership in the escape from the island of Java to the northern coast of Australia in an open boat with other members of his squadron, which in recent years has been re-told in vivid detail by Alain Charpentier, Lionel Lacey-Johnson and Geoffrey Jeudwine in their book '*Global Warrior, the Story of Group Captain JR Jeudwine DSO OBE DFC*' [published by L Lacey-Johnson, 1999].

The following day the Squadron was on standby for tactical support to the ground forces, but in the event were not called upon. On the 27th March, F/L Fox gave a lecture in the afternoon on the subject of the interrogation of German prisoners, and W/C MA Smith DFC,[28] a Master Bomber from RAF Coningsby and former flight commander on 619 Squadron, gave a talk on target marking.

The weather, either at base or over the Continent, precluded any further operations from the 28th March to the end of the month, and so on 31st '*the Squadron Commander addressed all aircrew on general matters pertaining to the Squadron*',[29] and they then made good use of their time, in traditional air force manner, by moving themselves and their

[28] W/C Maurice Smith, formerly of 619 Sqn, who after the War was Editor of Flight International.

[29] ORB entry for 31 March 1945.

kit from No 6 Site to Nos 1 and 5 Sites, '*so as all to get the whole of the Squadron onto those two sites*'.

And so began the last full month of the War.

10/11 APR **SW254 PG-S** **LANCASTER MK I**

Took off at 1831 from Strubby as part of a small Nos 5 and 8 Groups force to attack the *Wahren railway yards at Leipzig*, one of eleven aircraft despatched by 619 Sqn. Crashed at Löberitz roughly 20 km NE of Halle. The pilot and five of the crew were killed. Barely a month previously the pilot's brother had been killed on ops with 619 Squadron, the only brothers so far as is known to die with the Squadron. The rear gunner was an ex-Apprentice Clerk. The six who died are buried in the Berlin 1939-45 War Cemetery. Though not unique, it was unusual to have a crew of six officers, including both gunners.

Casualties:	F/L AE McMorran RCAF	Pilot	+
	F/L F Jackson	Flight Engineer	+
	F/L BA Williamson RCAF	Navigator	+
	F/S HJ Burke	Air Bomber	pow
	F/O FM Jackson RAAF	W/Op	+
	P/O JW Chambers	Air Gunner	+
	P/O CTW Perring	Air Gunner	+

25 APR 45 **LM756 PG-F** **LANCASTER MK III**

Took off at 0419 from Strubby for Berchtesgaden, part of a force of 359 Lancasters and 16 Mosquitoes of Nos 1, 5 and 8 Groups sent to attack the SS Barracks at *Eagle's Nest*, Hitler's mountain retreat in Bavaria. Only two aircraft were lost, one of them sadly Fg Off DeMarco and crew, on his 29th operation. For 619 and most of Bomber Command this was the last operational bombing mission of the War. Three of the crew survived as POWs.

Casualties:	Fg Off VT DeMarco RCAF	Pilot	+
	Sgt PJ Cole	Flight Engineer	pow
	WO2 NH Johnstone RCAF	Navigator	+
	F/S AH Shannon	Air Bomber	pow
	F/S JW Speers RCAF	W/Op	pow
	Sgt EW Norman	Air Gunner	+
	WO2 GV Walker RCAF	Air Gunner	+

During April 1945, the Squadron participated in ten operations, flying 118 sorties in 845.59 hours of operational flying and dropping 592 tons of bombs. In the process they lost two experienced pilots and crews: F/L AE McMorran RCAF, the brother of the pilot lost barely a month previously, and F/O WT DeMarco RCAF, who was on his 29th mission and was killed on the last major Bomber Command operation of the war.

On 4th April, the Squadron had despatched eighteen aircraft at 0600 hours as part of a mainly 5 Group operation [243 Lancasters and 1 Mosquito of No 5 Group and 8 Mosquitoes from No 8 PFF Group] for a daylight attack on German troop concentrations at *Nordhausen*. The German barracks and the town were badly damaged. The previous day 247 Lancasters and 8 Mosquitoes of No 1 and No 8 Groups had taken part in a similar raid on *Nordhausen*. Unfortunately, the barracks housed a large number of concentration camp prisoners who worked in the underground tunnels and workshops, and many were killed. The complex of tunnels and workshops had been constructed to house the rocket-research establishment following the successful raid against *Peenemünde* in August 1943 [in which operation No 619 Squadron had participated, losing three of its aircraft including that of its founding CO]. It is not known how many people were killed, but those who died were above ground, the survivors all being in the tunnels which acted as air raid shelters.

On the night of 7/8 April, No 5 Group attacked the power station and benzol plant at *Molbis*, near Leipzig, with a force of 175 Lancasters and 11 Mosquitoes. No aircraft were lost. No 619 Squadron contributed 14 aircraft, that figure having been reduced from the original 20 ordered earlier in the day by the simple expedient of removing from the list the least experienced crews. This was the first operation carried out from Strubby by both No 619 and No 227 Squadron, which was now based with the Squadron from which it had been spawned, and the use of the airfield by the two squadrons worked out well. On completion of this operation, F/O GG Runnals completed his tour of ops, the number of trips required for a tour to be satisfied having been reduced to 33. [It had originally been 30 but as the war progressed, and 'easier' targets became available following the Allied occupation of much of Europe, Bomber Command had decreed that some ops would only count as a third; there was an outcry, and the result was this compromise, though it will have been noted that there was still an appreciable risk in flying an ungainly heavy bomber loaded with fuel and bombs over enemy territory, particularly at night, and this persisted until the cease-fire].

On the night of 8/9 April, 231 Lancasters and 11 Mosquitoes of No 5 Group revisited the oil installation at *Lützkendorf*, and the refinery was put out of action. Six Lancasters were lost, but all 619's seventeen got back safely, though thick fog at the base meant a diversion to *RAF Abingdon*. Two aircraft [F/O FA Smith and W/O AV Potter] that got back close enough to call up base were diverted to *RAF Fulbeck*. F/O AR Taylor in LM657 PG-Q reported a combat over the target, and his rear gunner [Sgt DR Stirling] claimed a Me110 destroyed, as it was seen to spin into the ground. Two of the aircraft that had landed at Abingdon had to be left there when the others returned the following day, both because engine changes were needed, one [F/O JS Hunter RAAF in RA527 PG-M] having lost an engine soon after bombing.

On the night of 10/11th April, No 619 Sqn despatched eleven aircraft as part of a small No 5 and No 8 Groups force of 79 Lancasters and 19 Mosquitoes to attack the *Wahren railway yards at Leipzig*. Seven Lancasters were lost, including 619's SW254 PG-S [captain F/L AE McMorran RCAF, whose brother had been killed with the Squadron barely a month previously]. The eastern half of the yards was destroyed. This aircraft was one of 37 Lancasters built by Metropolitan Vickers and assembled by A.V. Roe between 24 Nov 44 and 22 Dec 45, with Merlin 24 engines. It says something about the state of the War that by the time this batch of aircraft came into service in early 1945, the danger of an aircraft being lost on ops had receded sufficiently that only three of the 37 were lost in this way, sadly SW254 being one of them. McMorran and five members of his crew died, only one [the Air Bomber, F/S HJ Burke] surviving as a POW. The dead rear gunner was P/O CTW Perring, an ex-apprentice [Ruislip Apprentice Clerk, 591253] who had enlisted in the 48th Entry at the age of 15 on 28 July

1937 and was 23 at the time of his death. His wife, Lilian Kathleen Perring, lived in Worthing, Surrey, and he is buried in the Berlin CWGC Cemetery. Of the 2,080 boys who enlisted as Apprentice Clerks between 1925 and 1942, when the scheme was put into mothballs following the evacuation of the RAF Record Office, where they were trained, from Ruislip to Gloucester, 455 of them served as aircrew, 318 were awarded decorations and 276 died in action or in active service. Of the 2,080, 819 were commissioned, four reaching air rank, and 1,061 reached warrant officer or SNCO rank. The author joined the RAF in the post-war 27th Entry of Administrative Apprentices in 1956, with the Apprentice Clerk number 593110, the apprentice clerk scheme having re-started in 1947. Many of the immediate pre-war apprentice clerks had to wait several years before being accepted as aircrew, because as one famous war-time Air Officer Commanding-in-Chief put it '*we can get as many aircrew as we like and train them quicker than we can get good trained clerks*' [*The 2080 Record of Service*, published privately by the Apprentice Clerk Association].

On 14/15 April 500 Lancasters and 12 Mosquitoes of Nos 1, 3 and 8 Groups had attacked *Potsdam*, the first time Bomber Command had entered the Berlin defence zone since March 1944, but with much of the Continent now in the hands of the Allies a safer route to and from the target could be flown and only one Lancaster was lost, falling victim to a night fighter, an amazing contrast with the situation during the winter of 1943/44 when squadrons like 619 were losing numerous aircraft and crews on an almost nightly basis as the Battle of Berlin had been waged. This was to prove to be the last raid of the war by Bomber Command on a German city. The aiming point was the centre of *Potsdam*, where the old German guards regiments had their depot and there were important railway yards. The raid was reasonably successful, as the author can testify from his own post-Cold War visits to *Potsdam*. Some bombs fell on northern and eastern districts of *Berlin*.

On 16/17th April, No 5 Group sent 222 Lancasters and 11 Mosquitoes on a precision attack against the railway yards at *Pilsen*. One Lancaster crashed in France. All of 619's fourteen aircraft reached the target, bombed and got back safely, though one [ME787 PG-X captain F/O JS Hunter RAAF] returned early with the port inner engine u/s.

On 17/18 April, 90 Lancasters and 11 Mosquitoes of No 5 Group attacked the railway yards at *Cham*, deep into eastern Europe and on the border with Czechoslovakia. The attack was once again devastatingly successful with track and rolling stock destroyed. No 619 Squadron despatched seventeen aircraft but one [ME787 PG-X captain F/L RJ Willitts] had to return early, this time with the port outer engine u/s. All the Group's aircraft returned safely. F/L GA Lavigne RCAF in RA521 PG-D returned with an engine feathered and F/O AP Reid RNZAF flew this operation in a borrowed No 227 Sqn aircraft [LM578].

After 17/18th April, there were no operations again until the daylight raid to *Flensburg* on the 23rd. In between various sessions of training, inspections and aircraft cleaning were arranged, with the HQ 5 Group Naval Liaison Officer, Lt Cdr Murdock, giving a talk on 'mining', which the ORB records was well attended and well received.

On 23rd, the Squadron provided twelve aircraft towards the 148 Lancasters No 5 Group despatched to attack the railway yards and port area of *Flensburg*. The raid was planned in two waves, with the 55 Base aircraft led by No 619 Squadron, flying behind 53 Base aircraft, and having as their aiming point a railway junction. Weather conditions were good until ten miles from the target when cloud conditions prevented bombing and the raid was called off, the aircraft returning to base with their bombs as instructed. With this operation, F/O GS Hatten completed his tour of ops.

On the 24th April, a Gardening effort for five aircraft was ordered but cancelled only two hours before take off. The Squadron was then ordered to prepare six aircraft for an attack on the SS Barracks at *Berchtesgaden*, Hitler's 'Eagle's Nest' Bavarian mountain retreat. The six were to be part of an attack by 80 other aircraft of 5 Group, including sixteen 617 Sqn aircraft dropping their last Tallboys.

The bomb load for the 619 Sqn aircraft was 1,000 lb M.C. bombs[30], and the briefing was in the early morning with a take-off time of 0410 hours. The attack took place in fine weather but with hazy conditions, and the crews found it difficult to observe the results. Eight *Oboe*-equipped Mosquitoes led the attack to assist with the marking, but the mountains around the target interrupted the *Oboe* signals and the Mosquitoes could not be used even though they were flying at 39,000 feet. Mist and the presence of snow on the ground also made accurate bombing difficult. Nonetheless, the bombing was thought to have been accurate [the Eagle's Nest was raised to the ground by American ground troops a couple of weeks later], and much of the Barracks are thought to have been destroyed. Within the Squadron, opinion was divided as to the effectiveness of the attack and as to the amount of opposition met. Flak was generally thought to have been moderate but accurate for height. No fighters were encountered, but, just in case, the attack was supported by three groups of American fighters.

The crews detailed by 619 Squadron were S/L PS Osborne [PG-A], F/O KR Taylor [PG-K], F/O NA Gampe RAAF [PG-O], F/O ET Pennells RCAF [PG-R], F/O G Greenway [PG-Y] and F/O VT DeMarco RCAF [PG-F]. The aircraft captained by Flying Officers Pennells and Greenway were slightly damaged by flak, and Greenway suffered slight injuries. LM756 PG-F with Flying Officer VT DeMarco RCAF and his crew failed to return, however. They were on their 29th sortie. And so, as this story began with the discovery of one PG-F [EE109] in1977, so it finishes with the last 619 Squadron aircraft loss of the War: another PG-F, [LM756].

This was to prove the last raid of the War for most of Bomber Command, and it was appropriate that the target should have been Hitler's mountain retreat in Bavaria, *Eagle's Nest*. The operation involved 359 Lancasters and 16 Mosquitoes of Nos 1, 5 and 8 Groups, including sixteen aircraft of No 617 Squadron dropping their last *Tallboy* bombs. The Master Bomber was W/C Maurice Smith, formerly

---

[30] Medium Capacity bombs with 30 minute delay fuses. These bombs looked like real bombs in that they had pointed noses and tails fins, whereas the more usual High Capacity [HC] or 'blast' bombs looked like large oil drums.

a flight commander on No 619 Squadron. No 619 despatched six crews, including F/O DeMarco. He was killed, along with three other members of his crew. Three survived as POWs.

Finally, that same night, a mine-laying operation was laid on to the *Oslo Fjord*, and No 619 Squadron sent four aircraft. Two of the four aircraft had to abort, one because the mine would not release, and the other with a faulty H2S set. One of the two successful mine drops was by F/L JH Johnston RCAF in RA521 PG-D, who with this mission thereby completed his tour of operations. The other was by F/O AP Reid RNZAF, in PA198 PG-J. When he landed back at Strubby at 0241 on 26th April, 1945, for No 619 Squadron the shooting war was over, and after 23 months of frenetic activity it had flown its last mission with hostile intent. In all the Squadron had dropped about 14,500 tons of bombs [no full accurate record exists], flown about 18,500 operational hours on just over 3,000 sorties, lost 85 aircraft and almost 500 men killed in action and won 125 awards for gallantry and duty.

Five days later, on 1st May, the Squadron was warned to have six aircraft ready for an early take off as part of *Operation Exodus* to collect former Allied prisoners of war, mainly Air Force, from *Moelsbroek* airfield, Brussels. This it did, bringing the former prisoners back to Wescott airfield in Oxfordshire. Before the end of the War, a few days later, a total of 469 flights had already been made by Bomber Command, and No 619 alone ferried 1,080 former prisoners back to England by the end of May, part of the staggering total of 75,000 men brought back by the quickest possible means within a month of the War ending. This contrasts with the situation in 1918 when many men were still not back by Christmas, but then, of course, there were no heavy bombers available for ready adaptation into the transport-trooping role. As soon as the uplift of prisoners of war had been completed, like other squadrons, No 619 began a series of '*bomb inspection damage tours*' by flying crews, and particularly ground crews, over Germany to see the devastation that had been wreaked on that country by the RAF and the USAAF, because of the egomania of a little Austrian corporal. For obvious reasons, these tours of inspection soon became known as *Cooks Tours*. At the same time, Bomber Command was heavily involved in getting supplies, especially food, to the former occupied countries, much of which had been ravaged by the ground battles following the Normandy landings ten months previously. In the part of Holland by-passed by the ground troops in the rush for the Rhine and Berlin, people were literally starving, and drops of food – *Operation Manna* - and other essentials were arranged, a truce being called by the German commander, to permit the drops to be made. During late April and the end of May some 6,672 tons of aid was delivered in this way.

The last Bomber Command losses occurred on 2/3rd May when two Halifax aircraft of 199 Squadron, No 100 [RCM] Group, each with eight men on board were lost while supporting Mosquito aircraft attacking Kiel. There were only three survivors from these sixteen men. The bomber war was now at an end.

On 30 April, 1945 Hitler committed suicide in his bunker in Berlin just off Wilhelmstrasse, near the Unter Den Linden, handing over the leadership to Admiral Dönitz, who was in the Keil-Flensburg area. On 4 May German officers came to Montgomery's Tactical Headquarters [21st Army Group] on Lüneburg Heath and signed the surrender document, effective from the following day. Following the collapse of the Soviet Union and the ending of the Cold War the part of the city of Berlin that had housed the Chancellory, the bunker and much of the departments of Government became open once more,[31] and the author was able to visit the site of Fascist megalomania. Today, a children's nursery stands on the site of the Chancellory, a much more savoury use of this part of a lovely city. Ironically, the one building that survived the bombing of Berlin relatively unscathed was the fabulous Air Ministry created by Göring, his grandiose vision at one time having taken in a

[31] This part of Berlin was in the Soviet-occupied zone, and though a mound of rubble was visible in the no-man's land visible from the West [and could be viewed from within the East when on official visits, escorted by the RAF Police from the P & SS Detachment at RAF Gatow], it was not until the fall of the Wall that a close-up inspection could be made.

building so large that an aircraft would be able to land on its flat roof. In this extravagance, of course, he competed with other members of the Nazi leadership, and we all now know of Albert Speer's plans for a domed Great Hall so large that it would have had its own internal climate and rainfall.[32] It was against this megalomania that the 55,573 dead of Bomber Command had fought...

> *'in an unselfish sacrifice made by thousands of young men, who came from all corners of the British Empire and from the occupied countries, to help grind out a painstakingly hard-fought struggle against a tyrannical regime'.*[33]

[32] For more information read Robert Harris' *Fatherland* [Arrow Books Limited 1993].

[33] W R Chorley, quoted on the back cover of *RAF Bomber Command Losses,* Vol 6 [Midland Counties Publications, 1998].

Table 4.1 The Phonetic Alphabet

A	Apple/Able	N	Nuts/Nab or Negat
B	Beer/Baker	O	Orange/Oboe
C	Charlie	P	Peter/Prep or Peter
D	Dog	Q	Queen
E	Edward/Easy	R	Roger/Robert or Roger
F	Freddie/Fox	S	Sugar
G	George	T	Tommy/Tare
H	Harry/How	U	Uncle
I	In/Item	V	Vic/Victor
J	Jug or Johnny/Jig or Johnny	W	William
K	King	X	X-ray
L	Love	Y	Yoke or Yoke/Yorker
M	Mother/Mike	Z	Zebra

Note: where two or more words are given, the first [to the left of the oblique stroke] was/were used until 1943 and the second from 1943 until 1956, when the current phonetics were introduced, though there were unofficial and idiosyncratic variances within squadrons.

Table 4.2 Commanding Officers of No 619 Squadron from April 1943 to July 1945

W/Cdr	I J	McGhie DFC	[32201][1]	20.4.43 to 17.8.43	[killed in action]
W/Cdr	W	Abercromby DFC and Bar	[44971][2]	20.8.43 to 4.12.43	[killed in action]
W/Cdr	J R	Jeudwine DSO OBE DFC[3]		4.12.43 to 22.5.44	[killed 19.10.45]
W/Cdr	J R	Maling AFC[4]		23.5.44 to 26.7.44	[POW 26.7.44]
W/Cdr	A R	Milward DFC and Bar	[37201][5]	28.7.44 to 21.2.45	
W/Cdr	S G	Birch DFC	[34120][6]	22.2.45 to 14.6.45	
W/Cdr	S E	Flett	[SR80042][7]	14.6.45 to 18.7.45	

[1] W/C McGhie, the founding CO, was killed on the Peenemünde raid on 17/18 Aug 43.

[2] W/C Abercromby was killed on 1/2 Jan 44 soon after leaving the Sqn to join No 83 [PFF] Sqn.

[3] W/C Jeudwine went on to be a Master Bomber and G/Capt station commander of RAF Strubby and RAF Little Staughton. He was killed on 19 Oct 45 while flying a single seat Typhoon 1B from Little Staughton.

[4] W/C Maling was shot down on 25/26 Jul 44 while on an operation to Stuttgart. He and three of his crew were taken POW, but three were killed.

[5] W/C Milward survived to complete his second tour of operations and has written to the author about this book.

[6] W/C Birch retired from the RAF as G/Capt MVO OBE. He died in 1979.

[7] W/C Flett, a Rhodesian, commanded the Squadron for its final month, during which it moved to Skellingthorpe and then disbanded a fortnight later. He joined No 44 [Rhodesia] Sqn, which in the 1960s flew Vulcan nuclear bombers from RAF Waddington as part of the 'V' Force.

Table 4.3 Operations in which No. 619 Sqn participated during 23 months of operational life

Date	*Target*	*Aircraft*			
		prepared	*took off*	*Ret early*	*missing*
11 Jun 43	Düsseldorf	12	12	-	1
12 Jun 43	Bochum	12	12	1	-
14 Jun 43	Oberhausen	6	6	-	1
20 Jun 43	Friedrichshaven[1]	5	5	-	-
21 Jun 43	Krefeld	7	7	1	1
22 Jun 43	Mulheim	5	5	-	-
23 Jun 43	Spezia	5	5	-	-
24 Jun 43	Wuppertal	9	9	1	-
25 Jun 43	Gelsenkirchen[2]	7	7	2	-
28 Jun 43	Köln	12	12	-	1
1 Jul 43	Gardening[3]	6	6	-	-
3 Jul 43	Köln	11	11	1	-
8 Jul 43	Köln	13	13	1	-
9 Jul 43	Gelsenkirchen	8	8	1	-
12 Jul 43	Turin[4]	11	11	-	-
24 Jul 43	Hamburg[5]	16	16	-	-
25 Jul 43	Essen	15	15	-	-
29 Jul 43	Hamburg	12	12	-	-
30 Jul 43	Remscheid	4	4	-	-
2 Aug 43	Hamburg[6]	14	14	2	-

---

[1] Sgt May, the bomb aimer in F/S McLeod's aircraft was killed by flak.

[2] It was on this op that Sgt Fuller and crew, flying in EE149 PG-U, were badly hit by flak but got back to base. The aircraft was crash-landed and written off.

[3] 'Gardening' was the codename for dropping anti-shipping mines in German coastal waters. In this case the mines were dropped in area Nectarine I [the Friesian Islands].

[4] On this raid a Ju88 was claimed [and confirmed] as shot down by the crew of EE106 PG-E, pilot F/L SEJ Jones DFM, mid-upper gunner Sgt G Cook, rear gunner P/O P Cartwright DFM.

[5] The first of the four raids on Hamburg known as Operation Gomorrah in which 8,620 tons of bombs were dropped on that city starting the fire-storm which has since made the name of Hamburg synonymous with death and destruction. For a full account of these raids read Martin Middlebrook's superbly researched book *The Battle of Hamburg* [first published Allen Lane 1980].

TABLE 4.3 OPERATIONS IN WHICH 619 SQN PARTICIPATED

Date	*Target*	*Aircraft*			
		prepared	*took off*	*Ret early*	*missing*
7 Aug 43	Milan[7]	10	10	-	-
9 Aug 43	Mannheim[8]	14	14	-	-
10 Aug 43	Nürnberg[9]	14	14	1	1
12 Aug 43	Milan	12	12	-	1
14 Aug 43	Milan[10]	6	6	-	-
15 Aug 43	Milan[11]	8	8	-	-
17 Aug 43	Peenemünde[12]	12	12	-	3
22 Aug 43	Leverkusen[13]	9	9	-	-
23 Aug 43	Berlin[14]	10	10	1	1
27 Aug 43	Nürnberg[15]	12	12	1	-
30 Aug 43	Mönchen Gladbach[16]	14	14	1	-

---

[6] The conditions this night were atrocious with severe icing, electrical storms and thick cloud. S/L Scorer jettisoned because of icing on his aircraft, F/O Joss after being hit by flak, and two other a/c returned early.

[7] Although all the Squadron's aircraft reached the target, bombed and returned safely, on the return journey the port inner engine of F/L Jones's aircraft caught fire and had to be feathered.

[8] The ORB records that several crews during debriefing said they had seen other aircraft being shot down. Large fires were seen from up to 150 miles away, and F/S Taylor had an aiming point photograph.

[9] The New Zealander F/L E Dampier-Crossley DFC RAAF, an experienced pilot, and his crew, were lost on this raid.

[10] A large explosion was noticed by crews at the Breda Works and F/S Taylor and F/L Aytoun had aiming point photographs.

[11] Six aiming point photographs were achieved by the eight crews of 619 Squadron.

[12] This was the night of the famous raid on the Experimental Rocket Establishment at Peenemünde, when G/Capt John Searby, an ex-Halton apprentice and pre-war NCO pilot, acted as Master Bomber. It was 619's worst night so far in nine weeks of operations, with three aircraft lost including that of its Commanding Officer, W/C John McGhie.

[13] The Squadron was led by its new Commanding Officer, W/C W [Jock] Abercromby, in this attack against the Chemical Factory at Leverkusen. The target was covered with 10/10ths cloud, but crews reported seeing a red glow through the clouds.

[14] Led by the 'A'Flight Commander, S/L Ronnie Churcher. Reported as a very concentrated attack with fires visible for up to 150 miles away during the return flight.

[15] A heavy concentration of bombing reported, directed by the Master of Ceremonies, and with fires seen to be merging into one great mass later on.

Date	*Target*	*Aircraft*			
		prepared	*took off*	*Ret early*	*missing*
31 Aug 43	Berlin[17]	13	13	1	2
2 Sep 43	Gardening[18]	5	5	-	-
3 Sep 43	Berlin	13	13	3	-
5 Sep 43	Mannheim[19]	10	10	-	1
6 Sep 43	München[20]	10	10	-	-
16 Sep 43	Antheor Viaduct[21]	6	6	-	1
22 Sep 43	Hannover[22]	13	13	-	-
23 Sep 43	Mannheim	11	11	-	-
27 Sep 43	Hannover[23]	12	12	1	-

---

[16] Several fires were started which gradually met until the whole target area was reported to be 'a mass of flames'. Anyone familiar with the post-war town of Mönchen-Gladbach will know that sadly very little of the old part of the town – the Altstadt – survived the war. Fighters were seen over the target area.

[17] F/S Bower and F/S Metcalfe and crews were lost this night.

[18] Again, against Nectarine I – the Friesian Islands.

[19] FS CA Goddard and crew were lost on this operation.

[20] The diarist recorded that the debriefed 619 Sqn crews 'doubted the success of this operation'. Middlebrook and Everitt in *The Bomber Command War Diaries* [first published Viking 1985] state that the Pathfinders found München covered in cloud and that neither their sky nor ground markers were very effective. The Main Force [257 Lancasters and 147 Halifaxes] could do no more than bomb on a timed run from the Ammersee, a lake 21 miles south west of the city, and, as a consequence, the bombing was mostly scattered over the southern and western parts of the city.

[21] This was a joint raid with 617 Sqn, led by W/C Jock Abercromby, the Commanding Officer of No 619 Sqn. It was an exercise designed 'to put 617 Sqn back into the saddle' after the disastrous raid on the Dortmund-Ems Kanal the previous night when they had lost five out of eight aircraft on their first operation since the Dams raid. The six 619 Sqn crews were specially selected and, in additon to Abercromby included the two Flight Commanders, S/Ls Churcher and Scorer, the two Deputy Flight Commanders, F/Ls Jones and Aytoun and F/O WED Bell. Bell had to jettison his bomb-load because of severe icing and F/L SEJ Jones had to ditch his aircraft off the coast of Portugal after being hit by flak over the target. He and his crew were interned but returned home soon afterwards to continue ops [though the navigator, F/O AD Holding, lost his life in Jan 44 with 617 Sqn while flying with an ex-619 pilot, F/L TV O'Shaughnessy]. Four of the returning aircraft landed at Predannack in Cornwall, almost out of fuel, after more then 10 hours in the air.

[22] The first of the four raids on Hannover in late Sep/Oct 43, in the last of which P/O Cyril Fuller and his crew were lost. Without them this book would not have been written.

TABLE 4.3 OPERATIONS IN WHICH 619 SQN PARTICIPATED

Date	*Target*	*Aircraft*			
		prepared	*took off*	*Ret early*	*missing*
29 Sep 43	Bochum[24]	10	10	-	1
1 Oct 43	Hagen[25]	12	12	-	1
2 Oct 43	München	7	7	-	-
3 Oct 43	Kassel[26]	5	5	-	-
4 Oct 43	Frankfurt[27]	7	7	-	-
7 Oct 43	Stuttgart[28]	9	9	1	-
8 Oct 43	Hannover[29]	9	8	-	-
18 Oct 43	Hannover[30]	12	12	2	1

---

[23] For once the weather over the target was clear, and the crews reported huge fires on the return flight that could be seen from the Dutch coast. Woodhall was clamped in by bad weather, and the returning aircraft had to divert to other airfields, six to Stradishall and one each to Feltwell, Framlingham, Chedburgh, Wratling Common and Great Sampford. One aircraft had returned early because of severe icing.

[24] On returning from this operation, P/O E Mearis in ED983 PG-W crashed in Cadwell Hill near Manby. Four of the crew were killed and one died in hospital. The other two were severely injured.

[25] On this night F/O Joss and his crew were lost when they crashed in the Bristol Channel. A newly arrived crew, captained by P/O JF Ward in EE170 PG-N, was hit by flak in the target area, which knocked out all their turrets, and they had to jettison bombs and later guns and ammunition but got back safely.

[26] On this night the rear gunner, Sgt GH Jackson, in P/O Nick Knilans' aircraft JB131 PG-T was killed by cannon fire in combat with an enemy fighter.

[27] Returning crews reported a plume of smoke over Frankfurt to a height of 6,000 ft and the fires could be seen from 200 miles away.

[28] The crews encountered 10/10ths cloud over the target, but it was thin enough for them to be able to bomb on the TIs. The success of the bombing was difficult to assess because of the red glow on the clouds from the many fires.

[29] ED839 PG-O captained by F/O Thompson crashed on take-off. None of the crew was injured. On return seven of the remaining eight aircraft had to land Coningsby and the eighth at East Kirkby because of the state of the weather at Woodhall. This was the night of the third of the four raids on Hannover and was the only one that was successful. The weather favoured the bombers, and amongst the buildings hit were the hutted barracks of Flak Batterie 3./521 on the Sportsplatz near the Stadionbruücke over the Leine river, and the Schloss Herrenhausen in which our King George I, King George II and other Royal Princes were born. Ten days later Flak Batterie 3./521 shot down Cyril Fuller and his crew in EE109 PG-F. During the course of the four Hannover raids this Batterie alone shot down a total of 12 RAF bombers [5 Lancasters, 4 Halifaxes and 3 Stirlings].

Date	*Target*	*Aircraft*			
		prepared	*took off*	*Ret early*	*missing*
20 Oct 43	Leipzig[31]	13	13	2	1
22 Oct 43	Kassel[32]	13	13	1	-
3 Nov 43	Düsseldorf	15	15	-	-
10 Nov 43	Modane[33]	13	13	2	-
18 Nov 43	Berlin[34]	19	19	1	-
22 Nov 43	Berlin	16	16	-	-
26 Nov 43	Berlin[35]	16	16	-	4

[30] This was the raid in which Cyril Fuller and his crew were shot down and killed over the target at 20.18.

[31] P/O C Firth and his crew in EE114 PG-B were lost this night [crashing near Langwedel] and two other aircraft had to jettison their 4,000 lb bomb [and one also 7 x 30 lb incendiaries] in order to remain in the bomber stream and reach the target. Two other aircraft returned early because of (1) instrument failure, and (2) failure of both inner engines and the rear turret. On return, four aircraft landed away from base.

[32] Good visibility over the target and the crews believed it to have been a successful attack. Middlebrook and Everitt, op cit, state that this was the most devastating attack on a German city since that on Hamburg in July with results that would not be exceeded until well into 1944. The rear gunner of EE111 PG-S [captain F/S EAL Smith] claimed a FW190 shot down at 20.36. On return, four aircraft landed away from base.

[33] The target was identified not only by ground markers but also visually by a timed run from a small lake 4 miles SW of Modane. The Squadron obtained five aiming point photographs.

[34] The target was covered with 10/10ths cloud and it was impossible to judge the success of the raid. DV335 PG-H [captain F/S RW Olsen] bombed on ETA without having seen any flares; JA867 PG-X [captain P/O KJ Mears] jettisoned on the defences at Stendal, both aircraft having been damaged by flak. JB131PG-T [captain F/O JWED McGilvray] returned early following the failure of the rear turret. On return three aircraft landed away from base, two in the south east of England [Manston and West Malling].

[35] This night the squadron lost four aircraft but only two crews. F/L Tomlin DFC and crew in EE168 PG-R crashed on return at Common Fal in Yorkshire. The aircraft was destroyed by fire but no injuries were reported. F/L WED Bell and crew in EE111 PG-S abandoned the aircraft over the Humber estuary. Again, no injuries were reported. The crews of P/O KJ Mears and F/L RD Rayment in DV336 PG-U and DV381 PG-B respectively were all killed, the former while trying to land at Elvington. Nine other aircraft landed away from base. The ORB also records for the first time that Nick Knilans was flying as a Lt USAAF, having now been commissioned in the American Air Force but opted to stay with 619 Squadron. That night his aircraft [PG-] was attacked and hit by two night fighters and lost an engine on the outward journey but the crew shot down a

TABLE 4.3 OPERATIONS IN WHICH 619 SQN PARTICIPATED

Date	*Target*	*Aircraft*			
		prepared	*took off*	*Ret early*	*missing*
2 Dec 43	Berlin[36]	10	10	-	2
3 Dec 43	Leipzig[37]	7	7	-	-
16 Dec 43	Berlin[38]	15	15	-	2
20 Dec 43	Berlin	15	15	1	-
29 Dec 43	Berlin[39]	15	15	-	-
1 Jan 44	Berlin[40]	14	14	1	-
2 Jan 44	Berlin[41]	10	10	1	2
5 Jan 44	Stettin[42]	12	12	-	1
14 Jan 44	Brunswick	11	11	-	-
20 Jan 44	Berlin	13	13	1	-
21 Jan 44	Magdeburg	7	7	-	-

Ju88 and ME110 and continued the target and got back safely. For this operation Knilans was awarded an immediate DSO. Recommended by W/C Jock Abercromby and the station commander G/Capt Johnson DFC AFC on 29/30 Nov 43 [copy of the citation held by the author].

36 On this night the two missing crews were those of P/O JF Ward and F/O JF Bowyer RCAF. Six members of Ward's crew were killed and three of Bowyer's. The AOC, G/Capt Patch, G/Capt Evans-Evans, W/C John Jeudwine [soon to take over command of the squadron from Jock Abercromby] and a medical branch A/Cdre attended the debriefing, and the American war correspondent, Mr Ed Murrow, flew to Berlin on this operation with the Sqn CO, W/C Abercromby, having previously visited the squadron on 30 November. Fires were seen burning in Berlin from 150 miles away.

37 W/C Jeudwine flew as 2nd Pilot with S/L R Aytoun on this operation.

38 P/O GB Loney and his crew in JA867 PG-X were lost this night. F/L AH Tomlin's EE150 PG-F, formerly a 617 Sqn aircraft, was damaged in a fighter attack and crashed-landed on return near the airfield's outer beacon. The crew were all safe, but the aircraft was written-off.

39 On this and the previous raid on Berlin thick cloud had obscured the target and so accurate assessment of the success of the raids was difficult.

40 Once again thick cloud [10/10ths] covered the target up to 20,000 ft and the returning crews thought it had not been a success. They were right. Middlebrook and Everitt, op cit, state that a lot of the bombs fell on the Grunewald and only 21 houses and one industrial building were destroyed. LM420 PG-R [captain P/O V Langford] returned early with three engines u/s.

41 On this night P/O JAF Heffernan RCAF and his crew [JB123 PG-B] were all killed. F/O JK Cox and three of his crew in LM423 PG-H were also killed and 3 taken POW.

42 On this night the squadron's veteran aircraft, ED977 PG-A *Nulli Secundus* with F/O AG Day and his crew on board, was lost with all the crew killed.

Date	*Target*	*Aircraft*			
		prepared	*took off*	*Ret early*	*missing*
27 Jan 44	Berlin	14	14	1	-
28 Jan 44	Berlin	14	14	-	-
30 Jan 44	Berlin[43]	11	11	-	-
15 Feb44	Berlin[44]	20	20	1	1
19 Feb 44	Leipzig[45]	19	19	-	-
20 Feb 44	Stuttgart	15	15	-	-
24 Feb 44	Schweinfurt[46]	18	18	-	1
25 Feb 44	Augsburg	13	13	1	-
1 Mar 44	Stuttgart	16	16	-	-
10 Mar 44	Chateauroux	10	10	-	-
15 Mar 44	Stuttgart[47]	16	16	-	-
18 Mar 44	Frankfurt	15	15	1	-
22 Mar 44	Frankfurt	18	18	-	-
24 Mar 44	Berlin[48]	18	18	1	1
25 Mar 44	Aulnoye[49]	1	1	-	-
26 Mar 44	Essen	13	13	-	-
30 Mar 44	Nürnberg	17	16	1	-
5 Apr 44	Toulouse	15	14	1	-

[43] On these last two raids on Berlin returning crews reported that Berlin appeared to be one mass of flames and that a large orange glow was visible for 100 miles on the return trip.

[44] On this night the squadron sent 20 aircraft and 21 crews into action – a squadron record. P/O K Roberts RAAF flew a 630 Sqn aircraft from East Kirkby, which crashed on return seriously injuring the rear gunner. The missing aircraft was DV330 PG-O, with F/O RM Rumble RCAF and crew aboard. All were killed.

[45] This night 619 Sqn borrowed an aircraft from 61 Sqn in order to put 19 crews into the air.

[46] The aircraft lost this night was LM419 PG-N with F/O EK Williams RCAF and crew on board. Three died and four were taken POW.

[47] When leaving the target area, F/L K Roberts RAAF and crew encountered a Ju88 night-fighter. All six guns of the mid-upper and rear turrets ceased to function. After violent corkscrewing evasive action by the pilot, the rear gunner [F/S King RAAF] managed to get one gun working and hit the fighter, which broke off with its port engine on fire and was claimed destroyed.

[48] This night DV328 PG-L, captain P/O P Thompson RNZAF, was shot down over Teltow, near Berlin. All were seven crew were killed. They were on their second op.

[49] W/C H Y Humphreys and crew, who were attached to 619 Sqn, made this trip.

TABLE 4.3 OPERATIONS IN WHICH 619 SQN PARTICIPATED

Date	*Target*	*Aircraft*			
		prepared	*took off*	*Ret early*	*missing*
10 Apr 44	Tours[50]	18	18	1	-
11 Apr 44	Aachen[51]	16	16	-	2
18 Apr 44	Juvisy	14	14	-	-
22 Apr 44	Brunswick[52]	16	16	-	-
24 Apr 44	München[53]	15	15	-	1
26 Apr 44	Schweinfurt[54]	15	13	-	2
28 Apr 44	Oslo	10	10	1	-
1 May 44	Toulouse	12	12	-	-
3 May 44	Mailly-le-Camp[55]	12	12	-	1
7 May 44	Salbris[56]	13	13	-	1
7 May 44	Gardening	1	1	-	-
9 May 44	Gennevilliers[57]	12	12	1	1
11 May 44	Bourg-Leopold	15	15	1	-
19 May 44	Amiens	16	16	-	-
21 May 44	Duisburg[58]	15	14	2	1

[50] On this raid, W/C JR Jeudwine, the CO of 619 Sqn, acted as Master of Ceremonies [Master Bomber].

[51] The two aircraft missing were LL784 PG-W, captain S/L JWED McGilvray DFC, and EE116 PG-Q, captain F/L HJ Moore, both with five killed and two POW.

[52] JB134 PG-G, captain Sgt DA Wadsworth, was attacked by a Ju88 night-fighter. The rear gunner, SGT FH Joy, returned fire and claimed the enemy aircraft destroyed. The elevators, fuselage and rear turret of PG-G had been hit by cannon shells and splinters.

[53] The missing aircraft was ME732 PG-X, captain W/O D Schofield DFM. All the crew were killed.

[54] The missing aircraft were LL904 PG-S, captain Sgt RF Whinfield, and LL919 PG-W, captain F/L GGC Gunzi. All eight crew in Schofield's aircraft were killed, including two RCAF and one RNZAF, and six members of Gunzi's crew were killed, with one taken POW. Earlier the detail for two more aircraft had been cancelled before take off.

[55] JB134 PG-G, captain P/O DA Wadsworth DFC was lost with eight crew killed.

[56] On this night S/L FE Fuller was lost in ND730 PG-O with eight crew [2 RCAF] killed. A new crew flew a Gardening op [Nectarine I]. W/C Jeudwine was controller, and enemy fighters were encountered. F/L John Howard, the gunnery leader and now Jeudwine's rear gunner, fired 4,211 rounds of ammunition.

[57] On this night LM446 PG-H, captain P/O JM Aitken RNZAF, was lost with seven killed and one POW.

Date	*Target*	*Aircraft*			
		prepared	*took off*	*Ret early*	*missing*
22 May 44	Brunswick	15	14	1	-
27 May 44	Cherbourg	14	14	-	-
31 May 44	Maisy	12	12	-	-
2 Jun 44	Wimereux[59]	14	14	-	-
5 Jun 44	La Pernelle[60]	16	16	-	-
6 Jun 44	Caen[61]	17	17	-	1
8 Jun 44	Pontaubault	14	14	1	-
9 Jun 44	Etampes	14	14	-	-
12 Jun 44	Caen[62]	16	16	-	-
14 Jun 44	Ornay sur Odon[63]	16	16	-	-
17 Jun 44	Beauvoir[64]	17	17	-	-
21 Jun 44	Wesseling[65]	17	16	-	6
24 Jun 44	Pommereval[66]	11	11	-	-
27 Jun 44	Marquise	14	14	-	-

[58] The missing aircraft was NN695 PG-X, captain F/O RH Redshaw, shot down by an intruder over East Anglia. Six died, but one member of the crew is believed to have parachuted to safety.

[59] On this occasion as happened so often at this time when the RAF was softening up the defences for the Normandy Landings a few days later, the aircraft all reached the target successfully but returned to base without bombing, as weather precluded accurate targeting. No chances were being taken.

[60] Once again, the 619 Sqn aircraft returned without bombing.

[61] This was the operation in which LL783 PG-C, captained by F/L Roberts RAAF, was lost. The ORB includes the fascinating comment that 'all aircraft took off to attack a road and rail bridge at Caen *where our paratroops were attempting to hold up enemy attempts to attack the beachhead.*'

[62] All sixteen aircraft reached the target but five were ordered not to attack and returned with some of the bomb loads intact [the remainder jettisoned to reduce landing weight].

[63] With this operation, flight commander S/L Bill Whamond completed his second tour of operations.

[64] This was an operation against a 'pilot-less plane' [ie flying bomb] launch site.

[65] This was the Squadron's blackest night with six aircraft missing, 32 aircrew killed and 12 taken pow.

[66] On returning to base, the ORB records, some 619 Squadron aircraft had 'to orbit base for a considerable time' because a 44 Squadron aircraft had burst a tyre on landing. [No 44 Sqn shared Dunholme Lodge with No 619 until the end of September 1944 when No 44 moved to Spilsby and No 619 to Strubby].

TABLE 4.3 OPERATIONS IN WHICH 619 SQN PARTICIPATED

Date	*Target*	*Aircraft*			
		prepared	*took off*	*Ret early*	*missing*
4 Jul 44	Creil[67]	18	18	2	-
7 Jul 44	St Leu D'Esserant[68]	16	16	-	1
12 Jul 44	Culmont Chalindrey	15	15	-	-
14 Jul 44	Villeneuve	13	13	-	-
18 Jul 44	Caen[69]	18	18	-	-
18 Jul 44	Revigny[70]	13	13	-	5
20 Jul 44	Courtrai	15	15	1	-
23 Jul 44	Keil[71]	12	12	-	1
24 Jul 44	Donges[72]	9	9	-	1
24 Jul 44	Stuttgart	6	6	1	-
25 Jul 44	Stuttgart[73]	14	14	-	1

[67] This night two aircraft returned early, one [DV326 PG-P, captain P/O RT Brown] with engine trouble; the other [ND932 PG-U, captain P/O NW Donnelley RNZAF] with a seriously wounded mid-upper gunner [Sgt A Bailes] after they had been attacked by a night-fighter. Sgt Bailes was admitted to hospital but appears to have recovered from his injuries. PG-U had been attacked over the primary target and was one of a number of 619 aircraft operating that night to have been fitted with both H2S and Monica Mk V.

[68] The missing aircraft was ME745 PG-L, captained by F/L CC Johnston. He and four other members of his crew evaded capture, but his two air gunners were killed. They were one of three 619 Squadron aircraft 'shot up' that night, for two others returned with combat damage [JB186 PG-O and PB245 PG-Z, captained by F/O CWA Coop RCAF and W/O J Patterson respectively].

[69] This operation is of significance, as it was the first carried out by 619 Sqn by day, a telling marking point in the air war, and something that had been presaged in a talk given the squadron a month previously by the Sqn CO, W/C Maling. In fact, for the crews, the effect of attacking by day was much like a night operation: the results could not be assessed, as the target was obscured by smoke and ground features could not be seen.

[70] This was also the first time the Squadron had flown two missions, using mainly the same crews, on the same day. Of the 13 crews flying to Revigny, ten had participated in the daylight attack on Caen earlier in the day. All five of the crews that went missing were included in that ten. It is perhaps dangerous to jump to conclusions, but the loss of almost 40% of aircraft despatched was another black day for 619 Sqn, coming as it did only a month after the other day of disastrous losses on the *Wesseling* operation.

[71] The aircraft lost was PB208 PG-S, with F/O J Parker and his crew. All were killed. Only one has a known grave.

[72] The aircraft lost was LM643 PG-E with F/O RW Orbell and his crew. All were killed.

Date	*Target*	*Aircraft*			
		prepared	*took off*	*Ret early*	*missing*
26 Jul 44	Givors[74]	11	11	-	1
28 Jul 44	Stuttgart[75]	13	13	-	1
30 Jul 44	Cahagnes[76]	14	14	-	-
31 Jul 44	Rilly St Montagne[77]	14	14	-	-
1 Aug 44	La Breteque/Siracourt[78]	12	12	-	-
2 Aug 44	Bois de Cassan[79]	13	13	-	-
3 Aug 44	Trossy St Maximin[80]	13	13	-	1

[73] On this occasion the aircraft lost was ND935 PG-K with the Squadron CO, W/C Maling and his crew. Three members of the crew were killed. Maling and three others were taken pow.

[74] The aircraft lost was LM484 PG-H with F/O R G Turvey RAAF and his crew. Another 619 Sqn aircraft, PB346 PG-J, was also lost on this raid, a 44 Sqn crew [captain F/O D N McKechnie] having borrowed it

[75] The aircraft lost was LM536 PG-Q with W/O J Patterson and his crew.

[76] All 14 aircraft reached the target but were ordered not to bomb and returned to base. This raid was the first involving the Squadron's new Commanding Officer, W/C RA Milward, who remained with the Squadron until 21 Feb 45 when he handed over to W/C SG Birch, who remained with the Squadron until the end of hostilities, relinquishing command on 14 Jun 45 to W/C Flett a month before the Squadron was disbanded. Today, W/C Milward usually takes the Chair at the annual reunions of the Squadron Association. W/C Birch retired as G/Capt MVO DFC and died in 1979. W/C Flett was a Rhodesian.

[77] All fourteen aircraft reached the target and bombed. The crews thought this was a successful attack. It involved 96 Lancasters and 6 Mosquitoes of 5 Group bombing the ends of a railway tunnel used for the storage of flying bombs. No 617 Sqn took part using their *Tallboy* bombs to cave in the ends of the tunnel with the rest of the aircraft cratering the approaches to the tunnel. Two aircraft were lost including one from 617 Sqn flown by F/L W Reid VC. He survived.

[78] All twelve aircraft reached the target successfully but were ordered not to bomb and so returned to base.

[79] All thirteen aircraft reached the target but four were ordered not to bomb. This operation involved the use of 1,114 aircraft: 601 Lancasters, 492 Halifaxes and 21 Mosquitoes, a massive organisational achievement and an indication of the strength and potential of Bomber Command in the final nine months of the War. It had taken five years for the RAF to catch up and overtake German industrial output and to match the Luftwaffe aircrew training system but the speed of the build up now was both startling and exponential.

TABLE 4.3 OPERATIONS IN WHICH 619 SQN PARTICIPATED

Date	*Target*	*Aircraft*			
		prepared	*took off*	*Ret early*	*missing*
5 Aug 44	St Leu D'Esserant[81]	14	14	-	-
6 Aug 44	Bois de Cassan[82]	13	13	-	-
7 Aug 44	Secqueville[83]	13	13	-	-
9 Aug 44	Chatelleurault[84]	13	13	-	1
10 Aug 44	Bordeaux	6	6	-	-
11 Aug 44	Givors	13	13	-	-
12 Aug 44	Brunswick[85]	3	3	-	1
13 Aug 44	Gardening[86]	5	5	1	-
14 Aug 44	Brest	15	15	1	-

[80] The missing aircraft was ME568 PG-F with W/O R Bennett and crew on board. They all died. Three other aircraft were badly shot up: PB297 PG-C [F/O EY O'Neill], LM209 PG-H [S/L MA Smith] and ND728 PG-N [F/O FR Maguire].

[81] All fifteen aircraft reached the target, a flying bomb storage site, and bombed successfully, but LM420 PG-R [F/L WF Jordan] was badly shot-up and the bomb aimer, F/S JC Speckman, died of wounds on landing.

[82] All thirteen aircraft reached the target successfully but were ordered not to bomb. PB297 PG-C [F/O EY O'Neill RAAF] was badly shot up by flak and jettisoned its bomb load, as also did three other aircraft, the remainder jettisoning only their heavier 'cookies'. This was the second time this aircraft and crew had been shot up in three days. F/O R Dickinson and his crew flew in a 44 Sqn aircraft [PB222 KM-U].

[83] All reached the target but only five bombed the remainder being instructed not to do so.

[84] The aircraft lost was ME866 PG-W with F/O LA Hall and crew on board. Six died, but the navigator, P/O HJ Cleland, escaped and evaded capture.

[85] The missing aircraft was ME855 PG-X with flight commander, S/L LB Gunter and crew on board. They were caught by a night-fighter whose fire smashed the rear turret and mortally wounded the rear gunner, F/S R A Willis MID. The other six members of the crew survived as POWs. As a F/L, LB Gunter had been at No 1661 CU, RAF Winthorpe, near Newark, Nottinghamshire as an instructor in 1943 when Cyril Fuller and his crew went through on heavy conversion training, though on another flight from them. He was, however, the instructor at that time of the late S/L JF Grime DFC, who went through training at the same time as Fuller and his crew, completed a tour on No 207 Sqn at RAF Langar and then went on to be a flying instructor [and acting CFI] at Winthorpe. John Grime was known personally to the author, in a capacity unconnected with the RAF, and the author attended his funeral in June 1997. Winthorpe airfield still exists and is used today by light aircraft and gliders. Part of the site is now the Nottinghamshire Air Museum and is well worth a visit.

[86] Code name Deodar: Bordeaux.

Date	*Target*	*Aircraft*			
		prepared	*took off*	*Ret early*	*missing*
15 Aug 44	Deelen	14	14	-	-
16 Aug 44	Stettin	16	16	1	-
18 Aug 44	L'Isle Adam[87]	17	17	-	-
20 Aug 44	Gardening[88]	3	3	-	-
25 Aug 44	Damstadt[89]	19	19	-	-
26 Aug 44	Königsberg[90]	15	15	-	-
29 Aug 44	Königsberg[91]	18	18	-	1
31 Aug 44	Auchy Les Hesdin[92]	16	16	-	-
2 Sep 44	Brest[93]	16	16	-	-
3 Sep 44	Deelen[94]	17	17	1	-
9 Sep 44	Mönchen-Gladbach[95]	16	16	-	-

[87] All seventeen aircraft reached the target, an oil storage depot at Bordeaux, and bombed, and all got back safely, though several suffered light flak damage.

[88] Mine-laying in area Cinnamon: La Rochelle.

[89] All nineteen aircraft bombed the target. Large fires reported.

[90] All fifteen aircraft bombed the target, an important German supply port. This was a long sortie with average times in the air of over 10 hours. The Squadron diarist records that this was the longest sortie undertaken by the Squadron, but this is not quite true: the Antheor Viaduct and some of the early sorties in the summer and autumn of 1943 were as long. Interestingly, however, on this trip none of the 15 pilots was of higher rank than flying officer.

[91] The missing aircraft was LM656 PG-M with F/O FE Eley and crew. On return, an aircraft burst a tyre on landing and several aircraft had to be diverted to Fiskerton.

[92] This night 601 aircraft went out to attack nine V-2 Rocket storage sites. Eight were found and destroyed.

[93] No 619's sixteen aircraft were part of a 5 Group force of 67 Lancasters that bombed Brest Harbour in clear weather. No aircraft were lost.

[94] On this night, although all the aircraft returned safely, most were hit by flak and Sgt LC Rennie, the Flt/Eng in F/O FR Maguire's aircraft [PB356 PG-G] was hit in the arm by shrapnel and had to be treated in Rauceby Hospital after the aircraft returned. The raid had been against the airfield at Deelen, and this crew had put their bombs down on the western intersection of the runways.

[95] All sixteen aircraft from 619 Squadron bombed the target. The ORB records that [the] '*report from the PRU later states that the target area was razed to the ground*'. [PRU = Photographic Reconnaissance Unit]. The author lived near Mönchen-Gladbach for two years in the 1970s, and it was clear then that much of the town had been rebuilt post-

Table 4.3 Operations in which 619 Sqn Participated

Date	*Target*	*Aircraft*			
		prepared	*took off*	*Ret early*	*missing*
10 Sep 44	Le Havre[96]	10	10	-	-
11 Sep 44	Darmstadt[97]	18	18	-	2
12 Sep 44	Stuttgart[98]	12	12	-	-
17 Sep 44	Boulogne[99]	16	16	-	-
18 Sep 44	Bremerhaven[100]	16	16	-	-
19 Sep 44	Mönchen-Gladbach[101]	16	16	-	1

1945, the Alt Stadt [Old City] having been destroyed and many medieval town houses lost.

[96] The operation against Le Havre involved 992 aircraft of Bomber Command and the bombing of eight German strong points. All were marked separately by the Pathfinders, and all were accurately bombed.

[97] The two missing aircraft were LM191 PG-O [F/O CB Dockrey RCAF and crew] and LM209 PG-X [S/L RA Squibbs and crew], both experienced crews. The sixteen returning crews reported heavy flak over the target and several crews returned with flak-damaged aircraft. It is almost certain that flak brought down LM191 and LM209. All 14 crew members were killed. The raid devastated Darmstadt, killing it is believed 12,300 and making anything from 49,200 to 70,000 homeless.

[98] This night some 217 aircraft of Bomber Command attacked Stuttgart while 387 more attacked Frankfurt. The northern and western areas of Stuttgart were erased in a concentrated attack that caused a firestorm. In Frankfurt the damage was equally devastating, with a troop train hit at the West Station and 469 people killed, 169 of them in a public shelter [a two-metre thick concrete wall was blown in by a high explosive bomb]. It was 48 hours before the last flames were extinguished.

[99] On this night the target for 762 aircraft of Bomber Command was German positions around Boulogne in preparation for an attack by Allied troops. 3,600 tons of bombs were dropped, and the German Garrison surrendered soon afterwards. Although all sixteen of No 619 Squadron's aircraft reached the target, only five were called upon to bomb, the remainder jettisoning their 1,000 lb and 500 lb bombs.

[100] On this night 213 aircraft of 5 Group destroyed Bremerhaven and destroyed it in a single blow with a comparatively small force of aircraft dropping only 900 tons of bombs, while fighters were successfully being kept at bay by the radio counter measures deployed by the aircraft of No 100 RCM Group. The centre of the town and the port area were both destroyed. 618 people were killed and 30,000 lost their homes.

[101] Mönchen-Gladbach and Rheydt were devasted by this attack, which involved 237 bombers of Nos 1 and 5 Groups. The Master bomber was W/C Guy Gibson VC DSO DFC, flying a 627 Sqn Mosquito from RAF Coningsby, but he and his experienced navigator S/L JB Warwick DFC were killed when their aircraft crashed near Bergen-op-Zoom on the return leg for reasons that have never been established. The aircraft may

Date	*Target*	*Aircraft*			
		prepared	*took off*	*Ret early*	*missing*
23 Sep 44	Handorf[102]	16	16	-	-
26 Sep 44	Karlsruhe[103]	18	18	-	1
27 Sep 44	Kaiserslautern[104]	16	16	-	-
4 Oct 44	Gardening[105]	5	5	-	-
5 Oct 44	Wilmelmshaven[106]	20	20	-	-

have been damaged by flak [it was over the target for a long time and was one of the last to leave] or there may have been engine failure. Aviation historian Alan Cooper, who has written a biography of Gibson, believes a simple mistake involving a failure to switch cocks from one fuel tank to another may have been to blame. The missing 619 Sqn aircraft was PB405 PG-S with F/O LW Leonard and his crew plus a newly arrived second bomb aimer, F/S JK Stobbs. All were killed.

[102] All sixteen of the Squadron's aircraft despatched reached the target, a German night-fighter airfield at Münster/Handorf, but only seven bombed, the others being instructed not to do so. This was one of three targets visited by Bomber Command that night, with only 113 aircraft going to Handorf. Some bombs fell on Münster itself but without casualties.

[103] All aircraft reached the target, and bombed, except ED602 PG-X, which disappeared without trace taking F/O R W Pettigrew RCAF and his crew and a new second pilot, F/O T E Kerslade, to their deaths. Kerslade had arrived on the Squadron three days previously. This was a veteran aircraft, issued from the manufacturer, Avro Manchester, in Feb 43 and having been flown by Nos 467, 83, 49 and 619 Squadrons.

[104] On this night 227 aircraft carried out the only major raid of the war on this medium sized city. The post-War British Bombing Survey Unit reckoned that 36% of the town's built-up area was destroyed. A local report says that 144 people, mainly women and children, were killed.

[105] On this night the aircraft of F/O DH Strachan RNZAF [LM681 PG-W] had to be crash-landed at Carnaby because the wheels and flaps could not be lowered as a result of enemy action. A cannon or rocket shell had hit the fuselage slightly forward of the mid-upper turret, burning a hole 3 ft long down the whole width of the aircraft. The hydraulics, intercom and emergency air supply were all put out of action, ammunition exploded and the bomb doors were holed. The mid-upper and rear gunners put out the fire, but the mid-upper gunner, Sgt F Webster, suffered extensive burns, which required hospitalisation. When this crew next flew, on the night of 28/29 October, it was with a replacement mid-upper gunner, Sgt FC McMillan. LM681 survived to be later converted into Civilian Tanker [G-AHJU] No 18, before being scrapped in 1950. This Gardening operation was carried out to deny Bergen to German U-boats that had been forced out of the Biscay ports following the Allied liberation of France.

[106] All twenty aircraft reached the target and bombed through 10/10ths cloud, relying on H2S, estimated position or visual sighting of other falling bombs. The local records show

Table 4.3 Operations in which 619 Sqn Participated

Date	*Target*	*Aircraft*			
		prepared	*took off*	*Ret early*	*missing*
6 Oct 44	Bremen[107]	20	20	-	-
11 Oct 44	Veere/Flushing[108]	14	14	-	-
14 Oct 44	Brunswick[109]	20	20	1	-
17 Oct 44	Westkapelle[110]	3	3	-	-
19 Oct 44	Nürnberg[111]	21	20	1	-
23 Oct 44	Flushing [Guns][112]	4	4	-	-
28 Oct 44	Bergen[113]	12	12	-	-

---

that the attack was scattered and that 12 people died. Only one Lancaster of the 227 taking part was lost.

[107] 246 Lancasters and 7 Mosquitoes carried out this attack on Bremen, the last of 32 major Bomber Command raids on Bremen during the War. Using the 5 Group marking techniques developed by No 617 and other specialist squadrons, the raid was an outstanding success. 1,021 tons of bombs were dropped and fires were started in the town centre and surrounding areas. Thus, a raid by only a quarter of Bomber Command's strength had finished off Bremen.

[108] Twelve of the aircraft attacked battery positions along the river Scheldt and two others the sea walls at Veere.

[109] In addition to over 2,000 sorties to Duisburg in less than 24 hours, Bomber Command now had the capacity to be able also to send 230 aircraft to Brunswick, including 20 from No 619 Sqn. It is claimed that 150 hectares of the town were destroyed and over 530 people killed. It could have been much worse, but fortunately, after about four hours of facing an impenetrable fire-wall, the town firemen got through and released townsfolk from the public shelters in which 23,000 people were hiding. Considerable help and aid was sent to Brunswick from Bavaria [which, by and large, had not suffered in this way].

[110] Three aircraft were despatched to attack the dykes at Westkapelle. Though the bombing was accurate it did not appear to have breached the walls.

[111] The raid was only a partial success, though swathes of the southern parts of the town were destroyed and over 300 people were killed, including 91 foreign workers and 65 Russian officer prisoners.

[112] Though all four aircraft got back to base from this daylight raid, they were not all unscathed. Aircraft ME787 PG-J [S/L RG Purnell and crew] was hit twice by flak while in the target area and a fire started in the bomb bay that resulted in the captain jettisoning the bomb load and giving the crew the order to bale out. Four of the crew did so over the target area [F/O KR Pearson, F/O RT Bates, F/O DB Fryer and F/S WI Bell] and two more over England [F/O SCW Lock and F/O FRA Young - and were treated in hospital for burns]. The pilot then crash-landed the aircraft at Woodbridge. The aircraft survived the crash-landing and went on to serve with 617, 106 and 189 Squadrons before being struck off charge in 1947.

Date	*Target*	*Aircraft*			
		prepared	*took off*	*Ret early*	*missing*
28 Oct 44	Gardening	6	6	1	-
30 Oct 44	Westkapelle[114]	9	9	-	-
1 Nov 44	Homberg[115]	18	18	-	1
2 Nov 44	Düsseldorf[116]	11	11	-	-
4 Nov 44	Dortmund-Ems Kanal[117]	13	13	-	-
6 Nov 44	Gravenhorst[118]	16	16	-	2

---

[113]On this night 244 aircraft of Bomber Command attacked the U-boat pens at Bergen. The area was covered by cloud and although the Master Bomber brought the force down to below 5,000 ft conditions were still not good, only 47 aircraft bombing before being ordered to return to base. One of the 47 was PB590 PG-O [F/O GM Proctor RNZAF and crew]. Local reports say that only four bombs hit the roofs of the U-boat pens and that operations were not disrupted. Thirty-five houses were damaged in the harbour area. No one was killed.

[114] On this night 110 aircraft of 5 Group attacked the gun positions at Walcheren in readiness for the attack by Allied ground forces the following day. The island fell after a week of fighting by Canadian and Scottish commandos.

[115] The squadron's 18 aircraft were part of a force of 228 aircraft of 5 Group that attacked the Meebeck oil installation at Homberg. Because of 10/10ths cloud over the target, the raid was not successful and had to be repeated a week later. The aircraft experienced intense flak over the target, and all except two of the Squadron's aircraft were hit, though only one seriously. That aircraft, PB540 PG-Z, with F/L LE Tanner and crew on board, was hit by heavy flak, and the port tail plane and aileron controls were severed. It was crash-landed at Woodbridge on return, where it burst into flames on landing and the captain and three other members of the crew [Sgt RJ Ward, Sgt MG Gibson and Sgt AP Goddard] were killed. The other three [Sgt JR Fletcher, Sgt JF Barton and Sgt R Ralston] were injured, the latter seriously.

[116] A thousand bomber raid [992, actually] and the last of the War on Dusseldorf. This was a heavy, concentrated attack, which fell mainly on the northern part of the city and destroyed 5,000 houses and some important industrial premises [steel works]. Of the nineteen aircraft lost that night, four came down behind the Allied lines in France and Belgium, and all except five of the 4 x 7 crewmen survived. The Allied presence on the Continent was beginning to change the air war in many subtle ways.

[117] The squadron's thirteen aircraft were part of a 5 Group force of 176 aircraft [174 Lancasters and 2 Mosquitoes] that revisited this notorious target, where previous damage in the section north of Münster had been repaired. The banks of both branches of the canal were again breached, leaving barges stranded and the canal unusable.

[118] Part of 242 aircraft of 5 Group [235 Lancasters and 7 Mosquitoes] that attempted to cut the Mittelland Kanal at its junction with the Dortmund-Ems Kanal. The marking

Table 4.3 Operations in which 619 Sqn Participated

Date	*Target*	*Aircraft*			
		prepared	*took off*	*Ret early*	*missing*
11 Nov 44	Harburg[119]	16	16	1	1
16 Nov 44	Düren[120]	16	16	1	-
21 Nov 44	Gravenhorst[121]	20	20	1	-
22 Nov 44	Trondjheim[122]	13	12	-	-
23 Nov 44	Gardening	4	4	-	-
26 Nov 44	München[123]	18	18	1	-

force had difficulty finding the target, and the crew of a low-flying Mosquito of 627 Sqn were so successful that their marker fell into the water and was extinguished. Only 31 aircraft bombed before the Master Bomber cancelled the raid. None of 619's aircraft bombed, and all jettisoned some bombs to reduce landing weight before returning to base. Two aircraft and crews were missing, LM742 PG-S [F/O EW Hookings] and NN723 [F/S JLB Webster]. Three of F/O Hookings' crew were killed [and the other four taken POW]; all of F/S Webster's crew were killed.

119 On this day 245 aircraft of 5 Group were sent to Harburg to bomb the Rhenania-Ossag oil refinery. It is not clear whether the oil refinery was put out of action or damaged but much damage was caused to local residential areas. The missing aircraft was PB356 PG-G [F/O PC Clapham].

120 This operation is of interest because it was carried out by day and because it was in support of the American ground troops in the area between Aachen and the Rhine, where the American First and Ninth Armies were facing the German lines. 1,188 Bomber Command aircraft attacked Düren, Jülich and Heinsberg, and 1,239 American heavy bombers attacked other targets in the area. Bomber Command lost four Lancasters and the USAAF none. Though massive damage and huge loss of civilian life was caused in the three towns attacked by the RAF, little of tactical advantage to the Americans was achieved, and their infantry advance was slow and costly.

121 Once again the target was the Mittelland-Ems Kanal, and this time the 128 aircraft of 5 Group [123 Lancasters and 5 Mosquitoes] were successful in breaching the banks, which had been repaired since the last raid earlier in the month. The one early return was because of an unserviceable Gee set.

122 This was an attack by 171 Lancasters and 7 Mosquitoes of 5 Group against the U-boat pens at Trondjheim, but the target was covered by a smoke screen and the Master Bomber ordered the raid to be cancelled. The crew [F/O JS Hunter] that failed to take-off was absolutely justified. When they got out to the dispersal they found that someone had forgotten to refuel aircraft [ND957 PG-M]. This must have been quite worrying for a raw crew that had arrived on the squadron only three weeks previously, and one can imagine that the F/S fitter in charge of the flight to which the aircraft belonged had some choice words of counselling for the person responsible.

Date	*Target*	*Aircraft*			
		prepared	*took off*	*Ret early*	*missing*
4 Dec 44	Heilbronn[124]	18	18	-	2
6 Dec 44	Giessen[125]	18	18	1	-
8 Dec 44	Heimbach[126]	14	14	-	-
10 Dec 44	Heimbach[127]	15	13	-	-
11 Dec 44	Heimbach[128]	15	15	1	-
14 Dec 44	Gardening	2	2	-	-
17 Dec 44	München[129]	17	17	3	-

[123] This attack on München by 270 Lancasters and 8 Mosquitoes of 5 Group was thought to have been highly successful. All the 619 Squadron aircraft reached the target and bombed, except one that turned back after an engine caught fire. One of the 619 Squadron aircraft was flown by a No 207 Squadron crew. Only one Lancaster was lost, in itself a remarkable commentary on the air superiority now being achieved.

[124] On this night 282 Lancasters and 12 Mosquitoes of 5 Group attacked Heilbronn for the first and only time. Heilbronn had little strategic significance except that it stood on the main north/south railway line. The 5 Group force once again delivered a devastating attack, the post-War British Bombing Survey Unit estimating that the 1,254 tons of bombs, dropped in a matter of minutes, had destroyed 82% of the town's built-up area, mainly as a result of fire, and that probably 7,000 people died. The two missing 619 Sqn aircraft were PB740 PG-O [F/O RH Schaeffer RCAF] and ND932 PG-X [F/O SV Chambers RCAF].

[125] Once again an entirely 5 Group force made up of 255 Lancasters and 10 Mosquitoes attacked in the railway yards and town centre at Giessen. Damage to the town and the railway yards was severe. PB699 PG-Z [F/O ET Pennells RCAF] received machine gun and flak damage.

[126] This operation was another 5 Group operation: this time against the Urft Dam at Heimbach, bombing by *G-H* through 9/10 cloud. Bombs were seen to land on the spillway and the dam walls. Seven of 619's aircraft were instructed not to bomb and jettisoned some of their load to reduce landing weight. Driving sleet led to all except four of the aircraft being diverted on return, mostly to Boscombe Down but one to Tarrant Rushden.

[127] Two aircraft collided while taxying and the remaining 13 were recalled after half an hour in the air.

[128] For the third time of asking 5 Group returned to the Urft Dam at Heimbach, near the then battle area in the region of Aachen. Though many direct hits were scored, the Dam was not breached.

[129] Another entirely 5 Group attack, using 280 Lancasters and 8 Mosquitoes. The returning crews reported extensive damage to the railway yards and old city centre. Only 4 Lancasters were lost, none from 619 Sqn. W/C RA Milward, who wrote the ORB this

TABLE 4.3 OPERATIONS IN WHICH 619 SQN PARTICIPATED

Date	*Target*	*Aircraft*			
		prepared	*took off*	*Ret early*	*missing*
18 Dec 44	Gydnia/Gardening[130]	14	14	1	-
21 Dec 44	Pölitz[131]	17	17	1	-
26 Dec 44	St Vith[132]	4	4	-	-
28 Dec 44	Horten[133]	5	5	-	-
30 Dec 44	Houffalize[134]	18	18	-	-

---

month, noted that '*this effort of early returns was the worst record the squadron has suffered for some time*'. [Two aircraft had returned with engine problems and one with navigational.]

[130] Eleven 619 Sqn aircraft took part in this attack by 236 Lancasters of 5 Group on the Baltic port of Gydnia, which caused considerable damage to shipping, installations and port facilities. F/O DH Strachan RNZAF in PB842 PG-Y and F/O KR Hickmott RCAF in PB205 PG-B attacked the German cruiser *Lutzen* visually. Three crews laid anti-shipping mines in the same area.

[131] On this night 207 Lancasters and 1 Mosquito of 5 Group attacked the oil refinery at Pölitz, near Stettin. Post-raid reconnaissance showed that the refinery had been seriously damaged. Only three Lancasters were lost in the raid, but five more crashed in England because of bad weather. [Only four of 619's aircraft got back to base, the others being diverted to Kinloss, Lossiemouth, Banff and Carnaby.] One aircraft returned early with a sick pilot and was diverted to Waddington.

[132] A daylight attack was laid on at such short notice that only four of 619 Squadron's aircraft could be bombed up in time. This came about because atrocious weather had prevented operations for several days, but at last, on Boxing Day, Bomber Command was able to involve itself in the Ardennes battle by attacking German troop positions. This was the first time aircraft had come together from all the Bomber Command groups [except No 100 RCM Group] for a single operation [294 aircraft, in roughly equal numbers of Lancasters and Halifaxes, led by 12 Mosquitoes] since the Spring.

[133] Five aircraft were detailed to attack shipping at Horten. Three aircraft from 57 Sqn and four from 630 Sqn also took off from Strubby for this raid. The Commanding Officer diarist noted that 'lively light flak had been encountered' but that all the aircraft had returned safely, though the success of the raid was doubted.

[134] This operation against a German supply bottleneck in the narrow valley of Houffalize was carried out after several delays during the course of the day by 154 Lancasters and 12 Mosquitoes of 5 Group. All the 619 Squadron aircraft got back safely, though only five had bombed, the others being instructed not to. One Lancaster from the force crashed in France. This turned out to be the last operation of the last full year of the War, an operation detailed for 31st December being cancelled at short notice. [Apart from one Gardening trip by F/O WJ Franks in ND957 PG-M, who returned at 2254 with one hour and 6 minutes to spare before the New Year.]

Date	*Target*	*Aircraft*			
		prepared	*took off*	*Ret early*	*missing*
31 Dec 44	Gardening	2	1	-	-
1 Jan 45	Mittelland Kanal[135]	19	19	-	-
4 Jan 45	Royan[136]	18	17	-	1
5 Jan 45	Houffalize[137]	12	10	-	-
6 Jan 45	Gydnia Harbour[138]	2	2	-	-
7 Jan 45	München[139]	16	16	-	1
13 Jan 45	Pölitz[140]	15	15	1	1

[135] The aircraft took off in very bad visibility and on return all except one had to be diverted to Tain in the north of Scotland. It was thought to have been 'a very successful raid'. Middlebrook and Everitt, op cit, state that '*half a mile of banks were pitted with bomb craters and some parts were breached*'.

[136] This raid was one of the almost inevitable cock-ups of War when a French town believed only to contain a German garrison that was refusing to surrender was bombed with devastating effect by 352 aircraft of Nos 1, 5 and 8 Groups of Bomber Command at the request of SHAEF and a large number of French civilians, probably resistance fighters, were killed. An American officer from a tactical air force unit was blamed for the mistake. Four Lancasters were lost and two more collided and crashed behind Allied lines. One of those lost was 619's ND728 PG-N with F/O D Gray and his crew.

[137] The Squadron having been stood down that afternoon after the previous night's operation, at 1730 without any warning they were ordered to get 12 aircraft ready for an operation that night to attack a concentration of enemy transport and troops reported by the Army. In the event only ten could be bombed up in time. On a clear frosty night they took off at around midnight. By they returned the weather had deteriorated and only one [LM657 PG-Q F/O Runnalls] landed at base, the remainder diverting to Topcliffe in Yorkshire. At the end of this operation, F/O Bateman and his crew completed their tour of operations.

[138] Two aircraft [F/O R Dickinson and F/O AE McMorran RCAF] took off at 1600 to lay mines in Gydnia Harbour. Visibility was poor at time of take-off but improved and both aircraft were able to land back at base at 0130.

[139] On a cold, fine day with a strong north wind, sixteen aircraft took off in only 14 minutes at around 1700. All reached the target and bombed, but only fifteen got back to base. News was received the next day that F/O Flockhart RAAF and crew in ND957 PG-M had crashed in France presumably because of weather. All were killed. This was the last major raid on München, and it caused severe damage.

[140] After three days of heavy snow and frost, when it had been necessary to activate the snow plan to keep the runways clear after two hours continuous fall on 10 January, operations were again ordered by Bomber Command. The target was an oil installation at Pölitz. One aircraft returned early with a u/s rear turret [PB699/G PG-Z F/L EJF Smith]

TABLE 4.3 OPERATIONS IN WHICH 619 SQN PARTICIPATED

Date	*Target*	*Aircraft*			
		prepared	*took off*	*Ret early*	*missing*
14 Jan 45	Merseburg[141]	14	14	-	-
16 Jan 45	Brux[142]	17	17	2	-
1 Feb 45	Siegen[143]	20	20	-	-
2 Feb 45	Karlsruhe[144]	20	20	2	1
7 Feb 45	Dortmund-Ems Kanal[145]	11	11	-	-

and one failed to return [PB842 PG-Y F/O BP Curran RAAF], one of only two Lancasters lost that night. It was a very accurate, entirely 5 Group, raid with low level marking by Mosquitoes. A photograph of PB842 PG-Y taking off from Strubby in 'late 1944' was published some years ago by Keith Woodcock, probably copied from an original in the Imperial War Musuem. The pilot had landed in Sweden, having come under fighter attack. The aircraft was repaired but scrapped in 1946.

[141] This was an attack on another oil installation, this time at Merseburg. The aircraft took off at around 1630 and it was reported by the crews as a most successful raid. Because of deteriorating weather at base, the crews all diverted to Middleton-St-George on returning. With this operation, F/O Strachan DFC RNZAF completed his tour.

[142] The target was a synthetic-oil plant at Brux in Czechoslovakia. This was the fourth in a series of raids against oil targets, all involving long flights to Eastern Germany. The crews reported that it was a highly successful attack, and they were right. After the War Albert Speer, Germany's Minister for Armanents, said that this raid had caused a severe setback to oil production. This raid also marked the return to ops with an almost entirely new crew of S/L RG Purnell, though on this night he was one of two pilots obliged to return early with technical problems. This was to prove the last operation of the month [January 1945] as repeated snow squalls and storms, with drifts of up to two feet deep, made further operations impossible.

[143] This was an attack on an important rail centre not far behind the ground troops frontline. Unfortunately, most of the attack was misdirected either because of strong winds or decoy fires and most of the bombs fell in the surrounding countryside, killing 128 people.

[144] Once again this was an entirely 5 Group affair, involving 250 Lancasters and 11 Mosquitoes. Cloud over the target caused the raid to be a complete failure. This was a lucky escape for Karlsruhe as it was the last major RAF attack of the war on this city. It cost the RAF, however, twelve Lancasters, four from No 189 Squadron, and one from No 619 Sqn [PB210 PG-V], F/L EJF Smith and crew. Smith survived as a POW, but the other six members of the crew were killed. They are buried at Dürnbach War Cemetery.

[145] This night, 177 Lancasters and 11 Mosquitoes of 5 Group returned once again to the Dortmund-Ems Kanal, 619's eleven all taking off at about 1600. Although the crews thought it had been a successful attack, later photographs showed that banks had not been damaged and most of the bombs had fallen in nearby fields. Three other crews went out on a mine-laying operation. All returned safely.

Date	*Target*	*Aircraft*			
		prepared	*took off*	*Ret early*	*missing*
7 Feb 45	Gardening	3	3	-	-
8 Feb 45	Pölitz/Gardening[146]	14	14	-	1
13 Feb 45	Dresden[147]	13	13	-	-
15 Feb 45	Leipzig[148]	15	15	-	-

[146] This was a large scale attack by Bomber Command, using 475 Lancasters and 7 Mosquitoes, in two waves; the first marked entirely using the 5 Group method of low marking, the second using Pathfinders of 8 Group. In good weather both waves were extremely successful, and much damage was caused to the synthetic-oil plant. Speer also mentioned this raid in his post-war interrogation. Twelve Lancasters were lost, one of them 619's ME314 PG-W [F/O HT Hesketh RAAF and crew]. Six members of the crew were killed, and only the rear gunner surviving as a POW. Only one of the dead has a known grave. Three of 619's crews laid mines in the area of Pölitz. PA180 PG-G [F/O R Dickinson] was attacked by a fighter while in the process of laying a mine, and abandoned the mission with a dead rear gunner, a seriously wounded W/Op and an injured M/Upper Gunner. Despite the aircraft sustaining heavy damage, the Pilot got it safely back to base.

[147] The thirteen aircraft were airborne in 9½ minutes. The crews' debriefings record that the target was lightly defended and no fighters were encountered. This first wave was an entirely 5 Group affair, using low level marking, 244 Lancasters dropping 800 tons of bombs. Because of cloud this attack was only moderately successful. A second wave three hours later in clear weather, using 8 Group Pathfinders to mark and 529 Lancasters to drop 1,800 tons of bombs, was fearfully accurate. The following day 311 aircraft of the USAAF dropped another 711 tons of bombs on Dresden. Dresden was destroyed and at least 35,000 people and probably more died in the firestorm that followed. More than any other operation of the War, this is the one that has since caused so much controversy, though the part the USAAF played is often forgotten, and blame is usually laid entirely on Harris's shoulders. This is unfair. The reasons for choosing Dresden that night are complex, and apart from Harris's determination to prove that area bombing could achieve all that he and others claimed of it, it is disingenuous to blame him alone. He was carrying out, albeit with enthusiasm, a strategy handed down to him. Bomber Command lost 6 Lancasters, with three others crashing, two in France and one in England. After the war, it suited the occupying Soviet Union and its puppet regime in the DDR to retain Dresden as a blackened ruin by way of anti-Western propaganda. When the author visited Dresden in 1991 and 1992, like so many other places in the East, including the Soviet sector of Berlin, it was only just beginning to emerge from ruins. The famous church is now at last being rebuilt, and Britain has made symbolic contribution towards the reconstruction. The Devil doesn't always, or perhaps ever, get the last laugh.

[148] Crews still resting from the previous night's operation were summoned by tannoy for this attack on another synthetic-oil plant, this time Rositz, south of Leipzig. They took

TABLE 4.3 OPERATIONS IN WHICH 619 SQN PARTICIPATED

Date	*Target*	*Aircraft*			
		prepared	*took off*	*Ret early*	*missing*
19 Feb 45	Leipzig[149]	18	18	-	-
20 Feb 45	Mittelland Kanal[150]	11	11	-	-
21 Feb 45	Mittelland Kanal[151]	13	13	-	-
23 Feb 45	Gardening[152]	3	3	-	-
24 Feb 45	Dortmund-Ems Kanal[153]	12	12	-	-

off around 1645, with F/O Hickmott taking a new pilot, W/O Potter as second pilot. All attacked and returned safely, but PG-J [F/O Dunsmore] was later than the others because he had attacked and returned on three engines, and F/L May landed at RAF Manston, Kent, with both inboard engines out of action and both tyres burst following an attack by a nightfighter. Once again, this was an entirely 5 Group affair, using 224 Lancasters and 8 Mosquitoes. Damage was caused to the southern end of the oil plant. Four Lancasters were lost, none from 619 Sqn.

[149] The eighteen 619 Sqn aircraft were part of another entirely 5 Group attack, consisting of 254 Lancasters and 6 Mosquitoes, this time against Böhlen near Leipzig. They took off late in the evening at around 2150. The raid failed, partly because only the faintest glow of a TI could be seen and partly because the Controller [Master Bomber], W/C EA Benjamin DFC and bar, was brought down by flak over the target. Post-raid reconnaissance showed that damage was superficial and very scattered. W/C Benjamin is buried in the CWGC 1939-1945 Cemetery in Berlin. Unusually, his aircraft, a Mosquito, was the only one missing that night. No Lancasters were missing.

[150] Once again 5 Group returned to the Mittelland Kanal at Gravenhorst with a force this time of 154 Lancasters and 11 Mosquitoes. The raid was abandoned because of cloud and all 619's aircraft returned safely with their bomb loads. No aircraft were lost.

[151] This night the take-off was earlier in a ten minute interval just after 1700, and the aircraft bombed the target in bright moonlight. F/O O'Brien in PG-R returned with the port wing damaged, and examination suggested that he had actually been struck by the fighter that had tried to attack him. S/L Osborne, the newly-promoted Flight Commander of 'B' Flight in PG-V crash-landed at Carnaby because of damage caused by a loose bomb which prevented him getting the undercarriage down. W/C SG Birch arrived today after an operational attachment with 50 Squadron at Skellingthorpe. He took over the Squadron the next day, 22 February, when W/C RA Milward completed his second tour of operations.

[152] Mine-laying in the Oslo Fjord.

[153] Once more 5 Group returned to the Dortmund-Ems Kanal, this time with 165 Lancasters and 12 Mosquitoes. No 11 Group [Fighter Command] supplied a fighter escort. No 619 Sqn contributed 12 of the Lancasters. All got back safely, but because cloud had cover the target they restricted themselves to each dropping one x 1,000 lb bomb and bringing the rest of the load back to base. Of the 5 Group force, nine Lancasters were lost and four crashed in France and Holland. One of those crashing in

Date	*Target*	*Aircraft*			
		prepared	*took off*	*Ret early*	*missing*
3 Mar 45	Dortmund-Ems Kanal[154]	15	15	-	-
5 Mar 45	Böhlen[155]	18	18	-	-
6 Mar 45	Sassnitz[156]	14	13	1	-

Holland was an 83 Sqn Lancaster captained by the RAF Coningsby Station Commander, G/Capt AC Evans-Evans DFC, a legendary figure with a huge personality and equally huge frame. His aircraft was shot down by a night-fighter, and he and the other seven members of the crew are buried at Eindhoven. He was 43 years of age, and his Navigator, S/L WG Wishart DSO, DFC and Bar, was 22. In addition to these two decorated officers, Evans-Evans' crew contained F/L WC Fitch with a DFC and a GM and F/O DAJW Ball with a DFM. Being shot down was largely a matter of luck, and fate took no account of crew experience.

[154] This was another all-5 Group attack, involving 212 Lancasters and 7 Mosquitoes, this time on the Ladbergen aqueduct of the Dortmund-Ems Kanal. The aqueduct was breached in two places and put out of use. No 619 Squadron contributed 15 aircraft, two of them detailed for a Gardening operation at the southern end of the Oslo Fjord. Seven Lancasters were lost, but all of 619's got back safely, although PB590 PG-O [F/O GM Proctor RNZAF] had an engine knocked out of its mounting by flak and RA527 PG-M [F/O R Dickinson] lost the use of an engine when its radiator was hit by flak over the target. W/C Birch's gunners in aircraft PD441 PG-B, Sgts JD Longworth and EM Martin, claimed a flying bomb shot down near the target area. It was probably aimed at the port of Antwerp. On return to base, enemy intruders were active, and although all the aircraft got down safely, the airfield was badly shot-up.

[155] This night saw another attack on the synthetic-oil plant at Böhlen, near Leipzig, and once again it was an entirely 5 Group operation, with 248 Lancasters and 10 Mosquitoes taking part. The target was covered by cloud, and the crews had difficulty seeing the wanganuis ordered by the Master Bomber. One of 619 Squadron's captains brought his bombs back because he had been unable to see the target, but some damage was done to the plant. Four Lancasters were lost, but all of 619's eighteen got back safely. The aircraft had had to climb to 15,000 ft on the way to the target to get above ice-producing cloud, and four aircraft sustained damage to the Perspex from ice flying off the propellers. Two aircraft had trouble with flak.

[156] This night 191 Lancasters and 7 Mosquitoes of 5 Group attacked the port and harbour installations, and shipping, at Sassnitz on the island of Rügen. Considerable damage was caused to the northern end of the town and three ships were sunk. No aircraft were lost. No 619 Sqn contributed 13 aircraft [it should have been 14, but F/L GM McMorran RCAF in NG286 PG-Y was unable to take off because the rear turret was completely unserviceable and also had a substantial oil leak]. F/O CP Sparkes RNZAF in PB699/G PG-Z was obliged to return early with the starboard outer engine feathered. The attack was only partially successful because of late arrivals, caused by a change in

Table 4.3 Operations in which 619 Sqn Participated

Date	*Target*	*Aircraft*			
		prepared	*took off*	*Ret early*	*missing*
7 Mar 45	Harburg[157]	16	16	-	2
11 Mar 45	Essen[158]	15	15	-	1
11 Mar 45	Gardening[159]	3	3	-	-
12 Mar 45	Dortmund[160]	16	16	-	-

---

wind strength, and cloud obscuring the TIs. One 619 Squadron captain brought his bomb load back. Three of 619's aircraft successfully laid mines in the area of the target. With the completion of this operation, two captains completed their tour of ops [F/O K Hickmott RCAF and F/O GM Proctor RNZAF].

[157] Once again 5 Group returned in force to the oil installation at Harburg with 234 Lancaster aircraft and 7 Mosquitoes. It was an accurate attack, but 12 Lancasters were lost, including two from No 619 Squadron and four from No 189 Squadron, which had lost a similar number on the Karlsruhe operation on 2 February, only a month previously. F/O ET Pennell's crew in NG503 PG-W claimed an Me410 shot down. The missing 619 aircraft were NG286 PG-Y [F/L GMS McMorran RCAF] and PB699/G PG-Z [F/O CP Sparkes RNZAF]. Four of McMorran's crew survived as POWs but all of Sparkes' crew were killed.

[158] On this day Bomber Command launched a 1,000 bomber raid on the city of Essen. No 619 Sqn contributed 15 aircraft, all taking off at around noon. There was little opposition and despite 10/10ths cloud over the target 4,661 tons of bombs were dropped accurately onto Essen by *Oboe*-directed sky markers. The Sqn ORB records that it was thought to have been a successful raid, and that the controller [Master Bomber] had directed the bombers onto red and blue puffs of smoke over the target. It was also the largest number of aircraft sent on a raid so far – 1,079, including 750 Lancasters! This was the last raid of the War on Essen, which was now in ruins, despite earlier raids having often produced disappointing and costly results. Essen's pre-War population of 648,000 had fallen to 310,000 by the end of the War, almost half having left for quieter parts. No 619 Sqn's missing aircraft was LM207 PG-E [F/O Hooper], which was wrecked in Belgium on the outward leg while attempting to land at Evere airfield and overshot the runway, fortunately without loss of life. The ORB records the aircraft as having landed at 1510 whereas the rest of the aircraft landed at around 1700. Presumably 1510 was the time down in Belgium. The ORB also states that: '*the attack was of great tactical value to our Western Front Armies in blocking communications behind the German front*'.

[159] Three crews the same evening planted 'vegetables' in Oslo Fjord. All returned safely.

[160] The ORB says that this was another raid of great tactical significance. This time 1,108 aircraft took part and only two were lost. Another record tonnage of bombs was dropped – 4,851 tons – and again the result was devastating. A post-War survey reported '*The final raid...stopped production so effectively that it would have been many months before any substantial recovery could have occurred*' [Webster and Frankland, *The Strategic Air Offensive against Germany 1939-45* HMSO 1961 Vol III p.264]. The sixteen aircraft of

Date	*Target*	*Aircraft*			
		prepared	*took off*	*Ret early*	*missing*
14 Mar 45	Lützkendorf[161]	15	15	1	-
16 Mar 45	Würzburg[162]	15	15	1	1
20 Mar 45	Böhlen[163]	15	15	1	1
21 Mar 45	Hamburg[164]	12	12	-	-

---

619 Sqn all got back safely but PD441 PG-B [F/O FW Seazell, on his first operation as captain] had its starboard outer petrol tank removed by a bomb dropped by a Halifax flying overhead near the target.

161 This was a night attack on a synthetic-oil refinery near Leipzig, involving 244 Lancasters and 11 Mosquitoes of 5 Group. PR suggested that moderate damage had occurred. 18 Lancasters were lost [7.4%], proving that even at this late stage of the War bombing distant targets was still a risky business. The early return was PA180 PG-G [F/O WD Cowling RCAF], the front escape hatch having blown off. Because of deteriorating weather the other aircraft were directed on return to RAF Upwood.

162 This was another entirely 5 Group operation involving 225 Lancasters and 11 Mosquitoes. No 619 Sqn contributed 15 aircraft to what turned out to be another devastating attack, the briefing and take-off in late afternoon being watched by officers from the RAF Staff College. 1,127 tons of bombs were dropped in only 17 minutes and a post-War survey suggested that 89% of this old cathedral city had been destroyed. Six Lancasters were lost, including 619's NG503 PG-W [F/O TE Farrow RCAF on his third operational trip] and two of 619's aircraft came back on only three engines [F/O GG Runnalls in LM657 PG-Q; and F/L JW May in NN751 PG-H]. The early return was S/L CM Palmer, a Rhodesian attached to the Sqn for operational experience, in LM649 PG-P with the port outer engine unserviceable.

163 This night the Squadron sent fifteen aircraft, taking off just before midnight, as part of another entirely 5 Group affair comprising of 224 Lancasters and 11 Mosquitoes, back to the synthetic-oil installation at Böhlen, near Leipzig. This accurate attack finally put the plant out of action, and it was still out of action when captured by American troops several weeks later. Nine Lancasters were lost including 619's PD425 PG-T [S/L CM Palmer, the Rhodesian on attachment to 619 for operational experience]. Palmer came from Marandellas in Southern Rhodesia. He and four members of his crew were killed, the other two being taken POWs. His Flight Engineer, F/O FJ Ricketts DFM had been decorated on a previous tour with 625 Sqn, and his navigator, F/L LC Raw, at the age of 35 was above the usual age for operational aircrew by this stage of the War. Another new pilot got back safely, however. LM657 PG-Q, piloted by F/S DR IrvineRCAF on his first trip as captain, was holed by a fighter attack but got back safely to base, landing 1¼ hours after the others. F/S Irvine was flying in the RCAF as also were three other members of his crew but three were RAF. F/O NA Gampe RAAF in PB590 PG-O returned early with the starboard inner engine feathered.

TABLE 4.3 OPERATIONS IN WHICH 619 SQN PARTICIPATED

Date	*Target*	*Aircraft*			
		prepared	*took off*	*Ret early*	*missing*
23 Mar 45	Wesel[165]	14	14	-	-
4 Apr 45	Nordhausen[166]	18	18	-	-
7 Apr 45	Molbis[167]	14	14	-	-

---

164 This was another night attack on enemy oil supplies, again an entirely 5 Group affair involving 151 Lancasters and 5 Mosquitoes. The target was the Deutsche Erdölwerke refinery near Hamburg. The attack was again accurate with twenty petrol storage tanks destroyed, so much so they were still out of action at the end of the War. Some of the bombs fell, however, on the Wilhelmsburg district of Hamburg and 31 German civilians were killed, together with about 100 foreign workers whose camp was hit. F/O AR Whittaker in NN751 PG-H lost an engine as he crossed the Danish coast on the outward leg but continued the attack on three engines and got back safely, an hour after the others.

165 On the evening of 23 March, No 619 Sqn despatched 14 aircraft as part of an attack in direct tactical support of No 21 Army Group by 5 and 8 PFF Groups, consisting of 195 Lancasters and 23 Mosquitoes. The Sqn ORB records that the attack was carried out in bright moonlight and was entirely successful as the Army was seen to cross the river and take the town of Wesel against only feeble opposition. The Stadt of Wesel claims to have been the most bombed town for its size of the entire war. It is said that 97% of the buildings were destroyed and that a population of 35,000 in 1939 had fallen to 1,900 by 1945. No aircraft were lost this night.

166 On 4th April, the Squadron's eighteen aircraft took off at 0600 hours as part of a mainly 5 Group operation [243 Lancasters and 1 Mosquito of No 5 Group and 8 Mosquitoes from No 8 PFF Group] for a daylight attack on German troop concentrations at Nordhausen. The German barracks and the town were badly damaged. The previous day 247 Lancasters and 8 Mosquitoes of No 1 and No 8 Groups had taken part in a similar raid on Nordhausen. Unfortunately, the barracks housed a large number of concentration camp prisoners who worked in the underground tunnels and workshops, and many were killed. The complex of tunnels and workshops had been constructed to house the rocket-research establishment following the successful raid against Peenemünde in August 1943 [in which operation No 619 Squadron had participated, losing three of its aircraft including that of its founding CO]. It is not known how many people were killed, but those who died were above ground, the survivors all being in the tunnels which acted as air raid shelters.

167 On the night of 7/8 April, No 5 Group attacked the power station and benzol plant at Molbis, near Leipzig, with a force of 175 Lancasters and 11 Mosquitoes. No aircraft were lost. No 619 Squadron contributed 14 aircraft, that figure having been reduced from the original 20 ordered earlier in the day by the simple expedient of removing from the list the less experienced crews. This was the first operation carried out from Strubby by both No 619 and No 227 Squadron, and the use of the airfield by the two squadrons worked out well. On completion of this operation, F/O GG Runnals completed his tour of ops,

Date	*Target*	*Aircraft*			
		prepared	*took off*	*Ret early*	*missing*
8 Apr 45	Lützkendorf[168]	17	17	-	-
10 Apr 45	Leipzig-Wahren[169]	11	11	-	1

---

the number of trips required for a tour to be satisfied having been reduced to 33. [It had originally been 30 but as the war progressed, and 'easier' targets became available following the Allied occupation of much of Europe, Bomber Command had decreed that some ops would only count as a third; there was an outcry, and the result was this compromise, though it will have been noted that there was still an appreciable risk in flying an ungainly heavy bomber loaded with fuel and bombs over enemy territory, particularly at night, and this persisted until the cease-fire].

[168] On the night of 8/9 April, 231 Lancasters and 11 Mosquitoes of No 5 Group revisited the oil installation at Lützkendorf, and the refinery was put out of action. Six Lancasters were lost, but all 619's seventeen got back safely, though thick fog at the base meant a diversion to RAF Abingdon. Two aircraft [F/O FA Smith and W/O AV Potter] that got back close enough to base to call up and seek landing instructions were diverted to RAF Fulbeck. F/O AR Taylor in LM657 PG-Q reported a combat over the target, and his rear gunner [Sgt DR Stirling] claimed a Me110 destroyed, as it was seen to spin into the ground. Two of the aircraft that had landed at Abingdon had to be left there when the others returned the following day, both because engine changes were needed, one [F/O JS Hunter RAAF in RA527 PG-M] having lost an engine soon after bombing.

[169] On the night of 10/11 April, No 619 Sqn despatched eleven aircraft as part of a small No 5 and No 8 Groups force of 79 Lancasters and 19 Mosquitoes to attack the Wahren railway yards at Leipzig. Seven Lancasters were lost, including 619's SW254 PG-S [captain F/L AE McMorran RCAF, whose brother had been killed with the Squadron barely a month previously]. The eastern half of the yards was destroyed. This aircraft was one of 37 Lancasters built by Metropolitan Vickers and assembled by A.V. Roe between 24 Nov 44 and 22 Dec 45, with Merlin 24 engines. It says something about the state of the War that by the time this batch of aircraft came into service in early 1945, the danger of an aircraft being lost on ops had receded sufficiently that only three of the 37 were lost in this way, sadly SW254 being one of them. McMorran and five members of his crew died, only one [the Air Bomber, F/S HJ Burke] surviving as a POW. The dead rear gunner was P/O CTW Perring, an ex-apprentice [Ruislip Apprentice Clerk, 591253] who had enlisted in the 48th Entry at the age of 16 on 28 July 1937 and was 23 at the time of his death. His wife, Lilian Kathleen Perring, lived in Worthing, Surrey, and he is buried in the Berlin CWGC Cemetery. Of the 2,080 boys who enlisted as Apprentice Clerks between 1925 and 1942, when the scheme was put into mothballs following the evacuation from Ruislip to Gloucester of the RAF Record Office, where they were trained, 455 served as aircrew, 318 were awarded decorations and 276 died in action or in active service. Of the 2,080, 819 were commissioned, four reaching air rank, and 1,061 reached warrant officer or SNCO rank. The author joined the RAF in the post-war 27th

TABLE 4.3 OPERATIONS IN WHICH 619 SQN PARTICIPATED

Date	*Target*	*Aircraft*			
		prepared	*took off*	*Ret early*	*missing*
13 Apr 45	Gardening [Keil]	4	4	-	-
16 Apr 45	Pilsen[170]	15	14	1	-
17 Apr 45	Cham[171]	17	17	1	-
23 Apr 45	Flensburg[172]	12	12	-	-
25 Apr 45	Berchesgaden[173]	6	6	-	1
25 Apr 45	Gardening[174]	4	4	-	-

Entry of Administrative Apprentices in 1956, with the Apprentice Clerk number 593110, the apprentice clerk scheme having been re-started in 1947. Many of the immediate pre-war apprentice clerks had to wait several years before being accepted as aircrew, because as one famous war-time Air Officer Commanding-in-Chief put it '*we can get as many aircrew as we like and train them quicker than we can get good trained clerks*' [*The 2080 Record of Service*, published privately by the Apprentice Clerk Association].

[170] On 16/17April, No 5 Group sent 222 Lancasters and 11 Mosquitoes on a precision attack on the railway yards at Pilsen. One Lancaster crashed in France. All of 619's fourteen aircraft reached the target, bombed and got back safely, though one [ME787 PG-X captain F/O JS Hunter RAAF] returned early with the port inner engine u/s.

[171] On 17/18 April, 90 Lancasters and 11 Mosquitoes of No 5 Group attacked the railway yards at Cham, deep into eastern Europe and on the border with Czechoslovakia. The attack was once again devastatingly successful with track and rolling stock destroyed. No 619 Squadron despatched seventeen aircraft but one [ME787 PG-X captain F/L RJ Willitts] had to return early, this time with the port outer engine u/s. All the Group's aircraft returned safely. F/L GA Lavigne RCAF in RA521 PG-D returned with an engine feathered and F/O AP Reid RNZAF flew this operation in a borrowed No 227 Sqn aircraft [LM578].

[172] On 23 April No 5 group sent 148 Lancasters to attack the railway yards and port area of Flensburg. The raid was planned in two waves, with the 55 Base aircraft led by No 619 Squadron, flying behind 53 Base aircraft, and having as their aiming point a railway junction. Weather conditions were good until ten miles from the target when cloud conditions prevented bombing and the raid was called off, the aircraft returning to base with their bombs as instructed. With this operation, F/O GS Hatten completed his tour of ops.

[173] This was the last raid of the War for most of Bomber Command, and it was appropriate that the target should have been Hitler's mountain retreat in Bavaria, *Eagle's Nest*. The operation involved 359 Lancasters and 16 Mosquitoes of Nos 1, 5 and 8 Groups, including sixteen aircraft of No 617 Squadron dropping their last *Tallboy* bombs. No 619 Squadron despatched six crews, including F/O VT DeMarco RCAF in LM756 PG-F and on his 29th operation. He failed to return and was killed, along with three other members of his crew. Three survived as POWs.

Date	*Target*	*Aircraft*			
		prepared	*took off*	*Ret early*	*missing*
TOTALS:	236 targets	3,035	3,019	81	85

Most aircraft despatched on a single raid: 20 [on eight occasions].

[174] That evening, mine-laying in Oslo Fjord followed the Berchtesgaden raid. Two of the four aircraft had to abort, one because the mine would not release, and the other with a faulty H2S set. One of the two successful mine drops was by F/L JH Johnston in PG-D, who with this mission completed his tour of operations. When at 0241 F/O AP Reid RNZAF, in PA198 PG-J, landed back at Strubby, the shooting war was over, and No 619 Sqn had flown its last mission with hostile intent.

Table 4.4 No 619 Squadron – Decorations and Awards

An asterisk [*] indicates an immediate decoration for a specific act of gallantry. [p] indicates a posthumous award.

Date	*Award*	*Recipient*	*Occupation*	*Captain's name*
Aug 43	DFC	F/L SE Harrison DFM	Pilot	
	DFC [bar]	F/L CSR Bell DFC	Pilot	
	DFM	F/S W McLeod	Pilot	
	DFM	Sgt DJ Coomber	Pilot	
	DFM	F/S WL Vander Dasson	A/B	S/L GR Scorer
	DFM [bar]	F/S TH Goacher DFM	A/Gun	F/L SE Harrison
Sep 43	Nil			
Oct 43	Nil			
Nov 43	DFC	S/L R Aytoun	Pilot	
	DFC*	W/O HR Cooke	A/Gun	F/L WED Bell
	DFM*	F/S PD Mitchell	A/Gun	F/S EAL Smith
	DFM	Sgt RT Hughes	Pilot	
Dec 43	DSO*	Lt HC Knilans USAAF/ RCAF	Pilot	
	DFC [bar]	S/L RG Churcher DFC	Pilot	
	DFM*	F/S RA Learmouth	A/Gun	Lt HC Knilans
	DFM	Sgt WR Tyrie	W/Op	F/O MacDonald
	DFM	Sgt CD Walton	W/Op	F/O Vickerstaffe
Jan 44	DFC	F/L AH Tomlin	Pilot	
	DFC [bar]*	F/L AH Tomlin DFC	Pilot	

Date	*Award*	*Recipient*	*Occupation*	*Captain's name*
	DFC	P/O TA Peatfield	Nav	F/L AH Tomlin
	DFM	F/S J Simkin	A/B	F/L AH Tomlin
	DFM [bar]*	F/S AE Brookes DFM	F/Eng	F/L SEJ Jones
Feb 44	DFC	F/L JA Howard	A/Gun	Gunnery Leader
	DFC	F/L PSF Walmsley	A/B	S/L GR Scorer
Mar 44	DFC*	P/O K Roberts RAAF	Pilot	
	DFM*	F/S GC King RAAF	A/Gun	P/O K Roberts
	DFM*	F/S D Schofield	Pilot	
	DFM*	F/S GE Hexter RCAF	A/B	F/S D Schofield
April 44	DFC*	P/O F Griffiths	Pilot	
	DFC	F/L J Sears RAAF	Nav	S/L RG Churcher
	DFC	P/O RE Knights	Pilot	
May 44	DFC*	W/C JR Jeudwine DSO OBE	Pilot	
	DFC [bar]*	S/L WN Whamond DFC	Pilot	
	DFC [bar]*	F/L JA Howard DFC	A/Gun	W/C JR Jeudwine
	DFC	F/L A Sandison	Pilot	
	DFC	F/L ACE Lance	Nav	F/L A Sandison
	DFC*	P/O D Wadsworth	Pilot	
	DFM	F/S LJ Birch RAAF	A/Gun	W/C JR Jeudwine
	DFM*	Sgt HG Brady	W/Op	P/O D Wadsworth
	DFM*	Sgt FH Joy	A/Gun	P/O D Wadsworth
	DFM*	Sgt JH Maltby	A/Gun	P/O D Wadsworth

Table 4.4 No 619 Squadron Decorations & Awards

Date	*Award*	*Recipient*	*Occupation*	*Captain's name*
June 44	DFC	F/L WED Bell	Pilot	
	DFC	F/O HL Vickerstaffe	Pilot	
	DFC	F/O WA Johnson-Biggs	A/Gun	W/C JR Jeudwine
	DFC	F/O T Wilkie	A/B	Bombing Leader
	DFC	F/O NB Morrison RCAF	Pilot	
	DFC	F/O PH Taylor RCAF	Pilot	
	DFC	P/O RT Boultbee RAAF	A/Gun	F/O Vickerstaffe
	DFC	P/O JP Hind RCAF	Nav	F/O Vickerstaffe
	DFC	P/O BTJ Hucks RAAF	W/Op	F/O A Sandison
	DFC	P/O GG Taylor	Pilot	
	DFC	P/O EK Alley	A/B	F/L NB Morrison
	DFC	P/O JI Johnston RCAF	A/Gun	F/L NB Morrison
	DFC	W/O RA Westad RCAF	W/Op/AG	P/O GG Taylor
	DFC	W/O PD Mitchell DFM RCAF	A/Gun	F/S EAL Smith
	DFC	W/O GG Turnbull RAAF	A/Gun	F/O A Sandison
	DFM	F/S JA Featherstone	Nav	F/L WED Bell
	DFM	F/S JH Bryant	Nav	F/O GS Stout
	DFM	Sgt MV King	F/Eng	F/O A Sandison
	MiD	F/S GT Short	A/Gun	S/L LB Gunter
	MiD	F/S RA Willis	A/Gun	S/L LB Gunter
	MiD	F/S ED Poulter	F/Eng	S/L LB Gunter
	MiD	F/S TA Gould	Engine Fitter	

Date	*Award*	*Recipient*	*Occupation*	*Captain's name*
	MiD	F/S FJ Mullins[1]	Airframe Fitter	-
	MiD	Cpl WF Copson	Engine Fitter	
	MiD	LAC RW Houghton	Airframe mechanic	-
	MiD	LAC J Lynch	Airframe mechanic	-
	MiD	LAC JJD Stevens	Engine mechanic	-
	MiD	LAC AC Turner	Engine mechanic	-
July 44	DFC*	F/O FF Molinas RAAF	Pilot	
	DFM*	Sgt TF Frogley	A/Gun	P/O NW Donnelly RNZAF
Aug 44	DFC	F/O P Buttar RCAF	Pilot	
	DFC	F/O LJ Warner RAAF	Pilot	
	DFC	F/O JC Dougherty	Pilot	
	DFC	F/O FG Secker	Pilot	
	DFC	F/O FL Chipperfield	Nav	F/O RW Olsen
	DFC	F/O RW Olsen	Pilot	
Sep 44	DFC	F/L SEJ Jones	Pilot	
	DFC	F/O KR Makin	W/Op	S/L W Whamond
	DFC	F/O RW Wood RCAF	A/B	F/O P Buttar
	DFC	F/O VP Kennedy	A/B	S/L W Whamond
	DFC	P/O JG Noble RCAF	Nav	F/O P Buttar
	DFM*	F/S CH Stewart RCAF	A/Gun	S/L MA Smith

[1] Flight Sergeant TA Gould and Flight Sergeant FJ Mullins were both ex-Halton apprentices.

Table 4.4 No 619 Squadron Decorations & Awards

Date	*Award*	*Recipient*	*Occupation*	*Captain's name*
	DFM	F/S T Fleetwood	W/Op	F/O P Buttar
	DFM	F/S GG Watt	F/Eng	F/O P Buttar
	DFM	F/S PVJ Lowen	Nav	P/O LJ Warner
	DFM	F/S T Aitken	A/B	P/O LJ Warner
	DFM	Sgt AM McInulty	F/Eng	P/O LJ Warner
	DFM	Sgt H Waterson	W/Op	P/O LJ Warner
Oct 44	DFC*	F/O DH Strachan RNZAF	Pilot	
	DFC	F/O A Whiteley	Pilot	
	DFC	P/O FS Garside	Nav	P/O JC Dougherty
	DFC	P/O GF Wilson	W/Op	P/O JC Dougherty
	DFM	F/S H Hope	A/B	P/O JC Dougherty
	DFM*	Sgt F Webster	A/Gun	F/O DH Strachan
	DFM	Sgt HD Campbell	F/Eng	P/O JC Dougherty
	DFM	Sgt AJ Griffee	A/Gun	P/O JC Dougherty
Nov 44	DFC [bar]	F/O RA Marshall	Nav	S/L W Whamond
	DFC	F/O NE Westergaard	Nav	F/O D MacDonald
Dec 44	Nil			
Jan 45	DFC	F/O AB Neilson RAAF	Pilot	
	DFC	F/O KH Youdale RAAF	Nav	F/O AB Neilson
	DFC	F/O WG Stevens RNZAF	Nav	F/O DH Strachan
	DFC	P/O JR Hill	W/Op	F/L PF Wingate
Feb 45	DFC	F/L EY O'Neill RCAF	Pilot	

Date	*Award*	*Recipient*	*Occupation*	*Captain's name*
	DFC	F/O AB Fleck RCAF	Pilot	
	DFC	F/O WSM Nash	A/B	F/O G Scripps
	DFM	Sgt AJA York	A/Gun	F/O DH Strachan
Mar 45	DFC*	S/L PS Osborne	Pilot	
	DFC	F/L TK Graves	A/Gun	S/L WF Jordan
	DFC*	F/O DJ Davies RAAF	A/Gun	F/L RT Brown
Apr 45	DFC	W/C IJ McGhie [p]	Pilot	
	DFC	P/O C Fuller [p]	Pilot	
	DFM	F/S FG Metcalfe [p]	Pilot	
	DFC	F/O GG Runnalls	Pilot	
	DFC	P/O RT Jouchin	W/Op	F/L JL Whiteley
May 45	DFC [bar]	W/C RA Milward DFC	Pilot	
	DFC	F/L PF Wingate	Pilot	
	DFC	F/O WJ Franks	Pilot	
	DFC	F/O JL Birtles RNZAF	A/B	F/O DH Strachan
	DFC	P/O HE Hayes	A/Gun	S/L WF Jordan
	DFC	P/O DR Attwood[2]	F/Eng	F/LAE McMorran

[2] As a W/O, P/O Attwood had flown as a member of the crew of F/L AE McMorran until the second week of Feb 45, when he appears to have completed his tour. Thereafter, until F/L McMorran was lost on 10/11 April, he had as his F/Eng first Sgt KG Couchman and then P/O S Love. On the fatal flight on 10/11 April, the F/Eng Leader, F/L F Jackson, went with him [Jackson having flown with F/L John Whiteley on the Dresden operation in Feb]. Earlier Whiteley and Jackson had given a talk to the squadron about 'looking after engines'.

TABLE 4.4 NO 619 SQUADRON DECORATIONS & AWARDS

Date	*Award*	*Recipient*	*Occupation*	*Captain's name*
	DFC	P/O JPW Heather-Hayes	Nav	F/O GG Runnalls
	DFC	W/O EG Nisbett	W/Op	F/O DH Strachan
June 45	DFC	W/O GE Deschaine RCAF	B/A	P/O GG Taylor
Dec 45	DFC	S/L RG Purnell	Pilot	
	DFC	F/L SCW Lock	W/Op	S/L RG Purnell
	DFC	F/L JL Whiteley	Pilot	

Totals:	
DSO	1
DFC	79 [including 8 bars]
DFM	35 [including 3 bars]
MiD	10
	125

In terms of number of awards the most decorated crews were those of F/O JC Dougherty and F/O DH Strachan RNZAF, six members of each receiving decorations.

Table 4.5 Aircraft Captains and crews[1] serving with No 619 Squadron During 23 months of operations – June 1943 to May 1945

Date In	*Captain*[2]	*Date Out*	*Remarks*
18 Apr 43	W/C IJ McGhie[3]	18 Aug 43	Killed on Peenemünde raid.
19 Apr 43	F/L CSR Bell DFC[4]	23 Jun 43	Completed this 2nd tour.
19 Apr 43	F/O SE Harrison DFM	13 Jun 43	Completed this 2nd tour.
19 Apr 43	Sgt W McLeod	23 Jun 43	Completed this 1st tour.
22Apr 43	A/S/Ldr R G Churcher DFC[5]	Feb 44	Rtd G/C DSO MVO DFC.
22 Apr 43	F/O E Dampier-Crossley DFC	11 Aug 43	Killed on Nürnberg raid.
22 Apr 43	A/F/L CO Taylor[6]	12 Jun 43	Shot down on first op [evd]

---

[1] In the interests of brevity and because some crews changed members during the course of a tour of ops, I have reluctantly restricted this list to the names of pilot captains only, as otherwise an unacceptable number of notes and qualifications would have been needed to support the entries. The other members of the crew were, of course, just as important as the pilots.

[2] The rank shown is the rank in which the captain arrived on 619 Sqn. Many sergeants were commissioned within days of arrival and others were rapidly promoted.

[3] W/C McGhie was posted in as Commanding Officer of the new Squadron from RAF Station Scampton and F/O GM Burdett was posted in from No 17 OTU to be Squadron Adjutant.

[4] Bell, Harrison, McLeod and their crews were the three experienced teams left behind at Woodhall Spa by No 97 Sqn to form the nucleus of the new squadron in April, 1943. On this day also F/L LC Mitcham was posted in from No 1485 B&G Flight as Squadron Engineering Officer.

[5] F/O acting F/L RC Churcher was posted in from 1660 CU to fill a S/Ldr post as 'A'Flight Commander. On this same day F/O PSF Walmsley was posted in from No 1654 CU to be Squadron Bombing Leader.

Table 4.5 No 619 Squadron Captains & Crews

Date In	*Captain*[2]	*Date Out*	*Remarks*
23 Apr 43	Sgt DV Jordan	22 Jun 43	Killed on Krefeld raid.
23 Apr 43	Sgt K McCulloch	15 Jun 43	Killed on Oberhausen raid.
23 Apr 43	Sgt T Metcalfe	1 Sep 43	Killed on Berlin raid. DFM.
23 Apr 43	Sgt DJ Coomber[7]	24 Aug 43	POW on Berlin raid.
6 May 43	S/L GR Scorer[8]	Mar 44?	Completed tour. Died 1964
8 May 43	F/O SEJ Jones DFM	Mar 44?	Tour comp; posted 617 Sqn
8 May 43	F/O AH Tomlin[9]	Mar 44?	Survived tour. DFC. d1981.
23 May 43	Sgt FW Shirley	9 Jun 43	Killed in training.
23 May 43	Sgt WJ Douglas	9 Jun 43	Killed in training.
23 May 43	Sgt RT Hughes	15 Nov 43	Posted to 630 Sqn
1 Jun 43	Sgt CA Goddard	6 Sep 43	Killed on Mannheim raid.
1 Jun 43	P/O WED Bell	Mar 44?	Survived W/C DFC d1966
3 Jun 43	Sgt OA O'Leary	18 Aug 43	Killed on Peenemünde raid.
6 Jun 43	Sgt TP Murphy	29 Jun 43	Killed on Köln raid.
8 Jun 43	P/O DM Joss	2 Oct 43	Killed on return Hagen raid

---

[6] F/O Dampier-Crossley and acting F/L Taylor were both ex-No 50 Squadron.

[7] Sgts Jordan, McCulloch, Metcalfe and Coomber and their crews were posted in as freshly trained crews from No 1660 CU. On Easter Monday, 26th April, F/O JD Henderson was posted in from No 57 Squadron to be the Squadron Navigation Officer and the following day, 27 April, F/O JA Howard was posted in from No 1485 B&G Flight to be the Squadron Gunnery Officer.

[8] S/L GR Scorer was posted in from Fiskerton to be the other ['B'] Flight Commander. On 1st May F/L Gilmour had been posted in as the Squadron Signals Leader. Thus, the Squadron Headquarters staff was now complete.

[9] F/O Tomlin was posted in from No 106 Sqn.

Date In	*Captain*[2]	*Date Out*	*Remarks*
14 Jun 43	Sgt C Fuller [DFC]	18 Oct 43	Killed on Hannover raid.
15 Jun 43	P/O O'Shaughnessy	30 Sep 43	Killed with 617 Sqn Jan 44.
15 Jun 43	Sgt AJ Pearce	18 Aug 43	Killed on Peenemünde raid.
15 Jun 43	F/O DA McDonald	Dec 43	Posted to East Kirby.
17 Jun 43	F/O A Sandison	Mar 44?	Completed tour. DFC.
17 Jun 43	Sgt HL Vickerstaffe	Mar 44?	Completed tour. DFC.
18 Jun 43	F/S GG Taylor[10]	Feb 44	Completed tour. DFC.
18 Jun 43	Sgt C Firth	21 Oct 43	Killed on Leipzig raid.
27 Jun 43	Sgt GW Bower RCAF	1 Sep 43	Killed on Berlin raid.
29 Jun 43	Sgt H C Knilans RCAF	6 Jan 44	To 617 Sqn DSO DFC.
30 Jun 43	Sgt RE Knights	6 Jan 44	To 617 Sqn DSO DFC.
7 Jul 43	F/L F Pullen	Not known	Crew posted to 50 Sqn.
9 Jul 43	P/O RD Rayment	27 Nov 43	Killed on Berlin raid.
9 Jul 43	F/O NB Morrison RCAF	Jan 44?	Completed tour. DFC.
14 Jul 43	F/L R Aytoun	Dec 43?	Completed as S/L. DFC.
14 Jul 43	Sgt JH Mason	Dec 43?	Completed tour?
27 Jul 43	F/O B Arden[11]		Survived W/C DFC d1979?

---

[10] A Cornishman from St Austell and a friend of Sgt Roy Trahair, the rear gunner in Cyril Fuller's crew.

[11] On returning from Milan on 13 Aug 43 [in JA844 PG-J] collided with Lancaster ED361 of No 207 Sqn off the Sussex coast. F/O Arden and four of his crew survived, and he re-crewed and completed his tour of ops, retiring in Oxfordshire after the War as a W/Cdr with a DFC. Believed now to be dead. The navigator of JA844, Sgt DV Jones drifted away from the dinghy after the crew came down in the sea, and the rear gunner, Sgt J Maddaford, died in Littlehampton Hospital after they were rescued by an RAF ASR launch.

Table 4.5 No 619 Squadron Captains & Crews

Date In	*Captain*[2]	*Date Out*	*Remarks*
Not known	Sgt JF Ward	Not known	Listed in ORB >22 Aug 43
15 Aug 43	F/O JA Heffernan RCAF	3 Jan 44	Killed on Berlin raid.
15 Aug 43	F/O EK Williams RCAF[12]	25 Feb 44	Killed on Schweinfurt raid.
19 Aug 43	P/O JG Thompson	Apr 44	Completed tour.
20 Aug 43	W/C W Abercromby DFC	4 Dec 43	Killed 2 Jan 44 Berlin op.
?? Aug 43	F/S VG Stabell RAAF	18 Aug 43	2nd pilot at Peenemunde.
5 Sep 43	F/O JK Cox	3 Jan 44	Killed on Berlin raid.
5 Sep 43	F/O ML Hamilton	16 Feb 44	To 617 Sqn.
5 Sep 43	P/O J Horne[13]	18 Oct 43	Killed on Hannover raid.
9 Sep 43	F/O RHE Foote	28 Nov 43	To 83 PFF Sqn.
23 Sep 43	F/O RM Rumble RCAF	16 Feb 44	Killed on Berlin raid.
27 Sep 43	Sgt RW Olsen	27 Apr 44	Completed tour.
27 Sep 43	P/O JF Bowyer RCAF	3 Dec 43	Killed on Berlin raid.[14]
Not known	P/O E Mearis	30 Sep 43	Killed returning Bochum.
?? Sep 43	P/O SPJ Thomas	28 Sep 43	Posted to 514 Sqn.
7 Oct 43	F/S EAL Smith RAAF	25 Nov 43	To new RAAF Sqn [463].
12 Oct 43	P/O V Langford	2 Feb 44	To 83 PFF Sqn.

[12] Four members of F/O Williams' crew survived as POWs.

[13] P/O James Horne died with Cyril Fuller and his crew over Hannover on the night of 18 Oct 43 when Horne was flying his second op as second pilot, the first having been on 4 Oct 43 with F/S GG Taylor. He left a young widow in South Brixham, Devon. His religion is recorded as Church of Scotland, suggested a Scottish connection. In 1945 Cyril Fuller's mother said that his young widow had still not accepted his death.

[14] Four members of F/O Bowyer's crew survived as POWs.

Date In	*Captain*[2]	*Date Out*	*Remarks*
13 Oct 43	F/S GB Loney RCAF	17 Dec 43	Killed on Berlin raid.
13 Oct 43	F/S P Buttar RCAF	Jun 44?	Completed tour. DFC.
21 Oct 43	F/O GS Stout[15]	23/24 Sep 44	Killed with 617 Sqn
22 Oct 43	F/O JWED McGilvray[16]	11 Ap 44	Killed on Aachen raid.
22 Oct 43	P/O FG Secker	14 May 44	Posted to 52 Base.
31 Oct 43	Sgt DH Shorter	11 Mar 44	Posted to 97 PFF Sqn.
15 Nov 43	Sgt LV Hall	Jun 44?	Completed tour.
?? Nov 43	P/O JW Nancarrow RAAF	25 Nov 43	Posted to 463 Sqn RAAF
1 Dec 43	Sgt JC Dougherty	Nov 43?	Completed tour. DFC
4 Dec 43	W/Cdr JR Jeudwine	15 May 44	To Master Bomber duties.
15 Dec 43	F/S D Schofield [DFM]	25 Apr 44	Killed on München raid.
15 Dec 43	Sgt F Griffiths	Apr 44	Completed tour. DFC.
23 Dec 43	F/O AG Day	6 Jan 44	Killed on Berlin raid.[17]
?? Dec 43	Sgt DA Wadsworth [DFC]	4 May 44	Killed Mailly-le-Camp.
30 Dec 43	Sgt GGC Gunzi	27 Apr 44	Killed Schweinfurt raid.
8 Jan 44	Sgt RF Whinfield	27 Apr 44	Killed Schweinfurt raid.
8 Jan 44	P/O K Roberts RAAF[18]	7 Jun 44	Killed Caen raid D Day.

[15] F/O Stout and his crew were posted in from 617 Sqn.

[16] As a S/L, JWED McGilvray DFC, was lost on the Aachen raid of 11 Apr 44.

[17] F/O Day and his crew had been on the squadron for only ten days. They were lost in the squadron's veteran aircraft, ED977 PG-A *Nulli Secundus*, which had completed 46 missions and flown 440 hours.

Table 4.5 No 619 Squadron Captains & Crews

Date In	*Captain*[2]	*Date Out*	*Remarks*
8 Jan 44	F/L FE Fuller	8 May 44	Killed [S/L] Salbris raid.
8 Feb 44	S/L WN Whamond[19]	14 May 44	DFC. Doctor after War.
13 Feb 44	Sgt J Parker	24 Jul 44	Killed on Keil raid.
20 Feb 44	F/L HJ Moore	12 Apr 44	POW on Aachen raid.
26 Feb 44	P/O GG Runnalls	7 Apr 44	Completed tour. DFC.
?? Feb 44	P/O LJ Warner RAAF [DFC]	28 Jun 44	Completed tour.[20]
8 Mar 44	P/O P Thompson RNZAF	25 Mar 44	Shot down over Berlin.
11 Mar 44	F/S JM Aitken RNZAF	10 May 44	Killed Gennevilliers raid.
11 Mar 44	F/S J Patterson	29 Jul 44	Killed Stuttgart raid.
13 Mar 44	F/S NW Donnelley RNZAF[21]	19 Jul 44	Killed on Revigny raid.
15 Mar 44	P/O A Whiteley	Aug 44?	Completed tour. DFC.

---

[18] In 1995 a memorial was unveiled in France at the site of the 1944 aircraft crash by the Mairie D'Auvers and was attended by members of F/L Kimberley Roberts' family and the two surviving crew members of the crew, the air bomber Reg De Veill and the Flight Engineer Jack Forrest. An interesting article also appeared in the Roberts' local [Bunbury] newspaper in Australia which included the information that F/L Roberts always wore around his neck as a lucky talisman a WWI German Iron Cross given him by a friend's father, a RFC pilot, who had been given it as a keepsake by a young WWI German pilot, Hermann Goering, after an aerial duel over Belgium on 8 June 1917 in which Goering had shot the RFC pilot down.

[19] With 619 Sqn, S/L Bill Whamond completed his second tour of ops. He survived the War and was a medical Doctor post-War. He died round about the Millenium.

[20] The ORB diarist notes that with the Marquise operation P/O L Warner had completed his first tour of 36 ops without once having to return early.

[21] P/O Donnelley RNZAF flew with a mixed crew of two RNZAF, one Rhodesian and four RAF.

Date In	*Captain*[2]	*Date Out*	*Remarks*
1 Apr 44	Sgt PH French	21 Apr 44	Killed La Chapelle.
15 Apr 44	P/O KE Crawford RAAF[22]	22 Jun 44	Killed Wesseling raid.
22 Apr 44	P/O F Young RNZAF[23]	26 Apr 44	POW Sweinfurt raid.
22 Apr 44	P/O P Johnson	22 Jun 44	Killed Wesseling raid.
27 Apr 44	F/S JA Buckley	22 Jun 44	Killed Wesseling raid.
28 Apr 44	F/O RH Redshaw	22 May 44	Killed Duisburg raid.
29 Apr 44	P/O GA Baker	22 Jun 44	Killed Wesseling raid.
1 May 44	P/O MHA Davis	22 Jun 44	Killed Wesseling raid.
1 May 44	F/S AB Neilson RAAF [DFC]	Dec 44?	Completed tour. DFC.
1 May 44	F/O RT Brown RAAF	Dec 44?	Completed tour.
2 May 44	P/O TN McCurdy	14 June 44	Posted to 97 Sqn PFF.
3 May 44	F/S R Bennett	3 Aug 44	Killed Trossy raid.
6 May 44	F/O DC Saunders	22 Jun 44	POW Wesseling raid.
9 May 44	P/O G Scripps	Dec 44?	Completed tour.
11 May 44	F/O PF Wingate	Dec 44?	Completed tour. DFC
12 May 44	F/S SB Morcom[24]	19 Jul 44	Killed on Revigny raid.
?? May 44	F/S K Goodwin	10 May 44	Killed as second pilot.

---

[22] P/O Crawford, an Australian himself, had a New Zealander and a Rhodesian in his crew and 4 RAF.

[23] P/O Young RNZAF was taken POW on his first op as second pilot with the crew of F/S Whinfield in LL904 PG-S, which was shot down during the raid of Schweinfurt. Young was the only survivor. Illustrating the confusion that often surrounded ranks when a pilot arrived on a squadron from training, it is interesting to see that in the F540 he is shown as a P/O and in the F541 as a F/S.

[24] Both P/O Morcom's gunners were RCAF, Morcom and the rest of the crew RAF.

Table 4.5 No 619 Squadron Captains & Crews

Date In	*Captain*[2]	*Date Out*	*Remarks*
18 May 44	F/O CWA Coop RCAF	12 Jul 44	Posted to 83 PFF Sqn.
22 May 44	P/O FF Molinas DFC RAAF	19 Jul 44	Killed on Revigny raid.
22 May 44	A/S/L LB Gunter	13 Aug 44	POW Braunschweig raid.
23 May 44	F/O LA Hall	10 Aug 44	Killed on Chatellerault raid.
23 May 44	W/C JR Maling[25] AFC	26 Jul 44	POW on Stuttgart raid.
30 May 44	F/O HJ Wilson RCAF	19 Jul 44	Killed on Revigny raid.
4 Jun 44	F/S AB Fleck RCAF[26]	Jan 45?	Completed tour. DFC.
6 Jun 44	F/O EA Orange	Oct 44?	Posted out?
8 Jun 44	F/L GM Howes	Jul 44?	Posted out?
12 Jun 44	P/O FR Maguire	Dec 44?	Completed tour.
12 Jun 44	S/L MA Smith[27]	Jan 45?	Completed tour. DFC.
15 Jun 44	F/L AR Squibbs[28]	12 Sep 44	Killed on Darmstadt raid.
16 Jun 44	P/O LW Leonard	20 Sep 44	Killed Mönchen-Gladbach.
16 Jun 44	Sgt DGF Lockwood		Posted out?

[25] The Squadron's fourth CO in a year of operations. He and his crew were shot down in ND935 PG-K during a raid on Stuttgart on 25/26 Jul 44. Three were killed and four, including Maling, were taken POW.

[26] F/O Fleck's crew consisted of four RCAF and three RAF.

[27] S/L Maurice Smith survived the war, leaving as a W/C with a DFC and for many years afterwards was the editor of 'The Aeroplane' magazine and was associated with Flight International. He died in Feb 1987.

[28] The remains of the aircraft in which S/L RA Squibbs and his crew were lost during a raid on Darmstadt was not discovered until 10 May 1947 when the authorities examined a large crater in a wood about 1 km south of Darmstadt and recovered the remains of the crew. They were initially taken to Neckargemünd but have since been interred in the Dürnbach War Cemetery.

Date In	*Captain*[2]	*Date Out*	*Remarks*
22 Jun 44	F/L CC Johnston	8 Jul 44	Came down St Leu op. Evd
23 Jun 44	F/O EY O'Neill RCAF[29]	Jan 45?	Completed tour. DFC.
27 Jun 44	F/O WF Jordan [S/L]	Jan 45?	Completed tour.
1 Jul 44	F/O RW Pettigrew RCAF	27 Sep 44	Killed on Karlsruhe raid.
7 Jul 44	F/O RW Orbell	25 Jul 44	Killed on Donges raid.
13 Jul 44	F/O CB Dockrey RCAF[30]	12 Sep 44	Killed on Darmstadt raid.
20 Jul 44	P/O R Mather[31]	Oct 44	Tour completed.
20 Jul 44	F/O RG Turvey RAAF	27 Jul 44	Killed on Givors raid.
21 Jul 44	F/S DH Strachan RNZAF[32]	14 Jan 45	Tour completed. DFC.
22 Jul 44	F/O JH Peck	Oct 44	Tour completed.
23 Jul 44	F/O R Bateman	6 Jan 45	Tour completed.
23 Jul 44	F/O WJ Franks	Mar 45?	Completed tour. DFC.
24 Jul 44	W/O SV Chambers RCAF[33]	5 Dec 44	Killed on Heilbronn raid.
25 Jul 44	F/O FE Eley	30 Aug 44	Killed on Konigsberg raid.
28 Jul 44	F/O GB White	Sep 44?	Posted out?
29 Jul 44	F/O R Dickinson	Jan 45?	Completed tour.

[29] F/O O'Neill's crew contained four RCAF and three RAF.

[30] F/O Dockrey's crew included four RCAF and three RAF.

[31] Though F/O Mather was serving in the RAF, his crew contained five RAAF members.

[32] F/O Strachan's crew contained three New Zealanders.

[33] W/O Chambers and three members of his crew were RCAF, the other three RAF.

TABLE 4.5 NO 619 SQUADRON CAPTAINS & CREWS

Date In	*Captain*[2]	*Date Out*	*Remarks*
29 Jul 44	W/C RA Milward[34]	21 Feb 45	Second tour completed.
29 Jul 44	F/O EJF Smith	3 Feb 45	pow Karlsruhe. Crew killed
??	F/O BJ Hines	27 Aug 44	Posted to 97 Sqn.
14 Aug 44	F/O JW May	Jan 45?	Completed tour.
14 Aug 44	F/O PC Clapham	12 Nov 44	Killed on Hamburg raid.
16 Aug 44	F/S GD Lean RNZAF	30 Oct 44	Posted to 189 Squadron.
17 Aug 44	F/O JD Cottman RAAF[35]	Attached from 97 Sqn	Ceased attch. 27 Sep 44.
26 Aug 44	F/O CWA Coop RCAF	Returned from 83 Sqn.	
29 Aug 44	F/S KR Allen RAAF	Oct 44	Tour completed.
6 Sep 44	F/O KR Hickmott RCAF[36]	7 Mar 45	Tour completed.
11 Sep 44	F/O GM Proctor RNZAF[37]	7 Mar 45	Tour completed.
12 Sep 44	F/O DW Martin	3 Nov 44	Posted to 189 Squadron.
14 Sep 44	F/O MW Bell	7 Oct 44	Posted to 227 Squadron.
15 Sep 44	F/S JLB Webster	7 Nov 44	Killed Gravenhorst raid.
18 Sep 44	Lt MH Meter SAAF	5 May 45	Posted to 617 Sqn.
23 Sep 44	F/O WR Carter RAAF	16 Oct 44	Posted to 227 Squadron.

[34] W/C RA Milward DFC was the Squadron's fifth Commanding Officer. He remained in post until 21 Feb 45 when he handed over to W/C SG Birch DFC who remained with the Squadron throughout the rest of the war, relinquishing command on 14 Jun 45 to W/C SE Flett [SR80042], a Rhodesian, a month before the Squadron disbanded on 18 Jul 45.

[35] F/O Cottman's crew was unusual for a mainstream RAF Squadron in that all members of the crew except the F/Eng were members of the RAAF.

[36] F/O Ken Hickmott RCAF, a present-day member of the Squadron Association, flew with five RCAF and two RAF members in his crew.

[37] F/O GM Proctor RNZAF flew with two RNZAF, one RAAF and four RAF in his crew.

Date In	*Captain*[2]	*Date Out*	*Remarks*
23 Sep 44	F/O TE Kerslake	26 Sep 44	Killed Karlsruhe raid.
26 Sep 44	F/O AE McMorran[38]RCAF	11 Apr 45	Killed Leipzig raid.
26 Sep 44	F/O GM McMorran RCAF	8 Mar 45	Killed Harburg raid.
28 Sep 44	F/O GA Lavigne RCAF	8 June 45	Repatriated via Rufforth.
28 Sep 44	W/C HR Black	7 Oct 44	Posted to 227 Sqn [as CO].
30 Sep 44	F/O BP Curran RAAF	14 Jan 45	Interned in Sweden.
5 Oct 44	F/O JH Johnston RCAF[39]	25 Apr 45	Completed tour.
12 Oct 44	F/O LW O'Brien RAAF[40]	Apr 45?	Completed tour?
15 Oct 44	F/O JM Grant RAAF[41]	Apr 45?	Completed tour?
16 Oct 44	S/L RG Purnell	Apr 45?	Re-crewed after crash.DFC.
6 Oct 44	F/L LE Tanner	1 Nov 44	Killed on Homberg raid.
17 Oct 44	F/L KC Davis	Apr 45	Completed tour?
20 Oct 44	F/O EW Hookings	7 Nov 44	POW on Gravenhorst raid.
20 Oct 44	F/O JL Whiteley	10 Apr 45	Completed tour. DFC.
22 Oct 44	F/O PS Osborne	Mar 45?	Completd tour as S/L DFC.
30 Oct 44	F/O WD Cowling RCAF	8 Jun 45	Repatriated via Rufforth.

[38] The two Canadian McMorran brothers were posted on to the Squadron together in September 1944 and were killed within a month of each other in the last few weeks of the War on 7 March and 9 April 1945. It is believed they were the only two brothers lost with No 619 Squadron during its 23 months of operations.

[39] F/O JH Johnston RCAF flew with a mixed crew of five RCAF and two RAF.

[40] F/O LW O'Brien RAAF flew with three RAAF, one RNZAF, one RCAF and two RAF in his crew.

[41] F/O JM Grant RAAF flew with three RAAF and four RAF in his crew.

Table 4.5 No 619 Squadron Captains & Crews

Date In	*Captain*[2]	*Date Out*	*Remarks*
?? Nov 44	F/O D Gray RAAF	5 Jan 45	Killed on Royan raid.
1 Nov 44	F/O JS Hunter RAAF	Apr 45?	Completed tour?
2 Nov 44	F/O VT DeMarco RCAF[42]	25 Apr 45	Killed Berchtesgaden raid.
5 Nov 44	F/S GS Hatten	23 Apr 45	Completed tour.
7 Nov 44	F/O RH Shaeffer RCAF	5 Dec 44	Killed on Heilbronn raid.
7 Nov 44	F/L KW Whitefield	11 Nov 44	Killed as second pilot.
20 Nov 44	F/O CK Flockhart RAAF	8 Jan 45	Killed returning München.
21 Nov 44	W/O AR Whittaker	1 Jun 45	Posted to 97 Sqn.
22 Nov 44	F/L RJ Willitts	11 Jun 45	Posted to 61 Sqn.
24 Nov 44	W/C JN Tomes	13 Dec 44	To 57 Sqn as CO.
27 Nov 44	F/O ET Pennells RCAF[43]	8 Jun 45	Repatriated via Rufforth.
8 Dec 44	F/O HT Hesketh RAAF	9 Feb 45	Killed on Pölitz raid.
5 Jan 45	F/O CP Sparks RNZAF	Apr 45	Completed tour?
7 Jan 45	F/O EH Hooker	21 Jun 45	Posted to 617 Sqn.
19 Jan 45	F/O NA Gampe RAAF	Apr 45	Completed tour?
7 Feb 45	F/O JG Taylor	21 Jun 45	Posted to 617 Sqn.
8 Feb 45	W/O AV Potter	1 Jun 45	Posted to 97 Sqn.
15 Feb 45	F/O AL Leriger RCAF	8 Jun 45	Repatriated via Rufforth.
16 Feb 45	F/O A Poole	[still operational at end of war]	

[42] F/O DeMarco's was the last crew to be lost in 23 months of operations. He was on his 29th Operation. His crew contained four RCAF and three RAF.

[43] F/O ET Pennells RCAF flew with four RCAF and three RAF in his crew.

Date In	*Captain*[2]	*Date Out*	*Remarks*
16 Feb 45	F/O G Greenway RCAF	8 Jun 45	Repatriated via Rufforth.
21 Feb 45	F/O LDB Hooper RNZAF	1 Jun 45	Posted to 97 Sqn.
21 Feb 45	W/C SG Birch	14 Jun 45	Posted to 44 Sqn.
Feb 45	F/O WH Muncy	[no trace of ops]	Posted out?
5 Mar 45	F/O FW Seazell	1 Jun 45	Posted to 97 Sqn.
9 Mar 45	F/O AR Taylor	1 Jun 45	Posted to 97 Sqn.
9 Mar 45	F/O TE Farrow RCAF	17 Mar 45	Killed on third operation.
10 Mar 45	F/O AP Reid RNZAF	1 Jun 45	Posted to 97 Sqn.
13 Mar 45	S/L CM Palmer [attchd for ops experience]	Killed Böhlen 21 Mar 45.	
11 Mar 45	F/S DR Irvine RCAF	8 Jun 45	Repatriated via Rufforth.
13 Mar 45	F/O BR Bartlett	[still operational at end of war]	
13 Mar 45	W/O ER Peterson RCAF	8 Jun 45	Repatriated via Rufforth.
13 Mar 45	F/O A Hill RCAF	8 Jun 45	Repatriated via Rufforth.
13 Mar 45	F/O RW Knape	[still operational at end of war]	
29 Mar 45	W/C Balm DSO DFC [attchd for ops exp]	Posted to 227 Sqn as CO.	
29 Mar 45	F/O FI Smith	[still operational at end of war]	
18 Apr 45	F/L F Holmes RCAF	8 Jun 45	Repatriated via Rufforth.
19 Apr 45	F/O E Cook		
24 Apr 45	F/L PL Edwards	1 Jun 45	Posted to 97 Sqn.
27 Apr 45	F/O T Jones		
8 May 45	W/O ML Whinfield	1 Jun 45	Posted to 97 Sqn.
8 May 45	F/S WC Newman	1 Jun 45	Posted to 97 Sqn.
13 May 45	F/O D Blan		
18 May 45	W/O CPC Dibley		

Table 4.5 No 619 Squadron Captains & Crews

Date In	*Captain*[2]	*Date Out*	*Remarks*
May 45	F/L Wilkinson	1 Jun 45	Posted to 97 Sqn.
13 Jun 45	F/O EG Gillette		
13 Jun 45	W/O AE Breedon		
13 Jun 45	W/O WN Thompson		
13 Jun 45	F/S TE Stubbs		
13 Jun 45	F/L JAE Lancaster		
13 Jun 45	F/L HI Palfreyman*		
13 Jun 45	F/L CWG Wilson*		
13 Jun 45	F/O TA Austin		
13 Jun 45	F/O JM Hobbs*		
13 Jun 45	F/O JD Hollingsworth*		
13 Jun 45	F/O BE Keeler*		
13 Jun 45	F/O HF Ford[44]		
25 Jun 45	P/O D Long		
25 Jun 45	W/O CA Garthwaite*		
25 Jun 45	W/O S Hill*		
25 Jun 45	W/O CC Mann*		
25 Jun 45	W/O H Mason*		
25 Jun 45	W/O M Porteous*		
25 Jun 45	W/O JC Worsey*		
25 Jun 45	F/S LJ Mee Chang*		

[44] This captain and crew and the eleven captains and crews above were all posted in from No 1661 Conversion Unit with effect from 13 June.

Date In	*Captain*[2]	*Date Out*	*Remarks*
25 Jun 45	Sgt T Cartwright[45]*		

[45] This captain and crew and the eight above were all were posted in from No 75 Base with effect from 25 June. Interestingly, of the total of twenty one crews posted in during June 1945, thirteen of the Flight Engineers, including Sgt Cartwright's, are shown as Pilot/Flight Engineer, signifying a shift in the training involved [The thirteen are marked with an asterisk *]. Flight Engineers had always received some training in how to take over an aircraft if the captain was incapacitated so as to be able fly in a straight line while the crew got out, but this was a more substantial shift in training, almost reverting to the early days when the heavy bombers had two pilots, rather than one pilot and a flight engineer. What it tells us is that the training machine had now gathered such momentum that it could afford to put two pilots in each aircraft.

Table 4.6. No 619 Squadron personnel killed in action (June 1943 to May 1945)

Rank / Name		*Number*	*Captain's Rank / Name*		*Date /Operation*
F/S	Adams, G.P.	R221003	F/O	Pettigrew, R.W	Missing 26/9/44 (Karlsruhe)
Sgt	Adsetts, J.		F/S	Murphy, T.P.	Missing 29/6/43 (Köln)
P/O	Aitken, J.M.	NZ39075	P/O	Aitken, J.M.	Missing 9/5/44 (Gennevilliers)
F/O	Anderson, F.V.	B132958	F/O	Joss, D.M.	Missing 1/10/43 Crashed in Bristol Channel. Killed.
Sgt	Archer, A.		F/O	Dockrey, C.B.	Missing 11/9/44 (Darmstadt)
Sgt	Archibald, D.W.		F/L	Rayment, R.D.	Missing 26/11/43. Believed to have ditched in North Sea.
Sgt	Arlett, G.W.		P/O	Ward, J.F.	Missing 2/12/43 (Berlin)
Sgt	Atkinson, J.		P/O	French, P.H.	Missing 20/4/44 (La Chapelle)
W/O	Aumell, A.D.	R141507	F/O	Parker, J.	Missing 23/7/44 (Kiel)
F/O	Awad, P.P.	J39979	F/O	Schaeffer, R.H.	Missing 4/12/44 (Heibronn)
F/S	Baker, A.B.		W/O	Schofield, D.	Missing 24/4/44 (München)
P/O	Baker, F.J.		F/O	Redshaw, R.H.	Shot down by intruder at East Wretham. Killed, 21/5/44.
P/O	Baker, G.A.		P/O	Baker, G.A.	Missing 21/6/44 (Wesseling)
P/O	Bale, C.F.	B141333	F/O	Joss, D.M.	Missing 1/10/43 (Crashed in Bristol Channel. Killed).
Sgt	Bambridge, J.H.	R147187	Sgt	Shirley, F.W.	Missing training flight 9/6/43.
F/S	Bandur, S.B.	R171571	F/O	Redshaw, R.H.	Shot down by intruder at East Wretham. Killed, 21/5/44.

Rank / Name		*Number*	*Captain's Rank / Name*		*Date /Operation*
Sgt	Banks, L.	B1531755	P/O	Loney, G.B.	Missing 16/12/43 (Berlin)
Sgt	Barrie, T.B.	B1366519	Sgt	Pearce, A.J.	Missing 17/8/43 (Peenemünde)
Sgt	Bartholomew, W.B.		F/O	Gray, D.	Missing 4/1/45 (Royan)
F/O	Bearcroft, A.B.		F/O	Heffernan, J.A.	Missing 2/1/44 (Berlin)
F/O	Begernie, A.H.J.		F/O	Begernie, A.H.J.	Missing 18/7/44 (Revigny)
Sgt	Bell, T.		F/O	Day, A.G.	Missing 5/1/44 (Stettin)
Sgt	Bengston, J.		P/O	Wadsworth, D.	Missing 3/5/44(Mailly-le- Camp).
Sgt	Bennett, L.W.		F/O	Clapham, P.C.	Missing 11/11/44 (Harburg)
W/O	Bennett, R.		W/O	Bennett, R.	Missing 3/8/44 (Trossy St. Maximin)
Sgt	Bicknell, E.S.	B1893452	F/S	Webster, J.L.	Missing 6/11/44 (Mittelland Canal)
Sgt	Billingham, J.A.F.		P/O	Mearis, E.	Killed in crash near Manby on return from Bochum 29/9/43.
Sgt	Birch, H.V.		P/O	Mears, K.J.	Crashed 26/11/43 on return from Berlin. Killed.
Sgt	Birks, W.S.	R193025	F/O	Begernie, A.H.J.	Missing 18/7/44 (Revigny)
F/S	Black, P.N.	NZ4213790	F/O	Sparkes, C.P.	Missing 7/3/45 (Harburg)
F/O	Blazer, F.H.		F/L	Dampier-Crossley, E	Missing 10/8/43 (Nürnberg)
Sgt	Blundell, D.W.		P/O	Mears, K.J.	Crashed 26/11/43 on return from Berlin. Killed.
Sgt	Bone, A.D.		F/O	Dockrey, C.B.	Missing 11/9/44 (Darmstadt)
Sgt	Booth, J.		S/L	Fuller, F.E.	Missing 7/5/44 (Salbris)
Sgt	Bowden, H.		F/L	Smith, E.J.F.	Missing 2/2/45 (Karlsruhe)
Sgt	Bower, G.W.	R104755	Sgt	Bower, G.W.	Missing 31/8/43 (Berlin)

Table 4.6 No 619 Squadron Personnel Killed in Action

Rank / Name		*Number*	*Captain's Rank / Name*		*Date /Operation*
P/O	Bower, J.	J20584	P/O	Bower, J.	Missing 2/12/43 (Berlin)
F/S	Bowering, J.E.R.	R195841	P/O	Davis, M.A.H.	Missing 21/6/44 (Wesseling)
Sgt	Brady, H.		P/O	Wadsworth, D.	Missing 3/5/44 (Mailly-le- Camp).
Sgt	Bright, E.G.		F/O	Begernie, A.H.J.	Missing 18/7/44 (Revigny)
F/O	Britten, A.G.	J27492	F/O	Wilson, H.J.	Missing 18/7/44 (Revigny)
Sgt	Brodie, B.H.	B1862111	F/S	Webster, J.L.	Missing 6/11/44 (Mittelland Canal).
F/S	Broll, J.		F/O	Parker,J	Missing 23/7/44 (Keil)
Sgt	Broomfield, J		Sgt	Broomfield, J	Crashed into sea off Hornsea on training mission. 23/4/44.
Sgt	Brown, R.		P/O	Johnson, P.	Missing 21/6/44 (Wesseling)
Sgt	Brown, R.		F/O	Gray, D.	Missing 4/1/45 (Royan)
F/S	Brunt, E.		W/O	Schofield, D.	Missing 24/4/44 (München)
Sgt	Bryce, J.		F/O	Sparkes, C.P.	Missing 7/3/45 (Harburg)
F/S	Buckley, A.J.		F/S	Buckley, A.J.	Missing 21/6/44 (Wesseling)
Sgt	Burden, D.	B1439217	F/L	Cox, J.K.	Missing 2/1/44 (Berlin)
Sgt	Burgess, J.R.		P/O	Wadsworth, D.	Missing 3/5/44 (Mailly-le- Camp).
Sgt	Burton, F.		Sgt	Jordan, D.	Missing 22/6/43 (Krefeld)
F/S	Butler, D.R.		W/O	Patterson, J.	Missing 28/7/44 (Stuttgart)
F/O	Butler, P.R.		F/L	Moore, H.J.	Missing 11/4/44 (Aachen)
Sgt	Cade, W.H.		Sgt	Coomber, D.J.	Missing 23/8/43 (Berlin)
Sgt	Campbell, J.I.G.		P/O	Thompson, P.	Missing 24/3/44 (Berlin)
F/S	Carlson, E.K.	R218011	F/O	Dockrey, C.B.	Missing 11/9/44 (Darmstadt)

Rank / Name		*Number*	*Captain's Rank / Name*		*Date /Operation*
Sgt	Carpenter, G.H.		F/O	Rumble, R.M.	Missing 15/2/44 (Berlin)
Sgt	Carpenter, R.		F/O	Day, A.G.	Missing 5/1/44 (Stettin)
Sgt	Carter, D.J.		F/O	Leonard, R.W.	Missing 19/9/44 (Mönchen Gladbach).
F/S	Cass, F.G.		F/L	Gunzi, G.G.C.	Missing 26/4/44 (Schweinfurt)
F/S	Castle, A.		Sgt	Coomber, D.J.	Missing 23/8/43 (Berlin)
P/O	Chambers, J.W.		F/L	McMorran, A.E.	Missing 10/4/45 (Leipzig)
F/O	Chambers, S.V.	J88244	F/O	Chambers, S.V.	Missing 4/12/44 (Heilbronn)
Sgt	Chapman, A.C.R.	B1579639	W/C	McGhie, I.J.	Missing 17/8/43 (Peenemünde)
Sgt	Cheshire, K.W.		F/O	Heffernan, J.A.	Missing 2/1/44 (Berlin)
Sgt	Chick, D.		F/S	Whinfield, E.	Missing 26/4/44 (Schweinfurt)
Sgt	Christy, E.F.	R212615	F/O	Hall, L.A.	Missing 9/8/44 (Chatellrault)
F/O	Clapham, P.C.		F/O	Clapham, P.C.	Missing 11/11/44 (Harburg)
Sgt	Cobb, W.		W/O	Bennett, R.	Missing 3/8/44 (Trossy St. Maximin).
Sgt	Cody, M.		W/O	Bennett, R.	Missing 3/8/44 (Trossy St. Maximin).
Sgt	Cole, J.P.V.		F/O	Rumble, R.M.	Missing 15/2/44 (Berlin)
F/O	Coleman, P.J.		F/O	Rumble, R.M.	Missing 15/2/44 (Berlin)
Sgt	Colley, E.L.		F/O	Hall, L.A.	Missing 9/8/44 (Chatellrault)
F/S	Cook, C.S.		F/L	Rayment, R.D.	Missing 26/11/43. Believed to have ditched in North Sea.
Sgt	Cook, P.J.		Sgt	Shirley, F.W.	Missing on training flight 9/6/43.
Sgt	Cooksey, J.		F/L	Cox, J.K.	Missing 2/1/44 (Berlin)
Sgt	Cooper, R.L.		P/O	Mearis, E.	Killed in crash near Manby on return from

TABLE 4.6 NO 619 SQUADRON PERSONNEL KILLED IN ACTION

Rank / Name		*Number*	*Captain's Rank / Name*		*Date /Operation*
					Bochum 29/9/43.
Sgt	Corbitt, D.	B1591475	P/O	Loney, G.B.	Missing 16/12/43 (Berlin)
Sgt	Cossey, H.J.		P/O	Baker, G.A.	Missing 21/6/44 (Wesseling)
Sgt	Coverley, J.C.		F/O	Eley, F.E.	Missing 29/8/44 (Königsberg)
Sgt	Cox, D.G.	B1575287	P/O	O'Leary, O.A.	Missing 17/8/43 (Peenemünde)
F/L	Cox, J.K.		F/L	Cox, J.K.	Missing 2/1/44 (Berlin)
Sgt	Cox, R.B.		F/O	Molinas, F.F.	Missing 18/7/44 (Revigny)
P/O	Crawford, K.E.	A23484	P/O	Crawford, K.E.	Missing 21/6/44 (Wesseling)
Sgt	Crookes, R.H.		Sgt	Bower, G.W.	Missing 31/8/43 (Berlin)
Sgt	Crookes, V.	B1677821	P/O	Fuller, C.	Missing 18/10/43 (Hannover)
F/S	Crossley, R.	B996783	P/O	O'Leary, O.A.	Missing 17/8/43 (Peenemünde)
Sgt	Curtis, A.E.		F/O	Molinas, F.F.	Missing 18/7/44 (Revigny)
Sgt	Cutting, J.		P/O	Crawford, K.E.	Missing 21/6/44 (Wesseling)
Sgt	Dalman, A.C.		P/O	Baker, G.A.	Missing 21/6/44 (Wesseling)
F/L	Dampier-Crossley, RAAF		F/L	Dampier-Crossley, E	Missing 10/8/43 (Nürnberg)
F/O	Danielson, G.D.	J38265	F/O	Eley, F.E.	Missing 29/8/44 (Königsberg)
Sgt	Davies, E.C.T.		W/O	Bennett, R.	Missing 3/8/44 (Trossy St. Maximin)
F/S	Davies, J.		F/O	Leonard, R.W.	Missing 19/9/44 (Mönchen Gladbach)
Sgt	Davies, R.T.		P/O	Mearis, E.	Killed in crash near Manby on return from Bochum 29/9/43.
Sgt	Davies, W.A.		Sgt	Jordan, D.	Missing 22/6/43 (Krefeld)

Rank / Name		*Number*	*Captain's Rank / Name*		*Date /Operation*
F/O	Davis, L.G.	B125310	Sgt	Pearce, A.J.	Missing 17/8/43 (Peenemünde)
P/O	Davis, M.A.H.		P/O	Davis, M.A.H.	Missing 21/6/44 (Wesseling)
Sgt	Davison, J.		S/L	Squibbs, A.R.	Missing 11/9/44 (Darmstadt)
F/S	Dawson, F.		F/L	Dampier-Crossley, E	Missing 10/8/43 (Nürnberg)
F/O	Day, A.G.		F/O	Day, A.G.	Missing 5/1/44 (Stettin)
Sgt	Dearden, R.F.	B1590663	P/O	Loney, G.B.	Missing 16/12/43 (Berlin)
Sgt	Demaine, D.	B1575924	P/O	Firth, C.	Missing 20/10/43 (Leipzig)
F/O	DeMarco, V.T.	J29166	F/O	DeMarco, V.T.	Missing 25/4/45(Berchesgaden)
Sgt	Depotex, H.J.		F/O	Dockrey, C.B.	Missing 11/9/44 (Darmstadt)
Sgt	Deugard, R.D.	B864810	Sgt	Pearce, A.J.	Missing 17/8/43 (Pennemünde)
F/O	DeVries, H.A.	B134208	P/O	Loney, G.B.	Missing 16/12/43 (Berlin)
F/O	DeVries, T.		F/O	Eley, F.E.	Missing 29/8/44 (Königsberg)
Sgt	Dickson, A.		F/O	Parker, J.	Missing 23/7/44 (Kiel)
Sgt	Dillnut, D.W.	B1078529	P/O	Firth, C.	Missing 20/10/43 (Leipzig)
F/O	Dockrey, C.B.	J35152	F/O	Dockrey, C.B.	Missing 11/9/44 (Darmstadt)
F/O	Donnelley, N.W.	NZ422269	F/O	Donnelley, N.W.	Missing 18/7/44 (Revigny)
Sgt	Douglas, W.J.		Sgt	Shirley, F.W.	Missing on training flight 9/6/43.
Sgt	Dring, F.F.		P/O	Aitken, J.M.	Missing 9/5/44 (Gennevilliers)
Sgt	Duncan, J.H.		P/O	Ward, J.F.	Missing 2/12/43 (Berlin)
Sgt	Durkin, J.A.		W/O	Schofield, D.	Missing 24/4/44 (München)
P/O	Eaude, L.	B149506	F/O	Fuller, C.	Missing 18/10/43 (Hannover)

TABLE 4.6 NO 619 SQUADRON PERSONNEL KILLED IN ACTION

Rank / Name		*Number*	*Captain's Rank / Name*		*Date /Operation*
F/O	Eley, F.E.		F/O	Eley, F.E.	Missing 29/8/44 (Königsberg)
Sgt	Emesley, E.G.		Sgt	Broomfield,J.	Crashed into sea off Hornsea, training mission. 23/4/44.
Sgt	Engel, P.	B1381754	F/O	Joss, D.M.	Missing 1/10/43 Crashed in Bristol Channel. All Killed.
F/S	English, L.F.	NZ415524	P/O	O'Leary, O.A.	Missing 17/8/43 (Peenemünde)
W/O	Evans, E.S.		F/O	Heffernan, J.A.	Missing 2/1/44 (Berlin)
W/O	Evans, L.G.	R115196	S/L	Squibbs, A.R.	Missing 11/9/44 (Darmstadt)
F/O	Eyles, C.E.		F/O	Sparkes, C.P.	Missing 7/3/45 (Harburg)
F/O	Eynon, B.W.		F/O	Sparkes, C.P.	Missing 7/3/45 (Harburg)
F/O	Farrow, T.E.	J38025	F/O	Farrow, T.E.	Missing 16/3/45 (Würzburg)
F/S	Feindell, L.	R163548	F/L	Gunzi, G.	Missing 26/4/44 (Schweinfurt)
F/O	Ferguson, R.N.	NZ4211910	F/O	Sparkes, C.P.	Missing 7/3/45 (Harburg)
P/O	Firth, C.	B146984	P/O	Firth, C.	Missing 20/10/43 (Leipzig)
Sgt	Flewelling, C.C.	R153462	F/L	Saunders, D.C.	Missing 21/6/44 (Wesseling)
F/O	Flockhart, C.K.	A428679	F/O	Flockhart, C.K.	Missing 7/1/45 (München)
Sgt	Forrest, R.A.		W/O	Bennett, R.	Missing 3/8/44 (Trossy St. Maximin)
Sgt	Forsdick, R.V.		F/S	Goddard, C.A.	Missing 5/9/43 (Mannheim)
F/O	Forshow, H.		P/O	McCullock, K.	Missing 15/6/43 (Oberhausen)
F/S	Fowler, J.A.		F/L	Rayment, R.D.	Missing 26/11/43. Believed to have ditched in North Sea.
Sgt	Fox, P.		Sgt	Shirley, F.W.	Missing on training flight 9/6/43

Rank / Name		*Number*	*Captain's Rank / Name*		*Date /Operation*
Sgt	Francis, C.B.	B1335172	Sgt	Pearce, A.J.	Missing 17/8/43 (Peenemünde)
Sgt	Frank, K.		F/L	Gunzi, G.	Missing 26/4/44 (Schweinfurt)
F/S	Fraser, W.F.	R217646	F/O	Eley, F.E.	Missing 29/8/44 (Königsberg)
P/O	French, P.H.		P/O	French, P.H.	Missing 20/4/44 (La Chapelle)
Sgt	Frogley, T.F.		F/O	Donnelley, N.W.	Missing 18/7/44 (Revigny)
P/O	Fuller, C.	B149517	P/O	Fuller, C.	Missing 18/10/43 (Hannover)
S/L	Fuller, F.E.		S/L	Fuller, F.E.	Missing 7/5/44 (Salbris)
Sgt	Fullwood, T.H.		F/O	Hesketh, H.T.	Missing 8/2/45 (Pölitz)
Sgt	Furnival, A.		S/L	Squibbs, A.R.	Missing 11/9/44 (Darmstadt)
F/S	Galbraith, T.F.	R172370	F/O	Turvey, R.G.	Missing 26/7/44 (Givors)
F/S	Galliard, J.D.		F/O	Chambers, S.V.	Missing 4/12/44 (Heilbronn)
F/O	Galloway, K.A.	NZ422277	P/O	Crawford, K.E.	Missing 21/6/44 (Wesseling)
Sgt	Garbutt, J.A.	R163217	F/O	Wilson, H.J.	Missing 18/7/44 (Revigny)
Sgt	Gardner, L.		Sgt	Coomber, D.J.	Missing 23/8/43 (Berlin)
F/O	Gay, D.F.		F/O	Eley, F.E.	Missing 29/8/44 (Königsberg)
Sgt	Geddes, J.	R209156	F/O	Begernie, A.H.J.	Missing 18/7/44 (Revigny)
P/O	Gennis, M.	J22054	P/O	Loney, G.B.	Missing 16/12/43 (Berlin)
Sgt	Gibson, M.G.		F/L	Tanner, L.E.	Killed in crash at Woodbridge, 1/11/44.
Sgt	Giddings, R.G.		F/L	Moore, H.J.	Missing 11/4/44 (Aachen)
Sgt	Gilliver, J.H.		F/O	Turvey, R.G.	Missing 26/7/44 (Givors)
F/O	Girdwood, W.M.		Sgt	Jordan, D.	Missing 22/6/43 (Krefeld)
F/S	Glazebrook, J.	A425640	F/O	Williams, E.K.	Missing 24/2/44 (Schweinfurt)

TABLE 4.6 NO 619 SQUADRON PERSONNEL KILLED IN ACTION

Rank / Name		*Number*	*Captain's Rank / Name*		*Date /Operation*
Sgt	Goddard, A.P.		F/L	Tanner, L.E.	Killed in crash at Woodbridge, 1/11/44.
F/S	Goddard, C.A.		F/S	Goddard, C.A.	Missing 5/9/43 (Mannheim)
Sgt	Goldberg, H.		F/S	Whinfield, E.	Missing 26/4/44 (Schweinfurt)
Sgt	Golding, D.W.		W/O	Schofield, D.	Missing 24/4/44 (München)
F/S	Goldsmith, P.M.	A5105	W/C	McGhie, I.J.	Missing 17/8/43 (Peenemünde)
F/S	Gollogy, R.W.		F/S	Metcalfe, F.	Missing 31/8/43 (Berlin)
F/S	Goodwin, K.		P/O	Aitken, J.M.	Missing 9/5/44 (Gennevilliers)
Sgt	Goodwin, C.W.		F/L	Saunders, D.C.	Missing 21/6/44 (Wesseling)
Sgt	Grace, R.A.		F/S	Murphy, T.P.	Missing 29/6/43 (Köln)
Sgt	Graham, E.		F/O	Turvey, R.G.	Missing 26/7/44 (Givors)
F/L	Graham, W.F.		S/L	Palmer, C.M.	Missing 20/3/45 (Böhlen)
F/O	Grant, D.I.	NZ405253	F/O	Donnelley, N.W.	Missing 18/7/44 (Revigny)
Sgt	Gratwick, B.F.		P/O	Thompson, P.	Missing 24/3/44 (Berlin)
Sgt	Graves, P.S.		F/O	Flockhart, C.K.	Missing 7/1/45 (München)
F/O	Gray, D.	A417746	F/O	Gray, D.	Missing 4/1/45 (Royan)
Sgt	Gray, D.M.		Sgt	Shirley, F.W.	Missing on training flight 9/6/43.
F/S	Gray, J.		P/O	Loney, G.B.	Missing 16/12/43, Berlin
Sgt	Greenley, D.		S/L	Squibbs, A.R.	Missing 11/9/44 (Darmstadt)
F/S	Griffiths, A.		W/O	Bennett, R.	Missing 3/8/44 (Trossy St. Maximin).
P/O	Grigg, G.A.		F/O	Parker, J.	Missing 23/7/44 (Kiel)
F/L	Gunzi, G.		F/L	Gunzi, G.	Missing 26/4/44 (Schweinfurt)
Sgt	Haberfield, I.R.F.	B1416572	S/L	McGilvray, J.W.E.	Missing 11/4/44 (Aachen)

Rank / Name		*Number*	*Captain's Rank / Name*		*Date /Operation*
F/S	Habergham, A.W.		F/O	Molinas, F.F.	Missing 18/7/44 (Revigny)
F/S	Hall, F.H.		W/O	Patterson, J.	Missing 28/7/44 (Stuttgart)
F/O	Hall, L.A.		F/O	Hall, L.A.	Missing 9/8/44 (Chatellrault)
Sgt	Halpin, J.L.		F/L	Saunders, D.C.	Missing 21/6/44 (Wesseling)
Sgt	Handford, A.J.		F/L	Saunders, D.C.	Missing 21/6/44 (Wesseling)
P/O	Hargreaves, E.T.		P/O	Ward, J.F.	Missing 2/12/43 (Berlin)
Sgt	Harmer, K.W.		F/O	Redshaw, R.H.	Shot down by intruder at East Wretham. Killed, 21/5/44.
P/O	Harper, E.		F/S	Murphy, T.P.	Missing 29/6/43 (Köln)
Sgt	Harper, J.		W/C	Maling, J.R.	Missing 25/7/44 (Stuttgart)
F/S	Harrison, J.A.	B1582271	F/S	Webster, J.L.	Missing 6/11/44 (Mittelland Canal).
Sgt	Harwood, R.T.W.		F/O	Donnelley, N.W.	Missing 18/7/44 (Revigny)
F/S	Hay, J. RAAF		P/O	Thompson, P.	Missing 24/3/44 (Berlin)
F/O	Heffernan, J.A.	J20361	F/O	Heffernan, J.A.	Missing 2/1/44 (Berlin)
F/O	Hesketh, H.T.	A29468	F/O	Hesketh, H.T.	Missing 8/2/45 (Pölitz)
Sgt	Hickling, R.E.		P/O	Aitken, J.M.	Missing 9/5/44 (Gennevilliers)
F/S	Hill, J.		S/L	Fuller, F.E.	Missing 7/5/44 (Salbris)
Sgt	Hillier, R.	B1851609	S/L	McGilvray, J.W.E.	Missing 11/4/44 (Aachen)
Sgt	Hinett, W.F.		F/O	Begernie, A.H.J.	Missing 18/7/44 (Revigny)
Sgt	Hodson, F.		Sgt	Bower, G.W.	Missing 31/8/43 (Berlin)
Sgt	Hogg, R.J.	B2211120	F/S	Webster, J.L.	Missing 6/11/44 (Mittelland Canal).
F/S	Holke, A.G.	R172997	S/L	Fuller, F.E.	Missing 7/5/44 (Salbris) 2nd Nav with S/L

Table 4.6 No 619 Squadron Personnel Killed in Action

Rank / Name		*Number*	*Captain's Rank / Name*		*Date /Operation*
					Fuller's crew.
Sgt	Holliday, Y.W.D.		F/O	Day, A.G.	Missing 5/1/44 (Stettin)
P/O	Horne, J.	B155799	P/O	Fuller, C.	Missing 18/10/43 (Hannover). 2nd Pilot with P/O Fuller.
W/O	Horne, J.	R150952	F/S	Whinfield, E.	Missing 26/4/44 (Schweinfurt)
F/S	Hosham, P.J.	B574342	W/C	McGhie, I.J.	Missing 17/8/43 (Peenemünde)
Sgt	Howe, B.		Sgt	Jordan, D.	Missing 22/6/43 (Krefeld)
Sgt	Howe, T.E.	R195676	P/O	Crawford, K.E.	Missing 21/6/44 (Wesseling)
Sgt	Hubbard, J.T.	B1488523	P/O	O'Leary, O.A.	Missing 17/8/43 (Peenemünde)
F/O	Hudson, R.A.		F/O	Hesketh, H.T.	Missing 8/2/45 (Pölitz)
Sgt	Humphrey, W.	B1416813	Sgt	Pearce, A.J.	Missing 17/8/43 (Peenemünde)
Sgt	Hunt, K.W.P.			Sgt Broomfield, J.	Crashed into sea off Hornsea on training mission. 23/4/44.
Sgt	Hunter, E.H.		W/O	Patterson, J.	Missing 28/7/44 (Stuttgart)
F/S	Insley, H.		F/O	Gray, D.	Missing 4/1/45 (Royan)
F/S	Ireland,E.K.		F/O	Farrow, T.E.	Missing 16/3/45 (Würzburg)
F/L	Jackson, F.		F/L	McMorran, A.E.	Missing 10/4/45 (Leipzig)
F/O	Jackson, F.M.	A417195	F/L	McMorran, A.E.	Missing 10/4/45 (Leipzig)
Sgt	Jackson, G.H.		Sgt	Knilans, H.C.	Killed by enemy fighter 3/10/43 (Rear Gunner).
Sgt	Jamieson, A.L.		F/S	Buckley, A.J.	Missing 21/6/44 (Wesseling)
Sgt	Johnson, A.		F/O	Gray, D.	Missing 4/1/45 (Royan)
F/S	Johnson, J.K.	R127811	F/O	Donnelley, N.W.	Missing 18/7/44 (Revigny)

Rank / Name		*Number*	*Captain's Rank / Name*		*Date /Operation*
P/O	Johnson, P.		P/O	Johnson, P.	Missing 21/6/44 (Wesseling)
Sgt	Johnson, W.		F/O	Leonard, R.W.	Missing 19/9/44 (Mönchen Gladbach).
Sgt	Johnston,, J.O.		F/L	Saunders, D.C.	Missing 21/6/44 (Wesseling), 2nd Air Bomber.
F/O	Johnston, J.D.	J45931	F/O	Farrow, T.E.	Missing 16/3/45 (Würzburg)
W/O	Johnston, N.H.	R185861	F/O	DeMarco, V.T.	Missing 25/4/45(Berchesgaden)
Sgt	Jones, D.V.		F/O	Arden, B	Killed on ditching on return from Milan (12/8/43).
Sgt	Jones, M.	5602070	P/O	Firth, C.	Missing 20/10/43 (Leipzig)
Sgt	Jordan, D.		Sgt	Jordan, D.	Missing 22/6/43 (Krefeld)
F/O	Joss, D.M.	B128952	F/O	Joss, D.M.	Missing 1/10/43 Crashed in Bristol Channel. All Killed.
Sgt	Joy, F.H.		P/O	Wadsworth, D.	Missing 3/5/44 (Mailly-le-Camp).
Sgt	Keatley, H.C.		F/O	Eley, F.E.	Missing 29/8/44 (Königsberg)
F/O	Keeling, L.S.		F/O	Heffernan, J.A.	Missing 2/1/44 (Berlin)
F/S	Keightley, R.W.		F/O	Flockhart, C.K.	Missing 7/1/45 (München)
F/O	Kellett, J.		F/L	Rayment, R.D.	Missing 26/11/43. Believed to have ditched in North Sea.
Sgt	Kellum, J.R.	R204911	W/C	Maling, J.R.	Missing 25/7/44 (Stuttgart)
Sgt	Kennedy, L.	B1784070	F/S	Webster, J.L.	Missing 6/11/44 (Mittelland Canal).
Sgt	Kersey, D.W.A.		Sgt	Broomfield, J.	Crashed into sea off Hornsea, training mission. 23/4/44.
Sgt	Kershaw, W.		F/S	Goddard, C.A.	Missing 5/9/43 (Mannheim)

TABLE 4.6 NO 619 SQUADRON PERSONNEL KILLED IN ACTION

Rank / Name		*Number*	*Captain's Rank / Name*		*Date /Operation*
F/O	Kerslake, T.E		F/O	Pettigrew, R.W.	Missing 26/9/44 (Karlsruhe) 2nd pilot.
Sgt	Kidd, E.D.		P/O	Baker, G.A.	Missing 21/6/44 (Wesseling)
Sgt	Kilburn, H.E.		F/S	Metcalfe, F.	Missing 31/8/43 (Berlin)
Sgt	Knights, W.W.N.		P/O	Mears, K.J.	Crashed 26/11/43 on return from Berlin. Killed.
F/O	Kommes, J.J.	J35044	F/O	Orbell, R.W.	Missing 24/7/44 (Donges)
Sgt	Kullberg, E.N.	R162250	P/O	Baker, G.A.	Missing 21/6/44 (Wesseling)
F/S	Lambert, V.W.		F/L	McMorran, G.M.	Missing 7/3/45 (Harburg)
Sgt	Lang, H.G.		F/L	Moore, H.J.	Missing 11/4/44 (Aachen)
F/S	Langridge, G.	R156812	F/S	Whinfield, E.	Missing 26/4/44 (Schweinfurt)
F/S	LeBatt, W.H.G.		F/O	Morcom, S.B.	Missing 18/7/44 (Revigny)
Sgt	Leger, A.C.		F/O	Hesketh, H.T.	Missing 8/2/45 (Pölitz)
Sgt	Leitch, A.		P/O	Bower, J.	Missing 2/12/43 (Berlin)
F/O	Leonard, R.W.		F/O	Leonard, R.W.	Missing 19/9/44 (Mönchen Gladbach).
Sgt	Letchford, T.		F/O	Flockhart, C.K.	Missing 7/1/45 (München)
Sgt	Levy, S.		P/O	Aitken, J.M.	Missing 9/5/44 (Gennevilliers)
F/O	Leyland, J.V.		P/O	Thompson, P.	Missing 24/3/44 (Berlin)
Sgt	Lilley, L.E.		W/O	Patterson, J.	Missing 28/7/44 (Stuttgart)
Sgt	Ling, S.W.		F/O	Donnelley, N.W.	Missing 18/7/44 (Revigny)
F/S	Little, R.H.		F/O	Rumble, R.M.	Missing 15/2/44 (Berlin)
Sgt	Lloyd, D.R.		F/O	Sparkes, C.P.	Missing 7/3/45 (Harburg)
F/O	Logan, R.		F/O	Wilson, H.J.	Missing 18/7/44 (Revigny)
P/O	Loney, G.B.	J18815	P/O	Loney, G.B.	Missing 16/12/43 (Berlin)

Rank / Name		*Number*	*Captain's Rank / Name*		*Date /Operation*
Sgt	Loose, W.A.		P/O	Crawford, K.E.	Missing 21/6/44 (Wesseling)
Sgt	Loosli, M.		F/O	Molinas, F.F.	Missing 18/7/44 (Revigny)
F/O	Loranger, N.A.	J24524	S/L	Fuller, F.E.	Missing 7/5/44 (Salbris)
F/O	Lord, W.C.J.		F/O	Heffernan, J.A.	Missing 2/1/44 (Berlin)
W/O	Lott, J.		P/O	Roberts, K.	Missing 5/6/44 (Caen)
Sgt	Lowe, J.	B196013	F/O	Joss, D.M.	Missing 1/10/43 Crashed in Bristol Channel. Killed.
Sgt	Lowe, P.C.		F/O	Pettigrew, R.W.	Missing 26/9/44 (Karlsruhe)
Sgt	Lucas, G.H.		F/O	Orbell, R.W.	Missing 24/7/44 (Donges)
F/S	Lyford, F.P.		W/O	Bennett, R.	Missing 3/8/44 (Trossy St. Maximin).
Sgt	Lynche, M.		F/L	Rayment, R.D.	Missing 26/11/43. Believed to have ditched in North Sea.
Sgt	Mabutt, J.		F/O	Leonard, R.W.	Missing 19/9/44 (Mönchen Gladbach).
F/S	Macdonald, J.L.	R264905	F/O	Hesketh, H.T.	Missing 8/2/45 (Pölitz)
F/S	MacDonald, K.M.		F/O	Heffernan, J.A.	Missing 2/1/44 (Berlin)
P/O	Mackay, A.		F/S	Murphy, T.P.	Missing 29/6/43 (Köln)
Sgt	Mackintosh, J.E.		F/O	Morcom, S.B.	Missing 18/7/44 (Revigny)
F/O	MacNair, E.J.A.	J27469	F/O	Dockrey, C.B.	Missing 11/9/44 (Darmstadt)
Sgt	Macpherson, J.		F/O	Farrow, T.E.	Missing 16/3/45 (Würzburg)
Sgt	Maddaford, L.T.		F/O	Arden, B.	Missing 12/8/43. Died in Hosp following rescue from N Sea.
Sgt	Maltby, J.H.		P/O	Wadsworth, D.	Missing 3/5/44 (Mailly-le-Camp).

TAELE 4.6 NO 619 SQUADRON PERSONNEL KILLED IN ACTION

Rank / Name		*Number*	*Captain's Rank / Name*		*Date /Operation*
Sgt	Mara, J.F.	R203234	F/O	Wilson, H.J.	Missing 18/7/44 (Revigny)
Sgt	Marper, W.A.		F/O	Begernie, A.H.J.	Missing 18/7/44 (Revigny)
F/S	Marsh, L.E.	R257967	F/O	Hesketh, H.T.	Missing 8/2/45 (Pölitz)
Sgt	Martin ???		Sgt	Broomfield, J.	Shot down by intruder 23/4/44 while on training flight.
Sgt	Maton, S.J.J.		F/L	McMorran, G.M.	Missing 7/3/45 (Harburg)
F/L	McBride, C.W.	J22700	F/O	Farrow, T.E.	Missing 16/3/45 (Würzburg)
F/O	McConnell, N.E.	J35578	F/O	Clapham, P.C.	Missing 11/11/44 (Harburg)
P/O	McCulloch, K.		P/O	McCulloch, K.	Missing 15/6/43 (Oberhausen)
F/S	McDonagh, B.		F/L	Johnston, C.C.	Missing 7/7/44 (St. Leu D'Esserant)
Sgt	McDonald, A.M.B.		F/O	Pettigrew, R.W.	Missing 26/9/44 (Karlsruhe)
W/C	McGhie, I.J.	B32201	W/C	McGhie, I.J.	Missing 17/8/43 (Peenemünde)
Sgt	McGill, W.		Sgt	Bower, G.W.	Missing 31/8/43 (Berlin)
S/L	McGilvray, J.W.E.	B134533	S/L	McGilvray, J.W.E.	Missing 11/4/44 (Aachen)
P/O	McKay, A.C.		P/O	Mearis, E.	Killed in crash near Manby on return from Bochum 29/9/43.
Sgt	McKay, R.A.		F/O	Redshaw, R.H.	Shot down by intruder at East Wretham. Killed, 21/5/44.
F/O	McKinnon, L.J.		F/S	Buckley, A.J.	Missing 21/6/44 (Wesseling)
P/O	McManaman, R.	J26840	P/O	Bower, J.	Missing 2/12/43 (Berlin)
F/L	McMorran, A.E	J25722	F/L	McMorran, A.E.	Missing 10/4/45 (Leipzig)
F/L	McMorran, G.W.	J36260	F/L	McMorran, G.M.	Missing 7/3/45 (Harburg)

Rank / Name		*Number*	*Captain's Rank / Name*		*Date /Operation*
P/O	McNie, D.C.	J92166	F/L	Smith, E.J.F.	Missing 2/2/45 (Karlsruhe)
P/O	Mearis, E.		P/O	Mearis, E.	Killed in crash near Manby on return from Bochum 29/9/43.
P/O	Mears, K.J.		P/O	Mears, K.J.	Crashed 26/11/43 on return from Berlin. Killed.
Sgt	Measor, R.		F/S	Metcalfe, F.	Missing 31/8/43 (Berlin)
F/O	Meredith, F.L.	J38814	F/O	Schaeffer, R.H.	Missing 4/12/44 (Heibronn)
F/S	Metcalfe, F.		F/S	Metcalfe, F.	Missing 31/8/43 (Berlin)
Sgt	Metcalfe, K.A.		F/S	Goddard, C.A.	Missing 5/9/43 (Mannheim)
Sgt	Mino, M.	R263463	F/O	Farrow, T.E.	Missing 16/3/45 (Würzburg)
Sgt	Minsull, L.		P/O	Thompson, P.	Missing 24/3/44 (Berlin)
Sgt	Mitchell, W.A.	B1426572	W/C	McGhie, I.J.	Missing 17/8/43 (Peenemünde)
Sgt	Moggridge, G.H.		P/O	Davis, M.A.H.	Missing 21/6/44 (Wesseling)
Sgt	Moir, A.		F/O	Pettigrew, R.W.	Missing 26/9/44 (Karlsruhe)
F/O	Molinas, F.F.	A425454	F/O	Molinas, F.F.	Missing 18/7/44 (Revigny)
Sgt	Monoghan, T.	B530301	F/O	Joss, D.M.	Missing 1/10/43 Crashed in Bristol Channel. All Killed.
F/O	Morcom, S.B.		F/O	Morcom, S.B.	Missing 18/7/44 (Revigny)
Sgt	Morgan, L.		F/O	Molinas, F.F.	Missing 18/7/44 (Revigny)
Sgt	Morley, E.A.		F/O	Gray, D.	Missing 4/1/45 (Royan)
F/O	Morrison, E.L.	J21181	F/O	Wilson, H.J.	Missing 18/7/44 (Revigny)
Sgt	Morrison, M.L.	R156858	F/S	Buckley, A.J.	Missing 21/6/44 (Wesseling)
F/O	Mortis, E.J.		F/L	Smith, E.J.F.	Missing 2/2/45 (Karlsruhe)

Table 4.6 No 619 Squadron Personnel Killed in Action

Rank / Name		*Number*	*Captain's Rank / Name*		*Date /Operation*
F/S	Mortlock, K.G.	31324729	F/O	Joss, D.M.	Missing 1/10/43 Crashed in Bristol Channel. All Killed.
F/S	Morton, C.K.		F/S	Webster, J.L.	Missing 6/11/44 (Mittelland Canal).
P/O	Moxham, P.C		F/L	Dampier-Crossley,E	Missing 10/8/43 (Nürnberg)
F/S	Moyle, J.F.	R184290	F/O	Hesketh, H.T.	Missing 8/2/45 (Pölitz)
Sgt	Mullen, T.		F/O	Wilson, H.J.	Missing 18/7/44 (Revigny)
W/O	Munro, A.	B1075155	S/L	McGilvray, J.W.E.	Missing 11/4/44 (Aachen)
F/S	Murdock, A.F.		F/O	Flockhart, C.K.	Missing 7/1/45 (München)
Sgt	Murphy, D.M.	R176578	F/O	Orbell, R.W.	Missing 24/7/44 (Donges)
F/S	Murphy, T.P.		F/S	Murphy, T.P.	Missing 29/6/43 (Köln)
Sgt	Musso, P.	R140864	Sgt	Bower, G.W.	Missing 31/8/43 (Berlin)
Sgt	Mycock, W.G.		F/S	Metcalfe, F.	Missing 31/8/43 (Berlin)
Sgt	Myres, A.		F/O	Morcom, S.B.	Missing 18/7/44 (Revigny)
Sgt	Naylor, A.		P/O	Wadsworth, D.	Missing 3/5/44 (Mailly-le- Camp).
Sgt	Nicholls, E.E.		F/S	Goddard, C.A.	Missing 5/9/43 (Mannheim)
Sgt	Nixon, G.		F/O	Clapham, P.C.	Missing 11/11/44 (Harburg)
Sgt	Norman, E.W.		F/O	DeMarco, V.T.	Missing 25/4/45(Berchesgaden)
Sgt	Norris, A.C.		F/O	Hookings, E.W.	Missing 6/11/44 (Mittelland Canal).
P/O	O'Leary, O.A.	J17836	P/O	O'Leary, O.A.	Missing 17/8/43 (Peenemünde)
F/O	Orbell, R.W.		F/O	Orbell, R.W.	Missing 24/7/44 (Donges)
Sgt	Osborne, A.G.	B1613719	P/O	Firth, C.	Missing 20/10/43 (Leipzig)

Rank / Name		*Number*	*Captain's Rank / Name*		*Date /Operation*
S/L	Palmer, C.M.	Rhod80048	S/L	Palmer, C.M.	Missing 20/3/45 (Böhlen)
F/O	Parker, J.		F/O	Parker, J.	Missing 23/7/44 (Kiel)
Sgt	Parkes, W.J.		Sgt	Jordan, D.	Missing 22/6/43 (Krefeld)
Sgt	Parrott, H.		W/C	Maling, J.R.	Missing 25/7/44 (Stuttgart)
F/O	Parry, J.F.		S/L	Squibbs, A.R.	Missing 11/9/44 (Darmstadt)
F/O	Parry, R.C.	J26844	F/O	Rumble, R.M.	Missing 15/2/44 (Berlin)
Sgt	Pascoe, A.		F/O	Chambers, S.V.	Missing 4/12/44 (Heilbronn)
Sgt	Pascoe, V.		F/O	Dickinson, R.	Killed by enemy action 8/2/45 (Gardening).
F/O	Pateman, W.H.C.		F/O	Rumble, R.M.	Missing 15/2/44 (Berlin)
Sgt	Patterson, G.		F/L	Dampier-Crossley,	Missing 10/8/43 (Nürnberg).
W/O	Patterson, J.		W/O	Patterson, J.	Missing 28/7/44 (Stuttgart)
Sgt	Patterson, J.E.S.	R216287	F/L	Johnston, C.C.	Missing 7/7/44 (St. Leu D'Esserant.)
Sgt	Patterson, R.		F/O	Clapham, P.C.	Missing 11/11/44 (Harburg)
Sgt	Payne, C.G.		F/L	Cox, J.K.	Missing 2/1/44 (Berlin)
Sgt	Pearce, A.J.	B1316551	Sgt	Pearce, A.J.	Missing 17/8/43 (Peenemünde)
Sgt	Pearce, J.G.	R190936	F/O	Turvey, R.G.	Missing 26/7/44 (Givors)
Sgt	Pearse, L.		P/O	Mears, K.J.	Crashed 26/11/43 on return from Berlin. Killed.
Sgt	Pedley, J.D.		P/O	Thompson, P.	Missing 24/3/44 (Berlin)
P/O	Perring, C.T.W.		F/L	McMorran, A.E.	Missing 10/4/45 (Leipzig)
F/O	Pettigrew, R.W.	J26098	F/O	Pettigrew, R.W.	Missing 26/9/44 (Karlsruhe)
Sgt	Pickstone, S.		F/L	Gunzi, G.	Missing 26/4/44 (Schweinfurt)
F/O	Plunkett, C.K.		S/L	Fuller, F.E.	Missing 7/5/44 (Salbris)

TABLE 4.6 NO 619 SQUADRON PERSONNEL KILLED IN ACTION

Rank / Name		*Number*	*Captain's Rank / Name*		*Date /Operation*
F/S	Pope, A.W.		F/O	Hall, L.A.	Missing 9/8/44 (Chatellrault)
F/O	Potts, J.R.	J28194	F/O	Dockrey, C.B.	Missing 11/9/44 (Darmstadt)
P/O	Powell, E.N		W/O	Schofield, D.	Missing 24/4/44 (München)
Sgt	Presland, J.R.		P/O	Aitken, J.M.	Missing 9/5/44 (Gennevilliers)
F/O	Prest, E.G	J15788	W/C	McGhie, I.J.	Missing 17/8/43 (Peenemünde)
F/S	Price, A.P.		Sgt	Shirley, F.W.	Missing on training flight 9/6/43
Sgt	Price, R.W.		F/O	Flockhart, C.K.	Missing 7/1/45 (München)
P/O	Pritchard, J.L.	B618572	S/L	McGilvray, J.W.E.	Missing 11/4/44 (Aachen)
F/S	Prunkle, R.	R202987	F/O	Chambers, S.V.	Missing 4/12/44 (Heilbronn)
F/S	Rackley, G.N.		P/O	Crawford, K.E.	Missing 21/6/44 (Wesseling)
Sgt	Ramsay, J.R.A.		F/L	Smith, E.J.F.	Missing 2/2/45 (Karlsruhe)
Sgt	Randall, J.W.		P/O	French, P.H.	Missing 20/4/44 (La Chapelle)
F/L	Raw, L.C.		S/L	Palmer, C.M.	Missing 20/3/45 (Böhlen)
F/L	Rayment, R.D.		F/L	Rayment, R.D.	Missing 26/11/43. Believed to have ditched in North Sea.
F/O	Redshaw, R.H.		F/O	Redshaw, R.H.	Shot down by intruder at East Wretham. Killed, 21/5/44.
Sgt	Reed, C.J.		F/O	Chambers, S.V.	Missing 4/12/44 (Heilbronn)
Sgt	Reid, R.C.		S/L	Fuller, F.E.	Missing 7/5/44 (Salbris)
F/S	Rex, E.A.		F/L	Smith, E.J.F,	Missing 2/2/45 (Karlsruhe)
Sgt	Rice, K.F.		F/S	Buckley, A.J.	Missing 21/6/44 (Wesseling)
Sgt	Rice, N.M.		F/O	Parker, J.	Missing 23/7/44 (Kiel)

Rank / Name		*Number*	*Captain's Rank / Name*		*Date /Operation*
F/S	Rice, S.D.G.		W/O	Patterson, J.	Missing 28/7/44 (Stuttgart)
F/S	Richards, J.T.		F/L	Rayment, R.D.	Missing 26/11/43. Believed to have ditched in North Sea.
Sgt	Richards, N.		P/O	McCullock, K.	Missing 15/6/43 (Oberhausen)
Sgt	Richardson, J.C.		F/O	Clapham, P.C.	Missing 11/11/44 (Harburg)
Sgt	Richardson, L.J.		F/O	Redshaw, R.H.	Shot down by intruder at East Wretham. Killed, 21/5/44.
F/O	Ricketts, F.J.		S/L	Palmer, C.M.	Missing 20/3/45 (Böhlen)
Sgt	Rivers, N.E.		F/S	Murphy, T.P.	Missing 29/6/43 (Köln)
F/L	Roberts, K.	A415358	F/L	Roberts, K.	Missing 5/6/44 (Caen)
Sgt	Robinson, W.A.		Sgt	Shirley, F.W.	Missing on training flight 9/6/43
Sgt	Rodger, R.		W/O	Patterson, J.	Missing 28/7/44 (Stuttgart)
F/S	Rothwell, L.	A419608	F/O	Turvey, R.G.	Missing 26/7/44 (Givors)
Sgt	Ruane, P.J.		P/O	McCullock, K.	Missing 15/6/43 (Oberhausen)
F/O	Rumble, R.M.	J21210	F/O	Rumble, R.M.	Missing 15/2/44 (Berlin)
P/O	Salt, G.G.		P/O	Mears, K.J.	Crashed 26/11/43 on return from Berlin. Killed.
Sgt	Sanders, J.G.D.		F/O	Clapham, P.C.	Missing 11/11/44 (Harburg)
F/O	Schaeffer, R.H.	J35883	F/O	Schaeffer, R.H.	Missing 4/12/44 (Heibronn)
W/O	Schofield, D.	B1217454	W/O	Schofield, D.	Missing 24/4/44 (München)
Sgt	Scott, J.R.		F/O	Orbell, R.W.	Missing 24/7/44 (Donges)
Sgt	Scott, J.W.		P/O	Ward, J.F.	Missing 2/12/43 (Berlin)
W/O	Shantz, I.W.	R171523	F/O	Chambers, S.V.	Missing 4/12/44 (Heilbronn)

Table 4.6 No 619 Squadron Personnel Killed in Action

Rank / Name		*Number*	*Captain's Rank / Name*		*Date /Operation*
Sgt	Sharp, W.A.		Sgt	Parker, J.	Missing 23/7/44 (Kiel)
Sgt	Shaw, J.H.	B1130438	P/O	O'Leary, O.A.	Missing 17/8/43 (Peenemünde)
Sgt	Shearsby, H.F.		F/L	Moore, H.J.	Missing 11/4/44 (Aachen)
F/S	Shenton, A.C.		P/O	Wadsworth, D.	Missing 3/5/44 (Mailly-le-Camp).
W/O	Sheridan, C.H.		F/L	Saunders, D.C.	Missing 21/6/44 (Wesseling)
Sgt	Shirley, F.W,		Sgt	Shirley, F.W.	Missing on training flight 9/6/43
Sgt	Sinclair, S.		F/O	Orbell, R.W.	Missing 24/7/44 (Donges)
F/S	Singer, J.		S/L	Squibbs, A.R.	Missing 11/9/44 (Darmstadt)
F/S	Smillie, R.		F/O	Hall, L.A.	Missing 9/8/44 (Chatellrault)
F/S	Smith, E.A.	A429268	F/O	Flockhart, C.K.	Missing 7/1/45 (München)
Sgt	Smith, H.E.		F/O	Pettigrew, R.W.	Missing 26/9/44 (Karlsruhe)
Sgt	Smithers, R.		P/O	Ward, J.F.	Missing 2/12/43 (Berlin)
Sgt	Snell, H.R.		Sgt	Coomber, D.J.	Missing 23/8/43 (Berlin)
F/O	Sparkes, C.P.	NZ4211731	F/O	Sparkes, C.P.	Missing 7/3/45 (Harburg)
Sgt	Sprackman, R.S.	B1315858	P/O	Fuller, C.	Missing 18/10/43 (Hannover)
F/S	Speckman, J.C.		F/L	Jordan, W.F.	Died of wounds on return from Ops 5/8/44.
S/L	Squibbs, A.R.		S/L	Squibbs, A.R.	Missing 11/9/44 (Darmstadt)
F/S	Stabell, V.G.	A413037	W/C	McGhie, I.J.	Missing 17/8/43 (Peenemünde)
Sgt	Stanley, E.		Sgt	Jordan, D.	Missing 22/6/43 (Krefeld)
P/O	Stevens, P.	B149698	P/O	Fuller, C.	Missing 18/10/43 (Hannover)
F/S	Stobbs, J.K.		F/O	Leonard, R.W.	Missing 19/9/44 (Mönchen Gladbach) 2nd A/B.
Sgt	Stuart, M.		F/O	Day, A.G.	Missing 5/1/44 (Stettin)

Rank / Name		*Number*	*Captain's Rank / Name*		*Date /Operation*
Sgt	Sumner, F.		F/S	Goddard, C.A.	Missing 5/9/43 (Mannheim)
Sgt	Sutherland, J.		F/O	Leonard, R.W.	Missing 19/9/44 (Mönchen Gladbach).
Sgt	Swanson, J.L.		F/O	Schaeffer, R.H.	Missing 4/12/44 (Heibronn)
F/S	Symonds, I.J.	A424572	F/O	Gray, D.	Missing 4/1/45 (Royan)
F/L	Tanner, L.E.		F/L	Tanner, L.E.	Killed in crash at Woodbridge, 1/11/44.
W/O	Tate, J.F.R.		F/O	Donnelley, N.W.	Missing 18/7/44 (Revigny)
Sgt	Taylor, A.W.		F/O	Hall, L.A.	Missing 9/8/44 (Chatellrault)
F/S	Templeton, P.B.	A428079	F/O	Hookings, E.W.	Missing 6/11/44 (Mittelland Canal).
Sgt	Thair, R.J.		F/O	Turvey, R.G.	Missing 26/7/44 (Givors)
F/S	Thomas, W.J.		F/O	Morcom, S.B.	Missing 18/7/44 (Revigny)
Sgt	Thompson, F.A.	R82736	W/C	McGhie, I.J.	Missing 17/8/43 (Peenemünde)
F/O	Thompson, J.W.	J28977	F/O	Pettigrew, R.W.	Missing 26/9/44 (Karlsruhe)
P/O	Thompson, P.	NZ422333	P/O	Thompson, P.	Missing 24/3/44 (Berlin)
Sgt	Thompson, R.		P/O	French, P.H.	Missing 20/4/44 (La Chapelle)
F/O	Thomson, J.S	NZ425776	P/O	French, P.H.	Missing 20/4/44 (La Chapelle)
F/O	Tilley, L.	J40470	F/O	Farrow, T.E.	Missing 16/3/45 (Würzburg)
Sgt	Timms, L.		P/O	McCullock, K.	Missing 15/6/43 (Oberhausen)
F/O	Tinker, E.T.	J23964	P/O	French, P.H.	Missing 20/4/44 (La Chapelle)
Sgt	Tofts, R.E.		P/O	McCullock, K.	Missing 15/6/43 (Oberhausen)
Sgt	Towse, F.A.		P/O	Aitken, J.M.	Missing 9/5/44 (Gennevilliers)
Sgt	Trahair, R.	B1386008	P/O	Fuller, C.	Missing 18/10/43 (Hannover)
Sgt	Tucker, F.L.		Sgt	Broomfield,J.	Crashed into sea off Hornsea, training mission.

Table 4.6 No 619 Squadron Personnel Killed in Action

Rank / Name		*Number*	*Captain's Rank / Name*		*Date /Operation*
					23/4/44.
F/S	Tucker, J.H.		F/L	Roberts, K.	Missing 5/6/44 (Caen)
F/S	Turner, P.		F/L	Smith, E.J.F.	Missing 2/2/45 (Karlsruhe)
F/O	Turvey, R.G.	A421645	F/O	Turvey, R.G.	Missing 26/7/44 (Givors)
Sgt	Underdown, T.	B1528690	P/O	O'Leary, O.A.	Missing 17/8/43 (Peenemünde)
Sgt	Van Camp, R.	R134679	P/O	McCullock, K.	Missing 15/6/43 (Oberhausen)
F/S	Vaughton, J.		P/O	Johnson, P.	Missing 21/6/44 (Wesseling)
Sgt	Veal, F.E.W.		Sgt	Broomfield, J.	Crashed into sea off Hornsea, training mission. 23/4/44.
P/O	Vlassie, N.	J28974	F/L	Gunzi, G.	Missing 26/4/44 (Schweinfurt)
P/O	Wadsworth, D.		P/O	Wadsworth, D.	Missing 3/5/44 (Mailly-le-Camp).
F/S	Walch, S.		F/O	Williams, E.K.	Missing 24/2/44 (Schweinfurt)
Sgt	Walker, A.J.		F/S	Buckley, A.J.	Missing 21/6/44 (Wesseling)
Sgt	Walker, G.V.	R212817	F/O	DeMarco, V.T.	Missing 25/4/45(Berchesgaden)
Sgt	Walker, J.H.W.	R64856	F/S	Murphy, T.P.	Missing 29/6/43 (Köln)
Sgt	Wallace, K.R.		Sgt	Coomber, D.J.	Missing 23/8/43 (Berlin)
Sgt	Wallis, J.R.		F/S	Buckley, A.J.	Missing 21/6/44 (Wesseling)
Sgt	Ward, A.E.		P/o	Crawford, K.E.	Missing 21/6/44 (Wesseling)
P/O	Ward, J.F.		P/O	Ward, J.F.	Missing 2/12/43 (Berlin)
Sgt	Ward, J.R.		F/O	Orbell, R.W.	Missing 24/7/44 (Donges)
Sgt	Ward, R.J.		F/L	Tanner, L.E.	Killed in crash at Woodbridge, 1/11/44.
Sgt	Wardle, J.		F/L	Dampier-Crossley,	Missing 10/8/43 (Nürnberg)

Rank / Name		*Number*	*Captain's Rank / Name*		*Date /Operation*
F/O	Warren, J.M.	B129595	Sgt	Pearce, A.J.	Missing 17/8/43 (Peenemünde)
Sgt	Watson, E.E.		F/O	Day, A.G.	Missing 5/1/44 (Stettin)
Sgt	Watson, W.		F/S	Whinfield, E.	Missing 26/4/44 (Schweinfurt)
W/O	Webster, J.		F/O	Leonard, R.W.	Missing 19/9/44(Mönchen Gladbach)
F/S	Webster, J.L.	B138861	F/S	Webster, J.L.	Missing 6/11/44 (Mittelland Canal)
Sgt	Weighell, G.M.	B567856	P/O	Firth, C.	Missing 20/10/43 (Leipzig)
Sgt	Weir, L.G.		F/O	Schaeffer, R.H.	Missing 4/12/44 (Heibronn)
Sgt	Wemyes, J.J.		Sgt	Shirley, F.W.	Missing on training flight 9/6/43.
F/L	Wesson, R.E.		F/O	Day, A.G.	Missing 5/1/44 (Stettin)
F/S	Whinfield, E.		F/S	Whinfield, E.	Missing 26/4/44 (Schweinfurt)
F/L	Whitefield, K.W.		F/O	Clapham, P.C.	Missing 11/11/44 (Harburg) 2nd pilot with F/O Clapham.
F/S	Whitehurst, S.		F/O	Morcom, S.B.	Missing 18/7/44 (Revigny)
F/S	Whittome, J.E.G.		F/L	Saunders, D.C.	Missing 21/6/44 (Wesseling)
F/S	Wickham, R.A.		F/S	Whinfield	Missing 26/4/44 (Schweinfurt)
Sgt	Wilcher, A.R.		P/O	Mears, K.J.	Crashed 26/11/43 on return from Berlin. Killed.
F/S	Wilks, G.T.		Sgt	Broomfield, J	Crashed into sea off Hornsea, training mission. 23/4/44.
F/O	Williams, E.K.	J22780	F/O	Williams, E.K.	Missing 24/2/44 (Schweinfurt)
F/S	Williams, L.E.		F/L	Roberts, K.	Missing 5/6/44 (Caen)
F/L	Williamson, B.A.	J13366	F/L	McMorran, A.E.	Missing 10/4/45 (Leipzig)
F/S	Willis, R.A.		S/L	Gunter, L.B.	Missing 12/8/44 (Braunschweig)

TABLE 4.6 NO 619 SQUADRON PERSONNEL KILLED IN ACTION

Rank / Name		*Number*	*Captain's Rank / Name*		*Date /Operation*
Sgt	Wilson, G.A.	B1161605	P/O	Fuller, C.	Missing 18/10/43 (Hannover)
F/O	Wilson, H.J.		F/O	Wilson, H.J.	Missing 18/7/44 (Revigny)
Sgt	Wiseman, P.C.		S/L	Palmer, C.M.	Missing 20/3/45 (Böhlen)
F/S	Withinshaw, R.		W/O	Schofield, D.	Missing 24/4/44 (München)
Sgt	Wood, E.F.		F/O	Hookings, E.W.	Missing 6/11/44 (Mittelland Canal).
F/O	Wood, P.M.		F/L	Moore, H.J.	Missing 11/4/44 (Aachen)
Sgt	Woodcock, J.H.		S/L	Fuller, F.E.	Missing 7/5/44 (Salbris)
Sgt	Wright, C.N.	R131827	P/O	Firth, C.	Missing 20/10/43 (Leipzig)
F/O	Wyand, G.H.		F/L	Roberts, K.	Missing 5/6/44 (Caen)

Table 4.7 619 Squadron Aircraft Losses By Callsign

PG-A [Able]		PG-B [Baker]		PG-C [Charlie]	
ED977[1]	5/6 Jan 44	DV381[2]	26/27 Nov 43	ED839[3]	8 Oct 43
		EE114	20/21 Oct 43	JA847	2/3 Dec 43
		ED978	14/15 June 43	LL783	6/7 Jun 44
				ME846[4]	21/22 Jun 44

[1] ED977 was one of the Squadron's first aircraft and the first to be named *Nulli secundus.* It had completed 46 operations when lost in January 1944. S/Ldr Ronnie Churcher often flew in this aircraft as 'A' Flight Commander, and it was in this aircraft that Cyril Fuller flew his first operation as second pilot on 21 Jun 43 [to Krefeld with Churcher] and his first operation with his own crew [to Mulheim] on 22 Jun 43.

[2] Believed crashed in sea on return from Berlin 27 Nov 43. The pilot, F/Lt RD Rayment had previously flown Manchesters with 106 Sqn.

[3] Crashed on take-off from Woodhall Spa 8 Oct 43 when bound for Hannover [the third of the four raids on that city in September and October 43].

[4] Failed to return from Wesseling 21/22 Jun 44.

Table 4.7 No 619 Squadron Aircraft Losses by Callsign

PG-D [Dog]		PG-E [Easy]		PG-F [Freddie]	
ED982[1]	17/18 Aug 43	EE106[2]	16/17 Sep 43	EE109[3]	18 Oct 43
JB123	2/3 Jan 44	LM643	24/25 Jul 44	EE150[4]	17 Dec 43
W4127	20/21 Apr 44	LM207	11 Mar 45	ME568	3 Aug 44
LL808	21/22 Jun 44			LM756	25 Apr 45

[1] Failed to return from Peenemünde 17/18 Aug 43.

[2] Failed to return from Antheor Viaduct 16/17 Sep 43. Ditched off Portugal and crew interned.

[3] The aircraft in which Pilot Officer Cyril Fuller and his crew were lost over Hannover on 18 October 1943.

[4] Crash-landed on approach to Woodhall Spa on return from Berlin 27 Nov 43 [no injuries reported]. EE150 was also flown by 617 Sqn and was the one in which Flt Lt Micky Martin, the famous low-level expert and dam-buster, had taken operational control of the remnant of 617 after Gibson's replacement as CO was killed on the first operation after the dams: the disastrous attack against the Dortmund-Ems canal on 14 September 1943 when five out of eight 617 Sqn aircraft and crews were lost including Wg Cdr George Holden and his crew, which included three of Guy Gibson's old crew. This was an even greater casualty rate than that suffered on the dams' raid itself. Flying in EE150 Martin took control of the remaining aircraft and made thirteen attempts to drop his huge 12,000 High Capacity bomb, before finally doing so but to no avail. This attempt to burst the banks of the canal involved circling the target for about an hour at very low level [150 ft]. Martin, promoted Squadron Leader on his return from this raid, offered to take the remaining crews back for another attempt on the canal the following night, but his superiors wisely declined his offer, and to get 617 'back into the saddle' they were sent instead a few nights later jointly with 619 Sqn on another mission, led by 619's CO, Wg Cdr 'Jock' Abercromby [who was to be killed during a raid on Berlin on the night of 1/2 Jan 44].

Table 4.7 No 619 Squadron Aircraft Losses by Callsign

PG-G [George]		PG-H [Harry]		PG-J [Johnnie]	
EE115	31 Aug 43	EE198	21/22 Jun 43	JA844[1]	13 Aug 43
JB134	3/4 May 44	LM423	2/3 Jan 44	LM387	18/19 Jul 44
LL969	18/19 Jul 44	LM446	9/10 May 44	PB346	26/27 Jul 44
PB356	11/12 Nov 44	LL977	21/22 Jun 44	NN723	5/6 Nov 44
		LM484	26/27 Jul 44		
		LM209	11/12 Sep 44		

PG- K [King]		PG-L [Love]		PG-M [Mother]	
EE113	9 Jun 43[2]	EE117	17/18 Aug 43[3]	LM656	29/30 Aug 44
ND935	25/26 Jul 44	JB133	5/6 Sep 43	ND957	7/8 Jan 45
		DV328	24/25 Mar 44		
		ME745	7/8 Jul 44		
		LM640	18/19 Jul 44		

[1] Collided over Sussex with Lancaster ED361 of 207 Sqn while returning from Milan.

[2] Disappeared without trace on air test on 9 Jun 43, probably crashing in the North Sea with the loss of Sgt Shirley and his crew, plus several members of the ground crew checking instruments. Thus, this loss,the Squadron's first, was in training.

[3] Failed to return from Peenemünde 17/18 Aug 43 with the loss of the Squadron's founding CO, Wg Cdr IJ McGhie DFC and his crew. This was 619's worse night to date, with three aircraft and crews lost.

Table 4.7 No 619 Squadron Aircraft Losses by Callsign

PG-N [Nuts]		PG-O [Orange]		PG-P [Peter]	
EE170	2/3 Dec 43	DV330	15/16 Feb 44	EE147[1]	17/18 Aug 43
LM419	24/25 Feb 44	ND730	7/8 May 44		
ND728	5 Jan 45	JB186	18/19 Jul 44		
		LM191	11/12 Sep 44		

PG-Q [Queenie]		PG-R [Robert]		PG-S [Sugar]	
EE116	11/12 Apr 44	JA848	31 Aug 43	EE111[2]	27 Nov 43
ME747[3]	23 Apr 44	EE168	27 Nov 43	LM418	30/31 Mar 44
LM536	28/29 Jul 44	ND792[4]	4 Feb 45	LL904	26/27 Apr 44
				ND986	21/22 Jun 44
				PB208	23/24 Jul 44
				PB405	19/20 Sep 44
				LM742	7 Nov 44
				SW254	10/11 Apr 45

[1] Failed to return from Peenemünde 17/18 Aug 43.

[2] Abandoned over Yorkshire coast on return from Berlin 27 Nov 43.

[3] Crashed in the North Sea during exercise on 23 Apr 44.

[4] Crashed while landing at Strubby during training on 4 Feb 45.

Table 4.7 No 619 Squadron Aircraft Losses by Callsign

PG-T [Tommy]		PG-U [Uncle]		PG-V [Victor]	
EE112	10/11 Aug 43	EE149[1]	25/26 Jun 43	ED981	23/24 Aug 43
PD425	20/21 Mar 45	EE110	1/2 Oct 43	ED859	21/22 Jun 44
		DV336[2]	27 Nov 43	PB210	2/3 Feb 45
		ND932	4/5 Dec 44		

PG-W [William]		PG-X [X-ray]		PG-Y [York]	
ED983[3]	30 Sep 43	JA867	16/17 Dec 43	PB842[4]	13/14 Jan 45
LL784	11/12 Apr 44	LM751	4/5 Dec 44	NG286	7/8 Mar 45
LL919	26/27 Apr 44	ME723	24/25 Apr 44		
NE151	21/22 Jun 44	NN695	21/22 May 44		
ME314	8/9 Feb 45	ME855	12/13 Aug 44		
ME866	9/10 Aug 44	ED602	26/27 Sep 44		
NG503	16/17 Mar 45				

---

[1] EE149 was an ex-617 Sqn aircraft. It was crash-landed by Cyril Fuller and his crew on returning from Gelsenkirchen on 25 Jun 43, after having been badly shot up by flak.

[2] One of four aircraft and two crews lost 27 Nov 43 during a raid on Berlin [see also notes 2, 6 and 11].

[3] Crashed in Lincolnshire on returning from Bochum on 30 Sep 44.

[4] Interestingly, the only two aircraft with the code letter *Z* [Zebra] to be lost by 619 Sqn both went missing within weeks of each other in early 1945, both on operations to Politz.

Table 4.7 No 619 Squadron Aircraft Losses by Callsign

PG-Z [Zebra]		Code letter not known			
PB245	18/19 Sep 44	ED980[5]	14/15 Jun 43		
PB540[6]	1 Nov 44	ED979	28/29 Jun 43		
PB699	7/8 Mar 45	ED597[7]	17 Mar 44		

[5] Failed to return from Oberhausen 14/15 Jun 43, crashing in Holland, where crew buried. The pilot was P/Off K McCulloch RAFVR, whose young son, a toddler at the time, is now Bishop of Manchester. This was the Sqn's first operational loss with casualties [the pilot of a previous loss on 11/12 Jun 43 having crashed in Belgium, evaded capture and returned to the squadron, though his crew became POWs]. There had also been a previous loss with nine fatalities during training before the squadron became operational.

[6] Crash-landed at Woodbridge on returning from Homburg 1 Nov 44.

[7] Crashed on take-off from Coningsby during training 17 Mar 44.

Table 4.8 Operations with 619 Sqn of Sgt (later F/Sgt then P/Officer) Gordon Taylor

Year	*Date*	*Aircraft*	*Callsign*	*Target*	*Comments*
1943	18 June				Posted in from 1660 OCU, RAF Swinderby, as Sgt Pilot
1943	28 June	EE112	PG-T	Cologne	Second pilot with Flt/Lt E Dampier-Crossley DFC RAAF.[1]
1943	01 July	ED982	PG-D	Gardening.[2] Nectarine I[3]	Crew: FSgt GG Taylor (Pilot), Sgt W Allison (F/Eng), Sgt FA Sturges (Nav), P/O WO Lumm (B/Aim), Sgt VS Day (W/Op), Sgt N Fleming (A/Gun), Sgt RA Westad (A/Gun). This a/c FTR from Peenemünde on 17/18 Aug 1943.
1943	08 July	EE106	PG-E	Cologne + Nickelling[4]	Same crew. Red TI in bombsight at time of bomb release. Took off at 22.49, bombed at 01.15 and landed at 03.47. This aircraft FTR Antheor Viaduct 16/17 Sep 1943.
1943	09 July	ED977	PG-A	Gelsenkirchen	Same crew. Returned early - generator failure.
1943	12 July	ED977	PG-A	Turin	This a/c FTR Berlin 5/6 Jan 1944. [pilot: F/O AG Day].
1943	09 Aug	JA847	PG-C	Mannheim	Sgt Weisberg replaced Fleming. This aircraft FTR Berlin 2/3 Dec 1943.
1943	12 Aug	JA847	PG-C	Milan	Same crew as for Mannheim. This a/c FTR Berlin 2/3 Dec 43 [pilot F/O JF Bowyer RCAF].

[1] EE112 and this crew were lost during the raid on Nürnberg on 10/11 Aug 1943. Though in the RAAF, Dampier-Crossley was a New Zealander.

[2] 'Gardening' was the codename for the laying of anti-shipping mines.

[3] Nectarine I involved mine-dropping off the Friesian Islands.

[4] Nickelling was the codename for the dropping of propaganda leaflets. The Trahair archive includes examples of these leaflets, complete with the names of the crew on the nights in question.

Table 4.8 Operations with No 619 Sqn of Sgt Gordon Taylor

Year	*Date*	*Aircraft*	*Callsign*	*Target*	*Comments*
1943	14 Aug	ED982	PG-D	Milan	Very successful attack. This a/c FTR from Peenemünde on 17/18 Aug [pilot: Sgt AJ Pearce].
1943	22 Aug	EE106	PG-E	Leverkusen	Successful attack on chemical works. W/Cdr Abercombie had taken command of Squadron two days previously when W/Cdr McGhie FTR Peenemünde in EE117 PG-L. This a/c FTR from Antheor Viaduct 16/17 Sep 43.
1943	27 Aug	JB123	PG-D	Nürnberg	First of many ops in JB123, which replaced ED982 as PG-D when latter FTR Peenemünde on 17/18 Aug. [crashed Baltic: Sgt AJ Pearce and crew all killed].
1943	30 Aug	JB123	PG-D	M Gladbach	One of 14 aircraft despatched.
1943	31 Aug	JB123	PG-D	Berlin	First of eight trips to 'the Big City.
1943	22 Sep	JB123	PG-D	Hannover	Sgt Donaldson replace Weisberg as air gunner on this trip.
1943	04 Oct	JB123	PG-D	Frankfurt	P/O Horne flew as 2nd pilot.
1943	07 Oct	ED977	PG-A	Stuttgart	One of nine aircraft despatched.
1943	08 Oct	JB123	PG-D	Hannover	One of 10 aircraft despatched, though one crashed on take off fortunately without casualties. F/O Bower flew as 2nd pilot.
1943	18 Oct	JB123	PG-D	Hannover	The operation on which EE109 FTR from Hannover with Cyril Fuller and crew.
1943	23 Nov	JB123	PG-D	Berlin	Fg Off P Ingleby flew as nav and WO Hulbert and P/Off Hammond as air gunners.
1943	16 Dec	DV328	PG-L	Berlin	Taylor's first trip after commissioning as a Pilot Officer. This aircraft FTR Berlin 24/25 Mar 1944. 15 aircraft were despatched on this night. F/Sgt JG Noble (Nav), F/Lt PSF Walmsley (B/Aim), F/Sgt GG King (A/Gnr) and Sgt E Booth (2nd Nav)

Year	*Date*	*Aircraft*	*Callsign*	*Target*	*Comments*
1943	30 Dec	LM378	PG-J	Berlin	Failed to take off: last minute snag.
1944	01 Jan	LM378	PG-J	Berlin	Cloud over target. Not a successful operation. This aircraft FTR from Revigny on 18/19 Jul 1944.
1944	02 Jan	JB134	PG-G	Berlin	The fifth briefing for Berlin in a fortnight. This night ten aircraft were despatched and two FTR, incl JB123 in which Taylor had flown eight ops. JB123 had completed ten trips to Berlin.
1944	14 Jan	LM378	PG-J	Braunschweig	Same crew as 2/3 January.
1944	21 Jan	LM378	PG-J	Magdeburg	One of seven aircraft despatched plus two more to Berlin.
1944	28 Jan	LM378	PG-J	Berlin	One of 14 aircraft despatched, all returning safely though not landing until 0800 the next day.
1944	15 Feb	LM378	PG-J	Berlin	Twenty squadron aircraft took off, this night, the most yet. One FTR and one returned early with engine trouble.
1944	19 Feb	LM378	PG-J	Leipzig	Nineteen aircraft were despatched and a twentieth crew flew a 61 Sqn aircraft. All returned safely, quite an achievement as this night no fewer than 81 aircraft were lost or crashed, including 47 Lancasters.[5]

[5] This appears to be Taylor's last operation with 619 Squadron. The Squadron's Operational Record Book records that he was awarded a non-immediate DFC in June 1944 and had by then been posted out from the Squadron. His air gunner, Warrant Officer RA Westad RCAF, was also awarded a non-immediate DFC. Taylor was 22 years of age when he completed his tour of operations with 619 Squadron. He left the RAF as a Flight Lieutenant in September 1946, but completed five years as a part-time weekend flyer in the reconstituted RAFVR between 1950 and 1955, while earning his living as a civilian pilot with Aer Lingus. Like Sergeant Roy Trahair, the rear gunner in Cyril Fuller's crew, he came from St Austell in Cornwall, and he wrote to Mrs Trahair, Roy's mother, after Cyril Fuller and his crew failed to return from the Hannover operation on 18 October 1943.

5. The Aftermath – The Squadron and the Families

Oh, I have slipped the surly bonds of earth
And danced the skies on laughter-silvered wings;
Sunward I've climbed, and joined the rumbling mirth
Of sun-split clouds – and done a hundred things
You have not dreamed of – wheeled and soared and swung
High in the sunlit silence. Hov'ring there,
I've chased the shouting wind along, and flung
My eager craft through footless halls of air.
Up, up the long delirious, burning blue
I've topped the windswept heights with easy grace
Where never lark, or even eagle flew.
And, while with silent, lifting mind I've trod
The high untrespassed sanctity of space,
Put out my hand, and touched the face of God.

P/O John Gillespie Magee RCAF [killed at the age of 19]

The aftermath

The Squadron had despatched twelve aircraft to Hannover that night. Only eleven returned, one of those returning early at 2006 with technical problems.[1] Against the entry in the operational record for EE109 PG-F, the diarist could only record 'nothing further heard from this aircraft'. The first the squadron would have known that anything was amiss was when the other ten aircraft had returned and landed, and there was still no sign of EE109. The first back was F/S Gordon Taylor, the fellow Cornishman and friend of Roy Trahair from St Austell, in JB123 PG-D. He landed at Woodhall at 2231, five hours and sixteen minutes after take-off. The last back at 2257 was F/O MA MacDonald in JA867 PG-X, last probably because he had been hit by flak over the target. He had been airborne for five hours and thirty-four minutes. It may be significant that MacDonald had bombed at 2018, precisely the time that EE109 was shot down. The two aircraft were possibly hit by flak at the same time. An hour after MacDonald's return, and after frantic phone calls to other stations, in case Fuller had diverted, it would have become evident that EE109 was officially 'missing' and this would have been written up on the aircraft state board. We will return to the night of 18th October, and the likely sequence of events, in a later Chapter. For the moment, suffice to say a full list of the aircraft despatched that night by the Squadron, their times of take-off, the times they bombed and landing times is given in Table 3 of Chapter 3.

Bomber Command had despatched 360 Lancaster aircraft to Hannover that night on the fourth, and last, of the series of attacks on Hannover that began on 22/23rd September. Only one attack was moderately successful and that was the third of the attacks on the night of 8/9th October, when much of the city centre was hit, including the barracks housing flak 3./521 batterie, which ten days later shot down

[1] This same aircraft [EE114 PG-B] and crew,captain P/O C Firth, with an average age of 22, was lost on the next operation flown by the Squadron, against Leipzig on 20 October. They came down not far from Hannover and are buried in the Limmer War Cemetery, where Roy Trahair also rests.

EE109. On the other raids, cloud obscured the targets and most of the bombs fell outside the city on farmland and in forests. It is also possible that decoy fires had been started by the Germans, in much the same way as we built decoy docks to protect Hull.[2] During the course of the four raids, flak batterie 3./521 shot down twelve RAF bombers, five Lancasters, four Halifaxes and three Stirlings. On the night EE109 was shot down, Bomber Command lost eighteen aircraft and a nineteenth got back badly damaged with one dead and two injured crewmen on board. The crew of one of the other eighteen survived after ditching off the Suffolk coast and drifting ashore two hours later. Of the 124 men who made up the remaining seventeen crews, 102 were killed and only 22 survived as POWs. Eight of the 102 dead were aboard EE109: Cyril Fuller and his crew, plus a new pilot, P/O James Horne, who was gaining operational experience before flying with his own crew.

The squadron in the summer & autumn of 1943

One of Cyril Fuller's contemporaries on 619 Squadron was the American pilot, Hubert 'Nick' Knilans, who had joined the Royal Canadian Air Force in the days before the United States of America was involved in the war. Later, he was to be transferred into the USAAF but he chose to complete his two tours of operations with the RAF, first with No 619 and then with 617 Squadron. [It was not without financial advantage to be transferred from the RCAF to the USAAF: Nick reckoned that as a First Lieutenant in the USAAF he received as much pay as his Station Commander, a RAF Group Captain.] His Air Bomber, now a retired schoolteacher, had trained in Southern Rhodesia with others on the squadron and thought be remembered Leo Eaude from a photograph I sent him. Knilans and his crew were in 'B' Flight, and so they had little contact with Fuller and his crew. Also though, like others I have spoken with, they had closed their minds to the losses so as not to dwell on

[2] A Building Inspector of English Heritage at a recent talk said that as much as one quarter of all Luftwaffe ordnance was drawn away by decoys of this kind. He also said that Guy Gibson's dog's grave outside Hangar 2 at RAF Scampton was now a listed monument 'because of its historic and iconic significance'.

them too much. If they had thought about them much, they could not have continued themselves. So effective was that 'closure', to use the modern jargon, that they now have no memories of the people they knew at that time except a few close friends or their own crew. Nick Knilans earned an immediate DSO with 619, the only one awarded in its brief history. He then gained a DFC with 617 Sqn. He also wrote a diary.

Reading Knilans' wartime diary, one is struck by the extraordinary courage these men had to summon up night after night. On one occasion during an attack on Berlin in November 1943, while skirting the searchlights of Frankfurt, Knilans and his crew were attacked twice by night-fighters. On the first occasion a Ju88 made five separate runs and came in as close as 150 yards, opening fire three times, before being shot down by Knilans' rear gunner. No sooner had this aircraft been disposed of – indeed while it was still falling to the ground in flames – than a second fighter, this time a Me110, attacked. Again the rear gunner fired, and the W/Op observed the burst pass straight through the enemy aircraft, which then went away and was not seen again. Six weeks previously their first rear gunner had been killed and the mid-upper injured in another attack, when cannon shells and bullets hit the rear turret, the fuselage and both wings. They continued to the target, bombed and on return Nick personally removed his dead gunner friend from his turret. The gunner, a Scotsman from Dumfries, was married and his wife had given birth to their first child, a son, the previous day. Knilans has recorded how in his first six months on 619 no crew completed a tour of operations, and how his friend 'Mac' went down with all his crew on his first op.[3] One Canadian pilot's hair turned from brown to grey before he was shot down and killed. Knilans also records how his flight commander on 619, Squadron Leader Gerry Scorer kept two 50mm machine gun bullets on the corner of his desk. If they were horizontal no operations were on that day. If they were upright, operations were on. Regarding the loss of his rear gunner, Nick has written of

---

[3] This is probably P/O K McCulloch, although he was actually on his second op.

the situation that confronted him after they landed at Woodhall. It is a story that has been told before, but these are his own words:

I told the crew they did not have to stay to see Jerry taken from his turret. They all left, except Roy, the other wounded gunner. The ambulance had its head-lights trained on the rear turret. The men from it [the ambulance] were unable to open the turret. There were two sliding panels that opened to let the gunner in or out of his turret. When closed, they overlapped to keep the gunner from falling out when his turret was at right angles to the fuselage.

The force of the cannon shells and his muscular reaction had driven Jerry hard against these panels. The inner one had been forced out and over the outer one. I obtained a long screwdriver from one of the attendants. I used it like a can-opener to pry apart the overlapping strips inch by inch. The panels slid open easily after I finished separating the strips. Taking hold of the collar of Jerry's flying suit, I was able to pull him backwards free of the turret.

I lowered his stiff body to the ground and took off his goggles, oxygen mask and helmet. His still features were unmarked. I brushed back a fallen lock of hair. His forehead was icy cold. The middle of his flying suit had been badly torn. It was blood stained. The ambulance helper became ill and walked away. The driver and I put Jerry on a stretcher. We put him in the ambulance, along with Roy, for the ride to the hospital.

I stayed behind in the darkness. I needed a few minutes alone to unwind. The walk back to the Briefing Room was time enough. The young Squadron doctor came along while I was being debriefed. He said that Jerry had been cut in half and must have died instantaneously. He gave me two sleeping pills. The WAAF transport driver who was assigned to take me back to my billet was a good friend of Jerry's. He had given her all of his personal effects to send to his parents if he failed to return. She was overcome by grief and unable to drive. I tried to console her and gave her my two sleeping pills. Another WAAF, offered to drive us to our separate quarters. I was depressed at losing my friend. Before drifting off to sleep, I sent off a prayer that

God would see Jerry into Heaven. I woke up to find that my crew had been given a 48 hour Pass, courtesy of the doctor.

This would be added to our nine days leave already scheduled to begin that day. Roy had left the hospital without permission. He had planned, previously, to see his girl up in the Lake District. His eyes had been cleared of Perspex fragments. He was not about to waste his leave time lying about in the hospital. I declined an invitation from Ken to visit his home on the Isle of Wight. Also, one from Les to spend time at his home in Norwich.

I would have liked to have met their families, but I decided against it. If the crew members became too close to me, it would interfere with my life or death decisions concerning them. A kind welcome by their families would add to my mental burden. It could lead to my crew thinking of me as unfriendly, but it could lead to their lives being saved, too. Many pilots had to decide about flying on to the target or turning back when crewmembers were wounded, including themselves. Some were called, "killers", for carrying out their assigned duty while wounded crewmen had to wait for medical aidBill Reid, a pilot friend of mine, once flew to the target after he and some of his crew were injured. He made a successful bombing run. He was severely wounded on the way back to base. Though semi-conscious, he did make a safe landing. He was awarded an immediate Victoria Cross, his country's highest decoration for valour. He was denounced by other aircrew members for putting his duty to carry on the attack ahead of his own crew's welfare. Some of his squadron when he entered the bar would turn their glasses upside down and leave. He was given the silent treatment or "sent to Coventry", I think the English called it. I, of course, defended the pilot's position of not stopping the attack to tend the wounded.

He has also written of one incident that illustrates graphically how slim was the thread that separated survival and death when flying a cumbersome, heavy bomber in the circumstances of the War:

Over Hamburg the searchlights whirled in circles instead of in steady motions. The flak barrage was widely scattered and exploding at many levels. Joe Tate, my bomb-aimer, made a good run over the target. He claimed that he had a cluster of green target indicators in his sights when he released his bombs. We set course for base. We saw no other a/c on the return flight, probably because my navigator, Harry Geller, a Canadian, made a ten degrees error in plotting our course for base. We left the main bomber stream off to one side. Fortunately, we were over the North Sea so no flak batteries zeroed in on us.

The wireless-operator, Les Knell, gave me the latest meteorological information from base. I set the new height indicator on my altimeter. I received permission to land as I entered the circuit over Woodhall Spa. I flew at 1,000-ft. above some low cloud cover as I dropped my undercarriage and flaps. I turned port toward the final approach. I was looking for the Flight Path Indicator. This device sent up three angled beams of light. They showed yellow if you were too high, red if too low, and green if you were descending at the correct angle.

What I took to be a thin cloud layer obscured my vision. I checked my instruments and noted that I was still at 1,000-ft.

"There's the ground", shouted Joe.

I slammed the four throttle levers full forward with my right hand and hauled back on the control column with my left hand.

"Wheels up", I shouted.

I could see the grey outlines of a gravel pit around us. We struck a sand bar between pools of water we had swum in on our days off. The Lanc staggered upwards barely above stalling speed. It slashed through the tops of a grove of trees. Airmen were hurtling out of doors and windows of barracks built under the trees. One branch ripped off the wires leading to the port wheel brake. The thunderous roar of the straining engines rattled the buildings and terrified the airmen.

I nursed the struggling Lanc back up to a higher altitude. The crew was silent as I flew a wide circuit and approached the flight path again. I ignored the altimeter and visually stayed at a safe height. I followed the green light down to the runway. I had to open up the starboard engines, the only ones serviceable and needed to stop the aircraft. I looked at the altimeter as we slowed down. It registered 960-ft.

"You son-of-a-bitch", I muttered to myself. I parked in our dispersal site. The ground crew called me to the port wing upon leaving the aircraft. They played their flashlights over the two port propellers. Everyone had their several tips bent back where they had struck the ground. It was 0435 hours. By 0900 hours we were back in the Flight Room and told we would be going out on ops again that evening. July 25, 1943.

He has also written about the experience of facing flak over the target:

I had come to the conclusion that if there was not too much flak bursting over the target it meant that the bandits were waiting over the target. They would let the first wave drop their bombs, which would start many fires around the city. They could silhouette incoming bombers on the flames below them. My plan, if this happened, was to speed up to the front of the stream, drop my bombs and get the hell out of there.

This was not the case as I flew towards Essen. Hundreds of flak shells were bursting directly over the city. Searchlights were seeking out their next victims. I slowed my Lanc down to let the first wave knockout these guns and searchlights, leaving a safer path for me to follow. Next, I looked to see if someone up ahead had been coned. There always were several unfortunates. One appeared off to my port. I steered toward it, hoping that I could slip by him while all the searchlights would be on him. I was a few hundred feet below him as I passed by. A dozen searchlights held him in their silvery beams. Hundreds of flak shells were hurtling upwards at him. Suddenly, he dove towards me. The light beams and flak followed him as he passed over me. We were hit several times in the brief passage. A few seconds later, the other Lanc exploded below us.

Ken, the flight engineer said, "The starboard-inner is overheating and I'm feathering it".

"Okay," I said and changed the throttle settings and trim tabs to compensate for the loss of that engine's power. I had trained Ken to feather any engine immediately, if he noticed it had been damaged. Overheated engines quickly caught fire. Some pilots did their own feathering and wasted time dangerously. "We're losing petrol from the

starboard main tank," reported Ken. "I will run all engines from it to use up as much as possible before it is empty." Ken was only eighteen but very competent at transferring petrol to and from the various tanks in each wing. Nor did he panic or become immobilized by fear.

We made our bombing run without further trouble. The bomb-aimers wanted a 60 second straight and level run up to their aiming point. After dropping the bomb load, they were briefed to ask the pilot for more level flying. Thus they could take a photograph of where the bombs fell. A large photo flash shell was in the bomb load and went off as it neared the ground. The photo would enable the target plotters to see where each load was dropped and the total area covered. Flying straight and level over the brightly lighted city was a nerve-wracking time for all crew members. Our aiming point was the centre of the city. A five mile or more error would be inside the target area. I decided to give my bomb-aimer, Joe Tate, from Yorkshire, thirty seconds on the bomb run and less for his photo.

High flying photo reconnaissance planes could take better pictures by daylight anyway. The less time spent in this most dangerous area of the sky the better for my survival. The higher-up officers had their way to fight and I had mine! I weaved our way into the darkness and set course for base. The Lanc flew quite well on three engines. We lost height slowly to keep up our speed and save petrol both. There was no problem back at base. Landing on three engines required a bit more skill on my part but it went well.

The Air Officer Commanding (AOC) 5 Group sent a message to Group Captain H.L. Patch. 619 Squadron had sent off thirty-one bombers in the past two nights. We had dropped a heavier load of bombs than any other squadron in the Group. All aircraft returned safely.

We checked our Lancaster later in the morning. The anti-aircraft shell that went through the main petrol tank had not exploded. It left a hole large enough for my leg to fit into. A piece of flak had cut one of the glycol lines to the radiator in the engine nacelle, which had caused it to overheat. Nobody had to fly three nights in a row. We spent the afternoon resting in our hut.

The stress of knowing what effect your bombs must be having on the people below was also beginning to tell:

Already the destruction of the cities I had helped to bring about was beginning to bother me. My idealism was weakening, I thought. The atrocity stories about enemy actions in Europe had caused my early enlistment. I wanted to return happiness to the children of Europe. Now, I was helping to destroy them. I knew the residents of the cities we were bombing were no front-line soldiers. They were older workers, women and children.

Of the attack on Hamburg [Operation Gomorrah, from which the firestorm developed] during the atrociously icy weather conditions of 2nd August, 1943, Knilans has written:

This was to be my sixth trip and my last one to Hamburg. We were briefed by the Met Officer that we might encounter some severe thunderheads. He expected the target to be clear. We had a 12,500-1b. bomb load. I took off in a heavy, gusty rainstorm. It was like flying into a bottle of ink. The unlighted radium-coated needles were all I could see on the Sperry instrument panel before me. Our lives depended on my following the artificial horizon to judge our altitude or position. I worked hard to gain altitude. The aircraft broke free from the clouds at 17,000-ft. There was enough starlight to see clear spaces between thunderheads towering above us. We approached Hamburg down the Elbe River. A massive thunderhead covered the city, which was still burning. I told Harry, the navigator, to plot our position and we would make a timed run from there into the storm cloud and over the target.

I barely had entered the storm cloud when the aircraft was caught in a strong down-draft. I pulled back on the stick, but we were still descending. Blue streaks of static electricity, St. Elmo's Fire, were flowing over the windshield and wings. Rime ice was forming on the wings and props only to break off and bang against the fuselage like flak. I kept struggling with the stick and rudder pedals while watching the altimeter unwind. It reached 14,000-ft.

"Drop the bombs and let's get the hell out of here", I said.

The six-tons dropped away as we struck the updraft on the other side of the thunderhead. I pushed the stick up against the instrument panel and applied full starboard rudder. We ascended rapidly. As we popped out at the top, the starboard wing was nearly vertical to the ground. The altimeter registered 21,000 ft. The crew sat in stunned silence. I had been too busy to be scared. I was relieved to get the old Lancaster back on a level course for home base, however.

My good friend Sgt. Bobby Knights made his run up the Elbe River, too. He wisely decided to go under the storm at 12,000-ft. Flak caused a fire in the fuselage of his aircraft. He flew his smoke-filled plane over the target. His crew put out the fire and they landed safely. Sqn/Ldr. Scorer, the next morning reprimanded him for risking the airplane at that low height. He should have been given a medal. (He later earned a DSO & DFC).

Of the attack on Milan on 7th August, Knilans said:

As we flew over occupied France, I could see someone on the ground blinking a light in the Morse Code sign for V-Victory. This defiant gesture by someone of our allies often occurred over Belgium and Holland, also. A full moon rose up to bathe the Alps in its bright glow. I could see Mt. Blanc off the port wing. A white plume of snow was blowing from its top. The sheer brown slopes below it looked barren in the cold light from the moon. Strong currents of air were blowing about the mountain peaks. One of them twisted my aircraft into a sharp twisting dive to port. I had to apply full starboard stick and rudder to counteract its force. This unsettling manoeuvre was repeated once more before our course left the Alps behind.

The weak Italian defences gave us no trouble as we bombed a cluster of green T.I.s. The Fiat Works was our primary target. I could see fires starting up in Turin as other bombers had flown there. We flew unmolested across southern France. No shells were fired at us by flak guns or bandits as we flew by the Cherbourg Peninsula and across the channel. I was quite tired as I made the touchdown at Woodhall Spa again. Eleven of our squadron aircraft returned safely to base. The twelfth aircraft had a mid-air collision with another Lanc at 5,000-ft. near Selsey Bill on the channel coast. F/O Arden's aircraft port wing tip was hit by a Lanc's port rudder as it crossed his track. It caused the wing to curl up. F/O Arden took evasive action in the shape of a diving turn to port. Somehow, his port and starboard outer engines caught fire. His Flight Engineer managed to stop the engines and extinguish these fires. The pilot decided he could not reach an airfield, so he turned out to sea again. Before he could attempt his ditching procedure, his port wing buckled suddenly at 500-ft. and they crashed into the water. They were a few hundred yards offshore from Littlehampton. Most of the crew managed to get into a dinghy. The navigator (Sgt. Jones, D.V.) drifted away from the dinghy and was not seen again. An Air Sea Rescue launch picked up the rest of the crew. The Rear Gunner, Sgt. Maddaford, died in Littlehampton Hospital shortly after admission.

Of the second of the series of four attacks on Hannover, Nick wrote:

Bad weather over the continent caused operations to be cancelled for the next three nights. I spent the evenings pub-crawling in the village. Always managed to be bedded down by eleven, tipsy and happy.

Operations on the 27th [September] were not to be cancelled. Some nights we would be all strapped in and ready to start the engines when a yellow flare would shoot up from the Control Tower. This meant the ops were scrubbed. Cheers would be heard from dispersals all around the perimeter as happy crews spilled out of their aircraft. No such luck this time as we took off for Hanover in Northern Germany.

Our course would take us toward Bremen, as a feint, then south to Hanover and straight back across Holland to the channel. I got us up to 20,000-ft. in the colder air of Autumn before the bomb run. It was clear and bright over the target. Joe reported that he had a good cluster of green T.I.s to drop our load on this time.

"Bomb doors open," I said.

"Left-left", said Joe as he took over for the run-up. It was always right or left-left so I would know by the sounds even if other crew members were shouting about bandits and searchlights near us.

"Bombs away, steady for the photo", yelled Joe.

"Bandits 12 o'clock high", shouted the Mid-Upper gunner.

I looked up to see an aircraft diving right at us. The thought flashed through my mind, "Boy he's making sure of us". I dove steeply to port.

"Don't shoot, it's a Halifax", I shouted.

"He missed my turret by two feet", said Jack from the rear turret.

The Halifax had been badly hit. We could see it burning fiercely on its way down. The crump of an exploding anti-aircraft shell near us startled me. The bits of flak rattled against the fuselage and windows.

"Any damage", I asked.

"I can see petrol leaking from the starboard auxiliary tank", said Ken, the Flight Engineer. I'll pump what I can save into the main tank".

There must have been more leaks. He and the navigator stated we would have enough only to reach south-east England. I would have to rely on some emergency procedure to get us down. I certainly did not want to ditch in the channel in the darkness. The alternative was to ask for a homing to some friendly airfield. All pilots had studied a poster depicting a small Negro lad pointing toward a lighted airfield. One had only to call out into the night and aid would be forthcoming. I gave it a try.

"Hello Darky, Hello Darky, Hello Darky, T-Tommy calling, I am low on petrol and need a course for an emergency landing".

No answer came back from the darkness about me. We were flying over London. I descended to 2,000-ft. The wailing of barrage balloon warning sirens rose and fell in my earphones. I could see the River Thames gleaming in the centre of the blacked-out metropolis.

"Hello Darky, Hello Darky, Hello Darky", I spoke again into the enveloping darkness. "T-Tommy here, I need a course to land". Nothing happened.

I thought, perhaps, I could ditch my a/c in the Thames below. I would have to dodge barrage balloons and bridges to do it. I did not fancy our chances. I tried one more broadcast.

"T-Tommy calling, Hello. Darky, xxxxxx where are you?" I yelled in exasperation. A sweet feminine voice replied, "I have you T-Tommy, steer 095 degree."

"Roger, flying 095," I replied in relieved tones. I flew toward the mouth of the Thames.

"There it is," said Joe as he lay in the nose. "I can see the runway lights."

I could barely make them out as I let down and circled below 1,000-ft. I came in to land and found it was a grass field with no runway. It was used by small fighters. The flare path were goose neck flares for small fighters. The field was near Gravesend. We were refuelled and able to fly back to Woodhall Spa the same morning.

Of the earlier attack on Hannover on 22nd September, he said:

Hanover, an important railroad centre, was the designated target. 13,436 pounds made up our bomb load of varying sizes. It would be three hours from take-off to the bomb run.

As usual Joe aimed for the centre of town and hoped to be within five miles of the aiming point! The target indicator flares were not overly accurate under the best of conditions. There was a tendency for the Bomb Aimers to drop their loads on the first ones that they could see or on fires from a previously dropped load. This could cause a steady creep-back as crews bombed short to turn off into the welcome darkness. The Bomb Aimers lay on their bellies looking down through clear plastic at the seething flames and violent explosions of the burning city. They saw the glare of fires, the searchlight beams, the hundreds of coloured tracer shells arcing upward and other aircraft being destroyed below them. Joe said that he felt like he was suspended in air while stark naked.

He told me the next day that our photograph was poor because the aircraft was not level at the time of exposure. Only too true, as I had not wasted time after the bomb run in making a speedy turn out of the glare. The gunners and I had seen several bandits engaging other bombers. Besides, nobody ever got a medal for a pretty picture.

He also mentions a spiritual experience during his tour of operations with No 619 Squadron:

I was in bed by one a.m. and back in the Flight Room by 9 a.m. Operations were scheduled for the evening again. The Flight Engineer, Ken Ryall, said we would have 11,180 pounds of bomb load. The Briefing Room map showed Mannheim in southern Germany to be our target. Our new Wingco, "Jock" Abercomby, told us the usual words about how important it was to destroy the city.

We took off at twilight. Our climb up to 20,000 ft. kept us in the lighter part of the sky as darkness settled in below and behind us.

The upper sky before me was still somewhat lighted. A figure of a woman several thousand feet high slowly emerged into my startled view. The face and figure became more distinct. I recognized this vision as that of a girl I had loved very much. She had died six years ago at the age of nineteen. I kissed her good-bye one evening and two days later her father telephoned me that she was dead from pneumonia and diabetes, both unsuspected until it was too late. I was one of her pallbearers.

She had a slight smile on her lips as I flew towards her. The vision slowly melted into the darkening sky around us. I was a bit uneasy though. I did not know if she had appeared to reassure me that she would keep me from harm or if she was welcoming me into her world of the hereafter. I certainly hoped it was not the latter.

This was my second vision. The first one had occurred during the funeral of my eldest brother. I was eight years old then and my brother was twelve. My brother Lawrence had drowned when he was at Y-camp on Phantom Lake in Walworth County. The graveside service was held on a day when the sky was overcast with clouds. I attended Sunday School regularly at Delavan Baptist Church, but I was not very sure about where people went when they died. The minister was giving his prayer for my brother's soul to rest in peace when a single shaft of sunlight burst through and lit up my brother's casket. I looked up along the sunbeam into the opening in the clouds, and all around the edges were seraphims and cherubims smiling down at me. I did not tell anyone what I had seen, but I knew my brother would be welcomed as he went up to Heaven. It was fifteen years before I thought about that vision again [author: following the previous vision].

I grew steadily calmer as we flew through the night. I kept climbing and descending, gently weaving from port to starboard, always on the lookout for bandits or flak bursts ahead. Joe picked out a cluster of green T.I.s near a bend in the river. This was the centre of the Mannheim. We bombed from 20,000-ft. two hours and forty-eight minutes after take off. It would take three hours to get back to Woodhall Spa. We had to fly through a gauntlet of fighter flares. These were dropped along both sides of the bomber stream by enemy bombers. They were extremely bright and slowly descended, held up by parachutes. The bandits could find us visually in this eerie lane of flickering flares. I tilted the wings to port and starboard frequently. This enabled the gunners to see if a bandit was sneaking up on us from below. We made it out of the gauntlet without being attacked. Still, the minutes seemed to drag by as we flew on tensely awaiting an assault from any quarter. It was a good feeling to land safely from my eleventh trip over enemy territory. I felt my vision was to be my future guardian angel.

Two months later on 6 November we were heading for an onslaught on Berlin. On the outward flight we were heavily attacked by enemy night fighters. One engine was knocked out and the tail was damaged. We were still 250 miles from Berlin. I could have jettisoned the 4,000 pound bomb and the 3,000 pounds of incendiaries, but I was a bit angry and decided to follow the RAF dictum 'press on regardless'. I flew forward on three engines, losing altitude from 20,000 down to 13,000 feet. As we approached Berlin the buildings began to take shape. It was a vivid and dramatic moment with the target-marking flares above us and hundreds of searchlights below us. Block-buster bombs, looking like 50 gallon oil drums were tumbling down past us from the bombers above. Twelve hundred anti-aircraft guns were firing their yellow and red shells. Amid all the buffeting and noise, my 18 years old flight engineer spoke up: 'Should we pray, skipper? ' 'No', I replied, 'not while we are about to bomb and kill more old men, women and children down there'. By then I was overtaken by a thought, by a dream if you like, that if I survived this mission and the rest of the war, I would try to do some type of public service to balance my personal books. After the war I changed my career to teaching and this is the work I followed until retiring. I guess that experience on the approach to Berlin, along with my visions told me where my destiny lay.'

Following the War, Nick Knilans obtained a BSc degree at the University of Wisconsin-Madison and completed 25 graduate courses at the Universities of Minnesota and California. He taught history at Corona High School, California for 25 years, working especially with Hispanic students. He served as the President of the League of United Latin citizens, on Corona Juvenile Commission and as an elder of the Corona Baptist Church. He served as counsellor to the California Rehabilitation Centre for Narcotic Addicts and as a representative on the County Council of Economic Opportunity. In 1960 he took sabbatical leave and travelled to India at his own expense to assist at the Cheshire Home for Crippled Children. Between 1963-65, he served as a Peace Corps volunteer in Northern Nigeria and received commendations for his work. He is now retired in his native Delavan, the town in which he was born and bred. He has balanced the books.

Another contemporary of Fuller's, who also went on to 617 Squadron was Bob Knights, mentioned by Nick Knilans in one of his stories above. He won a DFC with 619 and a DSO with 617, joining 619 as a sergeant pilot and leaving with a commission. After the War he was seconded to BOAC and left after 35 years as a senior pilot. He could not remember Cyril Fuller but thought that was understandable, given '*the pressure... life went on... you were in charge of a crew and that was the main concern...*'. He had known many of the big 'names', and his assessment was interesting: Willie Tait '*was self-effacing, no leader, no charisma, surrounded by a few yes men and cushioned to some extent*'; Cheshire '*was a charismatic leader, almost a prophet like Jesus Christ, he would not put men at risk if he could avoid it*'; Jeudwine '*he was a great CO, who had readily agreed and understood my wish to transfer to 617 Squadron and arranged for me to go for interview*'. He also told the author, as noted elsewhere, that at the end of the war No 617 Squadron was the only squadron in Bomber Command to have a precision bombsight. The RAF had gone to war with a primitive course setting bombsight [CSBS] that made no allowance for variations in drift or changes of course. Improvements were made to the CSBS, the final version being the Mk IX A, which resulted in there being several variants of this bombsight in service but not much improvement in bombing accuracy. The CSBS was replaced by the Stabilised Vector Sight, which was a bit better, but in 1942 Squadron Leader Dickie Richardson, the bombing expert whose experience dated back to the primitive era of WWI, was instrumental in introducing into service the Stabilised Automatic Bomb Sight Mk II [SABS], which incorporated a gyro and a sort of early computer, and this bombsight did begin to make a big difference in bombing accuracy. In skilled hands, the SABS allowed bombs to be dropped from 20,000 feet with an average error of only a hundred yards, a considerable improvement on what had gone before. Bob Knights remembers: '*the SABS was a precision sight...and though a few squadrons received it...eventually 617 Squadron was the only squadron in Bomber Command to have the Mark II A version, which permitted the data to be adjusted all the way to the target*'. '*617 Squadron was taught to use this sight by S/L Richardson, known to us as 'Talking Bomb*'.

Stan Jones was another former sergeant pilot, commissioned after a first tour with No 106 Squadron, with whom he was won a DFM. He arrived on No 619 Squadron on 8 May as a F/O captain in that first summer as the squadron was forming up and survived to leave at the end of his tour as a F/L with a DFC to add to his DFM. By coincidence, he was born in Ludlow, only two miles away from where this book is being written. Before he was of school age, his family moved from Ludlow to Wem in North Shropshire, where he attended the local grammar school. Having known Ronnie Churcher from his days on 106 Squadron, he and several others were 'recruited' by Ronnie for the new squadron being formed at Woodhall Spa. *'Ronnie, John McGhie, Jock Hayden......we all knew each other...we were a small clique, if that's the right word.'* According to Knights survival was all really a matter of luck. He remembers that at a dinner in the RAF Club [in London] after the War, Bomber Harris had told them that his assessment was that crews had a 5% chance of surviving a first tour of operations and 1% of that 5% stood a chance of surviving a second tour of operations.

On No 106 Squadron they had flown the twin-engined Handley Page Hampden medium bomber, and off-duty they usually went to a pub in Boston where '*the couple that ran it were extraordinarily kind to us*', but after a while they said '*please don't bring any more* [new crews] *in – we can't stand it*' [the losses that had become evident night by night as faces disappeared]. '*I had not realised how personally the landlady was taking the losses.*'

After the war, Stan Jones became an airline captain with BEA and distinguished himself by flying the first Viscount aircraft to Australia [in record time]. He now lives in the Channel Islands.

Again, though another well-known story, it is worth repeating that it was with No 619 Squadron that the war correspondent Ed Murrow was taken on his famous wartime trip to Berlin on 2/3 December 1943, in aircraft JB123 PG-D flown by W/C Jock Abercromby. Three other war correspondents despatched that night with other squadrons were all shot down, Captain Nordhal Grieg and Mr Norman Stockton being killed, and Mr Lowell Bennett, like Murrow an American, being taken prisoner of war.

The Squadron was also chosen for a visit in the summer of 1943 by Martha Gellhorn, wife of Ernest Hemingway and an American War Correspondent, for her research into a story to be broadcast by radio to the USA from London. A transcript of the broadcast covers four pages of A4 paper, and so I will not repeat it all, but it is a highly evocative account of life on a wartime bomber airfield and of the insouciance, as Miss Gellhorn saw it, or faraway politeness, of the crews who that evening would be departing for an operation against Germany. She watched them go and was there when they were de-briefed after they returned. She was amazed by the low-key British understatement of it all. This is part of what she broadcast:

> *'it was known now that all the planes [author, 13 that night] were back and all undamaged, and no one hurt. Everyone was tired, anxious to get through the questioning, back to the Mess to the famous*

operational egg, the fried potatoes, the marmalade, and the bread that seems to be partially of sand. And then to sleep.'

She followed them back to the Mess:

'They were standing at the mess bar, which is a closet in the wall, drinking beer and waiting for breakfast. They were talking a little now, making private jokes and laughing easily. Some of the men had saved their raid rations, a can of American orange juice and a chocolate bar, to eat now. They value them very much. There are those who drink the orange juice and eat the chocolate early, not wanting to be done out of them, just in case.

The Lancasters looked like enormous deadly black birds going off into the night, and somehow they looked different when they came back. The planes carried from this field thousands of pounds of high explosives, and the crews flew all night to drop the load as ordered. Now the trains would not run between France and Italy for a while, not through that place anyhow. Here are the men who did it, with mussed hair and weary faces, dirty sweaters under their flying suits, sleep-bright eyes, making humble comradely jokes and eating their saved-up chocolate bars.

After it is finished let them have that lovely life they want. Let those of us who have never been where they have been see to it.

[Martha Gellhorn, June 1943]

The families

The telegram was received at St Austell post office at 12.46 pm on 19 October 1943, OHMS Priority for Mr RT Trehair [sic] of 6 Colenso Place, St Austell. It read, like over 55,500 others to be received by the mothers, fathers and wives of Bomber Command crews during the course of the war, quite simply:

REGRET TO INFORM YOU THAT YOUR SON 1586008 SGT ROY TREHAIR IS MISSING AS THE RESULT OF AIR OPERATIONS ON 18/19 OCT 1943 LETTER FOLLOWS ANY FURTHER INFORMATION RECEIVED WILL BE

IMMEDIATELY COMMUNICATED TO YOU = 619 SQUADRON

In Sheffield a similar telegram was received by Mr and Mrs Crookes and in Bristol another by Mr and Mrs Sprackman at Shrubbery Farm. In Catford and Battersea in London others were received by Mr and Mrs Fuller and Mr and Mrs Wilson, and in Birkdale another by the elderly Mr Eaude and his wife. Two other telegrams were especially hard to bear. In South Brixham, Devon, Mrs James Horne was receiving the first intimation that her husband, after only two weeks on a squadron, would not be returning home, and in Beacontree, Essex the twenty-three year old Mrs Reg Stevens was receiving similar news.

The letters from W/C Jock Abercromby were written the next day, and the one to Mr and Mrs Trahair read:

It is with deep regret that I have to inform you that your son, Sergeant Roy Trahair, is missing following operations on the night of 18/19 October, 1943.

He was Air Gunner of an aircraft detailed to make an attack against Hanover. As is usual, silence was maintained after take-off and, therefore, it is not possible to determine, at the moment, the cause of its failure to return.

Your son was a member of an experienced crew and I have every confidence in him and in their Captain, P/O C. Fuller, who would, I know, have done everything possible to ensure their safety. There is, of course, every possibility that they abandoned the aircraft and have landed safely in enemy territory, and if this is the case news should reach you from the Air Ministry within the next few weeks. We can only hope and pray that they are safe, and the hearts of us all go out to you during this anxious period of waiting.

You will wish to know that I have arranged for your son's personal effects to be taken care of by the Committee of Adjustment Officer at this station, and they will be forwarded to you in due course. Any further information concerning the missing aircraft will be sent to you by the Air Ministry, but if, as often happens, you receive news from other sources, I shall be most grateful if you will let me know.

Sergeant Trahair won the regard of us all. He and his colleagues in the crew have individually and collectively shown themselves to be men of high quality. I have been proud to have him in my Squadron.

May I express the sincere sympathy which I personally and the members of my Squadron feel with you at this most distressing time.

I am,
Yours sincerely,
W ABERCROMBY
Wing Commander
Commanding No 619 Squadron

On the 22 October, the Squadron Leader Joint Secretary of the RAF Benevolent Fund wrote to Mr and Mrs Trahair offering sympathy and saying that:

I am to inform you that if your missing son was making you a voluntary allotment from his Royal Air Force pay, you will be entitled to continue cashing the orders in the Royal Air Force order book for a period. If however, you do not receive a communications from the Air Ministry regarding you title to a temporary allowance within three weeks from the date of this letter, you should communicate direct with the Director of Accounts, Air Ministry (Accounts 7KCas), Whittington Road, Worcester. If your son had not made you a voluntary allotment but was making you regular payments for your support through unofficial channels, you should inform the Director of Accounts for this effect without delay. Should you be in need of some temporary assistance either now or at any time in the future, kindly let me know and I will arrange for our Representative to interview you at the earliest opportunity, otherwise please do not trouble to answer this letter.

Six days later on 28 October, the Casualty Branch of the Air Ministry, based at 77 Oxford Street, London W1, wrote to Mr and Mrs Trahair 'at the command of the Air Council' to offer sympathy and to say that their son's failure to return from operations 'does not necessarily mean that he is killed or wounded' and that enquiries were being made through the International Red Cross to establish whether he might be a prisoner of war, but meanwhile 'if any information regarding your son is received by you from any source you are requested to be kind enough to communicate it immediately to the Air Ministry'.

The same day a letter was written from RAF Station Coningsby saying:

as the officer responsible for the supervision of your son's personal belongings I to want to assure you my very deep sympathy with you [sic] during this period of anxious waiting. Nothing is known yet beyond the fact that the aircraft failed to return from Operations over enemy territory, and we can only hope eventually we may hear that the crew is safe, even if prisoners of war. It is extremely hard for you to have to wait for more definite news and I should like you to feel that we both understand and sympathise with you in your great anxiety.

Your son's effects have been carefully packed and in accordance with Air Ministry Orders they are now being sent to:

The Central Depository,
RAF Station Colnbrook,
Slough, Bucks.

I have to advise you that certain Statutory formalities must be completed before any articles are released but you can send any enquiries to the Officer Commanding, The Central Depository, if you so wish.

A Post Officer Savings Book was found among the effects and in accordance with the usual procedures we have to follow in these cases, this had been duly sent to Air Ministry.

If there is anything further I can do to help, please to not hesitate to write me. Meanwhile, I express the hope that the future will bring good news.

The next letter was dated 3 November and came from the Air Ministry Accounts Branch in Worcester. This letter referred with regret to the fact that 'your son has been officially reported as missing on 18th October 1943 and in these circumstances you will wish to be informed with regard to the voluntary allotment of 8s. 9d. a week at present in payment to you. I am to state that the regulations permit the continuance of payment at the present rate for seventeen weeks from the date the casualty was notified (i.e. four weeks as an allotment from the airman's pay and thirteen weeks from public funds). If your son is still missing at the end of this period of seventeen weeks, the payment may continue for a further period of nine weeks, i.e. up to and including order number 6 (due for payment on 13th April 1944) unless in the meantime further information regarding him is received, when you will be notified of any amendment which may in consequence be necessary.'

Meanwhile, Mrs Trahair had written to the one person she knew personally at Woodhall Spa: the Cornish NCO pilot, now flight sergeant, Gordon Taylor from St Austell, who before the war had worked in the office of a Cornish clay mine with Roy's uncle. A reply was a while coming, for Taylor had been detached from the station for a few weeks, and did not receive Mrs Trahair's letter until his return at the end of November. On 29th November 1943 he wrote to Mrs Trahair, as follows:

> *I have been detached from this unit for a considerable time. Upon returning, I found your letter awaiting me. I sympathise and fully understand your anxiety about Roy being reported missing. It also came as a great shock to myself and members of the squadron who knew him. I was on the same operation that night and experienced intense enemy activity – anything could have happened, and it was impossible to tell exactly what was happening. As you will have seen from the press, a considerable number of our crews were lost that night.*
>
> *I am indeed very sorry that there is nothing at the moment I can do or let you know that would relieve the terrible anxiety I am sure you are experiencing just now. Until such time as you hear from the Air Ministry or Red Cross there is nothing we can both do but hope for the best. Roy was a very popular member of this squadron and is greatly missed by all, but from experience gained from other crews we are all very optimistic and are looking forward to the day when he and his crew will be back with us. I shall be pleased to call on you at Christmas to give you any information I have since gained.*

Trusting you will have already had good news of your son. Yours sincerely. G. Taylor.

On the 20 January 1944, Mr and Mrs Trahair received from the RAF Central Depository a small cardboard box containing the personal effects of their son, including his diary, two air gunner's brevets, his pipe [still 58 years on with a half-smoked bowl of tobacco], the letters to him from his mother and a few other small trinkets.[4] These were all carefully kept by his mother and are now in a suitcase of letters and memorabilia Roy's younger brother inherited when their mother died. The only item not retained was a white silk scarf, which had been carefully wrapped so as to disguise the vomit it contained. Roy usually wore this when on operations as rear gunner. When on leave a few days before his final flight, he had told his mother that like other aircrew he had on occasion been frightened to the point of sickness.

On 1 February 1944 Mrs Trahair wrote to W/C Jock Abercromby, Officer Commanding No 619 Squadron, RAF Woodhall Spa, saying 'my son was reported missing fifteen weeks ago today. We have received no further news of him and are getting very anxious. Do you know if any of the rest of the crew are prisoners of war. I feel I have waited long enough for news and must write someone, the suspense is unbearable at times. Would you let me know if any news has been received....news has reached this town [St Austell] of a boy that was reported missing as recently as Christmas...he is a prisoner of war...I pray my son is still alive, but I don't know what to think at times.'

The letter was returned to Mrs Trahair a few weeks later with the envelope marked *Wyton, Huntingdon* and stamped '*Return to Sender on*

[4] Also included was a letter to Roy from 1600093 Sgt LG 'Les' Stacey, written from RAF New Camp, Gibraltar on 21st September 1943. Roy and Les had obviously met during training and Stacey was now operating out of Gibraltar. Interestingly the letter has been censored in two places by 'RAF Censor 229: RW Hurwood' where it refers firstly to 'our complete tour consists of [blanked out]' and 'Of course it is not too bad for us aircrew who can get back for leave at pretty regular intervals but I should not [blanked out] out here for [blanked out]. The censor had NOT blanked out a comment 'News is not too plentiful, and bearing in mind the censor's pencil it is difficult to write a very interesting letter'.

Air Ministry Instructions'. For years the Trahair family thought there was some deep significance in the returning of this letter, which had obviously had been opened in order to obtain the return address, and that the authorities were covering something up. In fact, of course, the explanation was much more prosaic. Jock Abercromby had been posted from 619 Squadron to No 83 Squadron [Pathfinders] at RAF Wyton, near Huntingdon, on 4th December 1943 and had been killed less than a month later on 2nd January 1944 while on an operation to Berlin. The letter had been forwarded on from Woodhall to Wyton, who had sent it back to the sender because it could not be delivered to a dead addressee. A word of explanation would have stopped years of worry, but the postal clerk concerned was probably told only 'return letters addressed to Abercromby back to the sender'.

On 7th February 1944, the Trahairs received a letter they must have been dreading in response to one Mrs Trahair had written them on 3rd February. The Air Ministry Casualty Branch was replying to say that no news had been received about Roy but that 'unhappily the only news received regarding your son's crew is that according to German information forwarded by the International Red Cross, the air bomber Pilot Officer L. Eaude lost his life on the 18 October 1943… I am to assure you that enquiries are continuing from every possible source and that should any news be received… it will be passed on to you…in writing this I am to add an expression of the sincere sympathy of the Department with you in your grave anxiety.

By now the mothers of the missing crew, led by the formidable Mesdames Fuller and Trahair were not only in touch with each other but beginning to get irritated with what they saw as Air Ministry indifference or intransigence. The possibility of placing advertisements in newspapers appealing for any information about their missing sons was proposed [and was later acted upon]. Later the mothers were astounded to discover that Mrs Eaude did not know that the body of her son had been found, whereas the others all knew. At a meeting at the Air Ministry in early October 1944 Mrs Fuller 'banged the table' but was told that Mr Eaude had been told because he was the next of kin [and the inference was that he may have been protecting his wife by not telling her], but the belief in the families has always been that either the Air Ministry was incompetent, or, more likely, was covering something up that it did not wish to tell them.

Finally, on 8th May 1944 the Air Ministry Casualty Branch wrote to Mr Trahair – and the other families – to say that: 'I am directed to inform you, with great regret, that in view of the lapse of time and the absence of any news about your son.....the Department now propose to presume his death for official purposes.... before this action is taken it is requested that you will be good enough formally to confirm that you have received no evidence of his survival.' That formal confirmation received, the Casualty Branch wrote to Mr Trahair again on 24th May 1944 to say that death had now been presumed for official purposes with effect from 18th October 1943. The RAF Benevolent Fund then wrote again on 13th June, referring to their earlier letter, and offering sympathy and assistance if needed. On 20th June the Central Depository wrote to advise Mr Trahair that a Committee of Adjustment was being set up by that office to deal with the estate of their son, and that the Air Ministry, Accounts 13 Department, in Worcester would shortly be in touch about the 'service estate...e.g. cash found in effects, pay due etc'.

On 14 July 1944, a letter was duly sent to Mr Trahair with an account showing:

	£	*s*	*d*
Balance of Pay and Allowances	10	16	1
Service Post War credits @ 6d a day	17	1	6
Cash found in effects	4	13	8
Refund of Income Tax	14	0	0
	46	11	3
Less Mess Bill RAF Woodhall	1	2	11
	45	8	4

The letter went on to say that a Payable Order for this amount in favour of Mr and Mrs Trahair would be forwarded under separate cover within a few days.

On 22nd August, the Casualty Branch in reply to a further letter from Mrs Trahair, responded that it still had no news of the crew except that 'the name of Pilot Officer Eaude had been given on an official German death list as having lost his life on 18th October when a Lancaster aircraft was shot down' and that 'owing to the lapse of time and absence of news, this department can hold out little hope of your son's survival'.

A similar letter was sent by the Casualty Branch in response to a further letter from Mrs Trahair on 10th April 1945 and another on 12 June 1946, except that this latter one added the information that 'the body of Pilot Officer Eaude *according to captured German documents* [author's italics] had been washed up on the bank of the River Leine, Hanover'. [Requests by the author to view this document have been refused.] It also said that Mrs Trahair's request for her son's logbook had been referred to the Royal Air Force Record Office, Gloucester [a request that was well made, because the majority of the tens of thousands of unclaimed logbooks were destroyed by the Central Depository in the early 1960s after a notice was placed in newspapers saying this would happen if they were not claimed].

There is no trace in the Trahair archive of the letter believed to have eventually been sent to them saying that the body of their son had been found, but MOD Air Historical Branch has examined the casualty file [now held at Hayes] and told the author that No 4 Missing Research Enquiry Service[5] completed their investigation into the loss of that Lancaster on 17th October 1948 and that at least seven German witnesses had said that they had seen the bodies of two airmen being recovered from the crash site and that one of them was named Isahair

---

[5] After the War, a number of Missing Research Enquiry Units were set up in Germany to try to find out what had happened to the many missing Bomber Command aircraft and crews. They were not police units and were usually commanded by former aircrew. The quality of their enquiries varied according to the people in charge. No 4 MREU covered the Hannover area, and almost certainly relied on documents captured from the two local units responsible, one, for burying RAF aircrew, and the other for disposing of aircraft wrecks. AHB says it does know the whereabouts of these documents and nor does the modern Luftwaffe or Hannover City authorities. Their recovery would probably answer a lot of questions.

[sic] '*who was found in the garden of the corner house in Weddigen-Ufer, Emden Strasse*' [author's italics]. AHB went on to say that both airmen had been buried in Hannover Limmer Civil Cemetery within a few days of the crash. The other six missing men were recorded as having been lost with their aircraft in the River Leine. A search of Hannover Civil Cemetery had then been carried out, and the body of Sergeant Trahair was identified, disinterred and transferred to Hannover Limmer War Cemetery, where it was placed in grave No 7, Row C, Plot 3. [The author understands that the Hannover War Cemetery is on part of the site of the Hannover Civil Cemetery.] In 1948 no trace could be found of the body of Pilot Officer Leo Eaude, but we will return to this again in Chapter 6.

Isahair is, of course, an understandable mistake to have made in translating into Germanic script an English capital letter 'T', especially given that a contemporary photograph of the crew shows a handwritten name badge sewn onto the right hand side of the uniform jacket above the breast pocket.

In response to the author's observation that Mr and Mrs Trahair appear not to have been told of the finding of their son's body until the early 1950s, AHB said that this was not so and that a letter was sent to Mr Trahair and to the other seven next of kin on 11th June 1949 saying that Sgt Trahair's body had been identified, disinterred and placed in the grave plot mentioned above. AHB also say that Mr Eaude was told on 3rd January 1944 that a telegram had been received from the IRCC to the effect that his son had been killed. The author's request to examine the casualty file was refused.

On 22nd March 1951 the Commonwealth War Graves Commission at High Wycombe wrote to Mr and Mrs Trahair regarding the headstone that would be placed on the grave of their son. The crux of the message was that the headstone would be of a standard simple pattern so that 'every man, rich or poor, General or Private, will be honoured in the same way' A personal inscription could be selected by relatives, if they so wished, and 'some relatives had expressed the wish to pay for this personal inscription'. If they did not wish to pay, then the cost would be met by the Commission. The cost of the inscription, if relatives wished to pay, was the very modest sum of £1. It is a sensitively-written, touching, letter. A follow-up letter from the CWGC made it even clearer that relatives should not feel under any obligation to pay for an inscription unless they wished to do so.

The 'families support network' [for that is what we would call it today] was in place within ten days of the crew going missing, when on 28th October 1943, Mrs Mary Fuller, mother of Cyril, wrote to the other families expressing deepest sympathy 'we know how you must be feeling' and asking that should any news reach them of their son the Fullers please be told. Mrs Fuller is believed to have badgered the Air Ministry into giving her a list of the names and addresses of all the next of kin of the missing crewmembers. Four months later on 1st March 1944 Mrs Fuller wrote again, in response to a letter from Mrs Trahair, saying;

> *'I am only too pleased to hear from you or any of the crew's parents. I know just what your feelings are. I'm going through the same trying times. I got another letter from another poor mother this morning. I can only wish for all our sakes I could give you some good news. Did you receive a note from the Red Cross saying that Leo Eaude, the Bomb Aimer was killed in action? They may be prisoners of war. The Germans like to keep people waiting – only too pleased when they have killed one to let people know..........may God comfort you and all the mothers. M. Fuller.*

In September 1944, Mrs Fuller and her daughter, Nellie, spent a week on holiday in St Austell with the Trahairs, Mrs Fuller writing a thank you letter from 135 Thornsbeach Road, Catford on the 24th to say they had got back safely by train and Nellie writing from Eastbourne on the 25th to add her thanks.

A year on from the loss of EE109, Mrs Fuller wrote to Mrs Trahair on 9th October 1944 to say she was:

> *... thinking of you all this week... last year at this time, we all had our dear lads with us at home..... yes, Mr Fuller and I went to the Air Ministry on Tuesday ... they could tell me nothing... only that the plane had not been heard of since leaving the aerodrome on the 18th*

..... we saw an officer...I asked him how he could account for Mrs Eaude not being notified that her son was killed. The officer said as her husband was next of kin he would be told and no doubt he had kept the news from Mrs Eaude...I said I could hardly believe he could keep her suffering and wondering all this time...I don't think they or the Red Cross know anything... we are putting adverts in the paper to come out on the 18th and 20th [author: the anniversaries of the loss of EE109 and Cyril Fuller's 32nd birthday], the latter in local papers. Mrs Wilson put an advert in the Evening News... she got no reply ... we have just put the date they were missing... it is our boys we are enquiring about not the country's... Mrs Eaude told me in her last letter that she had thought of doing it but was advised to wait until the war was over... whenever that will be ... I feel we have waited long enough .... Mrs Stevens came to see me a week ago .... She tells me her daughter-in-law has just got a pension, also a gratuity... she can't understand why we have got neither pension or gratuity.... I have been told it is only wives who get it..... Mary Fuller.

Cyril's sister, Nellie Fuller, wrote to Mrs Trahair on 16th October, saying

'I expect by now you will have heard from Mum, so you will know that she and Dad did not get any satisfaction from the Air Ministry. They are a lot of bounders. My friend and I went to a whist drive last Friday and, whilst there, I got talking with an airman who is on the ground staff quite near, and he said we should not give up hope...a cousin of his had to wait nearly a year before she heard anything of her husband and he turned out to be a prisoner...

On 2nd November 1944 Mrs Fuller wrote again to Mrs Trahair, saying 'I suppose we will have peace one day' and enclosing cuttings from The Times and a local paper. The notices read:

FULLER – Missing from air operations over Germany, Oct. 18, 1943, Pilot Offr Cyril Fuller and crew. Any information gratefully received by Mr Fuller of 135 Thornsbeach-rd, Catford, S.E.6.

The five inches of newspaper cutting contained eight other similar notices, six of them for paratroopers and glider regiment pilots missing at Arnhem since 25th Sept 1944.

In the more frugal age in which people then lived, Mrs Fuller also sent an old pair of trousers so that they could be cut down to make a pair for Michael [then aged 5]. She also appears to accept for the first time that 'perhaps they are missing', which is almost certainly a euphemism for 'dead'.

The letters continue regularly through 1945, with Mrs Fuller expressing her own depression [which sometimes, she says, 'make me feel like screaming'] and Nellie of the prospects of writing to a friend of a friend in Holland to see whether they could find anything out about the crew. On 19th April, 1945 Mrs Fuller wrote to say that Cyril had been awarded a DFC, the notice in the *London Gazette* including the words 'with effect 18 Oct 1943 (since deceased)'. Mrs Fuller wrote:

> *'I jumped at the deceased at once and said why weren't we notified if he was dead… they tell me that is because he is presumed killed… I am not going with Dad to collect it… I've asked Nellie to go …. I've had enough'.*

By June 1945 the mothers were collecting cuttings from newspapers about servicemen who had been prisoners of war near Hannover and writing via the editors to the men concerned. Mr and Mrs Stevens had visited the Fullers on VE Day but, Mrs Fuller reported, they 'had very little hope' that Reg might still be alive. There is also a reference in one letter to Mrs Fuller asking Mrs Trahair 'will you be able to see Mr Taylor, the one who thought they didn't reach the target?' and also 'I wrote to Mrs Horne the other day… I feel very sorry for her… she always wrote full of hope … she felt sure her husband would come back to her'.

By now the letter are expressing, first, disappointment that nothing has been heard about their missing sons but, then, an increasing realisation that they are not going to return. Finally, in an undated letter written some time after the Trahairs found out [in June 1949, according to AHB] that Roy's body had been identified and interred in the

Hannover War Cemetery, Mrs Fuller wrote that 'I am afraid there is no chance of us hearing anymore' and expressing the hope that Mrs Trahair will be able to visit Roy's grave, as she knows what a solace that was for a friend who lost a son in WWI. In the early 1950s Mr and Mrs Fuller and Mr and Mrs Stevens hired a car to drive up to Lincoln to attend the dedication in Lincoln Cathedral of a memorial to the men of Bomber Command lost in the Second World War.

Two other piles of letters are really too private to publish in any detail. They are the ones from Mrs Trahair to Roy and from him to her. In an age before television and computers, or even the mass use of the telephone, people kept in touch by writing – regularly. Between early August and 18th October 1943 when Roy went missing he received seventeen letters from his mother, three of them after returning to Woodhall Spa from the week's leave at home in early October. The last letter written on Sunday, 17th October did not reach him. He was already dead when it arrived at RAF Woodhall Spa, and it was 'returned to sender on Air Ministry instructions' on 25th October by RAF Coningsby, the parent station.

Roy wrote four letters home between the 10th and 26th September and a further three between arriving back at Woodhall on Wednesday evening 13th October and taking off for Hannover on Monday 18th October. He tells his mother that he realises he is getting used to returning to base but that 'it will never become a pleasure'. He also tells her that…

> *'I met all the boys at King's Cross and it was good to see their smiling faces again after my usual hectic dash across London… we all had dinner on the train at Leo's expense…. and the journey didn't go badly… we made Boston in time to get back to camp and on arrival got your letter and paper… when you write please pass on Bob's address* [his brother in the Navy] *and let me know how Mick* [his four year old brother] *is doing…. Life here is not too bad and so with this and knowing that six weeks won't take too long to pass, we push along. This is all and so Goodnight and Good Luck to you all.'*

He signed off with kisses for his mother and separate kisses for Mick. He wrote again on Saturday 16th October, signing off…

> *…look after Mick…. Cheerio and all the best.*

It was to be his last letter home, but there was also one other special letter written that day. It was a letter from Roy to Mick:

> *'…you will learn your ABC soon and then you will be able to write me letters and tell me what you are doing… all the aeroplanes up here are OK and we fly them every day … I will tell you more about them when I come home again, which won't be long…*
> *Cheerio for now and all the very best…*
> *Be a good boy.*
> *Roy.'*

Mick did learn his ABC, qualified as an accountant, started his own business [Trahair and Geake (Accountants)] and has visited his brother's grave in Hannover.

6. The End of the Century and the Final Report

This Chapter is, in effect, the final police report that should have been written in 1977 and would have been had the RAF Police been allowed to pursue the case as thoroughly as they would have liked to have done. One day, when the official papers and casualty files presently locked away in the Ministry of Defence are eventually released to the public, someone may be able to add more to this account if they are able to find amongst the released papers the MRES[1] report of 17th October 1948 and the captured German documents on which it was based, which were probably taken from the German Air Force Burial Unit and the Luftwaffe Salvage Unit, both in 1943 based at Langenhagen, near Hannover.

The aim will be to summarise the evidence as it is now known by the author, most of it uncovered in only the last twelve months, and to draw conclusions as to what actually happened to Lancaster EE109 and its crew when it was hit by flak over Hannover on the night of 18th October 1943.

In 1977 we were hamstrung by not having access to the information already held on file by the Ministry of Defence. Had this information been available, questions could have been asked in a way that might

[1] No 4 Missing Research Enquiry Service was the unit set up in the Hannover area after the War by the RAF to try to find out what had happened to missing aircraft and crews and to collect bodies from the various scattered cemeteries to create the 1939-45 War Cemeteries. These units were not police units and were staffed mainly by former aircrew. Their effectiveness varied considerably, and their research relied heavily on captured German documents, the Luftwaffe being as thorough and meticulous in their book-keeping as most other German departments.

have filled gaps in knowledge and answered apparent contradictions. It is quite likely that some of the witnesses we saw in 1977 were the same people interviewed by the MRES in 1948. Because the two investigations were not correlated, their two reports, one from 1948 and the other from the RAF Germany pathologist in 1977 [submitted to the Ministry of Defence, via the Institute of Aviation Medicine in UK, but based on information that could only have come from the RAF Police in Germany], contain contradictions that will probably now never be resolved.

According to AHB, who have examined the casualty file[2] at the request of the author, the report from 1948 concluded that a number of German witnesses [at least seven] saw the bodies of two RAF airmen being recovered from the crash site. One airman, named Isahair [sic], was found in the garden of the corner house on Weddigen Ufer and Emden Strasse, and the other, named as Pilot Officer Eaude, was recovered from the river bank. As Trahair was the rear gunner and Eaude the bomb aimer, they would have been at the two extreme ends of the 70 feet of fuselage that made up a Lancaster, one in the tail turret and the other in the nose. The places from which they were recovered would fit with the aircraft having crashed in the Leine, after approaching it at right angles from the direction of, and immediately above, Emden Strasse. If these two bodies were recovered from the crash site, and there was no report of a massive fire destroying the aircraft – indeed, the fuselage was the one part that seemed to have survived recognisably intact – what happened to the other six crew members, who would have been situated five in the front cockpit area and one in the mid-upper turret? It is not likely that the Luftwaffe recovery units would have failed to recover bodies if this was at all possible.

The RAF Police files in Germany cannot now be found and have almost certainly been destroyed, particularly as the RAF Station at Gütersloh, from which the day-to-day control of the investigation was exercised, has closed down. Flight Sergeant Jim Condon, who led those day-to-day enquiries, retired as a Warrant Officer many years ago and

[2] File P409857/7/43, now held in the MOD archives at Hayes.

died in 1998. It is unlikely he would have kept any notes from the investigation, anyway. This means that the detailed notes made at the time of the investigation are not available to be consulted. Furthermore, no full or final report was ever submitted by the Provost & Security Services Headquarters in Germany to the UK RAF Police Headquarters, as the case was suspended in the summer of 1977 when it became clear that it could not be taken forward without the assistance of MOD [Operational Aircraft Records].

An interim report submitted by P & SS Germany in September 1977 does, however, provide tantalising clues as to how the investigation might have progressed had the investigators known the information already on file from 1948 at MOD. In 1977 some six or so witnesses were found in the immediate area of the crash site during door-to-door enquiries that could remember seeing the aircraft wreckage in 1943. The main points of their recollections were:

1. only one aircraft fell on Weddigen Ufer during the entire war.
2. most of the wreckage fell in a line along Emden Strasse at right angles to the river.
3. 'some' bodies were found in Emden Strasse and removed by the authorities.
4. the aircraft fell in late 1943 during a heavy attack on Hannover.

In addition, Dr Med Klaus Riehm, who in 1977 still lived in the house in Emden Strasse that he had occupied with his parents during the war, by reference to his late father's diary, could date the crash precisely to the evening of 18th October 1943. He also remembered seeing the body of at least one 'enemy flyer' the morning after the crash. [Another witness thought she had seen at least two.]

Another medical doctor, Professor Dr med Jürgen Probst, then a practising surgeon but now retired, could also date the shooting down of the Weddigen Ufer Lancaster to the night of 18th October, 1943, as he was employed as a fifteen year old, along with other boys of his class at High School, as a *Luftwaffenhelfer* on the flak battery that shot down EE109. By reference to an official list of aircraft shot down by his battery, he could also put a time on the shooting down: 2018 hours on 18th October 1943.

Readers will remember that the wreckage recovered in 1977 consisted of the remains of the centre section of an aircraft fuselage [the bomb bay], together with one in-line Mark 28 Merlin engine, the blade of a propeller and part of a wing, plus human bones.

In response to a letter, the author was first told by the MOD Air Historical Branch [AHB], who have succeeded OAR as custodians of the WWII casualty files, that:

> *the aircraft had been hit over the target area by German anti aircraft fire at 2021 hrs which resulted in the loss of the entire crew. The aircraft hit the roof of a house on the river bank and came to rest on top of a barge moored on the opposite bank of the river. The front of the aircraft was embedded in soft mud with the wings and the remainder of the aircraft sticking out across the river. On the day of the crash the body of P/O Eaude was found on the bank of the River Leine, sadly his burial details are missing and he is recorded as having no known grave. The body of Sergeant Trahair was also recovered from a garden in Emden Strasse and later buried in Hannover Limmer War Cemetery.*

Two years later, the author was told by AHB, in response to more detailed written questions, that:

- On 3 June 1946, a Missing Research Enquiry Unit had discovered captured German documents stating that the body of P/O Eaude had been recovered from the bank of the River Leine near Hannover. [Author: as a result of which, it is said, letters were sent to Mrs Trahair and the other next of kin saying that the search for other bodies continued, with a further letter being sent in December 1947 in a similar vein.] No 4 Missing Research Enquiry Service completed their investigation on [the aircraft] on 17 October 1948. This report confirmed that a number of German witnesses [at least seven] had been interviewed…who saw the bodies of two RAF airmen being recovered from the crash site. One by the name of Isahair [sic] was found in the garden of the corner house in

Wedding [sic] Ufer, Emden Strasse, and the second, P/O Eaude, whose body was recovered from the river bank. Both airmen were buried within a few days of the crash. The other six bodies were recorded as being lost with their aircraft in the River Leine. The final investigation, which included a précis of the seven witness accounts, enabled the investigating officer to complete his report. This report and that of the RAF pathologist [author: from 1977] are both on the casualty file, but are not available to the public.

- After a search of all the graves in the Hannover Limmer civil cemetery had been completed, a letter was sent to the next of kin of all eight crew members...this letter confirmed that the body of Sgt Trahair had now been identified and disinterred from the Hannover Civil Cemetery to the Hannover Limmer War Cemetery, where he now lies in Row C, Plot 3, Grave No 7. The date shown on these letters was 11 June 1949.
- The report dated 17 October 1948 also stated that Lancaster EE109 had crashed on Wedding [sic] Bank on the River Leine, near Fischer Street [author: Fischer Strasse is on the opposite side of the river from Emden Strasse]. The aircraft was completely disintegrated and a greater part of it had ended up in the water. Only three parts of it were found; the first consisting of part of the fuselage, half a wing and one engine were discovered outside a house at Wedding [sic] Ufer 15. The undercarriage was found at the corner of Moorweg [sic] Strasse and Fischer Strasse, and small pieces of debris from this aircraft were found in the garden of Ober Strasse 8 [author: about 600 metres away from Fischer Strasse]. All this wreckage was removed by the German Luftwaffe Salvage Unit based at Langenhagen. All other remains of the wreckage sank in the River. The bodies of P/O Eaude and Sgt Trahair were removed by a German Air Force Burial Unit from Langenhagen, and taken to the Hannover Limmer Civil Cemetery.
- Finally, during exhumations of all the graves at Hannover Limmer Civil Cemetery, a large communal grave was uncovered which was numbered 1973-1987. This grave, which was believed to contain

> the bodies of fifteen airmen, in fact contained the remains of two badly burnt bodies, some of which were found in an urn. The two bodies were removed and re-interred in Row C, Plot 3, Graves 10/11. Initially, the MRES believed these bodies to be those of 1807481 Sgt JW Grain, the flight engineer on Lancaster ED499, which was lost on the same night of 18 October 1943, and that of P/O L Eaude. However, the MRES officer who carried out this investigation was inexperienced in this type of work and had concluded that the bodies were Sgt Grain and P/O Eaude purely on the basis of elimination. A further investigation was then carried out in December 1948 by an experienced team, but no factual evidence was uncovered which would have allowed them to make a positive identification of these bodies, and it was finally agreed that they should be recorded as unknown airmen.

Readers will notice that the two accounts are contradictory, especially in respect of the state of the aircraft after it had crashed. The first account fits with the finding of the rear gunner in the garden of the house at the corner of Weddigen Ufer and Emden Strasse and the body of the air bomber on the river bank. The second account suggest that it is far more likely that the aircraft came down in pieces with only a few large bits landing at the Weddigen Ufer crash site. From the first account one could be forgiven for thinking that the aircraft had been flown down to the crash site, perhaps in an attempt to land on the open land on the other side of the river, but had clipped the corner house and, just, failed to make it. The second account suggests that the aircraft dropped out of the sky, no longer airworthy. The author, therefore, asked AHB for further elaboration.

In a third letter from AHB, he was told:

> *The two descriptions of the crash of Lancaster EE109 were taken from separate reports contained in the RAF Casualty file. The first.....is recorded in an Aviation and Pathology Report produced in 1977 by the RAF Institute of Pathology and Aviation Medicine [author: based near Aylesbury, Bucks], which in Annex B details the circumstances of the accident. The second description, which is de-*

scribed [in my second letter] was taken from No 4 MRES report dated 17 October 1948. During these investigations seven German civilians who witnessed the crash were interrogated by the MRES in 1948 and were added to several other witness statements, which were contained in captured documents to form the basis of the report.

The AHB letter goes on to say that:

> *The information gathered together by the Germans in 1943 and those of No 4 MRES in 1948 all point to the fact that only two bodies were ever recovered from the crash site in 1943.*

The author's request to examine the casualty file was refused. It seems likely that the information contained in Annex B of the 1977 report by the Institute of Pathology and Aviation Medicine would have been based on information supplied by the RAF Police in RAF Germany, as it is difficult to see how else it could have been obtained. It is unlikely that doctors based in Buckinghamshire carried out their own police enquiry in Germany. The author has not been allowed to see Annex B [or the rest of that report] and so can only speculate as to its origins. Were the original witness statements to be found from 1977 they might shed some light on this, and certainly it might then be easier to assess the weight to be given the contradictory reports.

Dr Jürgen Probst has been unable to find out anything about the crash in the Hannover Town Archives, and Herr Günter Leonhardt of the Luftfahrt-Museum Laatzen-Hannover has also been unable to find any wartime records. The Chief Reporter, Herr Wolfgang Steinweg, of the Hannoversche Allgemeine Zeitung newspaper has no archives to check as the RAF bombing on the third attack on Hannover on 8/9th October 1943 destroyed the Newspaper's offices and put it out of circulation for some months.

A Luftwaffe nightfighter pilot, who was shot down by his own flak on the night of 18th October 1943 over Hannover, has said that the normal technique in shooting down a bomber was to aim for the fuel tanks. This prevented the bomber blowing-up, as it would do if its bomb bay was hit [and still contained bombs], and also gave the crew some chance of getting out. In the case of EE109 the aircraft was hit by flak, but the principle is the same: an aircraft hit in belly with its bomb load intact would explode with such force that few recognisable pieces would reach the ground [the bomb load of a Lancaster bomber containing a weight of bombs of an entirely different order from that of, say, the terrorist bomb that brought down the Pan Am airliner over Lockerbie in 1988]. The technician who inspected the remains of the Lancaster bomb bay in 1977 when the wreckage was dragged from the river Leine was able to say from the position of the bomb release mechanism clips that the bombs had been released before the aircraft hit the ground. This does not mean, of course, that the aircraft had necessarily released its bombs before it was hit by flak, but it is probably more likely than not.

Dr Probst remembers this particular Lancaster aircraft coming 'straight down' after being hit. The flak battery was positioned only just over 2 kilometres from the crash site, and this does suggest that the aircraft was so badly crippled by the flak strike that it dropped almost straight down from its bombing height of 20,000 feet. It is not certain where the time of 2021 [which appears in the first AHB letter] has come from, but if that was the time the aircraft hit the ground and if the time of 2018 shown in the records of Flak Batterie 3./521 is the time of the flak strike then the aircraft came down from 20,000 feet in something like three or four minutes. Even if still more or less in one piece at the start its descent, it would not be by the time it reached the ground at that rate of descent.

The debriefing reports of the crews of the ten No 619 Squadron aircraft that returned from Hannover that night show that they all bombed at heights of between 21,300 feet and 19,500 feet, seven in a three minute period between 2018 and 2021 and the other three at 2023, 2027 and 2028 hours. Three of the crews that bombed in the first period of three minutes said they had seen an explosion [two at 2020 hours and one at 2021] lasting about 20 seconds, two from 20,500 feet and one from 21,000 feet. But there was almost complete cloud cover at 14,000 to 15,000 feet. Sadly, it seems likely the explosion they saw was EE109 exploding after being hit by flak, probably in the wings, and probably after releasing its bombs. The red [and blue] flash reported by these three crews was the high-octane fuel in the wing tanks exploding. The effect of this would have been to destroy the main cabin area, where five of the crew would be sitting, and possibly the section of the fuselage containing the mid-upper turret. This would explain why the only bodies recovered were those of the rear gunner and air bomber, who were furthest away from the explosion. It would also explain [if the MRES report is more accurate than the 1977 report from the Institute of Aviation] why so little of the wings and only one engine were recovered. The rest of the aircraft - and any bodies – probably fell into the part of Hannover being bombed that night, and so the failure to find more of the aircraft would be explained.

Finally, it will not have been forgotten that another aircraft of No 619 Squadron was hit by flak that night: JA867 PG-X, captained by F/O MA MacDonald, *which bombed at 2018 from 20,300 feet.* It is possible that this aircraft was hit by the same flak that brought down EE109 PG-F. Dr Probst says that they were told in training that a bursting flak shell would bring down an aircraft if it exploded within 12 metres of the aircraft. A direct hit was not needed. It is believed the flak guns were set to fire at 20,000 feet that night, using their *Sprechender Kanonier* anti-aircraft guns, linked to *FunkMessgerät Serie 1939 Fabrikat Telefunken "Würzburg"* radar. By the end of the War, four of Jürgen Probst's *Luftwaffenhelfer* classmates had been killed, and also the *Ober-leutnant* commanding the Flak Batterie, who died in Holland in 1945, and so it is unlikely other eye witnesses will be found.

Today, the police enquiry would be handled differently. The advent of DNA testing means that from the outset there would have been a greater incentive to try to contact the next of kin in order to identify the men whose remains had been found with the wreckage. More effort would have been made to establish just how much was known from 1943/1948. As a consequence, it is likely that the remains would have been identified – as were those of the Romanovs eighty years on from the Russian Revolution - and the bodies resting as unknown airmen in the War Cemetery in Hannover would today have names on their headstones. It is an intriguing question, but could the MOD refuse if relatives insisted on having the remains DNA tested? Presumably not?

There are no words with which I can do justice to the air crew who fought under my command. There is no parallel in warfare to such courage and determination in the face of danger over so prolonged a period...it was, moreover, a highly conscious courage, by which the risk was taken with calm forethought. It was the courage of the small hours, of men virtually alone, for at his battle-station the airman is virtually alone. It was the courage of men with long-drawn apprehensions of daily 'going over the top'. Such devotion must never be forgotten.

Air Chief Marshal Sir Arthur Harris,
AOC-in-C Bomber Command 1942-45

7. Envoi – Was it worth it?

> *"By early 1945 the [USAAF] 8th Air Force had achieved an average circular probable error of two miles on operations guided by H2S. All its blind-bombing missions through the winter of 1944, therefore, amounted in reality if not in name to area bombing."*
>
> *[Max Hastings]*

Much has been written in the years since the end of the Second World War about Bomber Command and the Strategic Bombing Offensive. Scholars and historians in particular have questioned whether the policy of 'area bombing' could be justified, either morally or strategically. Since the early 1970s, when they were released to the public domain, wartime records have been pored over, and the personalities and characters of the main RAF players have been scrutinised with varying degrees of accuracy, usually attributing to them more authority to determine strategic policy than they actually had. Armed with perfect 20/20 hindsight, and the knowledge that in the end we won, these armchair tacticians and strategists have re-fought the air campaign in the light of late Twentieth and early Twenty First Century thinking and technology. As a consequence, few people today have not read a book or seen a television programme about Bomber Command and the Second World War.

Because of this, most people are also familiar with the name of Bomber Command's most famous Commander-in-Chief, Air Chief Marshal Sir Arthur Harris, appointed by Chief of Air Staff Charles Portal, on 22 February 1942 at a time when the war was most definitely not going our way, and then dumped unceremoniously at the end of the War when the politicians started to clear their yardarms for the general election and post-War strategic analysis. [The shabby treatment meted out to Harris has been matched in the RAF's eighty-year history only by the equally shabby treatment of Hugh Dowding, C-in-C Fighter Command at the time the Battle of Britain, and his AOC 11 Group, Keith Park.] Between February 1942 and May 1945, Harris created the mightiest bombing force this country has ever seen and developed the science of air power to levels previously unknown. But it was a long haul, with air power taking the driving seat in war, as against land and sea power, for the first time in history. Quite apart from inter-service squabbling, which had been ever-present since the RAF came into being as a third force in 1918, the use of air power, strategic or tactical, was still very much a matter for debate, and the aircraft and the techniques for using them still very much at the development stage. It was far from being an accurate, or even an agreed, science. It was only as the Second World War was drawing to an end, and German opposition was fast fading, that one specialist RAF bomber squadron was able to mark targets sufficiently accurately that, given decent weather, the bulk of the main bombing force could put their bombs within a reasonable distance of the target. The USAAF was not much better, for all the attempts during and after the War to distinguish their operations from those of Bomber Command.[1]

To get to this point, the RAF hierarchy - the Air Council - and their political masters in the British Cabinet, had been obliged to find out the hard way during the difficult days of 1940 and 1941 that the pre-War maxim 'the bomber will always get through' was little more than wishful thinking, at least it was certainly wishful thinking when in the first eighteen months of the war the RAF had flown by day with inadequate aircraft that had been picked off all too easily by faster, more manoeuvrable and better armed Luftwaffe day fighter aircraft. From this rude awakening – but also because of a conjunction of other factors, such as Hitler's aerial bombing of European and British cities - was born, *faut demieux,* the policy of night bombing, by which means

[1] For example, Max Hastings, *Bomber Command* [Michael Joseph 1979], chapter XIV p340. "*By early 1945 the 8th Air Force had achieved an average circular probable error of two miles on operations guided by H2S. All its blind-bombing missions through the winter of 1944, therefore, amounted in reality if not in name to area bombing.*"

for three years from 1941 until the Normandy landings and the crossing of the Rhine six months later, the RAF took the war to the enemy in the only way then possible, given the fortress that was Europe.

With anything up to 10/10ths cloud covering German cities for much of the year, and no accurate navigational or bomb aiming equipment in their aircraft, the bomber crews could only do their best to drop their bomb loads as near as possible to the target. More often than not, their best efforts were not good enough, and bomb loads were often scattered over a massively wide area, sometimes making it difficult for the German authorities even to establish just what the target had been. But the RAF was not alone in these problems. In a Luftwaffe raid on Southampton, the bombing was so scattered that British intelligence concluded the target was Portsmouth. US crews arriving in Britain in 1942 were convinced they could 'drop a bomb in a pickle barrel from 30,000ft'.[2] They were soon disabused of this idea, as the huge Flying Fortress formations were decimated by German fighters, sadly at a great cost in young American lives. The awful realisation dawned on the American commanders that this would continue until they had long-range day fighter cover [not until 1944]. What is more, the USAAF's 'precision-bombing', despite the use of a superior bombsight, was not a lot more accurate than was Bomber Command's, and the difference between the British approach and the American approach was largely one of semantics: of the language in which the strategic objectives were couched. In their day role, the most important difference was that the American formations with much heavier firepower to protect them[3] could get to targets and back again without the aircraft and aircrew losses becoming totally prohibitive.

The lack of bombing accuracy did not affect only the Allies. Even the relatively advanced missile systems the Germans were able to bring into use in the final year of the War did not always get through British

---

[2] Quoted by Robin Neillands in an article *Ordering up the Whirlwind* [BBC History magazine Sep 2001].

[3] The Flying Fortress had a crew of ten, compared with the RAF heavy bomber's seven, and nine .5in guns. The price for this armament was a vastly inferior bomb load: 4,000 lbs compared to the Lancaster's 12,000.

defences, and they were certainly not accurate, whether fired from land-based launchers or the Heinkel III aircraft specially adapted to piggy-back them to within striking distance of targets. On 16 September 1944, for example, in perfect weather conditions, fifteen Heinkels set off to bomb London with piggy-backed Fieseler Fi 103s (V-1s), for launching close to the Thames estuary at London. Nine Fi 103s were got away successfully, three were destroyed before reaching the coast of England, two more were destroyed over land, two came down in open countryside in Essex and two reached Greater London, one falling in Woolwich and the other on Barking. Similarly, on 24 December 1944 fifty Heinkels carried their Fi 103s by night for an attack on Manchester [*Operation Martha*]; only eleven bombs came within fifteen miles of the centre of Manchester and only one came down within the city limits [killing 37 people and seriously injuring 67].[4] Just over ten thousand Fieseler flying bombs were launched against England in total, the great majority from ground launchers. Of the 7,500 that are believed to have crossed the English coast, almost 4,000 were shot down short of their targets. Of the rest, fewer than 2,500 reached London and about 30 Southampton and Portsmouth. One reached Manchester. [Nonetheless, they caused over 6,000 deaths and about 18,000 people were injured.]

Just when the menace of the V1 flying bombs was coming to an end with the capture of the launch sites by the allied armies, Hitler's second secret weapon started to descend on London and the South East of England. The V2 rockets carried a much heavier high explosive load than the flying bombs and approached their victims silently unlike the noisy chugging of the V1s. They were impossible to intercept [whereas Fighter Command had found a way of dealing with a goodly proportion of the V1s], but they were like the V1 in one respect: the V2 was totally indiscriminate. Rather like the Scud missiles of the Gulf War, there was little or no attempt at targeting. If you heard the bang, someone else was the victim.

[4] Dr Alfred Price *The Last Year of the Luftwaffe* [Arms & Armour Press 1991], p87.

It took until the last days of the war to capture the sites from which the V2s were being fired, and in 177 days a total of 1,050 rockets fell on or around London at the rate of about seven a day, producing several mass carnages during the last and very cold winter of the War. Such was the horror these weapons inspired that Churchill believed the Germans had forfeited all humane consideration by the use of them, and toyed with some fairly wild schemes for retaliatory strikes, included the use of gas and chemical weapons.[5] The era of smart bombs was quite simply not yet upon us. Moral assessments of the War Cabinet's strategic directives, and Harris's implementation of them, have to be made in the light of circumstances of the time and the perceived threat.

It has been said that the RAF, and Harris[6] in particular who was the Air Officer Commanding-in-Chief of Bomber Command during the critical period from 22 February 1942 until the end of the War, in so single-mindedly pressing the case for strategic bombing were fundamentally wrong: that they were motivated by inter-Service rivalry, even internal RAF rivalries, and were desperately trying to prove the previously untested belief that air power alone could bring about the defeat of an entrenched and well-armed enemy, without having to expose ground troops to the sort of attrition the senior commanders of the Second World War remembered only too well from their youth in the trenches during the Great War.

The post-1945 revisionist argument goes something like this: that the strategic bombing campaign wasted resources and men that could have been better deployed in other ways; that it did not bring about a

---

[5] Roy Jenkins *Churchill* [Macmillan 2001].

[6] Air Chief Marshal Sir Arthur Travers Harris Bt, GCB, OBE, AFC, LLD – 'Bert' to his friends; 'Butch' to his bomber crews; 'Bomber' to the public. Remarkably for a senior commander who rarely strayed from his HQ at High Wycombe, Harris inspired a confidence and loyalty in his bomber crews similar to that Monty inspired in his Army in North Africa. I have always thought – and in this I am probably influenced by my post-War conversations with the many former Bomber Command aircrew then still serving in the RAF – that the reason for this was quite simply that Harris understood what was at stake: nothing less than the winning of the war and the minimising, in total, of British casualties. His crews paid for his objectives with their lives, but they understood the risk, and their courage and sacrifice should, therefore, be all the more treasured and honoured.

terminal collapse in enemy morale; that until late 1944, at least, it did not reduce significantly the enemy's capacity to wage war; that morally it was reprehensible. The morality debate has seemed at times to be not so much 'did the bombing offensive succeed in helping to bring about the collapse of an evil regime' as 'should it have been waged at all'. It makes for good television documentaries and, of course, the 'what if' genre of history it is fertile ground for devil's advocates.

It is true that the passing of the years makes it easier to put into context and to view dispassionately the historic events of half a century ago [whose origins go back another half century], but the passage of time also dilutes the instinctive response of the ordinary man and woman, who en masse may not be able critically to analyse what they know but can usually be relied upon to know what they know and to get right instinctively, with shrewd hall-mark British common sense, what they can see in front of their noses. Because few families were untouched by the War, or the Great War that preceded it, they knew quite well in 1945 just how close run a thing it had been for so much of the six years of the Second World War, and that even after the D Day landings until the final few weeks of hostilities there was no telling what new technological rabbits Hitler might pull out of the hat. Any one of the many developments we now know to have been in the pipeline, had it come to fruition sooner or been put to better operational use, could have tilted things back in Hitler's favour.[7] Most people thought at the time and for twenty years or so afterwards that Hitler was simply reaping, in Harris's famous words, 'the whirlwind' unleashed in 1939/40. *Morality is a thing you can indulge in an environment of peace and security, but you can't make moral judgements in war, when it's a question of national*

[7] Dr Alfred Price in his book *The last Year of the Luftwaffe* [Arms & Armour Press 1991] has written at length, using German sources, of the many 'white hopes' or secret weapons Hitler hoped would turn the tide. No fewer than ten defensive and six offensive weapons systems for the Luftwaffe alone were being tested or made operational during 1944 [see Price, Chap 9]. During September 1944 alone, the Luftwaffe took delivery of seventeen new types of aircraft, totalling 3,821aircraft in all.

survival [Charles Patterson, Bomber Command Pilot[8]]. Those of us who lived through the Cold War will remember that for years the black humour in the West was that 'our' German rocket scientists were better than 'their' German rocket scientists [the Soviet Union's]. Lest we forget, Dr Werner von Braun who played such a pivotal role in America's post-war race for Space, had also been a major figure at Peenemünde in 1943.[9]

It is difficult, perhaps impossible, always to make distinctions in total war between combatants and those who support and supply them.

> *A factory that makes aeroplanes or makes guns or submarines has got to be staffed by blood and guts men that make them, and if you are going to win a total war there is no way you can do that job without killing civilians*
>
> [Jim Verran, Bomber Command pilot][10]

Hitler, in bombing Manchester and other British cities during the 1940 Blitz, did so because they were industrial centres making weapons of war or in other ways sustaining the British war effort. He probably also thought bombing was a way of demonstrating to the British people the futility of resisting German domination of Europe. The densely packed, terraced houses of the Mancunian industrial workers and their families[11] were part and parcel of the British war effort. In any event, German strategic bombing was no more accurate than was British or

---

[8] Quoted by Richard Overy in his book *Bomber Command 1939-45* [HarperCollins 2000].

[9] For a full account of the RAF raid on the Experimental Station at Peenemünde on the night 17/18 Aug 43 there can be no better or balanced reading than Martin Middlebrook's book of that name, first published by Allen Lane in 1982. For the posthumously-published memoirs of the master bomber on the Peenemünde raid, Gp Capt John Searby, DSO DFC, readers should get hold of a copy of *The Everlasting Arms* [William Kimber 1988], which traces Searby's career from RAF apprentice in 1929, FSgt Pilot in 1939, Gp Capt in 1943 and Air Commodore when he retired from the RAF in 1964.

[10] Quoted in Overy, op cit, p200.

[11] The author was five months old when war was declared and lived with his family in Salford, about four miles from the centre of Manchester, throughout the war. His earliest memory is of an air raid on Manchester.

American bombing three years later. *In War the correct tactics are those that achieve the aim for the lowest cost in men and materials.*[12] Fighting an unprincipled aggressor does pose enormously difficult moral dilemmas for a principled opponent, as the democratic world still knows to its cost in the Twenty First Century when facing international, or sometimes even national, terrorism.[13] *Any country that was faced with Nazi Germany did everything it could to make sure they lost...... war is horrible; war is immoral...... but you fight it the way you can.* [Air Marshal Sir John Curtiss, Bomber Command navigator.][14] Few who lived through the six years of the Second World War, a generation that had already lost fathers and sons in the trenches of the First World War, ever doubted the necessity of fighting this second war with whatever weapons were to hand, no matter how technically imperfect. If in 1943 and 1944 Bomber Command had had the ability to deliver 'smart' bombs directly onto strategically important individual buildings, without losing a disproportionate slice of its aircraft and aircrew in the process[15],

---

[12] 'In war the correct tactics are those that achieve the aim for the lowest cost in men and materials' [Price, op cit p.147].

[13] By remarkable coincidence, on the day that Arab terrorists attacked the World Trade Centre, New York, and the Pentagon, Washington, The Times newspaper in London that morning carried an article in its series **On this Day**, copied from the paper's pages of 11 Sep 1940, with the summary: '*For the third night in a row, the City of London had been the target of Luftwaffe bombs. But for many workers, despite the damage, it was ' business as usual'.* ***The raids continued for a further 54 consecutive nights and by May 1941 the Blitz had killed 43,000 people*** [Author's emphasis]. *But were Londoners downhearted? No'.* The actual report of 11 Sep 1940 included the story: *'When the Prime Minister, inspecting damage that had been done to streets and buildings, was recognised by the people, someone raised the old cry of "Are we downhearted?" There was an immediate and vigorous reply of "No!" from the thousands of City workers.'* [The Times, page 17, on 11 Sep 2001].

[14] Quoted in Overy, op cit, p200.

[15] Even so, the loss rates were horrendous: of the 125,000 aircrew that served in Bomber Command between 1939 and 1945, 55,573 were killed on operations or accidents, a further 8,403 were injured or wounded and another 9,838 taken prisoner of war [source: Middlebrook and Everitt, *The Bomber Command War Diaries*, first published by Viking in 1985, p708; Bill Chorley, *The Bomber Command Losses* series published by Midland Publishing Ltd 1991-2002]. Thus, a total of 73,814 or almost 60% were lost, one way or another. As a general rule, loss rates on individual raids of less than 5% were not viewed with too much concern. It was when they exceeded these limits – for example, during the

there can be no doubt it would have done so[16] [and so would the Luftwaffe in 1940/41]. The truth is that Bomber Command did not have the technical skill to do so, and the choice, quite simply, was between area bombing to sap the enemy's capacity and will to wage war, and to reduce his materiel ability to do so, or not bombing Germany at all, and thereby contributing to the likelihood that Hitler would succeed. Speaking to the author, one Lancaster pilot who completed a tour with 619 Squadron as part of 5 Group's 'Main Force' and then went on to fly another tour with 617 Squadron said

> *'You do realise that there was only one precision bombing squadron in the RAF – and that's not a reflection on the others – but only one squadron had a bomb sight capable of putting a bomb in the right place......I tried so hard during my tour with 619, but I doubt whether I ever got a bomb within two hundred yards of the target...... but the 617 Squadron bombsight was marvellous'*
>
> [Flight Lieutenant Bob Knights DSO, DFC]

Knights' assessment of 'within two hundred yards of the target' is probably itself optimistic, though it has to be said that Knights was a particularly skilled pilot. The Butt Report of 1941 had concluded that most bombs dropped by the RAF up until that stage of the War had landed anywhere up to 75 miles from their target and that, without better navigation, better target-finding equipment and better target-marking techniques, accuracy was not likely to improve very much.

daylight attacks in 1940 and early 1941, or the raids on Leipzig on 19/20 Feb 1944 and Nürnberg on 30/31 Mar 44 – that questions were asked. It was generally thought that a bomber crew had about a one in five chance of surviving a first tour of thirty operations and a smaller chance of surviving a second tour. F/L Stan Jones DFC DFM told the author that he remembers hearing 'Bomber' Harris at an aircrew dinner in London after the War say that he reckoned bomber crews had a one in five chance of surviving a first tour [of 30 ops] but that only 1% would survive a second tour [of 20 ops]. This sets into context the remarkable achievement of men like Cheshire and Gibson, who accumulated a total in excess of 100 operations each.

16 Chaz Bowyer, *Bomber Barons* [Book Club Associates 1983] puts the survival rate as no better than one in three for a first tour, getting slimmer with each successive tour [p24].

In his classic account of the story behind the first thousand bomber raid on Köln on 30/31 May 1942, Ralph Barker[17] tells the story of a bombing competition between rival RAF squadrons at Hinaidi, near Baghdad soon after the First World War, in the presence of the Air Officer Commanding Iraq, Air Vice-Marshal Sir John Salmond, who had ordered the competition to settle the claims of the CO of 45 Sqn that it was possible to put bombs down within fifteen yards of a circle drawn in the sand. Fifteen yards! At this stage of the RAF's development, things were still pretty primitive. The twin-engined Vicker Vernon aircraft flown by 45 Squadron were a development of the old Vickers Vimy bomber in which Alcock and Brown had flown the Atlantic only four years previously. Like most of his officers in Iraq, Salmond was aware of the extravagant claims made by the squadron commander of 45 – to the irritation and ridicule of the other bombing squadron commanders in Iraq - of which there were seven, flying a mixture of aircraft: Vernons, DH9a's and Bristol Fighters. These other squadrons had been happy to keep their average error down to between one and two hundred yards. Now, under the impartial eye of the AOC the extravagant claims of 45 Squadron would be exposed in a competition between two crews from each of the eight squadrons.

The issue at stake was that the CO of 45 Squadron had devised an entirely new way of aiming bombs. The crews of 45 Squadron aimed their bombs from the prone position, rather than by peering over the side of the cockpit WWI-fashion as did the crews of the other seven squadrons. In 45 Squadron, the second pilots or observers lay flat on their bellies in their khaki shorts on the unyielding floor beneath the high cockpit of the Vernon, and with the aid of a standard drift sight and a rectangular hole cut in the plywood nose of the aircraft, aimed their bombs. It was a job for only the most experienced airmen, and as the two Vernon aircraft of 45 Squadron banked ponderously and settled into their bombing runs, the men stretched out on the floor of the aircraft were respectively the squadron commander and his deputy.

---

[17] Barker, *The Thousand Plan* [first published by Chatto & Windus Ltd in 1965].

The competition started soon after dawn to reduce difficulties created by hot air currents later in the day, and soon the 13 lb practice bombs, filled with stannic chloride to give off a tell-tale white puff when they hit the ground, were tumbling from the sky. The results were unexpected. Only two crews had managed to drop their bombs anywhere close to the target, and this in daylight, in peace-time conditions, without interference from flak or night-fighters. They were, of course, the two crews of 45 Squadron, and they had pointed the way to the future. Their average error in the competition was less than twenty yards, whereas their nearest rivals were four times as far away from the target. At no great expense, and with a little ingenuity and thought, a revolution in aerial bombing had started. The vindicated Squadron Commander and bomb-aimer in the leading 45 Squadron Vickers Vernon was Wing Commander AT Harris, 'Bert' to his colleagues.[18] His deputy and bomb-aimer in the second aircraft was Squadron Leader Bob Saundby.[19] Twenty five years later, they were to complete the revolution.

At the end of WWI, the RAF had a serving strength of more than 240,000 officers and men and at least 22,600 aircraft. Five years later in 1923 the figures were 30,000 and 36 squadrons of aircraft [probably about 650 in all]. By 1938 the numbers had built up to 6,218 officers and 67,049 airmen, giving a total serving strength of 73,267, and a total of 1,982 aircraft. By 1945 the total strength of officers and airmen was 1,115,523 and aircraft 27,443.[20] This enormous increase was to be expected after six years of total war, but it does provide some idea of the almost total unpreparedness of the RAF for war in the late 1930s.[21]

---

[18] Barker, ibid, p 1-3. Barker says that Harris was nicknamed 'Bert' while living in an Officers' Mess in Baghdad full of ex-Naval Air Service men. In the Navy, just as all Wilsons were called 'Tug' and all Millers 'Dusty', so all Harrises were called 'Bert'.

[19] Air Vice-Marshal RHMS Saundby, Harris's deputy at HQ Bomber Command during WWII [later Air Marshal Sir Robert Saundby].

[20] Ken Delve, *The Source Book of the RAF* [Airlife Publishing Ltd 1994], p.272.

[21] Perhaps surprisingly, such basic statistics as the strengths of men and aircraft at any given stage of the RAF's history are not certain. A different source puts the number of aircraft in 1945 at 61,584! [ibid p273].

This is not the place to discuss the reasons for that unpreparedness, save to say that, in matters of finance and procurement, responsibility by the nature of things lies with politicians rather than Service chiefs. Meanwhile, in the 21 years between the two world wars, the RAF had fought a rearguard action to remain in being as a separate military force. There seems little doubt that but for Trenchard's tenacity and Churchill's support, the RAF and its men and machines would have been swallowed back into the Army and Navy from whence they had come. Certainly, the military and naval hierarchy were never keen supporters of the RAF, and even in the years since WWII – with the possible exception of the 13 years or so when the 'V' Force of the RAF was the United Kingdom's sole nuclear strategic deterrent – the siren voices from time to time have called for the abolition of the third force and its absorption back into the original two services. As recently as June 2001[22], the letters pages of The Times newspaper contained letters arguing this case, and only four years before that, in 1997, a former [Army] Chief of Defence Staff[23] added his voice to this call. There is nothing new in this. Anyone who has looked even briefly at RAF history [which is all most RAF officers have ever done] will know that to the Generals, aircraft have never been anything more than airborne tanks and to the Admirals merely a useful extension of the ship's weapons and reconnaissance system [but, the story goes, 'where is the driver?' said the cavalry officer to his friend, when his cavalry colleague,

[22] The Times, 28 Jun 2001, letter from a retired Naval officer.

[23] Field Marshal Lord Carver DSO MC, letter in The Times 27 Jun 1997, who wrote 'that the existence of a third armed service had introduced aggravating complications to command and control of operations'. It may also lie behind his view that the three separate single-Service, third tier gallantry awards [DSC, MC and DFC] should be merged into one [letter in The Times 24 Aug 2001]. Interestingly, on the same day as Lord Carver's second letter was published, Admiral of the Fleet Sir Henry Leach also wrote a letter taking the opposite view and expressing the hope that '*our Government would have deployed to better purpose the intelligence of its Civil Service in addressing the problems of the railways, the London Underground, the road congestion or the NHS*' than have them '*fiddling on the margins*' of medal award arrangements '*and in the process depersonalising the three Services*'.

completing a tour as a pilot with the Army Air Corps, offered him a trip in his helicopter in Northern Ireland].

At the outbreak of war with Nazi Germany in September 1939, RAF Bomber Command was barely three years old, having come into being as a separate Command within the RAF on 14 July 1936. With its headquarters at RAF Uxbridge, the old RAF Depot, the new Command had as its first Air Officer Commanding-in-Chief, Air Chief Marshal Sir John Steel. He was succeeded in September 1937 by Air Chief Marshal Sir Edgar Ludlow-Hewitt. At this time, the Command consisted of three Groups, with a total of 32 squadrons between them, all operating biplane bombers little different from those flown during the Great War. With the highest spending priorities for pre-war expansion being allocated to the Royal Navy, followed by RAF home defence, Bomber Command's re-equipment with more modern aircraft was slow. It was not until 1936 onwards that the Air Ministry's specifications from 1932 - 1936 for twin and multi-engined monoplane bombers began to bear fruit with aircraft such as the Vickers Wellington, the Armstrong Whitworth Whitley, the Handley Page Hampden, the Bristol Blenheim and the Fairey Battle entering squadron service. In September 1939, the Command's operational strength in Britain was put under serious pressure by the detachment of all ten squadrons of Fairey Battles – the whole of No 1 Group – to France as tactical support for the British Expeditionary Force [BEF]. This left Bomber Command with only 23 operational squadrons – 370 aircraft – with which to engage in any form of aerial offensive against the enemy.[24] There were also other restrictions: *political* [the need not to provoke a response we could not handle], *tactical* [the crews were obliged to carry out their raids by daylight because it was believed they could self-protect if they flew in formations] and *moral* [not to engage a target unless they could see it clearly and at all costs – including their own lives – to avoid any

[24] Bowyer, op cit, p 18; Max Hastings, *Bomber Command* [first published Michael Joseph 1979], p49-51, gives the figures as 608 front-line fighters and 536 bombers as at September 1939, compared with the Luftwaffe's 1,215 and 2,130 respectively, with 160 of the bombers – the Fairey Battles - being sent to France as the Advanced Air Striking Force, leaving 376 available for the aerial offensive.

civilian casualties]. Ludlow-Hewitt, a teetotal, Christian Scientist of acute humanitarian sensitivities[25], was not the most inspiring or popular of leaders, and there was general relief when he retired and was replaced by Charles Portal.

Sir Charles succeeded Ludlow-Hewitt as C-in-C Bomber Command on 4th April 1940, but six months later in October 1940, Sir Cyril Newall retired as Chief of Air Staff, and he was succeeded by Portal, who remained CAS until the end of 1945 and was therefore in charge of the RAF for most of the war[26]. Sir Richard Peirse, a proponent of 'precision' bombing [as opposed to Harris, the arch proponent of 'strategic' bombing], and a protégé of Charles Portal, succeeded Portal as C-in-C of Bomber Command. Peirse remained in charge of Bomber Command, by this time at its new Headquarters at High Wycombe, Buckinghamshire, until Harris took over on 22nd February, 1942.

Meanwhile, the Air Ministry and Bomber Command had had to undergo a shift of seismic proportions in their thinking about the way bomber aircraft were used. From the pre-war notion that the bomber would always get through and could be sent by day to find and bomb specific targets and then fly safely home back to base, a new realism had dawned. Not only might the bomber not get through, it would probably not find the target and, even if it did, would not be able to hit it accurately, for want of decent target finding or target marking equipment. If, through the remarkable skill of the crew, the target was found and hit, the likelihood of the aircraft and crew surviving to get back to base could be as low as 50/50.[27] In the period 1939/40 the Battles, Blenheims, Whitleys, Hampdens and Wellingtons of Bomber Com-

---

[25] Max Hastings, ibid, p54.

[26] ACM Sir Cyril Newall KCB CMG CBE AM was CAS from1 Sep 37 to 25 Oct 40; MRAF Sir Charles Portal was CAS from 25 Oct 40 to 1 Jan 46.

[27] On 18 Dec 39, twenty-four Wellingtons of Bomber Command were sent on a reconnaissance operation to Wilhelmshaven in broad daylight without any form of fighter protection in the belief, held since WWI, that a tightly-formated bomber force could self-protect. They were totally outgunned and out-run by the Luftwaffe fighters, whose pilots could not believe their good fortune in being presented with a target in such perfect formation, and proceeded to tear the formation apart. Fifteen [62.5%] of the twenty-four Wellingtons were lost that day. It was not the crews' fault.

mand and the AASF[28] sometimes lost over 50% of their aircraft in actions against the enemy and in support of the BEF. The aircraft were inadequate for the task to which they were being put, but they were all we had. Not until late 1940 did some of the new aircraft commissioned in the last few years of peace begin to arrive at Bomber Command stations: No 7 Squadron reformed at RAF Leeming on 1 Aug 1940 to receive the Short Stirling heavy bomber and bring it into service at RAF Oakington from 29 Oct 1940; No 207 Squadron re-equipped with the inadequately-powered, twin-engined Avro Manchester on 1 November 1940 at its base at RAF Waddington; No 35 Squadron reformed at Boscombe Down on 5 Nov 1940 to receive the first of the Handley Page Halifax heavy bombers and bring it into service at Leeming on 20 Nov 1940. Not until another thirteen months had passed did the first of the Avro Lancasters begin to reach the squadrons, three aircraft arriving at Waddington on Christmas Eve 1941. Even then, it was then a further two months before the receiving squadron, No 44 [Rhodesian], flew their first operation in the new aircraft on 3rd March, 1942 [a 'gardening'[29] trip to the Heligoland Bight]. The Lancaster went on to become the best[30] and certainly the best known of the war-time trio of heavy bombers, and the backbone of Bomber Command. Ironically, it was a success story that grew out of failure. So chronically underpowered was the Manchester with its trouble-prone twin Vulture engines that something had to be done to salvage the aircraft. The 'something' was the Merlin-powered, four-engined Lancaster, and the rest is history.

Chaz Bowyer in his History of the RAF writes of the maxim that *old men make wars and young men fight them*[31]. The RAF was, and still is, a very young service.[32] By 1939 it was only 21 years of age, a neat para-

---

[28] Advanced Air Striking Force, the bomber force that accompanied the BEF into France.

[29] 'Gardening' was the codename for the dropping of anti-shipping mines in enemy coastal waters.

[30] 'The greatest single factor in winning the War', said Sir Arthur Harris after the War.

[31] Bowyer, *History of the Royal Air Force* [Bison Books Ltd 1977].

[32] The RAF came into being on 1 April 1918 [and has suffered from the April's Fool joke ever since] as a political expedient to deal with the Zeppelin and Gotha aircraft attacks on

digm as this was the same sort of age as its young pilots and crews. The small corps of regular officers and airmen available at the outset of war for the air defence of Great Britain, or deployment with the BEF or for offensive attacks against the enemy, had been trained and tested for the two decades after the Great War, in the deserts of the Near and Middle East, and against the tribesmen of the North West Frontier, that is, against enemies with no air forces or sophisticated arsenals of war. Air power was a very recent invention, and there was little clear agreement as to how it should be used or where it would be going in the future. The RAF's first CAS, Hugh Trenchard[33], the Italian General Guilo Douhet, Billy Mitchell in America, Liddell Hart and Fuller in 1920s London and other thinkers and writers of the time contributed to the debate. Fuller and Liddell Hart [at first] foresaw aerial bombing in a future conflict as a blunt but unstoppable instrument of war that would bring the enemy's people to their knees, and cause them to put pressure on their Government to sue for peace. Others deplored such a barbaric use of military power[34], which they felt would amount to terrorism

London, Kent and Essex. Although a Joint War Air Committee, under the Chairmanship of Lord Derby, had been established in February 1916 and an Air Board under Lord Curzon had succeeded that body, these were seen by the Army and Navy as merely instruments of operational control and coordination, and the Generals and Admirals viewed the formation of the Royal Air Force by the Lloyd George government as an unfortunate but temporary War-time necessity. The Government after all had been under pressure 'to do something'. An attack on London by fourteen Gotha aircraft in June 1917 had resulted in 118 high explosive bombs being dropped in the city, with a direct hit on Liverpool Street Station that killed nearly a 150 people and injured more than 350. More than 90 British aircraft took off to intercept the bombers but not a single one was shot down and all returned safely to their bases. The RAF was born out of the ensuing political pressure [as also was the myth that 'the bomber will always get through']. Three individuals in particular were instrumental in [1] bringing about the formation of the separate RAF and [2] keeping it in being after the Great War ended. To General Jan Smuts, who with Prime Minister Lloyd George in 1917 had formed a Committee to examine defence arrangements and had recommended a separate air force, is owed thanks for [1]; and to Hugh Trenchard and Winston Churchill thanks for [2]. At the end of hostilities in November 1919 the Admirals and Generals wanted their aircraft back.

[33] Maj Gen Sir Hugh Trenchard KCB DSO, later MRAF Lord Trenchard [d. 1956].

[34] It should be remembered, too, that it was only just over twenty years since the sinking of the Lusitania off the coast of Ireland on 7 May 1915 by a torpedo fired from a German

from the air.[35] Even the RAF's own senior commanders were divided in their views, and the Army and Navy hierarchy were almost unanimously hostile. The debate continued up to and well beyond the outbreak of the Second World War, and on through the period of the 'Phoney War', when it was still hoped we would be able to step back from the brink. Memories of German aerial bombing of London and other targets in the south and east and the coastal regions during WWI were still fresh in the minds of the older officers, the generation now filling the senior staff and operational appointments. In the RAF, of course, these senior officers had all served before 1918 in either the Army or the Navy, and so they had personal experience of war, often in the trenches. This cannot be over emphasised, because it coloured their views about the use of air power during the second world conflict. They, and the population as a whole, knew only too well the price in young lives that had been paid a quarter of a century previously in the trenches, and anything that prevented that kind of carnage was better than more of the same. It was Prime Minister Stanley Baldwin, speaking in a debate in the Commons in November 1932, who made famous the phrase 'the bomber will always get through'. Part of what he said bears repeating, for it records from an era that now seems almost primeval something of the thinking from which Bomber Command operations gradually grew in the years up to 1943:

> *I think it is well for the man in the street to realise that there is no power on earth that can protect him from being bombed. Whatever people may tell him, the bomber will always get through. The only defence is in offence, which means that you have to kill more women and children more quickly than the enemy if you want to save yourselves.*

Prime Minister Baldwin went on to say that he could not but help reflect that after millions of years of the human species on Earth it was

---

submarine had led to world-wide revulsion and condemnation [and indirectly to the United States joining the War]. The killing of 1,200 civilians, even at a time of war, was considered a moral outrage. Armies [and navies] fought each other, not civilians.

[35] See, for example, Hastings, op cit, Chapter 1: British bombing policy 1917-1940.

only in the past generation that mastery of the air had been secured, with all this might entail for the future, and that this was not a cheerful thought for his generation.

Hastings and Bowyer are fairly critical of the failure of the Air Staff until the mid-1930s to appreciate the speed with which technology was advancing. Specifications for new equipment, especially aircraft, barely improved on older models already in use, and the more unconventional scientific minds, such as that brought to bear on aeronautics by Barnes Wallis [of bouncing bomb fame], were dismissed as freaks. When Wallis first suggested the use of big bombs in the 1930s, Air ministry bureaucrats said that they doubted it would be possible to detonate properly large quantities of explosive[36]. The early bombsight with which the RAF went to war had within it no provision for compensating for the gyrations of an aircraft and consequently required the pilot to approach the target in an absolutely straight and level run, taking no account of operational conditions. The RAF had no effective target finding equipment, no target marking equipment ….. and the list goes on. Hastings puts much of this down to the Trenchardian faith that 'all would be right on the night'. This is a harsh judgement. It is easy to be too critical of the senior officers of the still-fledgling RAF. They faced enormous odds in trying to keep the RAF together as a separate force, with minimal budgets, and it is not surprising they were able to achieve this only in the inadequate state in which they were eventually obliged to go to war. That they did not foresee many of the problems of using aircraft against an enemy with equally – indeed, at first, considerably superior – equipment is also not surprising. Few people, on this side of the North Sea at any rate, had that gift of foresight in sufficient time to be able to do anything about it. The RAF had been looking over its shoulder since 1919. It not only had to do things more cheaply than the Army or Navy, but it had demonstrably to be seen to be doing so. This was still true in the RAF the author knew from 1956 to 1979. In Northern Ireland, for example, in the 1970s it was much easier to get

---

[36] Thirty years later other Whitehall bureaucrats could not see a future for swing-wing aircraft, and so Wallis's design went to America, and the RAF almost ended up buying American swing-wing aircraft.

essential [non aircraft] equipment through the Army than through the RAF. It used to be said in jest that the reason was that the Chief of Air Staff was having to save up all his box-tops for another aircraft. On one occasion we wished to get RAF Policemen on guard duties out of their standard RAF working blues and white webbing, so as to make them less of a target for terrorists at night. A bid to Bomber Command's successor Headquarters, Strike Command, for the policemen to be issued with disruptive pattern 'cabbage kit' uniforms seemed to be quite non-contentious until a RAF staff officer, motivated no doubt by financial considerations, sent a signal back saying that disruptive pattern clothing was not suitable for the climate of Northern Ireland. The author's retort that in that case he would tell the GOC[37] because he had made the mistake of issuing that same uniform to some 20,000 soldiers in the Province, led to a swift change of heart. A few years previously, travelling to the Gulf in an RAF VC10 transport aircraft, the author found himself sitting next to a civilian auditor. The auditor said that, in his experience of working with all three services, the difference between them was this: when the government ordered defence cuts of say 10%, the RAF would come back three months later and say it had made them, the Army would set up a working party which three years later would still be thinking about it, and the Navy would simply ignore the order. There is more than a grain of truth behind this story, even if it is perhaps apocryphal. Outside the periods 1939-1945 and 1956-69, the RAF has always feared that it would only be allowed to remain in being as a separate force for as long as it was politically expedient for the Government to allow it so to remain. Its senior officers are usually less politically minded than those of the other two services, and on the whole less personally ambitious. Most of them, in the flying branches particularly, are only there because they enjoy the flying and the travel this brings, and as inevitably, and quite rightly, most of the top posts are held by pilots [or other aircrew[38]], this breeds

[37] The General Officer Commanding [GOC], based at the Army HQ at Lisburn, at that time General Sir Frank King of Arnhem fame.

[38] Theoretically, at least, most operational flying appointments are open to other aircrew – for example, navigators – as well as to pilots, but in practice most are held by pilots. The

a rather different sort of officer from those in the other services. Hastings is right, therefore, to highlight the atmosphere of caution and 'separateness' that marked the new service in the inter-war years as being different from the other two, but Trenchard and his senior officers had, in fairness, good reason for being the way they were.[39] Though perhaps not excusing them of all responsibility, it also explains why such a large proportion of the RAF budget was spent on building the new permanent stations – an investment, incidentally, which post-1970 has so benefited the Army as the RAF has reduced in size and the Army has moved into so many former RAF stations. As for 'the fat' pre-War Air Ministry [Hastings estimates that in the 1930s there were three civil servants for every aircraft, and that 20% of the budget was spent on buildings] one wonders what the proportions would be today. Not until 1938 did the RAF's share of the combined services budget become the lion's share [40%]. During the inter-war years it had averaged about 17%, or less than one-fifth of the total, when it had to provide from that figure for a whole series of new aircraft, new airfields and new barracks. Even then, a new aircraft cost a lot of box-tops, compared with the kit required by most army units [the problem of the high cost of ships was something the Navy had learnt to live with since the time of the *Mary Rose*].

---

author has to admit, however, to at least three of his station commanders having been navigators. During WWII, the captain of a multi-crewed aircraft was invariably the pilot, regardless of rank, and so a Sgt pilot in the air would command commissioned officers if they were members of his crew.

[39] Trenchard's lasting testament to the RAF was the establishment of the Flight Cadet and Apprentice training schemes, which produced for the RAF a steady supply of the finest officers and NCOs, the latter mainly mechanics/fitters, but also clerks, of the highest calibre. Some 60% of all the apprentices trained under the scheme were later commissioned, both as aircrew and in ground branches, and they were the backbone of the RAF until the 1990s when the RAF was seduced by modern management-speak to abandon an arrangement that had served it immensely well. It is too easy to brush aside Trenchard's legacy: it was enormous. Many of the 'Bomber Barons' started their careers as apprentices [see, for example, Chaz Bowyer, 'Bomber Barons', first published William Kimber 1983, to get some idea of just how important Trenchard's training scheme was to the RAF and the country].

That RAF bomber aircraft development should have outstripped [considerably] RAF fighter/defence aircraft development was also not surprising, given the received wisdom of the day. Yes, of course, there were dissenting voices, but that is true in almost any sphere of human activity.[40] Someone can always be found with a dissenting view [and we hear them nightly on the radio and television – it makes for 'balanced' reporting and spins out a thin news night]. That later they are found to have been right, may mean they had wisdom and foresight. It may simply be luck. Most of us are right some of the time. Few are wrong all the time. Given these pressures, it is not surprising that the number of modern fighter aircraft available by 1940 to fight the Battle of Britain was barely sufficient for the job, given the lateness of political awareness that war was inevitable. None of this, however, is a reflection on the senior RAF officers, like Harris, who strove so hard throughout the 1930s to build an effective bomber force and an effective fighter defence force before it was too late[41]. The 'civilised' Western World was moving into totally new territory, and concepts or war were going to have to change. No longer would there be combatants and non-combatants.

On the other hand, for those senior RAF standard-bearers, the 1920s and 1930s offered good training in battling against the odds. It produced a kind of unsophisticated, apolitical doggedness from which arose the two officers who more than any other, except perhaps General

[40] See for example Hastings, op cit, chapter I p49, in which Sir Thomas Inskip, Minister for the Co-ordination of Defence, is cited as having declined in December 1937 to accept a plan for a substantial increase in the bomber force because the cost was reckoned to be too great and the number of fighter aircraft proposed too few.

[41] In a letter to Lord Beaverbrook, the Minister responsible for war material production, in February 1941, Harris was typically blunt and forthright, writing: "*For twenty years everybody on the stations and squadrons has been screaming for runways without avail. The maximum consolation obtained from Air Ministry when I was a Group Commander in the days of peace was a long dissertation on the potentialities and a promise of 'worm action' towards making our new aerodromes fit for the bombers to live on.......... Every other nation throughout the world has long been convinced of the necessity for runways, but we ourselves have always been apparently just as convinced that our view* [author: as to the unwarranted cost] *is right. We alone are the only soldier in step in the entire battalion.*" [PRO document AIR19/492].

Bernard Montgomery, helped turn the tide at vital moments of the War, Hugh Dowding and Bert Harris [in 1940, and 1943-44, respectively]. For this reason, it is not altogether surprising that they were treated so badly and dumped with trivial reward when they had completed the tasks set by Whitehall. Anyone who has read Dowding's letter urging Whitehall not to waste any more fighter aircraft on the lost cause of France, because if they did he would not be responsible for what this would do for the air defence of Great Britain, or knows of the determination, bordering on obsession, with which Harris pursued the case for the strategic bombing of Germany, can see why these two men were not popular with their superiors; but nor was Monty, 'the messianic monk of war'.[42] They were military professionals and not politicians or diplomats. What is more they were usually right. Churchill never forgave 'Stuffy' Dowding for being right about France and nor did he give 'Bomber' Harris the protection he deserved for pursuing so well the policy that Churchill and the War Cabinet had required of him.[43]

It has been said many times that the bombing of Germany failed to break German morale, just as the Luftwaffe bombing of London and other British cities had failed to break British morale during the Blitzes of 1940/41. Because of this, it is claimed, Harris failed in his grand strategy. His critics say that he should instead have given greater priority

[42] In a recent response to Nigel Hamilton's revised biography of Montgomery *'The Full Monty'* [Penguin Press 2001], Alex Danchev, co-author of Alanbrooke's unexpurgated war diaries [Weidenfeld & Nicolson], quotes the novelist Anthony Powell in describing Monty: *'the faint and faraway reminder of the clergy; parsonic, yet not in the least numinous, the tone of the incumbent ruthlessly dedicated to his parish, rather than the hierophant celebrating divine mysteries'. 'That', says Hamilton, 'was Monty to a tee – the messianic monk of war'.* [The Times, section 2, p4, 19 Sep 2001]. Harris was rather more earthy and blunt, but the effect was much the same.

[43] As Hastings noted, op cit, in Chapt XV, writing 30 years ago, the former aircrew of Bomber Command felt very keenly that they had been let down by their political masters after the War and been allowed to carry the can for a strategy that in an assured peace could seem barbaric. That no separate medal was given bomber crews still rankles, and that their former 'chief' Harris was so badly treated [yet maintained a dignified silence once he had written his memoirs in 1947] is also a source of much bitterness. The aircrew of Bomber Command, and Harris, have been very badly let down.

to the Transport Plan and the attacks on oil plants.[44] But Harris demurred [his critics would use a stronger verb] and so, it is said, an opportunity was lost. Albert Speer, Hitler's successful if mercurial Minister of Armaments[45], writing after the war, said that by not pursuing their attacks against oil installations '*the Allies threw away success when it was already in their hands*'.[46] Adolf Galland, the war-time Luftwaffe fighter pilot and General, and post-War West German Air Force Chief of Staff, wrote in a similar vein when he said '*looking back, it is difficult to understand why the Allies started this undertaking* [attacking fuel supplies] *so late*'. He thought the attacks on the sources of fuel supply had been the single most successful campaign of the entire Allied air strategy. Speer also thought that Bomber Command's attacks against the oil installations were more effective than those of the USAAF because the larger bombs caused more damage. Harris never disputed that the question of the oil attacks had been the source of friction between himself and his boss, the Chief of the Air Staff, Sir Charles Portal. Max Hastings records Harris as telling him that the only serious row he ever had with Portal was about the Oil Plan.[47] [Hastings also goes on to say that because, in his view, Portal failed to stand up to Harris in late 1944/early 1945, the chance of using Bomber Command in a more effective way was lost; if Hastings is right – and these things can never be proved – then Dresden would almost certainly not have happened, and the main beneficiary of a different policy – in terms of reputation - would have been Harris himself and his bomber crews.] If only…but then maybe not. Maybe not, because it is no more than wishful thinking. Until late 1944 the RAF did not have the equipment or the operational conditions over Europe to fight a tactical war. That they were able to do so from the autumn of 1944 onwards was the prize

---

[44] In November 1944 the weight of bombs delivered against oil targets by Bomber Command accounted for 24.6% of all their effort [Hastings, *Bomber Command,* p.331, Michael Joseph Limited 1979].

[45] It occurs to me as I write this that Speer and Beaverbrook had more in common than just their similar roles in supporting the war efforts of their two countries.

[46] Speer, *Inside the Third Reich.*

[47] Hastings, op cit, p334.

they had won by the earlier strategic campaign. The two were not alternatives: the one followed the other.

More recently, in his book *The Bomber War*, Robin Neillands, a journalist like Hastings, has done much to redress the balance.[48] He draws heavily on the testimonies of the fast-dwindling band of Bomber Command veterans and devotes an entire chapter to the moral issues. His conclusions are remarkably similar to those I had written in this chapter before I read his book. If I may paraphrase Neillands, he says that one cannot separate one strand of events in a situation as fluid as total war from others: that one cannot know what the effect would have been had a different emphasis been placed on one strategy rather than another. The Allied strategic bombing campaign tied down German men and resources that would otherwise have been free for use in other ways. The balance would have been changed, and the outcome would – must – have been different. Because of this one cannot rewrite history. The consequences may not have been at all what hindsight would seem to suggest. Neillands also picks up on a theme I had noticed myself during my service in the post-War RAF and have long since held to be a basic principle of leadership. The men above a commanding officer or an air officer commanding may have the wool pulled over their eyes, and frequently do have, but the men below are usually much shrewder in their judgement. They know whether their boss is any use or not. The boss may be able to impress his superiors, but he will not impress his subordinates for very long unless he knows what he is about. The aircrew of Bomber Command trusted Harris almost to a man, and the veterans I have spoken with still hold him in high regard fifty five years on, and see the attacks on his reputation as a slur on themselves. That is Harris's real record and his testimony. He did something positive about the War at a time when, goodness knows, something positive was desperately needed. And so to answer the question with which I opened this chapter: yes, it was worth it. The sacrifice of the aircrew of 619 Squadron and the aircrew of the many other, now unknown, squadrons like 619, which sprang up throughout Lincolnshire and East Anglia

---

[48] Robin Neillands *The Bomber War* [John Murray Limited, 2001].

almost overnight to meet the demands of the Strategic Bombing Campaign in the two years 1943-1945 and were then disbanded almost as quickly, when their job was done and the War was won, did more – collectively - than any other arm of the Services to bring about the end of the War and the defeat of Hitler. Their Squadron serial numbers may not be known today even in the Service to which they belonged, but their loss continues to touch families throughout this country and the world. Children grew up in the post-War years without fathers. Others did not know the uncles - or the offspring cousins - they would have known had the War – like the Great War before it - not denied so many young men the opportunity of getting married and enjoying a normal family life. This time, however, the Allied losses, dreadful though they were, did not run into the millions of the trenches of the Great War, and that was what Harris had intended. War is not a business that any right-minded person would choose, but sometimes the choice is taken out of one's hands.

The Old Alleynian accountant Cyril Fuller, his flight engineer George Wilson from Battersea, the London policeman Reg Stevens, the Southport-born local government clerk Leo Eaude, the Bristol farmer's son Dick Sprackman, the apprentice bricklayer Vinny Crookes from Sheffield, the Cornish clay-mine accounts clerk Roy Trahair and their companion for the night, the second pilot James Horne - a 31 years old married man on his second operational trip - did not die in vain. Without them, there might not have been an Allied Landing on the Normandy Beaches in June 1944. The Allies might not have won the War. The outcome might have been very different. There might not have been a Cold War, because there might not have been a need for it. There may have been nothing left.

> *'The Luftwaffe ...... started the war as the best-equipped and most powerful air force in the world, but following the initial relatively easy victories in Poland and Norway and in the West, Hitler ...[became] ... too ambitious. By the end of 1941 his nation was at*

war not only with Britain but also with the USA and the Soviet Union.'[49]

A desperate dictator will do anything to reverse his fortunes.

[49] Price, op cit, p 183/184.

Epilogue

What is needed is a humanity strong in will and firm in the determination to preserve itself. Freedom must discover its virility.
[Thomas Mann. The Coming Victory]

Today, of course, it would all be different. Wouldn't it? Well, yes, it would. We would probably have lost, because we would not have been able in a democracy to sustain a war for six years in the face of a media with an unquenchable thirst to fill its time slots with round the clock news entertainment, which would have given equal weight to the press releases of Dr Goebbels' propaganda ministry as to those of Bomber Command's chief press officer, would have sought interviews with the housewives of Hamburg, Berlin and Düsseldorf [and London, Bristol and Manchester] and would have destroyed the will of the British people to fight the war, in a way that would not have hampered the German dictatorship. The voices of the relatively few dissenters – people like Bishop Bell of Chichester and Canon Collins, the RAF Bomber Command Chaplain, whose outspoken opposition to the bombing campaign are now fairly well known - would have been heard by a much wider audience at the time, and we would have found it difficult to sustain the will to continue the war to its conclusion.[1] We would have been under pressure to find some form of appeasement, which may have saved some lives in the short-term but would almost certainly have cost more in the long run. Peace is not, of course, merely

[1] I have not attempted here to discuss the concept of the 'just war', a set of moral precepts originally set out by St Thomas Aquinas in the Thirteenth Century and refined by Christians over the centuries, which prescribe a number of principles that should be met before a War can be thought, in Christian terms, to be just. I have not done so, because I think most people then, and probably now, thought WWII to be a just war.

the absence of war. Sooner or later, and probably sooner, we would have discovered that appeasement was only a sticking plaster. As Professor Probst has said, 'you could not negotiate with Hitler'. But by then it would have been too late. It now remains to be seen whether, in the Twenty First Century, democracies are still able to stand up to non-democracies in the glare of constant media coverage. Jonathan Sacks, the Chief Rabbi, and a wise man, has written in his recent book:

> *'Sooner or later my freedom will conflict with yours. If I am free to steal, you are not free to own. If I am free to attack, you are not free to walk without fear. Freedom for the pike means death to the minnows. A society based on hofesh – what is today called a libertarian society – will be one in which the strong will prevail over the weak, the many over the few, the powerful over the powerless.'*[2]

[*Hofesh* is one of many Hebrew words meaning freedom – in this case individual freedom.] As someone who was involved professionally in counter-terrorism, and in particular in countering terrorist aircraft hi-jackings in the 1970s, I can only say that the sudden upsurge of hi-jackings - from a handful to ten times as many in a period of little more than 12 months – was only contained and then reversed when enough countries and airlines had taken firm action to make hi-jacking an unattractive proposition.

If we are not careful, terrorist attacks and dictators' megalomania will become little more than television entertainment, and a Twenty First Century means of pressuring democratic nations into doing whatever the undemocratic terrorist wishes to be done. One cannot help but think that Hitler and Goebels would find it much easier now than they did in 1940.

---

[2] Dr Jonathan Sacks, '*Radical Then, Radical Now – The Legacy of the World's Oldest Religion*' [HarperCollins Publishers 2000].

Postscript

On 1st August, 2002 the author and the retired German Professor, who as a boy had helped shoot down EE109, laid flowers on the grave in Hannover of the rear gunner, Sergeant Roy Trahair, and the two unnamed crew members buried there in 1978. The Professor laid a single red rose on Roy's grave. When the author thanked him, he replied 'it is a soldier's duty'. We also paid our respects at the graves of the crew of EE114 PG-B [captain P/O Christopher Firth], shot down 48 hours after EE109 and the only other 619 Squadron members buried in the CWGC cemetery in Hannover. It was a moving occasion and brought to an end 25 years of investigation.

Appendix 1. The Organisation of RAF Bomber Command in 1943

Headquarters Bomber Command	Based at RAF High Wycombe and commanded by Air Marshal Sir Arthur Harris KCB OBE AFC [later Air Chief Marshal GCB OBE AFC] from 22nd February 1942 until the end of the War. *In 1943*, the Command contained some 93 operational squadrons, and two flights functioning like squadrons, on some 61 stations. The squadrons were spread throughout eight operational Groups, usually two squadrons per station, as follows:
No 1 Group	in Lincolnshire, commanded by Air Vice-Marshal EAB Rice CB CBE MC, with sixteen squadrons on ten stations;
No 2 Group	in Norfolk, commanded by Air Vice-Marshal JH D'Albiac CB DSO, with twelve squadrons on nine stations [No 2 Group moved into Fighter Command on 1 June 1943];
No 3 Group	in Bedfordshire, Huntingdonshire, Norfolk, Cambridgeshire, Leicestershire and Norfolk, commanded by [1] Air Vice-Marshal The Hon RA Cochran CB CBE AFC and [2] Air Vice-Marshal R Harrison CB CBE DFC AFC with twelve squadrons on nine stations;
No 4 Group	in Yorkshire, commanded by Air Vice-Marshal CR Carr CBE DFC AFC, with ten squadrons on eight stations;
No 5 Group	mainly in Lincolnshire, but with two stations in Nottinghamshire and one in Leicestershire, commanded by [1] Air Vice-Marshal WA Coryton CB MVO and [2] Air Vice-Marshal Sir Ralph A Cochran KBE CB AFC, with fourteen squadrons on eight stations;
No 6 [Canadian] Group	in Yorkshire, commanded by Air Vice-Marshal GE Brookes OBE, with fourteen squadrons on ten stations;
No 8 [Pathfinder] Group	based around Huntingdon, commanded by Air Commodore DCT Bennett DSO [later Air Vice-Marshal CB CBE DSO], with ten squadrons on seven stations;
No 100 [Special Duties]	in Norfolk, commanded by Air Commodore EB Addison

Group	CBE [later Air Vice-Marshal CB CBE], with five squadrons and two flights on three stations.
Operational Training Units [OTUs]	23 units in three Groups as follows:
	No 91 [OTU] Group commanded by Group Captain HSP Walmsley OBE MC DFC [later Air Vice-Marshal, CBE MC DFC];
	No 92 [OTU] Group commanded by Group Captain HA Haines OBE DFC;
	No 93 [OTU] Group commanded by Air Commodore AP Ritchie AFC [25 Feb 43].

Bomber Command Stations

Operational RAF stations, then as now, were usually commanded by an officer of Group Captain rank. Stations were small townships, with perhaps some 1,500 or more men and women working on them in all the various trades and branches needed to support the aircraft and their crews. In addition to the wing commanders and squadron leaders on the operational squadrons, there would also be a number of other officers of those ranks filling senior station appointments. By 1943 stations were being clustered together into groups known as 'Bases', each consisting of a major airfield and two or three satellites. Thus, RAF Woodhall Spa was part of No 54 Base[1], with the Base Com-

[1] 54 Base was commanded by A/Cdre Bobby Sharpe and contained within it at RAF Coningsby a training unit known as 54 Base Flight, where No 5 Group's Master Bombers were trained in a highly sophisticated link-trainer type device known as the Jordan trainer, which replicated the effect of flying over a German city at night while a raid was in progress. Master Bombers had an especially dangerous job to perform, as they were obliged to remain over the target directing and re-directing the attack, often arriving first and departing last. Guy Gibson, who is generally reckoned to have pioneered the master bomber technique during the raid on the Dams in May 43, was killed when his aircraft crashed in Holland on returning from acting as Master Bomber on an operation to Mönchen-Gladbach on 19 Sep 44. The technique was also used by John Searby, CO of 83 [Pathfinder] Sqn, during the Peenemünde raid in Aug 43. Searby was later succeeded by John Jeudwine, a former CO of 619 Squadron [83 Sqn having been transferred with 97 from No 8 Pathfinder Group to 5 Group to set up the main force 5 Group's own

mander, an Air Commodore, at RAF Coningsby. RAF Waddington, near Lincoln, was the centre of another Base cluster, and so on.

Bomber Command Squadrons

Bomber squadrons were located on RAF stations along most of the East coast of England, mainly at the rate of two per station, for example, Nos 467 and 463 [Australian] Squadrons were based at RAF Waddington; Nos 218 and 623 at RAF Downham Market; Nos 50 and 61 at Skellingthorpe; Nos 12 and 626 at RAF Wickenby; Nos 7 and 627 at RAF Oakington; Nos 57 and 630 at RAF East Kirby, and so on. So thickly was East Anglia covered with airfields and runways that it was once referred to as '*a large aircraft carrier anchored off the coast of Europe*'. In the late 1960s, when stationed at Waddington, the author asked one of the 'V' Force squadron commanders, whose own flying experience as a navigator went back to the immediate post-War years, '*how on earth did crews ever find their way back to their own airfields*', and he replied '*they often didn't ...... they landed wherever they could!*'

A few words about RAF officer rank structure might not go amiss. A reader unfamiliar with the RAF might expect, as the rank structure would seem to suggest, that squadrons would be commanded by squadron leaders and flights by flight lieutenants. This had been the intention when the RAF officer rank titles were invented in 1918, and fighter squadrons were usually still so commanded during WWII. But by the 1930s, bomber squadrons were invariably commanded by wing commanders, for example: No 82 Squadron in 1940/41 by Paddy Bandon [the Earl of Bandon, and the author's C-in-C in the Far East in the late 1950s]; No 10 Sqn by Bill Staton in 1940/41; No 106 by Guy

---

specialist marker unit], and he in turn by John Woodruffe [the author's station commander at RAF Wittering in 1957/8] from 61 Sqn, who has been described as the greatest master bomber of them all [for example, see *The Bomber Command War Diaries*, Middlebrrok and Everitt, published by Viking in 1985, p575]. Strictly speaking, the master bombers were really called 'master of ceremonies' or 'controllers'. W/C Willie Tait from 83 Base and W/C Simpson from 97 Sqn were posted in as controllers to 54 Base Flight at the same time as Jeudwine, and W/C Joe Northrop, yet another ex-apprentice Bomber 'name', was also a controller at this time.

Gibson in 1942/3; No 76 by Leonard Cheshire in 1943; No 617 by Gibson, Cheshire and Willie Tait 1943-45; No 619 by John McGhie, Jock Abercromby, John Jeudwine, Dick Maling and Robert Millward in the 23 months of its operational life 1943-45; and so on. A final word about officer ranks: rank titles are common to officers of all branches, whether pilots or not, whether flying or not. Thus, a pilot officer is not necessarily a pilot and a flying officer does not necessarily fly.

Bomber squadrons were further sub-divided into usually two but sometimes three flights, each commanded by a squadron leader. This sub-division was more for administrative and disciplinary convenience – to reduce the breadth of command – than for operational reasons, as squadron aircraft flew as part of the squadron rather than as part of a flight. In any event, once in the air each crew was on its own and made its own way to the target and back, albeit as part of a bomber 'stream' that could stretch out over several miles and had taken over 30 minutes to form up off the East Anglian coast. The presence in close proximity of so many aircraft could be as much of a risk to the Bomber Command crews as enemy flak and night-fighters. Many accidents are known to have occurred, and many more probably occurred but were not reported as no one survived to tell the tale. In addition to the flight commanders, other members of the squadron could also hold the rank of squadron leader, for the example, the Squadron Navigation Leader, the Squadron Bombing Leader, the Squadron Gunnery Leader etc.

Later in the war, some specialist bomber squadrons were commanded by Group Captains. For example, John Searby, the ex-apprentice master bomber, commanded 83 Pathfinder Squadron as a group captain at the time of the Peenemünde raid in August 1943 [but he had control on that raid of over 450 aircraft and 3,200 aircrew]. By 1945 there were often more, sometimes many more, than one officer of wing commander rank on an operational bomber squadron. The author has seen a titled photograph, with ranks and names given, of No 7 Squadron at RAF Oakington in the final weeks of the War, and counted at least six wing commanders posing in the front row of the photograph. Some may have been station rather than squadron officers, but a wartime aircrew member of the Hereford and Marches Branch of the Aircrew Association assured the author that 'wing commanders were ten a penny' by that time. He may have been joking.

The number of aircraft on the '*establishment*' of the squadrons also varied considerably. The usual total was about 18, but some squadrons had an establishment of many more, in one case, at least, of 30. The '*strength*' of aircraft depended, of course, on how many had been lost in the past few days and how quickly their replacements reached the squadron. Sometimes a new aircraft would reach a squadron from the factory only to be sent to another squadron immediately, because there was a greater need somewhere else [as happened to Lancaster Mk I, DV338, issued new from the manufacturer, Metropolitan Vickers, to 619 Sqn, RAF Woodhall Spa, in Oct 43 and transferred immediately to 467/463 Sqn, RAF Waddington; with the latter squadron it was lost four months later on 19/20 Feb 44 with 186 flying hours on the clock].

Bomber Command by 1945

By 1945, Bomber Command still contained the same number of groups [Nos 1, 3, 4, 5, 6, 8, 100 and the OTUs - No 2 Group having been transferred to Fighter Command], but by then the Command had a total of 110 operational squadrons on 73 stations.

Specialist Techniques & Equipment

Bomber Command began the War with such basic equipment that crews had the greatest difficulty finding or hitting targets. As the war progressed the equipment became steadily more sophisticated and eventually specialist crews were able to identify targets in all but the worst of weather conditions. By this time also most aircraft were fitted with H2S radar, Monica, an early warning device to counter marauding night fighters [Wilde Sau], which took the heaviest toll of RAF and USAAF aircraft until the final months of the War when a combination of Luftwaffe fuel shortages and the introduction of fast, long-range American fighters gave the Allies, first, considerable and, eventually, almost total air superiority.

Appendix 2. The Organisation of the Luftwaffe in World War II

Luftwaffe Flying Units

Kommando	a *Kommando* was an ad hoc unit, often named after its commander and serving in a specialised role. Its strength was usually less than that of a *Staffel.*
Staffel	at first a *Staffel* had an establishment of nine aircraft and was the smallest combat unit of the *Luftwaffe*. Later, a *Staffel* could be larger or smaller than that. In the autumn of 1944 many *Staffeln* had their establishment increased to 16 aircraft. A *Staffel* was commanded by a *Staffkapitän*, usually a *Leutnant*, *Oberleutnant* or *Hauptmann*.
Gruppe	A *Gruppe* was the normal flying unit of the *Luftwaffe* for operational purposes, initially consisting of three *Staffeln* of nine aircraft each plus a *stab* [staff] unit of three aircraft, making 30 in all. The nearest RAF equivalent was a fighter wing of two squadrons. Individual *Gruppen* varied in size enormously, and later some fighter *Gruppen* had over twice as many aircraft. A *Gruppe* commander was known as a *Kommandeur* and would usually be of *Hauptman* or *Major* rank.
Geschwader	A *Geschwader* was the largest flying unit of the *Luftwaffe*, initially consisting of three *Gruppen*, with a total of 90 aircraft. Later, many fighter *Geschwader* and all bomber *Geschwader* had a fourth *Gruppe* added. The *Geschwader* commander held the title *Kommodore* and was usually a *Major*, *Oberstleutnant* or *Oberst.*

Abbreviated Descriptions of Luftwaffe Units

A Luftwaffe unit was usually described by its Staffel, or Gruppe, and Geschwader. For example, 3./NJG1 would be the 3rd Staffel of the 1st Night Fighter Geschwader. III/NJG1 would be the 3rd Gruppe of the 1st Night Fighter Geschwader.

Luftwaffe Terminology

Bf	Bayersiche Flugzeugwerke [aircraft type]
Fw	Feldwebel
Fw	Focke-Wulf [aircraft type]
Hptm	Hauptmann
Jagd-	Fighter
Jagdbomber	Fighter-bomber
Ju	Junkers [aircraft type]
Kampf	Bomber
Lt	Leutnant
Nachtjadg-	Night fighter
Nachtschlacht-	Night ground attack
Maj	Major
Me	Messerschmitt [aircraft type - the German abbrev was Bf]
Oblt	Oberleutnant
Ofw	Oberfeldwebel
Schnellkampf-	Fast bomber
Sturm	Heavily armed Fw 190 fighters
Sturzkampf	Dive-bomber
Uffz	Unteroffizier
Wilde Sau	Wild Boar [a type of night-fighter operation]
Zerstörer	Twin-engined fighter

Equivalent RAF, Luftwaffe & British Army Ranks

Royal Air Force	*Luftwaffe*	*Army*
Aircraftman	Fleiger / Gefreiter	Private
Leading Aircraftman	Obergefreiter Haupgefreiter	Lance Corporal
Corporal	Unteroffizier Unterfeldwebel	Corporal
Sergeant	Feldwebel	Sergeant
Flight Sergeant	Oberfeldwebel	Staff Sergeant Warrant Officer II
Warrant Officer	Stabsfeldwebel	Warrant Officer I
Pilot Officer	Leutnant	Second Lieuten- ant
Flying Officer	Oberleutnant	Lieutenant
Flight Lieutenant	Hauptmann	Captain
Squadron Leader	Major	Major
Wing Commander	Oberstleutnant	Lieutenant Colonel
Group Captain	Oberst	Colonel
Air Commodore	Generalmajor	Brigadier
Air Vice-Marshal	Generalleutnant	Major General
Air Marshal	General der Fleiger	Lieutenant General
Air Chief Marshal	Generaloberst	General
Marshal of the RAF	Generalfeldmarschal	Field Marshal

The crew of EE 109 PG-F standing in front of the aircraft in the summer of 1943 [Trahair].

The crew ....ditto.... with ground crew [Trahair].

Nose of EE 109 showing bombing symbols and the Meathound logo and the pilot looking out of cockpit [Trahair].

Studio photograph of Cyril Fuller's posthumous DFC [Trahair].

Studio photograph of Vinny Crookes [19] in RAF Sergeant Air Gunner's uniform [Crookes family].

View of EE109 from the front showing the nose and four engines [with more bombing symbols] [Trahair].

Roy Trahair's grave in Hannover War Cemetery [Trahair].

Professional RAF publicity photograph of S/L Ronnie Churcher standing in front of ED977 Nulli Secundus in 1943 [Gp Capt R G Churcher].

American pilot Nick Knilans and crew [Knilans]. L-R (front) Harry Geller, Nick Knilans, Joe Tate, Les Knell (rear) Gerry Jackson, Ken Ryall, Roy Learmouth.

Air crew sitting outside the Mess with pint pots in hand, based around W/C John Jeudwine [John Howard].

Christian Names: Hubert Clarence

Surname: Knilans

Rank: 1st Lieutenant (USA A.F.)

Official No:

Command or Group: No.5 Group, Bomber Command.

Unit; No.619 Squadron

Total hours on operations:	109.59
Number of sorties:	17
Total hours flown on Operations since receipt of previous award:	N/A
Number of sorties since receipt of previous award:	N/A
Recognition for which recommended:	Immediate Distinguished Service Order.
Appointment held:	Pilot.

Particulars of meritorious service for which recommendation is made: In an attack on Kassel on 3rd October, 1943, this officer was captain of a Lancaster which was attacked on the route to the target by an enemy fighter. In spite of the rear turret being put out of action and the gunner killed, he carried on and bombed the target. On 26th.November, 1943, Lt. Knilans was Captain of an aircraft taking part in the attack on Berlin when two enemy fighters intercepted. One damaged the mid-turret and put an engine out of action. In spite of this, the captain manoeuvred his aircraft so that no further damage was sustained while one of the fighters went down on fire and the other was damaged by the fire of the rear gunner. Although still well over two hundred miles from the target, the captain decided to continue, bombed from a low height and obtained a photograph of the target. On return to this country it was found that one wheel was badly damaged but in spite of this, the aircraft was landed successfully in bad weather. Lt. Knilans has made seventeen sorties and has throughout shown outstanding airmanship and captaincy.

Date: 29th. November, 1943.

JOCK ABERCROMBY

Wing Commander, Commanding,
No. 619 Squadron, R.A.F.

Remarks of Station Commander: In the attack on Berlin on 26.11.43, this officer displayed courage and leadership of the highest order. In spite of damage which would have caused many pilots to jettison their bombs he attacked the enemy capital on three engines and from a low altitude. Throughout his tour he has been an outstanding captain of aircraft. He is strongly recommended for the immediate award of the Distinguished Service Order.

JOHNSON

Date: 30th November, 1943.

Group Captain, Commanding,

Citation for Knilans' immediate DSO [Knilans].

Jurgen Probst with his classmates in Luftwaffenhelfer uniform outside the flak barracks in 1943 at the time EE 109 was shot down [Probst]

Damage to the flak battery's huts caused by the RAF bombing on 8/9 Oct 1943 [Probst].

German Radar scanner showing the RAF aircraft silhouette 'kill' symbols, including the Lancaster that can be identified as EE 109 [Probst].

Jurgen Probst in uniform in close up [Probst].

Newspaper photograph of the bomb disposal leader holding upright the blade of a propeller from the aircraft wreckage after being dredged from the River Leine, Hannover, in March 1943 [Hannoversche Allgemeine Zeitung].

Aerial photograph of bombing in progress over Hannover [taken by an Australian pilot] on 8/9 Oct 1943, on the one clear night of the four raids, from which the locations of the flak battery and the crash site of EE 109 can be identified [Hannoversche Allgemeine Zeitung].

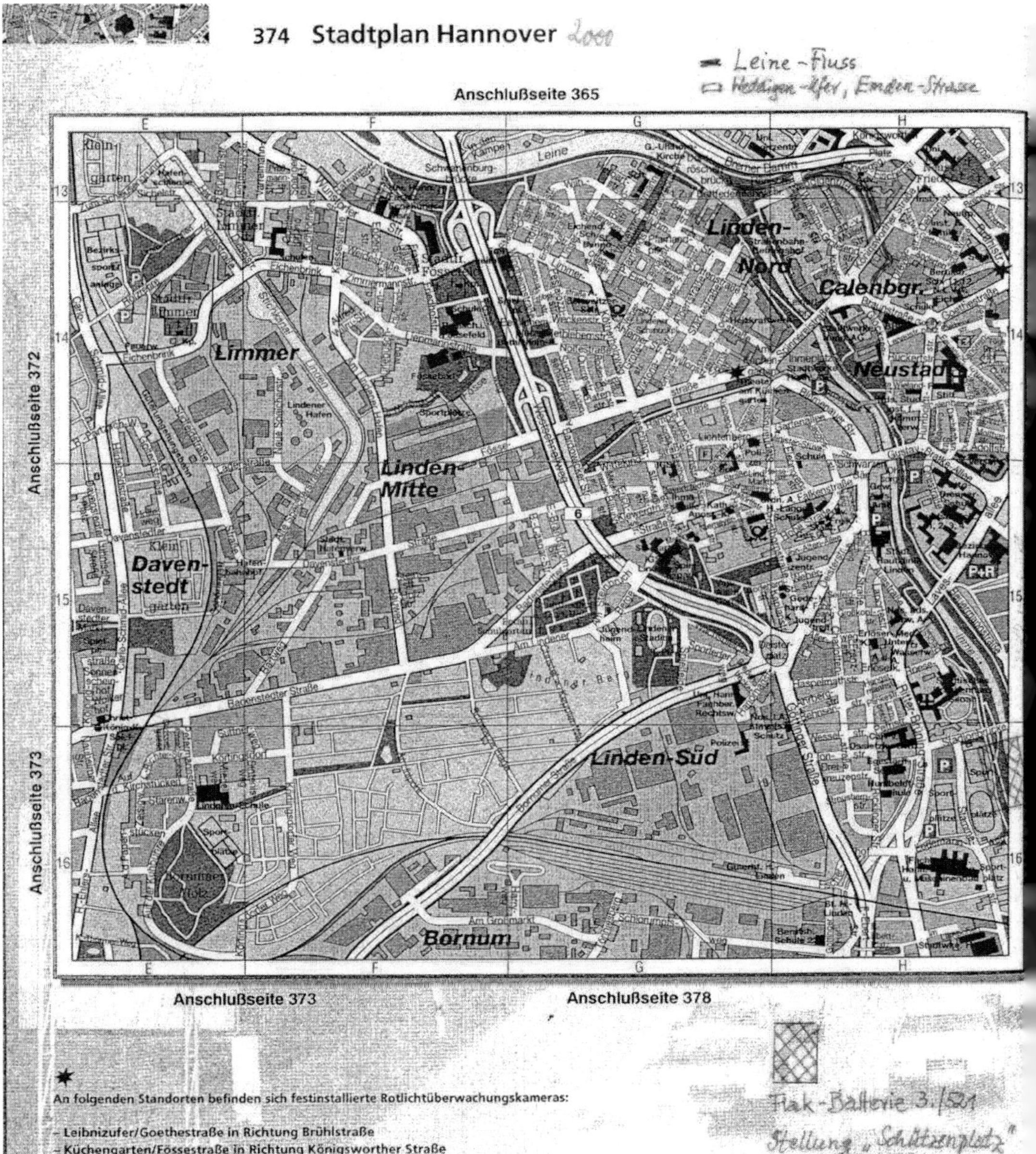

Street plan of Hannover showing the locations of the flak battery and crash site [Probst].

Abschussliste für schwere Flakartillerie der Luftwaffe.

Dem Luftwaffenoberhelfer Jürgen Probst, geboren am 19. Januar 1927 in Hannover, wird bestätigt, dass er vom 15. Februar 1943 bis 9. September 1944 bei der Flakartillerie der Luftwaffe eingesetzt war und in dieser an folgenden Abschüssen feindlicher Flugzeuge im Heimatkriegsgebiet beteiligt ist :

I. Abschüsse :

Tag	Zeit	T y p	Aufschlagort	Fnkt. (Funktion)	P.	laut Verfügung etc.
1943						
26/7	12,25	Short Stirling	Nindorf/Visselhövede		2	
"	12,45	Fortress B 17 F	Bümmerst.Moor(Oldbg.)		2	
22/9	22,35	Short Stirling	1,5km so Gestorf		2	
"	22,45	Halifax	1km n Hüpede		2	
"	22,50	Halifax	1km sw Voremberg	B 5	2	→ „Sprechender" Kanonier
"	22,58	Halifax	1km sw Bemerode	FuMG	2	→ = FunkMessGerät = Radar
27/9	23,05	Lancaster	b.Gross-Förste	39 T	2	→ = Serie 1939 Fabrikat Telefunken „Würzburg"
"	23,13	Lancaster	b.Gross-Giesen		2	
"	23,16	Short Stirling	500m n Bhf.Ronnenberg		2	
"	23,34	Short Stirling	2km s Eldagsen		2	
9/10	1,37	Halifax	500m o Bhf.Hainholz		2	
"	1,41	Lancaster	Ronnenberg		2	
18/10	20,18	Lancaster	Hannover-Weddigenufer		2	
"	20,35	Lancaster	2km n Rehburg		2	
22/11	21,40	Short Stirling	Kerstenhausen/Fritzl.		2	
2/12	21,29	Lancaster	Hannover-Döhren		2	
1944						Alle Abschüsse aus Stellung „Schützenplatz"
30/1	12,10	Fortress B 17 F	1,5km o Ottbergen		2	
1/2	19,34	Mosquito	nw Pattensen		2	
10/2	12,06	Fortress B 17 F	nw Eldagsen		2	
24/2	14,05	Fortress B 17 F	Gross-Munzel		2	
				B 3		→ Richtkanonier Höhenwinkel
				FuMG		→ Serie 1941 „Mannheim"
				41 T		

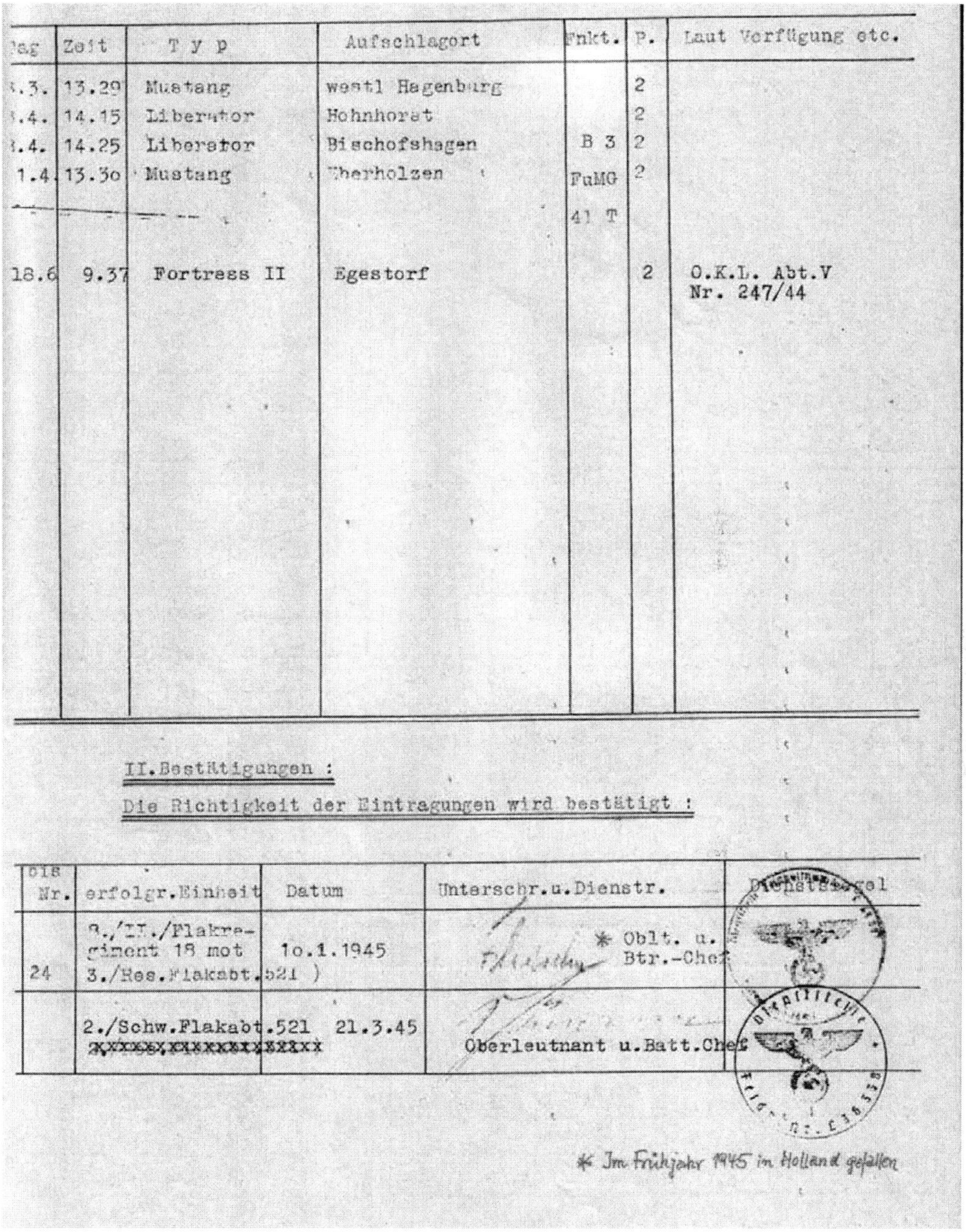

Tag	Zeit	T y p	Aufschlagort	Fnkt.	P.	Laut Verfügung etc.
.3.	13.29	Mustang	westl Hagenburg		2	
.4.	14.15	Liberator	Hohnhorst		2	
.4.	14.25	Liberator	Bischofshagen	B 3	2	
1.4.	13.3o	Mustang	Uberholzen	FuMG 41 T	2	
18.6	9.37	Fortress II	Egestorf		2	O.K.L. Abt.V Nr. 247/44

II.Bestätigungen :

Die Richtigkeit der Eintragungen wird bestätigt :

bis Nr.	erfolgr.Einheit	Datum	Unterschr.u.Dienstr.	Dienstsiegel
24	3./II./Flakregiment 18 mot 3./Res.Flakabt.521)	1o.1.1945	* Oblt. u. Btr.-Chef	
	2./Schw.Flakabt.521 xxxxxxxxxxxxxxxxxxxx	21.3.45	Oberleutnant u.Batt.Chef	

* Im Frühjahr 1945 in Holland gefallen

Official, signed, Abschussliste of aircraft shot down by Flak Batterie 3./521, listing all 25 aircraft shot down between 26 Jul 43 and 18 Jun 1944 [Probst].

The author and Prof Probst at the graves of the two unknown crew members of EE109 [Author]

Prof. Probst laying flowers on the grave of Roy Trahair in August 2002 [Author].

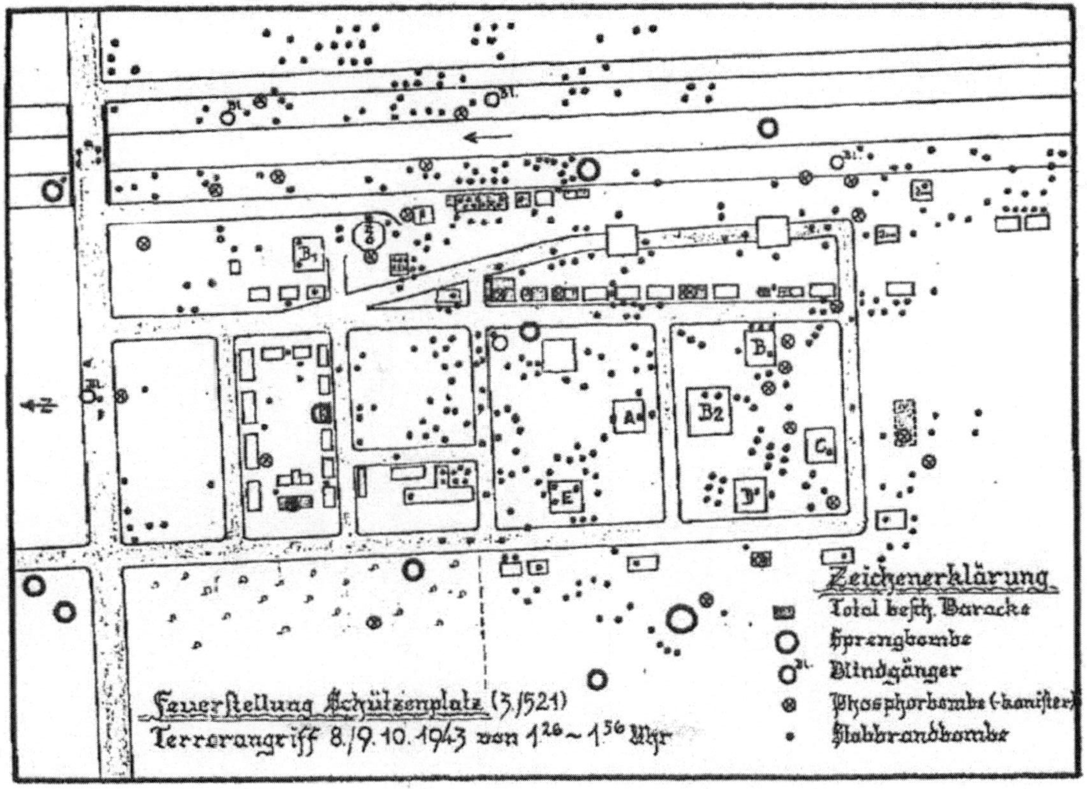

Scale plot made by the Hannover Flak batterie authorities in 1943 of the hundreds of bomb hits received on site during the raid on the night of 8/9 Oct 1943 [Probst].

All that remains of the domestic site at Woodhall, rescued by the Thorpe Camp Visitor Centre volunteers. [Author]

Street scene in modern-day Hannover. [Author]

The Blue Bell public House, just outside the station boundary, where the landlord opened the bar in the early hours of the morning for crews returning from operations. [Author]

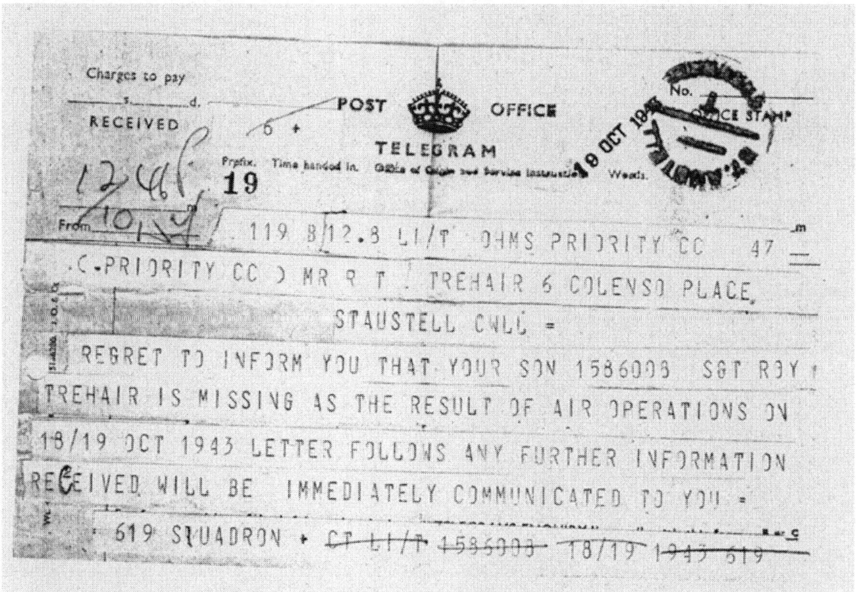

Charges to pay
s. d.
RECEIVED

POST OFFICE TELEGRAM

Prefix. Time handed in. Office of Origin and Service Instructions. Words.
19

From
119 B/12.8 LI/T OHMS PRIORITY CC 47
C.PRIORITY CC) MR R T . TREHAIR 6 COLENSO PLACE
STAUSTELL CWLL =
REGRET TO INFORM YOU THAT YOUR SON 1586008 SGT ROY
TREHAIR IS MISSING AS THE RESULT OF AIR OPERATIONS ON
18/19 OCT 1943 LETTER FOLLOWS ANY FURTHER INFORMATION
RECEIVED WILL BE IMMEDIATELY COMMUNICATED TO YOU =
619 SQUADRON + CT LI/T 1586008 18/19 1943 619

Telegram informing Mr and Mrs Trahair that their son Roy is missing [Trahair].

War memorial at Hannover CWGC Cemetery. [Probst]

Also published by Woodfield...

The following titles are all available in high-quality softback format

Cyril Wild: The Tall Man Who Never Slept • **James Bradley**'s biography of a Japanese-speaking British officer who helped many POWs survive on the infamous Burma railway. **£9.95**

Desert War Diary • **John Walton's** diary and photos record the activities of the Hurricanes and personnel of 213 Squadron during WW2 in Cyprus and Egypt. **£9.95**

Espionage Behind the Wire • former POW **Howard Greville** tells the story of how he worked as a spy for British intelligence (MI6) from inside a German POW camp. **£9.95**

Fly High, Fly Low • the life story of **Les Colquhoun DFC**, who enjoyed 3 aviation careers: as a PRU pilot in WW2; a postwar test pilot with Supermarine; and a Hovercraft pioneer with Vickers. **£9.95**

From Fiji to Balkan Skies • Spitfire/Mustang pilot **Dennis McCaig** recalls eventful WW2 operations over the Adriatic/Balkans with 249 Sqn in 43/44. **£9.95**

From 1 to 1000 Horsepower • **Fergus Davidson** reveals how he went from cavalryman with the Scottish Horse to RAF fighter pilot with 534, 91 and 239 Squadrons and was later a POW. **£9.95**

Get Some In! • The wartime adventures of **Mervyn Base**, a WW2 RAF Bomb Disposal expert **£9.95**

Hunt Like a Tiger • **Tom Docherty** a WW2 history of 230 squadron, equipped with Sunderland flying boats, which were put to many uses in many theatres. **£9.95**

Just a Survivor • Former Lancaster navigator **Phil Potts** tells his remarkable tale of survival against the odds in the air with 103 Sqn and later as a POW. **£9.95**

Memoirs of a 'Goldfish' • The eventful wartime memoirs of former 115 Sqn Wellington pilot **Jim Burtt-Smith**, who ditched into the North Sea and became a POW. **£9.95**

Nobody Unprepared • The history of No 78 Sqn RAF is told for the first time by **Vernon Holland** in this absorbing account of the Whitley/Halifax squadron's World War 2 exploits. **£14.95**

No Brylcreem, No Medals • RAF MT driver **Jack Hambleton**'s account of wartime escapades in England & Middle East blends comic/tragic aspects of war in uniquely entertaining way. **£9.95**

Nobody's Hero • Former RAF Policeman **Bernard Hart-Hallam**'s extraordinary adventures with 2TAF Security Section on D-Day and beyond in France, Belgium & Germany. **£9.95**

One of Butch's Boys • **Philip Turner** tells the story of Allen Clifford, a navigator with 218 Squadron based at Methwold in Norfolk during WW2 who later became a POW at Stalag Luft 6. **£9.95**

Operation Pharos • **Ken Rosam** tells the story of the RAF's secret bomber base/staging post on the Cocos Keeling islands during WW2 and of many operations from there. **£9.95**

Over Hell & High Water • WW2 navigator **Les Parsons** survived 31 ops on Lancasters with 622 Sqn, then went on to fly Liberators in Far East with 99 Sqn. **£9.95**

Pacifist to Glider Pilot • **Alec Waldron** tells how he renounced the pacifism of his Plymouth Brethren parents and went on to pilot gliders at Sicily & Arnhem with the GPR. **£9.95**

Pathfinder Force Balkans • Pathfinder F/Engineer **Geoff Curtis** saw action over Germany & Italy before baling out over Hungary. He was a POW in Komarno, Stalags 17a & 17b. **£9.95**

Per Ardua Pro Patria • Humour and tragedy are interwoven in these unassuming autobiographical observations of **Dennis Wiltshire**, a former Lancaster Flight Engineer. **£9.95**

Ploughs, Planes & Palliasses • Entertaining recollections of RAF pilot **Percy Carruthers**, who flew Baltimores in Egypt with 223 Squadron and was later a POW at Stalag Luft 1 & 6. **£9.95**

RAF/UXB The Story of RAF Bomb Disposal • Stories contributed by wartime RAF BD veterans that will surprise and educate the uninitiated. *"Amazing stories of very brave men."* **£9.95**

Railway to Runway • The wartime diary & letters of Halifax Observer **Leslie Harris,** killed in action with 76 Sqn in 1943, discovered by his son 50 years later and turned into a moving book. **£9.95**

Seletar Crowning Glory • The history of the RAF base in Singapore from its earliest beginnings, through the golden era of the flying-boats, WW2 and up to its closure in the 1970s. **£15.00**

The RAF & Me • Former Stirling navigator **Gordon Frost** recalls ops with 570 Sqn from RAF Harwell, including 'Market-Garden' 'Varsity' and others. **£9.95**

Training for Triumph • **Tom Docherty**'s very thorough account of the achievements of RAF Training Command, who trained over 90,000 aircrew during World War 2. **£9.95**

To Strive and Not to Yield • A detailed account of the involvement of No 626 Squadron RAF Bomber Command in the 'Battle of Berlin' (1943/44). **£9.95**

Under the Red Eagle • **Frank Pearce** catalogues the many achievements of the Kittyhawks and Mustangs of 239 Wing of the Desert Air Force in Africa, Sicily and Italy during WW2. **£9.95**

Un Grand Bordel • Air-gunner **Norman Lee**'s real-life adventures in occupied France with the Maquis and US Special Forces after being shot down are told with a wry sense of humour. **£9.95**

UXB Vol 2 • More unusual and gripping tales of bomb disposal during WW2 and afterwards. **£9.95**

Wot! No Engines? • Alan Cooper tells the story of the RAF glider pilots who served on Operation Varsity in 1945. A large and impressive book with many photos. **£15.00**

While Others Slept • Former Hampden navigator **Eric Woods** tells the story of Bomber Command's early years and his tour of duty with 144 Squadron flying Hampdens. **£9.95**

WOMEN & WORLD WAR TWO

A WAAF at War • Former MT driver **Diana Lindo**'s charming evocation of life in the WAAF will bring back happy memories to all those who also served in World War 2. **£9.95**

Corduroy Days • Warm-hearted and amusing recollections of **Josephine Duggan-Rees**'s wartime years spent as a Land Girl on farms in the New Forest area. **£9.95**

Ernie • **Celia Savage**'s quest to discover the truth about the death of her father, an RAF Halifax navigator with 149 Sqn, who died in WW2 when she was just 6 years old. **£9.95**

In My Father's Footsteps • **Pat Bienkowski**'s moving account of her trip to Singapore & Thailand to visit the places where her father and uncle were both POW's during WW2. **£9.95**

Lambs in Blue • **Rebecca Barnett's** revealing account of the wartime lives and loves of a group of WAAFs posted to the tropical paradise of Ceylon. *"A highly congenial WW2 chronicle."* **£9.95**

Radar Days • Delightful evocation of life in the wartime WAAF by former Radar Operator **Gwen Arnold**, who served at Bawdsey Manor RDF Station, Suffolk. *"Amusing and affectionate."* **£9.95**

Searching in the Dark • The amusing wartime diary of **Peggy Butler** a WAAF radar operator 1942-1946 – written when she was just 19 yrs old and serving at Bawdsey RDF station in Suffolk **£9.95**

Tales of a Bomber Command Waaf (and her horse) • entertaining book composed of wartime letters received and sent by **Sylvia Pickering**, a Waaf at RAF Cottesmore and Coningsby. **£9.95**

More Tales of a Bomber Command Waaf (and her horse) • The second part of **Sylvia Pickering**'s war spent at HQ 5 Group (Bomber Command). More entertaining reminiscences. **£9.95**

Why Did We Join? • **Eileen Smith** recalls the camaraderie, excitement and heartbreak of working as a Waaf at an operational Bomber Command Station – RAF East Kirkby in Lincolnshire. **£9.95**

MILITARY MEMOIRS & HISTORIES – THE POST-WAR PERIOD

A History of the King's Flight & The Queen's Flight • An illustrated history of the RAF unit responsible for the air transport of the Royal family from 1936 to its disbandment in 1995. **£15.00**